C000072340

THE FOUNDATIONS OF POSITIVE AND NORMATIVE ECONOMICS

The Handbooks in Economic Methodologies Series

The Foundations of Positive and Normative Economics: A Handbook
Edited by Andrew Caplin and Andrew Schotter

In collaboration with Center for Experimental Social Science, New York University

THE FOUNDATIONS OF POSITIVE AND NORMATIVE ECONOMICS

A HANDBOOK

Edited by

ANDREW CAPLIN
and
ANDREW SCHOTTER

OXFORD
UNIVERSITY PRESS

OXFORD
UNIVERSITY PRESS

Oxford University Press, Inc., publishes works that further
Oxford University's objective of excellence
in research, scholarship, and education.

Oxford New York
Auckland Cape Town Dar es Salaam Hong Kong Karachi
Kuala Lumpur Madrid Melbourne Mexico City Nairobi
New Delhi Shanghai Taipei Toronto

With offices in
Argentina Austria Brazil Chile Czech Republic France Greece
Guatemala Hungary Italy Japan Poland Portugal Singapore
South Korea Switzerland Thailand Turkey Ukraine Vietnam

Copyright © 2008 by Oxford University Press

Published by Oxford University Press, Inc.
198 Madison Avenue, New York, New York 10016
www.oup.com

First issued as an Oxford University Press paperback, 2010

Oxford is a registered trademark of Oxford University Press

All rights reserved. No part of this publication may be reproduced,
stored in a retrieval system, or transmitted, in any form or by any means,
electronic, mechanical, photocopying, recording, or otherwise,
without the prior permission of Oxford University Press.

Library of Congress Cataloging-in-Publication Data
The foundations of positive and normative economics: a handbook
edited by Andrew Caplin and Andrew Schotter.
p. cm.
Includes bibliographical references and index.
ISBN 978–0–19–974485–5
1. Economics—Methodology.
I. Caplin, Andrew.
II. Schotter, A.
HB131.H353 2008
310—dc22   2007036915

1 3 5 7 9 8 6 4 2

Printed in the United States of America
on acid-free paper

Andrew Caplin: To Ruth, Ann, and Olivia,
in order of first meeting. Love heals.

Andrew Schotter: To Anne, Geoffrey, and Liz for
keeping life interesting.

ACKNOWLEDGMENTS

That we are not alone in our belief in the importance of putting constructive methodological discussion onto the agenda is evidenced by the enthusiastic response of our publishers at Oxford University Press, Terry Vaughn and Niko Pfund in particular, to whom great thanks are due. We also thank Deans Richard Foley and George Downs for their foresight in helping to create the Center for Experimental Social Science, which has developed into the most rewarding and open of research environments. We thank several of our NYU colleagues, most notably Paul Glimcher of the Center for Neuroscience and Guillermina Jasso of the sociology department, for encouraging us in our determination to use methodological levers to expand interdisciplinary communication. We thank Rajiv Advani for the work he put into organizing the NYU conference of August 2006 at which all authors presented early drafts of their chapters, and Mark Dean for his central role not only in organizing the conference but also in organizing and essentially coediting this book.

Contents

. . . .

PART IV. NEW DIRECTIONS FOR POSITIVE ECONOMICS

CONTRIBUTORS

....

Benhabib, Jess: Department of Economics, New York University

Bernheim, B. Douglas: Department of Economics, Stanford University

Bisin, Alberto: Department of Economics, New York University

Camerer, Colin: Division of Humanities and Social Sciences, California Institute of Technology

Caplin, Andrew: Center for Experimental Social Sciences, Department of Economics, New York University

Crawford, Vincent P.: Department of Economics, University of California–San Diego

Gabaix, Xavier: Stern School of Business, New York University

Gale, Douglas: Department of Economics, New York University

Glaeser, Edward L.: Department of Economics, Harvard University and National Bureau of Economic Research

Gul, Faruk: Department of Economics, Princeton University

Haisley, Emily: Tepper School of Business, Carnegie Mellon University

Hausman, Daniel: Department of Philosophy, University of Wisconsin–Madison

Köszegi, Botond: Department of Economics, University of California–Berkeley

Laibson, David: Department of Economics, Harvard University

Loewenstein, George: Department of Social and Decision Sciences, Carnegie Mellon University

Pesendorfer, Wolfgang: Department of Economics, Princeton University

Rabin, Matthew: Department of Economics, University of California–Berkeley

Rangel, Antonio: Division of Humanities and Social Sciences, California Institute of Technology

Rubinstein, Ariel: School of Economics, Tel Aviv University, and Department of Economics, New York University

Salant, Yuval: Graduate School of Business, Stanford University

Schotter, Andrew: Center for Experimental Social Sciences, Department of Economics, New York University

Spiegler, Ran: Department of Economics, University College London

Series Introduction

Durable contributions to economic thought that focus purely on methodology are few and far between. Absent substantive progress, methodological reflections are widely seen as fruitless, while the methodological importance of successful research is seen as self-evident. Yet as the chapters written for this book attest, there are increasing signs of methodological ferment within the profession. We see this as long overdue, and for that reason we are editing a series of handbooks in a deliberate effort at raising methodological awareness. We believe that the next few decades will produce important advances in social scientific methodology. Improvements in our professional knowledge base and in the technology that is available to us have radically expanded potential avenues of research. By engaging in a collective discussion of the newly feasible options, we will improve our ability to exercise and explore the most fruitful among them. While we will surely start out on a wide variety of different research paths, a new consensus will form far more rapidly if we appreciate the motives of those forging these distinct routes.

While the direct goal of these handbooks is to engage with current researchers as they contemplate new research opportunities, we aim also to reach some who have yet to set out on their research journeys. Moreover, we hope that the books will be of interest to researchers in disciplines other than economics. We view the expansion of research technology as opening the door to the formation of research teams that cross traditional field boundaries. We are confident enough in the value of our intellectual traditions to believe that a well-thought-through and fully articulated "economic" methodology would serve as the best center point for such endeavors.

Volume Introduction

Background

The timing of this series was influenced by an almost unprecedented burst of interest in issues of economic methodology. The publication that did most to provoke this interest was that of Gul and Pesendorfer that opens this volume. Observing and experiencing the intense intellectual passions that their work unleashed on its release in working paper form, we invited key players to a conference at NYU in August 2006. Preliminary papers were outlined by participants, and dialog was opened. This volume contains the final papers as completed over the ensuing months. To our delight, many of the chapters in this volume are best seen as opening gambits in a larger game that will be played out in the leading journals in economics and related disciplines in the coming years.

The issues at stake in this methodological dialog are foundational. What are the goals of economic analysis, and what methods will best serve the achievement of these goals? Prominent researchers have recently been developing models that rely heavily on psychological intuitions. They have sometimes sought support for these models based on data that have not previously been subjected to economic analysis, relating to such variables as eye fixations and responses to questions concerning subjective states. Taking the next step, in 2005 Camerer, Loewenstein, and Prelec cast neuroscientific data as likely to induce a revolution in economic methodology.[1] Gul and Pesendorfer made strong counterclaims, and this volume presents many different points of view on the issues raised in the course of the ensuing debate.

Setting the Stage

While other social sciences may take pride in their methodological diversity, most economists perceive our long-standing methodological unity as a source of depth and power. This opens the door to debate concerning how best to incorporate new measurement technologies of potential importance to our understanding of choice behavior. On the one hand, there must be room for exploration. On the other hand, there is great value to continued coherence of approach. It is this trade-off that provides the backdrop for the debate detailed in the first two sections of this volume.

Part I contains the chapter by Gul and Pesendorfer (henceforth GP), which stresses the value of maintaining various limits on the domain and range of economics. GP make three broad assertions concerning the appropriate limits to be placed on positive and normative economics that may be crudely paraphrased as follows.

- **Assertion 1: Positive Economics and Choice Data.** Positive economics concerns only choices. If different theories make the same predictions concerning choices, they are economically identical, whereas if they make different predictions, choice data can in principle be used to differentiate among them. Since economic models concern only choices, psychological intuitions and nonchoice data can be used only to provide background inspiration, and cannot be used to accept or reject these models. Interest in psychology extends only insofar as it has implications for choices.
- **Assertion 2: Positive Economics and Choice Theory.** Economists should strive to fully characterize the implications of their theories for standard choice data. As much as possible, these models should characterize agents as making choices that maximize some fixed objective function.
- **Assertion 3: Normative Economics.** The traditional normative economic question concerning how to design policies to forward some definition of the good inappropriately treats economics as social therapy. The only significant role of normative economics should be to highlight interesting questions for positive economics, such as how best to model the forces accounting for apparent failures of Pareto optimality. Given that normative economics is designed only to suggest new approaches to positive economics, it too must be centered around theories of choice.

Part II contains five chapters that present more or less direct responses to GP, focusing mainly on assertions 1 and 2. Part III contains chapters that address issues associated with how to conduct normative welfare analysis within the framework set by economics and psychology. Part IV contains six chapters that pursue largely independent themes in relation to the future methodology of positive economics. While the chapters in Parts III and IV are self-contained, all authors display an awareness of the larger methodological issues.

PART II: THE DEBATE

In the opening chapter of part II, Colin Camerer argues that enhanced understanding of nonchoice data is essential for the development of robust models of choice, in direct opposition to assertion 1 of GP. Moreover, he exposes the remarkable proliferation of nonstandard data sources open to economists seeking to understand the decision-making process. These data include such well-known sources as Mouselab, but extend far further to include data relating to bodily and neurological functions and the genetic makeup of the decision maker. Camerer surveys examples in which these data appear to materially increase our understanding of decision making, and indicates why he believes this to be merely the tip of the iceberg. He also argues that economists should be prepared to import into our discipline theoretical constructs that have provided durable value in the theory and practice of psychology, and that in so doing we will help to dissolve somewhat arbitrary lines between disciplines. In Camerer's view, not only can conventional rational choice theory be enriched by new psychological constructs, but so can normative economics. He ends his article with some direct criticisms of the GP chapter, which includes equally blunt criticisms of some of Camerer's own work.

Andrew Schotter argues in chapter 3 that analyzing choice data should be seen as one method of deriving more fundamental economic understanding, rather than as the main end in and of itself. He sees it as having been placed historically on such a high pedestal more for technological than for intellectual reasons. As richer sources of evidence become ever more available, he proposes incorporating them into our vision as seamlessly as possible. Indeed, Schotter argues that the practicing economist faced with the limited information content of standard choices does this anyway as a matter of routine. He also questions the value in practice of much standard choice data. If framing of options influences choice and the relevant frame is not recorded, the attempt to provide a frame-free inference concerning behavior may be fundamentally flawed. As to the uses to which nonstandard data can be put, Schotter outlines a recent study in which neuroscientific fMRI data was used to produce a hypothesis concerning auction design, which hypothesis was supported when put to the test.

In chapter 4, Ran Spiegler addresses the second assertion of GP, concerning the appropriate methods of modeling choice data. While arguing that the axiomatic methods they highlight can represent only one arrow in the methodological quiver, Spiegler indicates respect for their role as diagnostic tools. He shows by example that in the absence of axiomatic exploration, models based on psychological intuition may have weak or even counterintuitive implications for behavior. Even if one rejects the view that use of the "revealed preference" method of classical decision theory is a prerequisite for satisfactory economic theory, it may be of great value in clarifying behavioral implications of such theories. Despite this, Spiegler argues against the focus on modeling behavior as reflecting constrained optimization. He provides a vivid example to illustrate his argument that whether or not one views a particular model of behavior as optimizing depends on how that model is interpreted rather than on its purely technically characteristics.

As does Spiegler, Ariel Rubinstein and Yuval Salant focus their full attention in chapter 5 on the second assertion of GP relating to the methods of positive economic theory. They, too, argue strongly against the implied downgrading of psychological intuition as extratheoretical. They also reject any claim that models of constrained maximization deserve a privileged place in choice theory. Rubinstein and Salant view all economic models as being at the same time models of the mind, and see no reason to privilege any such models as ideals. In particular, they argue that procedural models have just as much claim to our interest as do those based on constrained optimization.

In chapter 6, Daniel Hausman provides comprehensive arguments against all three of the assertions of GP. He documents an interpretation of their work as centering on the relevance thesis, relating to the centrality of standard choice data. He places this thesis in methodological context in relation to the principle of revealed preference, as originally put forward by Paul Samuelson [1938][2] and Milton Friedman [1953].[3] He examines various justifications for this thesis and finds them wanting on logical grounds. On the normative role of economics, he argues that while current attempts to find alternative welfare criteria can be rightly criticized, this is not enough to damn the entire project as futile.

PART III: NEW DIRECTIONS FOR NORMATIVE ECONOMICS

The standard interpretation is that normative economics is the study of how best to make policy decisions for an individual or a group whose motivations are known to the policy maker. The assertions of GP rejects this interpretation as outside the economic canon. They argue against viewing those involved in the policy process as having distinctive normative goals. By contrast, chapters in part III are written by those who see the development of new forms of normative economics as among the most intellectually exciting challenges facing those who are interested in economics and psychology.

Douglas Bernheim and Antonio Rangel in chapter 7 ask how the history of individual choices can be used as the basis for normative economics in situations in which these individual choices reveal apparent inconsistencies. A paradigm example involves an individual who changes choice based on a seemingly irrelevant change in the method of framing a given decision. They are particularly concerned with a policy maker who has deep respect for private choice and for consumer sovereignty. They extend the standard concepts of Pareto optimality and consumer and producer surplus to cover the case of inconsistent choices by extracting all coherent information from choice, leaving indeterminacy only in areas in which inconsistencies have arisen. They consider possible choice-based methods of adjudication in the presence of such indeterminacy, as well as the possibility of relying on additional nonchoice sources of evidence for adjudication. They are currently engaged in research to further clarify the interplay among logic, evidence, and normative principles in an overarching framework.

The psychologically astute socially motivated policy maker's choice problem is greatly simplified if certain of the decisions can be identified as mistakes, and downgraded appropriately. In chapter 8, Botond Köszegi and Matthew Rabin ask how one might go about identifying mistakes while relying to the maximum extent possible on data from actual choices. Observing mistake-ridden behavior need not be a bar to understanding the preferences of a decision maker whose mistakes are systematic. They provide a clear motivating example illustrating how to separate preferences from beliefs in the case of a decision maker subject to the gambler's fallacy. Köszegi and Rabin suggest that similar methods may be applicable when beliefs incorporate systematic errors in the prediction of future behavior. Important examples in this regard involve decision makers who hold the false belief that they will in the future have more self-control, and those who inappropriately believe that future preferences will be close to current preferences.

George Loewenstein and Emily Haisley present in chapter 9 a robust defense of normative research based on the principles of economics and psychology. They detail the many applied domains in which economics and psychology are beginning to affect policy, and argue that applications of this form are set to increase exponentially. In fact, Loewenstein and Haisley argue that the challenges that economics and psychology raise call for giving more rather than less attention to questions of policy design. They outline policy proposals that are already identified with normative behavioral economics, and specify the overarching criteria that gave rise to these proposals. Not all such criteria involve selecting what the decision maker would have chosen if suitably informed. Loewenstein and Haisley argue that there are times when the policy maker would do better to simply override what is seen as systematically flawed decision making rather than trying to incorporate these flaws into the policy system.

PART IV: NEW DIRECTIONS FOR POSITIVE ECONOMICS

The chapters in part IV present various agendas and methodologically oriented manifestos for future research in economics and psychology. The goal of all authors contributing to this part is to influence the evolution of positive economics. While there are important distinctions among the proposals, several propose expanding the data to be modeled beyond that implicit in assertion 1 of GP, while retaining some form of discipline on the modeling process.

In chapter 10, Vincent Crawford details a research agenda in which nonchoice data are modeled alongside data on choices made in various games. The work that he outlines involves simultaneously measuring and modeling various types of search in strategic settings, with a view to understanding choices in a wide class of games in which lack of experience renders the assumption of equilibrium play both unreasonable and wildly inaccurate. Crawford shows that data deriving from the information search may have great predictive power for choices made in the corresponding games. Hence, highly predictive models that characterize the search process appear to classify decision makers in an empirically valid manner. The broader agenda of the research is to classify individuals' strategic behavior on the basis of these nonstandard search data, and to use these to predict later choices in a variety of games.

Douglas Gale in chapter 11 considers models of boundedly rational choice data generated in an intricate experimental protocol. The research he describes has the feature that constrained optimization is hypothesized to guide behavior. Specifically, it is assumed that the decision maker is endowed with a small number of heuristic decision-making procedures, and that the margin of choice is not between final options, but rather among these fixed heuristics. Choice data are used not only to back out preferences per se, but also to infer heuristics, which are treated as primitives of the model. This body of research elevates psychological intuition to a higher level than that implied by assertion 2 of GP, according to which psychological intuition is presumed only to inspire models, rather than to feature in them.

As the above discussion makes clear, there are vibrant research programs in positive economics that allow for nonchoice data and that directly incorporate psychological constructs. What criteria should be used to judge the success or failure of such nonstandard research? In chapter 12, Xavier Gabaix and David Laibson outline a set of modeling principles of universal importance across scientific disciplines. While the importance of these principles may be agreed by most economists, Gabaix and Laibson propose a rebalancing of priorities. They argue that specificity of predictions and tightness of the model's fit to the data have traditionally been downplayed. Economists may have become so used to the low explanatory power of our models that we artificially deflate such power as a criterion for discriminating among theories. While sharing common ground on issues such as parsimony, the Gabaix and Laibson ideals reflect an entirely different methodological stance than do those of Gul and Pesendorfer. In essence, they suggest that methodology is better defined by acceptance of a universal set of values by which to judge the output of models than it is by statements concerning the inputs with which the models were constructed.

What considerations are involved in deciding whether and how to incorporate novel nonstandard sources of data as objects of study? Edward L. Glaeser in chapter 13 provides some reasons for concern if the field opens up too rapidly to new and unfamiliar forms of data. He outlines several realistic features of the research process that remain underappreciated. His broad theme is that published research findings are self-selected from among a large mass of possible such findings. Those that the author chooses to produce are far from random, yet the mode of selection is typically ignored in stated interpretations of the published results. The dangers involved in self-selection of this type are particularly severe in the case of neuro-scientific data, which is unfamiliar to most and subject to many transformations in the course of empirical analysis.

In chapter 14, Jess Benhabib and Alberto Bisin provide another argument in favor of exercising discipline as we consider new and unfamiliar sources of data. They are explicit in rejecting both of the positive assertions of GP. They stress the importance of allowing psychological elements to guide the development of economic models, and they support the use of neuroscientific data and process data as providing valid insights into model performance. Yet they are wary of the unbridled use of such nonstandard data and propose that theory rather than measurement needs to take the lead in the expansion process. They argue that nonstandard data and psychological intuitions are permissible guides to those building economic models, yet the resulting models should not to be used in an informal or qualitative manner. Rather, rigorous modeling of nonstandard data sets in conjunction with choice data should be the central concern of the next generation of work in economics and psychology.

Andrew Caplin shares with Benhabib and Bisin a concern that unstructured expansions in the data that economists model will yield little by way of economic insight. He is also concerned with the breakdown in the ability to communicate across subdisciplines that may result without a common methodology. He places a particularly high value on ensuring that such communication not only is retained within economics but also is increasingly shared with other social sciences. With this goal of increased connectivity in mind, in chapter 15 Caplin proposes a minimalist methodology as an ideal to guide the next generation of research in economics and psychology. This methodology requires that axiomatic methods be pursued as the most unambiguous method of introducing elements of psychology into economic models. Minimalism places no restrictions either on the data to which such axioms may apply or on the theoretical concept underlying this axiomatization. Caplin provides examples of this methodology in action from his joint work with Mark Dean. In a sense, this proposal brings us full circle, differing from that of Gul and Pesendorfer only in the willingness to expand the data, and in the deliberate elevation of axiomatic methods above the principle of constrained optimization.

CONCLUDING REMARKS

The scholarly contributions in this volume strongly suggest that methodological debate will vitally inform the future path of economics, and possibly of other social sciences. Modern technology enables much new data to be generated of possible interest to social scientists. How best to use these new data is far from obvious. Possibilities range all the way from open embrace of all new possibilities to outright rejection of the unfamiliar. Intermediate positions involve structuring the incorporation of new data to allow for new insights that are broadly communicable. There are many positions that one might take on how best to provide such structure, as the chapters in this volume make abundantly clear. These are exciting methodological times in the social sciences. The underlying questions will not be resolved quickly. We look forward to tracking methodological progress in future handbooks in this series.

NOTES

1. Camerer, Colin F., George Loewenstein, and Drazen Prelec. 2005. Neuroeconomics: How Neuroscience Can Inform Economics. *Journal of Economic Literature.* 34(1): 9–64.

2. Samuelson, Paul. 1938. A Note on the Pure Theory of Consumer's Behavior. *Economica.* 5: 61–71.

3. Friedman, Milton. 1953. The Methodology of Positive Economics. In Friedman, *Essays in Positive Economics,* 3–43. Chicago: University of Chicago Press.

PART I

SETTING THE STAGE

CHAPTER 1

THE CASE FOR MINDLESS ECONOMICS

FARUK GUL AND
WOLFGANG PESENDORFER

NEUROECONOMICS proposes radical changes in the methods of economics. This chapter discusses the proposed changes in methodology, together with a neuroeconomic critique of standard economics. Our definition of neuroeconomics includes research that makes no specific reference to neuroscience and is traditionally referred to as psychology and economics. We identify neuroeconomics as research that implicitly or explicitly makes either of the following two claims:

> Assertion 1: Psychological and physiological evidence (e.g., descriptions of hedonic states and brain processes) is directly relevant to economic theories. In particular, it can be used to support or reject economic models or even economic methodology.
>
> Assertion 2: What makes individuals happy ("true utility") differs from what they choose. Economic welfare analysis should use true utility rather than the utilities governing choice ("choice utility").

Neuroeconomics goes beyond the common practice of economists to use psychological insights as inspiration for economic modeling or to take into account experimental evidence that challenges behavioral assumptions of economic models. Neuroeconomics appeals directly to the neuroscience evidence to reject standard economic models or to question economic constructs. Camerer, Loewenstein, and Prelec [2005] (henceforth CLP [2005]) express the neuroeconomics critique as follows: "First, we show that neuroscience findings raise questions about the usefulness of some of the most common constructs that economists commonly use, such as risk aversion, time preference, and altruism" [31–2].

In this chapter, we argue that assertion 1 of the neuroeconomic critique misunderstands economic methodology and underestimates the flexibility of standard models. Economics and psychology address different questions, utilize different abstractions, and address different types of empirical evidence. Neuroscience evidence cannot refute economic models because the latter make no assumptions and draw no conclusions about the physiology of the brain. Conversely, brain science cannot revolutionize economics because the former has no vehicle for addressing the concerns of economics. We also argue that the methods of standard economics are much more flexible than assumed in the neuroeconomics critique and illustrate this with examples of how standard economics deals with inconsistent preferences, mistakes, and biases.

Neuroeconomists import the questions and abstractions of psychology and reinterpret economic models as if their purpose were to address those questions. The standard economic model of choice is treated as a model of the brain and found to be inadequate. Either economics is treated as amateur brain science and rejected as such, or brain evidence is treated as economic evidence to reject economic models.

Kahneman [1994] asserts that subjective states and hedonic utility are legitimate topics of study. This may be true, but such states and utilities are not useful for calibrating and testing standard economic models. Discussions of hedonic experiences play no role in standard economic analysis because economics makes no predictions about them and has no data to test such predictions. Economists also lack the means for integrating measurement of hedonic utility with standard economic data. Therefore, they have found it useful to confine themselves to the analysis of the latter.

The neuroeconomics program for change in economics ignores the fact that economists, even when dealing with questions related to those studied in psychology, have different objectives and address different empirical evidence. These fundamental differences are obscured by the tendency of neuroeconomists to describe both disciplines in very broad terms: "Because psychology systematically explores human judgement, behavior, and well-being it can teach us important facts about how humans differ from the way traditionally described by economics" [Rabin, 1998: 11].

Note the presumption that across disciplines there is a single set of constructs (or facts) for describing how humans are. Rabin omits that economics and psychology study different kinds of behavior and, more important, focus on different variables that influence behavior. Realistic assumptions and useful abstractions when relating visceral cues to behavior may be less realistic or useful when relating behavior to market variables. Consider the following two statements:

Much aversion to risks is driven by immediate fear responses, which are largely traceable to a small area of the brain called the amygdala. [Camerer, Loewenstein, and Prelec, 2004: 567] (henceforth CLP [2004])

A decision maker is (globally) risk averse, . . . if and only if his von Neumann-Morgenstern utility is concave at the relevant (all) wealth levels. [Ingersoll, 1987: 37]

Which of these statements is (more) true? Which provides a better understanding of risk aversion? Most researchers recognize the various terms in the second statement as abstractions belonging to the specialized vocabulary of economics. Though less apparent, the language of the first statement is equally specialized in its use of discipline-specific abstractions. The terms "immediate fear" and "traceable" are abstractions of psychology and neuroscience. Moreover, the term "risk aversion" represents a different abstraction in the two statements above. For Ingersoll [1987], risk aversion is an attitude toward monetary gambles. For CLP [2004], risk aversion seems to be a much broader term that is readily applied to decisions involving airplane travel. It makes little sense to insist that the economic notion of risk aversion is false while the psychological notion is true.

We also discuss assertion 2 of the neuroeconomics critique in this chapter. We argue that the assertion misunderstands the role of welfare analysis in economics. Standard economics identifies welfare with choice; that is, a change (in consumption) is defined to be welfare improving if and only if, given the opportunity, the individual would choose to make that change. The neuroeconomic critique of standard welfare analysis mistakes the economic definition of welfare for a theory of happiness and proceeds to find evidence against that theory. The standard definition of welfare is appropriate because standard economics has no therapeutic ambition; it does not try to improve the decision maker but tries to evaluate how economic institutions mediate (perhaps psychologically unhealthy) behavior of agents.

Standard welfare economics functions as a part of positive economics. It provides a benchmark for the performance of economic institutions at aggregating individual preferences. Economists use welfare analysis to explain the persistence of some (efficient) institutions or to identify problems and anomalies in models of other (inefficient) institutions. For example, observing that an existing institution leads to Pareto efficient outcomes may increase the researcher's confidence in his model, whereas noting that the institution leads to Pareto inefficiency may lead researchers to seek explanations for the persistence of that institution. Within this conception of welfare economics, what is relevant are the agents' interests (or preferences) as perceived by the agents themselves. An institution's effectiveness at maximizing the true happiness of its participants cannot justify the persistence of that institution if the criterion for true happiness conflicts with the participants' revealed preferences. After all, only the latter plays a role in behavior.

Neuroeconomists expect recent developments in psychology and brain science to yield answers to age-old philosophical questions, such as "What is happiness?" "Should we be willing to take actions contrary to a person's wishes if we happen to know that such actions will make them happier?" And neuroeconomists insist on a new notion of welfare based on these answers.

Perhaps a therapist or a medical professional is guided by her answers to the two questions above; she may fashion her advice to advance the perceived objectives of the patient or to increase the patient's true happiness, as defined by the therapist herself.[1] Neuroeconomic welfare analysis assumes a relationship between the economist and economic agents similar to the therapist–patient relationship. Normative economics is therefore identified with effective therapy. The economist/therapist can influence individuals' happiness by dispensing compelling advice or by influencing the decisions of powerful (and perhaps paternalistic) intermediaries. For example, Kahneman [1994: 20] suggests that there is "a case in favour of some paternalistic interventions, when it is plausible that the state knows more about an individual's future tastes than the individual knows presently." Hence, the goal of welfare economics and perhaps the goal of all economics is to affect changes that result in greater happiness to all. In this endeavor, neuroeconomists plan to enlist the support of the state—a stand-in for a benign therapist—who may, on occasion, conceal facts and make decisions on behalf of the individual's future selves.

Neuroeconomists seek a welfare criterion that is appropriate for an economist who is part social scientist and part advocate/therapist, someone who not only analyzes economic phenomena but also plays a role in shaping them. Neuroeconomists assert that the standard economic welfare criterion is not adequate for this task. Our response to this criticism is simple: the standard welfare criterion is not intended to facilitate advocacy for therapeutic interventions. The standard approach assumes a separation between the economist's role as social scientist and the role that some economists may play as advisers or advocates. This separation is valuable because it enables economists to analyze and compare different institutions without having to agree on the answers to difficult philosophical questions.

Besides the two assertions stated above, neuroeconomists pose an additional challenge to standard economics: they argue that economics should take advantage of recent improvements in neuroscience, in particular, improvements in measurements. They claim that these improvements may facilitate the unification of economics and brain science:

> This "rational choice" approach has been enormously successful. But
> now advances in genetics and brain imaging (and other techniques) have made
> it possible to observe detailed processes in the brain better than ever before. Brain

scanning (ongoing at the new Broad Imaging Center at Caltech) shows which parts of the brain are active when people make economic decisions. This means that we will eventually be able to replace the simple mathematical ideas that have been used in economics with more neurally detailed descriptions. [Camerer, 2005: 1]

We then discuss the unification argument. Our main point is that the separation of economics and brain science is a consequence of specialization around different questions and different data; it has little to do with technological limitations in measuring brain activity. Therefore, there is no reason to expect improvements in such technologies to lead to a unification.

In this chapter, we do not assess the contributions or promise of neuroeconomic research. Instead, we offer a response to the neuroeconomic critique of standard economics. Our conclusion is that the neuroeconomic critique fails to refute any particular (standard) economic model and offers no challenge to standard economic methodology.

In the next section, we define the standard approach (or standard economics) and the neuroeconomics approach. We then discuss how the different goals of psychology and of economics necessitate different abstractions. As an example, we contrast the economic concepts of "complements" and "externalities" with the psychological concept of a "cue." Next, we present an example of each approach to illustrate our classification and highlight the differences in the concerns and abstractions of standard economics and neuroeconomics. We then discuss the three main arguments of the neuroeconomics critique.

The Two Approaches: Definitions and Objectives

Standard Economics

The standard approach to behavioral economics extends standard choice-theoretic methods to analyze variables that are often ignored. Some of these extensions are modest and entail little more than specifying a richer set of preferences over the same economic consequences. Others necessitate novel descriptions of the relevant economic outcomes. Yet, in most cases, the subsequent analysis is very similar to what can be found in a standard graduate textbook.

In the standard approach, the terms "utility maximization" and "choice" are synonymous. A utility function is always an ordinal index that describes how the individual ranks various outcomes and how he behaves (chooses) given his constraints (available options). The relevant data are revealed preference data, that is, consumption choices given the individual's constraints. These data are used to calibrate the model (i.e., to identify the particular parameters), and the resulting calibrated models are used to predict future choices and perhaps equilibrium variables such as prices. Hence, standard (positive) theory identifies choice parameters from past behavior and relates these parameters to future behavior and equilibrium variables.

Standard economics focuses on revealed preference because economic data come in this form. Economic data can—at best—reveal what the agent wants (or has chosen) in a particular situation. Such data do not enable the economist to distinguish between what the agent intended to choose and what she ended up choosing; what she chose and what she ought to have chosen. The standard approach provides no methods for utilizing nonchoice data to calibrate preference parameters. The individual's coefficient of risk aversion, for example, cannot be identified through a physiological examination; it can only be revealed through choice behavior. If an economist proposes a new theory based on nonchoice evidence, then either the new theory leads to novel behavioral predictions, in which case it can be tested with revealed preference evidence, or it does not, in which case the modification is vacuous. In standard economics, the testable implications of a theory are its content; once they are identified, the nonchoice evidence that motivated a novel theory becomes irrelevant.

As its welfare criterion, standard economics uses the individual's choice behavior, that is, revealed preferences. Alternative x is deemed to be better than alternative y if and only if, given the opportunity, the individual would choose x over y.[2] Hence, welfare is defined to be synonymous with choice behavior.

In standard economics, an individual's decisions may improve when a constraint is relaxed. For example, an agent may make better decisions if he is given better information, more resources, or more time to make his decision. However, standard economics has no therapeutic ambition; that is, it does not try to evaluate or improve the individual's objectives. Economics cannot distinguish between choices that maximize happiness, choices that reflect a sense of duty, or choices that are the response to some impulse. Moreover, standard economics takes no position on the question of which of those objectives the agent should pursue.

The purpose of economics is to analyze institutions, such as trading mechanisms and organization structures, and to ask how those institutions mediate the interests of different economic agents. This analysis is useful irrespective of the causes of individuals' preferences. Standard economics ignores the therapeutic potential of economic policies and leaves it to therapists, medical professionals, and financial advisers to help individuals refine their goals.

Neuroeconomics

"This new approach, which I consider a revolution, should provide a theory of how people decide in economic and strategic situations," said Dr. Aldo Rustichini, an economics professor at the University of Minnesota. "So far, the decision process has been for economists a black box." [Blakeslee, 2003]

Later, in the same article, the author explains that

> in a study published in the current issue of the journal *Science*, Dr. Cohen and his colleagues, including Dr. Alan G. Sanfey of Princeton, took images of people's brains as they played the ultimatum game, a test of fairness between two people. In the ultimatum game, the first player is given, say, $10 in cash. He must then decide how much to give to a second player. It could be $5, the fairest offer, or a lesser amount depending on what he thinks he can get away with. If Player 2 accepts the offer, the money is shared accordingly. But if he rejects it, both players go away empty-handed. It is a one-shot game, and the players never meet again. Most people in the shoes of Player 2 refuse to take amounts under $2 or $3, Dr. Cohen said. They would rather punish the first player than feel cheated. "But this makes no economic sense," he said. "You're better off with something than nothing."

As the quotes above illustrate, neuroeconomics emphasizes the physiological and psychological processes underlying decision making. The objective is to relate the decision-making process to physiological processes in the brain or to descriptions of emotional experiences. From its predecessor, psychology and economics,[3] neuroeconomics inherits the idea of modeling the decision maker as a collection of biases and heuristics susceptible to systematic errors (effects) and inconsistencies (reversals). Hedonic utilities (true utilities) are primitives, defined independently of behavior, while behavior is determined by biases and heuristics. The focus is on showing how factors that have no effect on these true utilities—or at least affect these utilities in a manner that is ignored by standard economics—influence behavior.

Neuroeconomics is therapeutic in its ambitions: it tries to improve an individual's objectives. The central questions of neuroeconomists are: How do individuals make their choices? How effective are they at making the choices that increase their own well-being? By contrast, economists analyze how the choices of different individuals interact within a particular institutional setting, given their differing objectives.

DIFFERENT OBJECTIVES DEMAND DIFFERENT ABSTRACTIONS

Neuroeconomists argue that the time is ripe for the methodology of economics to be brought in line with the methods and ideas of psychology and neuroscience. The neuroeconomics critique begins with the implicit or explicit assumption that economics, psychology, and possibly other social sciences all address the same set of questions and differ only with respect to the answers they provide:

> More ambitiously, students are often bewildered that the models of human nature offered in different social sciences are so different, and often contradictory. Economists emphasize rationality; psychologists emphasize cognitive limits and sensitivity of choices to contexts; anthropologists emphasize acculturation; and sociologists emphasize norms and social constraint. An identical question on a final exam in each of the fields about trust, for example, would have different "correct" answers in each of the fields. It is possible that a biological basis for behavior in neuroscience, perhaps combined with all-purpose tools like learning models or game theory, could provide some unification across the social sciences. . . . [CLP, 2004: 572–573]

Contrary to the view expressed in the quote above, economics and psychology do not offer competing, all-purpose models of human nature. Nor do they offer all-purpose tools. Rather, each discipline uses specialized abstractions that have proven useful for that discipline. Not only is the word "trust" much less likely to come up in an economics exam than in a psychology exam, but when it does appear in an economics exam, it means something different and is associated with a different question, not just a different answer. Far from being an all-purpose tool, game theory is a formalism for stripping away all strategically irrelevant details of the context, details that Gintis [2003] describes as central for psychologists. Similarly, a learning model in economics is different than a learning model in psychology. For an economist, a theory of learning might be a process of Bayesian inference in a multiarmed bandit model. This theory of learning is useful for addressing economic phenomena such as patent races but may be inappropriate for cognitive psychologists.

Once the goals of economics and psychology are stated in a manner that makes it seem as if the two disciplines address the same questions and deal with the same empirical evidence, it becomes reasonable for neuroeconomists to inquire which discipline has the better answers and the better tools for providing answers.

CLP [2005: 23] assert that "neuroscience findings raise questions about the usefulness of some of the most common constructs economists commonly use, such as risk aversion, time preference, and altruism." Risk aversion and time preference are indispensable concepts for modern economics. The authors really intend to question the validity of these concepts; in essence, they are asserting that there is no such thing as risk aversion or time preference. "Time preference" and "risk aversion" are useful economic abstractions just as "cue-conditioned cognitive process" or "hedonic forecasting mechanisms" are abstractions useful in neuroscience and psychology. The truth (or falsehood) of an abstraction cannot be evaluated independently; the only way to assess these abstractions is by assessing—within each discipline—the theories that use them.

Consider the reverse procedure of using evidence from economics in brain science. Suppose that we find that drug addicts generally satisfy the strong axiom of revealed preference in their demand behavior. Can we argue that since addicts maximize some utility function, there are no separate brain functions and conclude then that the "limbic system" does not exist? This line of reasoning is, of course, absurd because brain science takes no position on whether or not choices satisfy the strong axiom of revealed preference. The argument that evidence from brain science can falsify economic theories is equally absurd. CLP [2005] write:

> For neuroeconomists, knowing more about functional specialization, and how regions collaborate in different tasks, could substitute familiar distinctions between categories of economic behavior (sometimes established arbitrarily by suggestions which become modeling conventions) with new ones grounded in neural detail. For example, the insula activity noted by Sanfey et al. in bargaining is also present when subjects playing matrix games are asked to guess what other subjects think they will do. [15]

Economists who are not interested in the physiological mechanism behind economic decisions will not find the level of insula activity useful for classifying behavior. What CLP [2005] consider "distinctions based on arbitrary modeling conventions" are likely to be much more useful to economists, given their own objectives and given the type of data that are available to them.

The presumption that economics and psychology have the same goals and rely on the same data facilitates three types of critiques of standard economics:

1. *Failure of rationality:* Economic models of choice fail to take account of psychological or physiological phenomena or evidence.
2. *Inadequacy of rationality:* Rationality—defined to mean some sort of consistency in the behavior and preferences of individuals—is not an adequate starting point for economics because consistency of behaviors does not mean that these behaviors will lead to good outcomes.
3. *Unification:* Recent advances in neuroscience provide rich new sources of data. Economics must take advantage of these developments.

We address each of these arguments in specific sections below. We illustrate in the remainder of this section how the different goals psychology and economics and the different data available to these two disciplines necessitate different abstractions.

A Cue or a Complement?

The concept of a "cue" offers a good illustration of how abstractions from psychology are inappropriate for economics and, conversely, how the corresponding economic concepts are inappropriate for psychology and neuroscience. Psychologists call a stimulus that triggers a desire or a craving for a particular consumption or activity a "cue" or a "cue-elicited craving." For example, eating a hamburger may be a cue that triggers a craving for french fries. Drinking coffee may trigger a craving for cigarettes. Visiting the location of previous drug consumption may trigger a craving for drugs. As the example of drug consumption illustrates, cues may be determined endogenously through a process of conditioning.[4] Psychologists find the concept of a cue useful because they think of cues as exogenous variables in experimental settings. They investigate the physiological mechanisms behind the development of and the reaction to cues. For economists, the notion of a cue is not useful because it lumps together two distinct economic phenomena: *complements* and *externalities.*

Hamburgers and fries are complementary goods just like forks and knives. Forks do not generate a craving for knives, and therefore psychologists would not consider the fork/knife complementarity to be the *same* phenomenon as the hamburger/fries complementarity. For economists, the physiological distinction between the two examples is unimportant. What matters is that demand for those goods responds in a similar way to price changes.

Another form of complementarities is the one associated with nonseparable preferences over consumption streams. For example, consider an individual who enjoys building matchstick models and, as a result of this hobby, develops a complementary demand for matches and glue. The complementary demand for matches and glue is acquired through learning a hobby, while the complementary demand for coffee and cigarettes is acquired through a process of conditioning. For a psychologist, who is interested in the underlying causes of preferences, the coffee/cigarette and glue/matchsticks complementarities represent distinct phenomena. The first is an example of conditioning, while the second is an example of learning. However, both examples are similar in terms of the variables that economists observe and care about (prices, demand).

In the cue–response pairs above, the individual controls both the cue and the response. However, some cues are not under the control of the individual. For example, a former drug addict may experience a craving for drugs as she observes drug dealers in her neighborhood. In economics, this effect is captured by the notion of an externality. For economists, the neighborhood effect on drug addicts is similar to the effect of an improved network of roads on car buyers. Both are examples of an externality that causes a shift in the demand for a good. For psychologists, the craving for drugs by seeing drug dealers in the neighborhood is similar to the craving for cigarettes caused by drinking coffee. On the other hand, they would consider it absurd to describe the car buying example and drug addiction example as being the same phenomenon because the underlying psychological mechanisms are very different. It would be equally absurd to insist that economists treat the neighborhood effect on drug demand as the same phenomenon as the cigarette/coffee complementarity. In economics, there are important reasons for distinguishing between complementarities and externalities. For example, externalities often suggest market failures, while complementarities do not.

Economists and psychologists use different abstractions because they are interested in different phenomena and must confront different data. "Cue-triggered responses" is not a useful abstraction in economics because it lumps together distinct economic phenomena. Conversely, the economic abstraction of a complement is not useful in psychology because it lumps together phenomena with different psychological mechanisms.

THE TWO APPROACHES: EXAMPLES

In this section, we illustrate the standard approach to novel behavioral phenomena with a discussion of "Temporal Resolution of Uncertainty and Dynamic Choice Theory" by Kreps and Porteus [1978]. We illustrate the neuroeconomics approach with a working paper by Köszegi and Rabin [2004] titled "A Model of Reference-Dependent Preferences."

The Standard Approach: Resolution of Uncertainty

An individual goes to the hospital on Friday to have a biopsy of a suspicious mass. In case the biopsy detects cancer, surgery will be scheduled for the following Monday. When given a choice between waiting a few hours to learn the result or going home and learning the result on Monday, the individual chooses to wait. The decision to incur the cost of waiting seems plausible but is inconsistent with standard theory. Standard expected utility maximizers are indifferent to the timing of resolution of uncertainty.

Kreps and Porteus [1978] (henceforth Kreps-Porteus) expand the standard model of decision making under uncertainty to include anxious individuals such as the patient in the example above.[5] Suppose there are two dates $t = 1, 2$ and a finite set of prizes Z that will be consumed at date 2 ("surgery" or "no surgery" in the example above). Standard decision theory under uncertainty defines lotteries over Z as the choice objects. But this description does not differentiate between lotteries that resolve at date 1 and lotteries that resolve at date 2—and therefore cannot capture the anxious patient described above.

Let D_2 be the lotteries over Z and let D_1 be lotteries over D_2. Hence, D_1 is the set of lotteries over lotteries over Z. We refer to elements of D_1 as date 1 lotteries and elements of D_2 as date 2 lotteries. We can describe the problem of the anxious patient as a choice between two lotteries in D_1. Suppose the probability of surgery is α. Waiting for the results until Monday corresponds to a date 1 lottery where, with probability 1, the individual will face the date 2 lottery that yields surgery with probability α and no surgery with probability $1 - \alpha$. Learning the result on Friday corresponds to the date 1 lottery where, with probability α, the individual faces a date 2 lottery that yields surgery with probability 1 and, with probability $1 - \alpha$, the individual faces a date 2 lottery that yields surgery with probability 0.

Let p, q denote elements in D_2 and μ, ν denote elements in D_1. For simplicity, we consider only lotteries with finite supports. Let $\mu(p)$ be the probability that μ chooses the lottery $p \in D_2$. Standard expected utility theory identifies μ with the implied probability distribution over prizes, that is, the probability distribution $q \in D_2$ that assigns probability

$$q(z) = \sum_{D_2} \mu(p)p(z) \tag{1.1}$$

to prize $z \in Z$. Therefore, standard expected utility theory cannot accommodate the patient's strict preference for learning the test results on Friday.

The Kreps-Porteus model takes as a primitive an individual's preferences $\succeq$ (choices) over the date 1 lotteries, D_1. Some date 1 lotteries yield a particular date 2 lottery with probability 1. We call such lotteries degenerate date 1 lotteries. In the example above, learning the test results on Monday corresponds to such a lottery. Restricting the preference $\succeq$ to degenerate date 1 lotteries induces a preference on D_2, the date 2 lotteries. Let δ_p denote the date 1 lottery that yields the date 2 lottery p with probability 1. The induced preference $\succeq_2$ (on D_2) is defined as follows: ·

$p \succeq_2 q$ if and only if $\delta_p \succeq \delta_q$

Kreps-Porteus assume that $\succeq$ and $\succeq_2$ satisfy the standard von Neumann-Morgenstern axioms; hence, the preferences are complete and transitive and satisfy the independence axiom and an appropriate continuity assumption. Kreps-Porteus show that the preferences on D_1 satisfy those assumptions if and only if there are utility functions u and W such that $\mu \succeq \nu$ if and only if

$$\sum_{D_2} W \left[\sum_{z \in Z} u(z)p(z) \right] \mu(p) \geq \sum_{D_2} W \left[\sum_{z \in Z} u(z)p(z) \right] \nu(p).$$

The formula above applies the standard expected utility formula twice. The term in brackets is the expected utility formula for lotteries that resolve at date 2, whereas the outer term is the expected utility formula for lotteries that resolve at date 1.

The Kreps-Porteus formalism yields a precise definition of a new phenomenon: preference for early (or late) resolution of uncertainty. Let μ, ν be two elements of D_1 that imply the same distribution over prizes. The lottery μ resolves all uncertainty at date 1, while the lottery v resolves all uncertainty at date 2. In the example above, μ corresponds to the situation where the patient learns the test result on Friday, and v corresponds to the situation where the patient learns the test result on Monday. The individual has a preference for early resolution of uncertainty if he prefers μ over v. Kreps-Porteus show that a preference for early resolution of uncertainty implies (and is implied by) the convexity of W.

Note the key steps in the modeling exercise: Kreps-Porteus start with a novel psychological phenomenon and identify the economically relevant consequences of that phenomenon. Once the economically meaningful consequences are identified, the psychological causes become irrelevant. For the patient above, the source of the preference for early resolution of uncertainty is anxiety. But there could be many other reasons for a preference for early resolution of uncertainty. Suppose, for example, the agent owns a lottery ticket that will either yield a large reward (with small probability) or nothing. Prior to the lottery drawing, the agent must decide which car to purchase. The outcome of the lottery will typically affect the optimal car buying decision, and therefore, the agent would be better off if the lottery drawing was held earlier. Hence, the induced preferences over lotteries imply a preference for early resolution of uncertainty. In this case, the agent has perfectly standard preferences. The preference for early resolution of uncertainty comes about because the agent has a second payoff-relevant decision to make after choosing a lottery.

In the two examples, the causes of the decision maker's preference for early resolution of uncertainty are different. In the first example, the patient is trying to avoid anxiety, while in the second decision problem, he is trying to make a better informed decision. For a standard economist, this distinction is irrelevant because standard economics does not study the causes of preferences. For standard theory, the only relevant distinctions between the two examples are the ones that can be identified through the decision makers' preferences.[6]

The Kreps-Porteus theorem identifies a formula that resembles standard expected utility applied separately at each decision date. While the formula is suggestive of a mental process, this suggestiveness is an expositional device not meant to be taken literally.[7] The formula encapsulates the behavioral assumptions of the theory in a user-friendly way and thereby facilitates applications of the theory to (more complicated) economic problems.

The theory is successful if preference for early resolution of uncertainty turns out to be an empirically important phenomenon, that is, if models that incorporate it are successful at addressing economic behavior. The role of the axioms is to summarize the empirical content of the theory independently of the specific application. The generality of the representation theorem, the usefulness of the key parameters, the ease with which the parameters can be measured and, most important, the empirical success of the model at dealing with economic evidence determine the extent to which the theory succeeds.

The Kreps-Porteus model has been generalized and applied to macroeconomics and finance [see Epstein and Zin, 1989, 1991]. These fields analyze dynamic consumption choice under uncertainty. The primitives of the Kreps-Porteus model (dated lotteries) are easily adapted to match closely the objects studied in macroeconomics and finance. The fact that Kreps-Porteus strip all economically irrelevant details from their model is essential for the success of this adaptation.

Neuroeconomics: Reference-Dependent Utility

In a well-known experiment [Thaler, 1980], a random subset of the subjects are assigned one unit of some object, and then all subjects' reservation prices for this object are elicited. The price at which subjects who were assigned a unit are willing to sell it typically exceeds the price at which the remaining subjects are willing to buy a unit. This phenomenon is referred to as the endowment effect and has motivated models that add a reference point to the utility function.

Köszegi and Rabin [2004] (henceforth Köszegi-Rabin) propose a novel reference-dependent preference theory. To understand the Köszegi-Rabin theory, consider a finite set of choice objects X. A reference-dependent utility function U associates a utility with each reference point $z \in X$ and each choice object $x \in X$. Hence, $U : X \times X \to \mathbb{R}$, where $U(x, z)$ is the utility of x given the reference z. In Köszegi-Rabin, these choice objects are risky prospects, and the utility function U is analogous to a von Neumann-Morgenstern utility index. Here, we consider the simpler deterministic case.

The reference-dependent utility formulation is not new; the novelty is in the adoption of Köszegi [2005]'s notion of a personal equilibrium to determine the reference point. In this setting, a personal equilibrium for an decision maker facing the choice set A is any $x \in A$ such that

$$U(x, x) \geq U(y, x) \tag{1.2}$$

for all $y \in A$. Hence, Köszegi-Rabin define the reference point as the x that ultimately gets chosen. It follows that an alternative $x \in A$ is optimal (i.e., a possible choice) for a Köszegi-Rabin decision maker if (and only if) condition 1.2 above is satisfied. Köszegi-Rabin assume that U has the form

$$U(x, y) = \sum_{k \in K} u_k(x) + \sum_{k \in K} \mu \left[u_k(x) - u_k(y) \right], \tag{1.3}$$

where μ is an increasing function with $\mu(0) = 0$, and K is some finite set indexing the relevant hedonic dimensions of consumption. Köszegi-Rabin note that these consumption dimensions "should be specified based on psychological principles."

There are certain striking differences between the approaches of Kreps-Porteus and Köszegi-Rabin. In Kreps-Porteus, the formula is an "as if" statement and the assumed restrictions on choice behavior (axioms) are the content of the theory. In contrast, Köszegi-Rabin interpret the procedure associated with computing a personal equilibrium (i.e., finding x that satisfy equation 1.2) as a description of the underlying psychological process. Köszegi-Rabin focus on psychological evidence supporting this procedure and the various assumptions on the function U.

The revealed preference analysis answers the following question: Suppose the modeler could not determine the individual ingredients that go into the representation. How can she check whether or not the decision maker behaves in a manner consistent with such a representation? Or, to put it differently, how is the behavior of a Köszegi-Rabin decision maker different from a standard decision maker? For the case of deterministic choice, the answer is that the Köszegi-Rabin decision maker may fail transitivity.[8]

In contrast, Köszegi-Rabin treat the relevant dimension of hedonic utility and the values of the various options along these dimensions as observable and quantifiable. They emphasize that this quantification requires craft and an understanding of psychological principles:

> While we believe applying the model is straightforward in most cases, the necessity of using some psychological and economic judgment—for instance, in choosing the appropriate hedonic dimensions and the appropriate notion of "recent expectations"—leaves us significantly short of an entirely formulaic way to extend the classical utility model. [6]

The assumptions of many theoretical models are based on intuition rather than direct evidence. But in standard models, any future test of the assumptions and the underlying intuitions requires direct (revealed preference) evidence. Where Köszegi-Rabin differ from standard economics is that psychological principles and (nonchoice) evidence are viewed as an alternative form of evidence, and it is this type of evidence that is the focus of their attention.[9]

In Köszegi-Rabin, utility indices (u_k values) and attachment disutilities (measured by μ) are hedonic utilities and are distinct from choice utilities. The Köszegi-Rabin representation is not only a theory of choice but also a description of the underlying psychological process:

> That, by all intuition and evidence, is a real hedonic experience, and making choices reflecting that real hedonic experience is partly rational. But as interpreted by Loewenstein, O'Donoghue, and Rabin [2003], people seem to over-attend to this experience because they ignore that the sensation of loss will pass very quickly—behaving as if they would spend much time longing for the mug they once had. [37]

Hence, measured feelings are inputs in the Köszegi-Rabin analysis. The authors believe that these measurements will enable the analyst to identify hedonic utilities that capture the intrinsic satisfaction of consuming the good (i.e., the u_k's) and hedonic utilities that capture the real loss associated with giving up the good.

Moreover, they expect hedonic measurements to distinguish behavior that results from rational assessment of utilities from behavior that results from overattending to utilities.

Köszegi-Rabin plan to calibrate the model using psychological insights and evidence. They view the Kreps-Porteus–type insistence on calibrating through revealed preferences as an unnecessary demand for formulaic applicability. The model's success is judged by the extent to which the psychological process suggested by their formula matches psychological evidence.

The Failure of Rationality

Neuroeconomists share with many other critics of economics the view that individual rationality is an empirically invalid assumption. Over the years, critics of rationality have identified various economic assumptions as "rationality." The independence axiom, probabilistic sophistication, monotonicity of payoffs in the agent's own consumption, and the independence of payoffs from the consumption of others have all been viewed as implications of rationality before the emergence of economic models that relax these assumptions.

More recent criticisms of rationality focus on the fact that individuals make systematic mistakes even in situations where the right choice is clear. The most ambitious critics of rationality argue that the idea of utility maximization is flawed because individuals do not maximize any preference relation. Below, we argue that these criticisms typically underestimate the flexibility revealed preference methodology. In particular, we illustrate how standard economics deals with "mistakes." Then, we focus on the evidence reported by neuroeconomists in support of their criticism. We observe that much of this evidence misses its target because economic models make no predictions about physiological processes that underlie decision making.

The Neuroeconomic Case against Preference Maximization

CLP [2004] offer a shortlist of neuroeconomic evidence against the "standard economic concept of preference." The list begins with the following item:

> Feelings of pleasure and pain originate in homeostatic mechanisms that detect departures from a "set-point" or ideal level, and attempt to restore equilibrium. In some cases, these attempts do not require additional voluntary actions, e.g., when monitors for body temperature trigger sweating to cool you off and shivering to warm you up. In other cases, the homeostatic processes operate by changing momentary preferences, a process called "alliesthesia" [Cabanac, 1979]. When the

core body temperature falls below the 98.6°F set-point, almost anything that raises body temperature (such as placing one's hand in warm water) feels good, and the opposite is true when body temperature is too high. Similarly, monitors for blood sugar levels, intestinal distention and many other variables trigger hunger. Homeostasis means preferences are "state-dependent" in a special way: The states preferences and act as information signals which provoke equilibration. [562]

No observation in the above quote contradicts any principle of preference maximization. Economic models make no predictions or assumptions about body temperature, blood sugar levels, or other physiological data, and therefore, such data cannot refute economic models. Standard economics is not committed to a particular theory of what makes people feel good. Nor does it assume that feeling good is what people care about.

The second item challenges the adequacy of revealed preference data:

Inferring preferences from a choice does not tell us everything we need to know, and may tell us very little. Consider the hypothetical case of two people, Al and Naucia, who both refuse to buy peanuts at a reasonable price [cf. Romer, 2000]. The refusal to buy reveals a common disutility for peanuts. But Al turned down the peanuts because he is allergic: Consuming peanuts causes a prickly rash, shortens his breath, and could even be fatal. Naucia turned down the peanuts because she ate a huge bag of peanuts at a circus years ago, and subsequently got sick from eating too much candy at the same time. Since then, her gustatory system associates peanuts with illness and she refuses them at reasonable prices. While Al and Naucia both revealed an identical disutility, a neurally detailed account tells us more. Al has an inelastic demand for peanuts—you can't pay him enough to eat them!—while Naucia would try a fistful for the right price. [563]

It is often impossible to infer preferences from a single decision. In fact, finding a small class of such experiments to identify the individual's utility function is the central concern of revealed preference theory. Hence, not buying peanuts at a single price does not imply "Al and Naucia both revealed an identical disutility," and while "a neurally detailed could "tell us more," the economically meaningful information can only be elicited with a change in prices. In standard economics, the reasons for a particular ranking of alternatives is irrelevant. That Al might die from consuming peanuts and Naucia simply doesn't like consuming them matters only if at some price Naucia is willing to do so and Al is not, and even then, it is the latter fact and not the underlying reasons that are relevant.

We delay the discussion of the third item to the next section, where we discuss welfare analysis. The fourth item discusses what standard economics would consider a form of money illusion: decision makers may derive "direct" utility from money, beyond the utility they derive from the goods purchased with money:

A fourth problem with preference is that people are assumed to value money for what it can purchase—that is, the utility of income is indirect, and should be derived from direct utilities for goods that will be purchased with money. But roughly speaking, it appears that similar brain circuitry—dopaminergic neurons in the midbrain—is active for a wide variety of rewarding experiences—drugs, food, attractive faces [cite], humor [cite]—and money rewards. This means money may be directly rewarding, and its loss painful. [565]

There are straightforward economic tests for identifying money illusion. Such a test would entail changing prices and nominal wages in a manner that leaves the set of feasible-consumption, labor supply pairs unchanged. Then, we could check if this change has shifted the labor supply curve. But the issue cannot be addressed by investigating the brain circuitry and the midbrain, since economic models are silent on the brain activity associated with decision making.

The fifth and final item deals with addiction:

Addiction is an important topic for economics because it seems to resist rational explanation. . . . It is relevant to rational models of addiction that every substance to which humans may become biologically addicted is also potentially addictive for rats. Addictive substances appear therefore to be "hijacking" primitive reward circuitry in the "old" part of the human brain. Although this fact does not disprove the rational model (since the recently evolved cortex may override rat brain circuitry), it does show that rational intertemporal planning is not necessary to create the addictive phenomena of tolerance, craving, and withdrawal. It also highlights the need for economic models of the primitive reward circuitry, which would apply equally to man and rat. [565–566]

That substances addictive for rats are also addictive in humans is not relevant for economics because (standard) economics does not study rats.[10] It also does not study the causes of preferences. To say that a decision maker prefers x to y is to say that he never chooses y when x is also available, nothing more. Hence, addiction can be identified as a distinct economic phenomenon only through its distinct choice implications, not through the underlying brain processes. The fact that addictive substances appear to be "hijacking primitive reward circuitry" fails to disprove the rational model not because the cortex may override the rat brain circuitry but because the rational model addresses neither the brain circuitry nor the cortex.

What the authors describe as evidence is in fact a statement of their philosophical position. They have decided that the cortex represents planned action rational choice, while certain processes in other parts (presumably in the midbrain) represent overwhelming physiological influences (i.e., the hijacking of the primitive reward circuitry):

Many of the processes that occur in these systems are affective rather than cognitive; they are directly concerned with motivation. This might not matter for economics were it not for the principles that guide the affective system—the way that it operates—is so much at variance with the standard economics account of behavior. [25–26]

Hence, every decision that is associated with the latter types of processes is interpreted as evidence that rational choice theory is wrong. This critique fails because standard economics takes no position on whether a particular decision represents a manifestation of free will or a succumbing to biological necessity. Rationality in economics is not tied to physiological causes of behavior, and therefore, the physiological mechanisms cannot shed light on whether a choice is rational or not in the sense economists use the term. Brain mechanisms by themselves cannot offer evidence against transitivity of preferences or any other choice-theoretic assumption. Therefore, evidence that utility maximization is not a good model of the brain cannot refute economic models. Discussing decision making under uncertainty, Camerer [2005: 1] writes:

> For example, when economists think about gambling they assume that people combine the chance of winning (probability) with an expectation of how they will value winning and losing ("utilities"). If this theory is correct, neuroeconomics will find two processes in the brain—one for guessing how likely one is to win and lose, and another for evaluating the hedonic pleasure and pain of winning and losing and another brain region which combines probability and hedonic sensations. More likely, neuroeconomics will show that the desire or aversion to gamble is more complicated than that simple model.

Camerer assumes that there is one set of correct abstractions for both economics and neuroscience and tries to identify whether the ones currently used in economics belong to that set. The conceptual separation between probabilities and utilities is very important for expected utility theory. This separation need not have a physiological counterpart. Even if it did, mapping that process into the physiology of the brain and seeing if it amounts to "one [process] for guessing how likely one is to win and lose, and another for evaluating the hedonic pleasure and pain of winning and losing and another brain region which combines probability and hedonic sensations" is a problem for neuroscience, not economics. Since expected utility theory makes predictions only about choice behavior, its validity can be assessed only through choice evidence. If economic evidence leads us to the conclusion that expected utility theory is appropriate in a particular set of applications, then the inability to match this theory to the physiology of the brain might be considered puzzling. But this puzzle is a concern for neuroscientists, not economists.

Standard economics does not address mental processes, and as a result, economic abstractions are typically not appropriate for describing them. In his 1998 survey, Rabin criticizes standard economics for failing to be a good model of the mind, even though standard economics never had such ambitions: "Economists have traditionally assumed that, when faced with uncertainty, people correctly form their subjective probabilistic assessments according to the laws of probability. But researchers have documented many systematic departures from rationality in judgment under uncertainty" [24].

Many economists (including the authors of many introductory economic textbooks) are aware that most people do not think in terms of probabilities, subjective or otherwise. Nor does standard economics assume that consumers know Bayes's law in the sense that a graduate student in economics would be expected to know it. Economic models connect to reality through economic variables, prices, quantities, and so on, and not through their modeling of the individual's decision-making process. Evidence of the sort cited in neuroeconomics may inspire economists to write different models, but it cannot reject economic models.

Our central argument is simple: neuroscience evidence cannot refute economic models because the latter make no assumptions or draw no conclusions about physiology of the brain. Conversely, brain science cannot revolutionize economics because it has no vehicle for addressing the concerns of the latter. Economics and psychology differ in the questions they ask. Therefore, abstractions that are useful for one discipline will typically be not very useful for the other. The concepts of a preference, a choice function, demand function, GDP, utility, and so forth, have proven to be useful abstractions in economics. The fact that they are less useful for the analysis of the brain does not mean that they are bad abstractions in economics.

Mistakes

Individuals sometimes make obviously bad decisions. Neuroeconomists use this fact as proof of the failure in revealed preference theory. Bernheim and Rangel [2004] provide the following example:

> American visitors to the United Kingdom suffer numerous injuries and fatalities because they often look only to the left before stepping into streets, even though they know traffic approaches from the right. One cannot reasonably attribute this to the pleasure of looking left or to masochistic preferences. The pedestrian's objectives—to cross the street safely—are clear, and the decision is plainly a mistake. [1561–1562]

Standard economics has long recognized that there are situations where an outsider could improve an individual's decisions. Such situations come up routinely when agents are asymmetrically informed. Hence, standard economics deals with "mistakes" by employing the tools of information economics.

Consider the following thought experiment. A prize ($100) is placed either in a red or in a blue box, and the agent knows that there is a 60% chance that the money is in the red box. Confronted with a choice between the two boxes, the agent chooses the red box. An observer who has seen that the money was placed in the blue box may think that the agent prefers choosing red to getting $100. This inference is obviously incorrect because "choose $100" is a strategy that is not available to the agent. The observer who thinks the agent prefers red to $100 has not understood the agent's constraints. Given the agent's constraints, his choice of the red box is optimal.

Many situations in which agents systematically make mistakes can be interpreted as situations where agents face subjective constraints on the feasible strategies that are not apparent from the description of the decision problem. The strategy "only cross the street when no car is approaching" may be unavailable in the sense that it violates a subjective constraint on the set of feasible strategies. Hence, a standard economic model of the street-crossing problem would add a constraint on the set of feasible strategies as part of the description of the agent.

Suppose the economist asserts that the American tourist prefers not being run over by a car but finds it more difficult to implement that outcome in the United Kingdom than in the United States. As evidence for this assertion, the economist could point to data showing that American tourists in London avoid unregulated intersections. That tourists incur a cost to cross at regulated intersections suggests (i) they are unable to safely cross the street without help and (ii) they are not suicidal.

Framing effects can be addressed in a similar fashion. Experimenters can often manipulate the choices of individuals by restating the decision problem in a different (but equivalent) form. Standard theory interprets a framing effect as a change in the subjective constraints (or information) faced by the decision maker. It may turn out that a sign that alerts the American tourist to "look right" alters the decision even though such a sign does not change the set of alternatives. The standard model can incorporate this effect by assuming that the sign changes the set of feasible strategies for the tourist and thereby alters the decision. With the help of the sign, the tourist may be able to implement the strategy "always look right then go," while without the sign this strategy may not be feasible for the tourist.

For standard economics, the fact that individuals make mistakes is relevant only if these mistakes can be identified through economic data. That behavior would have been different under a counterfactual scenario in which the agent did not make or was prevented from making these mistakes is irrelevant.

THE INADEQUACY OF RATIONALITY

Neuroeconomists criticize both standard positive economics and standard normative analysis. In the preceding section, we describe and respond to the neuroeconomic critique of positive economics. Here, we address the neuroeconomic critique of normative economics.

Kahneman [1994: 20] notes that "the term 'utility' can be anchored in the hedonic experience of outcomes, or in the preference or desire for that outcome." Because agents make mistakes, neuroeconomists conclude that a person's choices do not maximize the hedonic consequences of these choices. More generally, neuroeconomists argue that choices do not maximize the individual's well-being or happiness.

The neuroeconomic critique of standard welfare analysis relies on two related arguments: first, what people choose often fails to make them happy; second, proper welfare analysis should be based on what makes people happy, and such measurements necessitate neuroscientific input. Even if direct measurement of happiness through brain scans is not yet feasible, neuroeconomists believe that such measurement will eventually be possible.

> A third problem with preferences is that there are different types of utilities which do not always coincide. . . . For example, Berridge and Robinson [1998] have found distinct brain regions for "wanting" and "liking," which correspond roughly to choice utility and experienced utility. The fact that these areas are dissociated allows a wedge between those two kinds of utility. . . . If the different types of utility are produced by different regions, they will not always match up. Examples are easy to find. Infants reveal a choice utility by putting dirt in their mouths, but they don't rationally anticipate liking it. Addicts often report drug craving (wanting) which leads to consumption (choosing) that they say is not particularly pleasurable (experiencing). Compulsive shoppers buy goods (revealing choice utility) which they never use (no experienced utility). [CLP, 2004: 564]

Neuroeconomists use such evidence and related (thought) experiments to suggest that the concept of a preference that simultaneously determines behavior and "what is good for the agent" can be wide of the mark. Hence, neuroeconomists distinguish between "decision utilities," which generate behavior, and "experienced utilities," which indicate what makes the agent happy.

Below, we discuss and respond to this neuroeconomic critique of standard welfare analysis. We then consider two examples of substantive rationality in the literature: recent proposals for paternalism and welfare analysis in multi-self models. First, we provide a brief summary of standard welfare analysis.

Standard Welfare Analysis

Economists use welfare analysis to examine how institutions mediate the interests of the participating individuals. Welfare-improving changes to an economic institution are defined to be changes to which the individual(s) would agree. Policy x is deemed better than policy y for an individual if and only if, given the opportunity, the individual would choose x over y. The choice of x over y may be motivated by the pursuit of happiness or a sense of duty or religious obligation or may reflect an impulse. In all cases, it constitutes an improvement of economic welfare.

Economic welfare analysis is a tool for analyzing economic institutions and models. For example, economic analysis of a trading institution may establish that the institution yields Pareto efficient outcomes, and therefore, there is no institutional change that will improve the economic welfare of all participants. Economists view such results as successes of their theories because the results demonstrate that the economic model of the institution is "stable"; there are no changes that are mutually agreeable to all participants. Conversely, models of economic institutions will raise suspicion if there are obvious welfare-improving changes (changes that all individuals would agree to) because the availability of such changes suggests that the model misses important aspects of the underlying reality.

Economists use the revealed preference of individuals as a welfare criterion because it is the only criterion that can be integrated with positive economic analysis. For example, consider the economic analysis of farm subsidies. Economists have found that U.S. farm subsidies are inefficient; that is, farm subsidies could be eliminated, and farmers could be compensated in a way that would increase the economic welfare of all U.S. households. The most interesting aspect of this observation is that farm subsidies persist despite their inefficiency. Motivated by this and related observations, economists have examined the mechanisms (political and economic) that lead to the persistence of inefficient policies.

The example of farm subsidies is typical for the use of welfare analysis in economics. Normative statements (farm subsidies are inefficient) are used to define new positive questions (what makes farm subsidies persist?) that lead to better models of the underlying institution. Economists use welfare analysis to identify the interests of economic agents and to ask whether existing policies can be interpreted as an expression of those interests or whether the understanding of the institutional constraints on policies remains incomplete. This use of welfare analysis requires the standard definition of economic welfare. There is no reason for economic agents to gravitate toward policies and institutions that yield higher welfare if the underlying notion of welfare does not reflect the interests of agents as the agents themselves perceive these interests.

Neuroeconomic Welfare Analysis

Neuroeconomists treat the economists' definition of welfare as if it were a theory of happiness and proceed to find evidence against this theory. CLP [2005: 36] write:

> Economics proceeds on the assumption that satisfying people's wants is a good thing. This assumption depends on knowing that people will like what they want. If likes and wants diverge, this would pose a fundamental challenge to standard welfare economics. Presumably welfare should be based on "liking." But if we cannot infer what people like from what they want and choose, then an alternative method for measuring liking is needed, while avoiding an oppressive paternalism.

Welfare in economics is a definition and not a theory (of happiness). Therefore, the divergence of "liking" and "wanting" does not pose any challenge to the standard definition of welfare, no matter how the former is defined. Standard economics offers no substantive criterion for rationality because it has no therapeutic ambition; it does not attempt to cure decision makers who make choices that do not generate the most pleasure. The more modest economic definition of welfare is mandated by the role of welfare analysis in economics.

To compare this role with the role envisaged by neuroeconomists, suppose that a trading institution is found to be (economically) inefficient. Typically, this will imply that someone can set up an alternative institution and make a profit. Hence, we can expect this change to take place without a benevolent dictator, simply as a result of self-interested entrepreneurship. Suppose a psychologist argues that an inefficient trading institution leads to higher "experienced" utility than an efficient one and that agents are mistaken in their preference for the economically efficient institution. Whether or not this assertion is true, the economic analysis of the trading institution is valid. The economically efficient trading institution is still the one we can expect to prevail. Moreover, since agents perceive their own interests to coincide with the economic welfare criterion, there is no obvious mechanism (economic or political) by which the psychologically superior institution could emerge.

Neuroeconomists would argue that even though a welfare criterion based on the individuals' own "preferences or desires" may be relevant for positive analysis, a substantive criterion is needed for normative theory. For neuroeconomists, the goal of welfare analysis is to advocate changes that improve decision makers' well-being. To achieve their goal, neuroeconomists can either try to convince people to want what is good for them (therapy) or make the right choice on their behalf (paternalism). Kahneman [1994: 27] summarizes both of these positions as follows:

> However, truly informed consent is only possible if patients have a reasonable conception of expected long term developments in their hedonic responses . . . . A more controversial issues arises if we admit that an outsider can sometimes predict an individual's future utility far better than the individual can. Does this superior knowledge carry a warrant, or even a duty, for paternalistic intervention? It appears right for Ulysses' sailors to tie him to the mast against his will, if they believe that he is deluded about his ability to resist the fatal call of the sirens.

The neuroeconomic view of welfare analysis builds on an inappropriate analogy between an economist and a therapist. It may be the case that sometimes outsiders know more about the future utility of an individual than the individual herself. But the goal of economics is not to prepare the economist for service at times when she finds herself in the role of that outsider.

If economists were in the business of investment counseling, it might make sense for neuroeconomists to focus on the conflict between what the typical consumer/investor wants to do now and what will make him happy in the future. But economists do not deal with patients (or even clients). Therefore, it is not clear who the recipient of their counseling would be. The neuroeconomics view of the economist as a therapist is inappropriate both as a description of what economists do and as a description of what they could be doing.

Of course, one could argue that economists should identify a substantive criterion for rationality (i.e., a criterion for measuring what really makes individuals happy) and advocate changes that increase welfare according to this criterion regardless of whether or not they have the means to convince the potential beneficiaries to follow this advice, the hope being that someone other than the potential beneficiary might be convinced to implement the policies. This view is apparent in Kahneman's [1994] search for a benevolent paternalistic figure in his examples:

> The physician could probably ensure that the patient will retain a more favorable memory of the procedure by adding to it a medically superfluous period of diminishing pain. Of course, the patient would probably reject the physician's offer to provide an improved memory at the cost of more actual pain. Should the physician go ahead anyway, on behalf of the patient's future remembering self? [32]

In the same article, Kahneman suggests that there is "a case in favour of some paternalistic interventions, when it is plausible that the state knows more about an individual's future tastes than the individual knows presently" [20]. When economists or political scientists model the government, they do so either by endowing the government with certain objectives or by modeling government as an institution where conflicting incentives of various agents interact. In Kahneman's analysis, the government is a benign and disinterested agent whose only role is to serve as the object of the modeler's lobbying efforts.

Welfare analysis for neuroeconomics is a form of social activism; it is a recommendation for someone to change her preferences or for someone in a position of authority to intervene on behalf of someone else. In contrast, welfare economics in the standard economic model is integrated with the model's positive analysis; it takes agents' preferences as given and evaluates the performance of economic institutions.

Regardless of one's views on the importance and efficacy of social activism, there are advantages to separating the role of the economist as a researcher from the role a particular economist might play as an advocate. This separation enables the positive analysis to proceed without having to resolve difficult philosophical problems such as figuring out what makes people happy or who is more deserving of happiness. It also enables other researchers to assess and critique a particular piece of analysis without having to evaluate the merits of the underlying moral philosophy or the effectiveness of the researcher's activism.

Proposals for Paternalistic Welfare Criteria

Two recent articles outline plans for welfare economics based on paternalistic principles. In both articles, the authors are motivated by evidence showing that the specification of the default option affects individual choices of retirement plans. Rates of enrollment in 401(k) plans are significantly higher when the default option is to enroll than when the default option is not to enroll.

A standard interpretation of the 401(k) problem would argue that the default matters for the decision problem as perceived by the individual. The employee's set of feasible strategies changes with the default just as the feasible strategies of the American tourist in London change when a sign is placed at the side of the road alerting the tourist to look right. The welfare-maximizing default option is the one that agents would choose when asked to choose among defaults.

Thaler and Sunstein [2003] (henceforth TS) seek paternalistic principles for choosing a default option. They advocate libertarian paternalism and suggest the following three guiding principles: "First, the libertarian paternalist might select the approach that majority would choose if explicit choices were required and revealed." Hence, the libertarian paternalist is to substitute the predicted preferences of the majority for the preferences of the individual. "Second, the libertarian paternalist might select the approach that would force people to make their choices explicit." Finally, "the libertarian paternalist might select the approach that minimizes the number of opt-outs" [178]. TS offer no arguments for why their principles are likely to lead to greater happiness. In fact, they offer no defense of these principles. They simply say that the libertarian paternalist might choose to use them.

The fact that the TS principles are not particularly compelling as moral philosophy is a side issue. The real issue is that it is difficult to see what question their proposal addresses. To put it differently, it is unclear who they have in mind as the potential beneficiary of their philosophical argument. The TS motivation for paternalism seems to be that it is inevitable: "The first misconception is that there are viable alternatives to paternalism. In many situations, some organization or agent must make a choice that will affect the choices of some other people" [175]. Clearly, the decisions of one agent may affect the utility of others. Economic analysis suggests that the interests of the agent in control are a good place to start when analyzing such situations. For example, in order to maximize profits, firms may wish to make their benefit plans as attractive as possible to their future employees. In that case, firms will choose plans (and their default options) in accordance with how the employees would choose them. It may be impractical to ask prospective employees about their preferred default option on the retirement plan, and therefore the firm will use its best subjective assessment of the employees' preferences.

Of course, employers may have different objectives and may choose a plan that differs from their best guess of the employees' preferred plan. Presumably, they would do so to increase their own welfare. In this situation, as in the situation of the pure profit-maximizing employer, there is no role for the TS principles. The TS argument amounts to telling employers that when they face incomplete information, they should adopt a different objective. Standard economics would predict that employers will take the best action given their own objectives and given what they know about the preferences of the employees.

In a recent Camerer, Issacharoff, Loewenstein, O'Donoghue, and Rabin [2003] (henceforth CILOR) introduce and advocate the notion of "asymmetric paternalism": "A regulation is asymmetrically paternalistic if it creates large benefits for those who make errors, while imposing little or no harm on those who are fully rational" [1212]. CILOR do not explain which preferences reflect bounded rationality and which reflect full rationality, when benefits are large and when there is little or no harm. Nevertheless, their implicit welfare criterion is familiar. As we describe above, the mistakes of boundedly rational agents can be modeled as a subjective informational constraint facing these agents. With this reinterpretation, the CILOR principle amounts to a (ϵ) version of the Pareto principle: help the uninformed without hurting the informed (too much). However, there is an important difference between the CILOR version of the Pareto principle and the Pareto principle in standard economics: CILOR view their principle as a framework for activism. They urge their readers to adopt their modified libertarian philosophy in place of the purely libertarian philosophy that they perceive as guiding many economists (and perhaps some lawyers) or the unabashed paternalism favored by behavioral economists:

> Our paper seeks to engage two different audiences with two different sets of concerns: For those (particularly economists) prone to rigid antipaternalism, the paper describes a possibly attractive rationale for paternalism as well as a careful, cautious, and disciplined approach. For those prone to give unabashed support for paternalistic policies based on behavioral economics, this paper argues that more discipline is needed and proposes a possible criterion. [1212]

Of course, it is legitimate for TS and CILOR to engage employers or the legal and economics professions in a moral debate. But this has little to do with welfare economics, which is not concerned with moral philosophy or with providing a disciplined guide for social action.

Standard economists spend little time or effort advocating normative criteria even when they feel that the right normative criterion is unambiguous. For example, many economists and decision theorists believe in the importance of making decisions under uncertainty consistent with some subjective probability assessments. Moreover, hardly anyone would question the normative appeal of using Bayes's law when updating probabilities. There are many research papers where agents are endowed with subjective probabilities and use Bayes's law. The purpose of these papers is not to advocate the use of subjective probabilities or Bayesian revision; rather, the normative appeal of the Savage model serves as a starting point for the positive analysis. The ultimate value of Savage's contribution depends not on the ability of his followers to convince individual economic agents or benign planners to adopt his view of probability but on the success his followers have at developing models that address economic data.

Preference Reversals and Multi-Selves

There is evidence that individuals resolve the same intertemporal trade-off differently depending on when the decision is made.[11] Researchers, starting with the work of Strotz [1955], have argued that this phenomenon requires modeling the individual as a collection of distinct selves with conflicting interests. Such models represent a major departure from the standard economics conception of the individual as the unit of agency. For example, if the individual cannot be identified as a coherent set of interests, then the economists' welfare criterion is not well defined. Hence, for neuroeconomists, preference reversals constitute an empirical validation of the psychologist's—as opposed to the economist's—view of the individual.

Consider the following example: In period 1, the agent chooses the consumption stream $(0, 0, 9)$ over $(1, 0, 0)$ and chooses $(1, 0, 0)$ over $(0, 3, 0)$. In period 2, the agent chooses $(0, 3, 0)$ over $(0, 0, 9)$. Suppose the agent faces the following decision problem: he can either choose $(1, 0, 0)$ in period 1 or leave the choice between $(0, 0, 9)$ and $(0, 3, 0)$ for period 2. Confronted with this choice, the agent picks $(1, 0, 0)$.

In Gul and Pesendorfer [2001, 2004, 2005], we propose a standard, single-self model that accounts for this behavior. To illustrate the approach, define $\mathcal{C}$ to be the set of second-period choice problems for the individual; that is, an element $C \in \mathcal{C}$ consists of consumption streams with identical first-period consumption levels: $(c_1, c_2, c_3), (c'_1, c'_2, c'_3) \in C \in \mathcal{C}$ implies $c_1 = c'_1$. In period 2, the individual chooses a consumption stream from some C. In period 1, the individual chooses a choice problem C for period 2. Choosing $(1, 0, 0)$ in period 1 corresponds to $\{(1, 0, 0)\}$, while the option of leaving it to period 2 to choose between $(0, 3, 0)$ and $(0, 0, 9)$ is described as

$$C = \{(0, 3, 0), (0, 0, 9)\}.$$

With this notation, we can summarize the (period 1) behavior as

$$\{(0, 0, 9)\} \succ \{(1, 0, 0)\} \succ C = \{(0, 3, 0), (0, 0, 9)\} \sim \{(0, 3, 0)\}.$$

Note that choosing between $\{(0, 3, 0)\}$ and $\{(0, 0, 9)\}$ is not the same as choosing from the set $C = \{(0, 3, 0), (0, 0, 9)\}$. In the former case, the consumer commits to a consumption path in period 1, while in the latters she chooses in period 2. The preference statements above indicate that the individual prefers a situation where she is committed to $(0, 0, 1)$ to a situation where she chooses from C in period 2.

When such a commitment is unavailable, and the agent is confronted with C in period 2, she chooses $(0, 3, 0)$.

Standard economics models identify choice with welfare. Therefore, the choice of $(0, 3, 0)$ from C in period 2 is welfare maximizing, as is the choice of $\{(0, 0, 9)\}$ over $\{(0, 3, 0)\}$ in period 1. The interpretation is that, in period 2, the agent struggles with the temptation to consume three units. Temptation is costly to resist, and therefore consuming (rather than holding out for nine in period 3) is the optimal (and welfare-maximizing) choice in period 2. In period 1, higher period 2 consumption is not tempting, and therefore, the agent prefers $\{(0, 0, 9)\}$ over $\{(0, 3, 0)\}$. Period 1 behavior reveals that the individual's welfare is higher in all periods when she is committed to $(0, 0, 9)$ than when she must choose from C in period 2.[12]

The multi-self model abandons the revealed preference approach to welfare and constructs paternalistic welfare criteria. Consider again the three-period model. In each period, the individual's preferences are described by a utility function, U_t. For concreteness, assume

$$U_1(c_1, c_2, c_3) = c_1 + \beta\delta c_2 + \beta\delta^2 c_3,$$

$$U_2(c_1, c_2, c_3) = c_2 + \beta\delta c_3, \tag{1.4}$$

$$U_3(c_1, c_2, c_3) = \delta c_3,$$

where $\delta = \beta = 1/2$. While different papers postulate different welfare criteria for such situations, the common argument is that preference reversals necessitate a criterion for trading off the utility of the various selves. The most common practice in this literature is to treat the following U_0 as the welfare criterion:

$$U_0(c_1, c_2, c_3) = c_1 + \delta c_2 + \delta^2 c_3$$

This particular welfare criterion may seem odd. After all, U_0 quite arbitrarily sets $\beta = 1$ and assigns a higher welfare to $(1, 0, 11)$ than to $(2, 3, 0)$ even though selves 1 and 2 prefer $(2, 3, 0)$. The multiple-selves literature interprets U_0 as the preferences with the "present bias" removed.[13] In other words, $\beta < 1$ is diagnosed as a defect, and the role of policy intervention is to cure this defect.

Note that hyperbolic discounting (or time inconsistency) is not necessary for generating conflict among the various selves of the individual: Consider again the three-period example above but now let $\beta = 1$. The resulting utility functions describe standard preferences with exponential discounting. Consider the two consumption streams, $(1, 0, 0)$ and $(0, 0, 4)$, and note that $U_1(1, 0, 0) = U_1(0, 0, 4)$ but $U_2(1, 0, 0) < U_2(0, 0, 4)$ and $U_3(1, 0, 0) < U_3(0, 0, 4)$; that is, the allocation $(1, 0, 0)$ is Pareto dominated by the allocation $(0, 0, 4)$ even though the usual welfare criterion of the multi-selves literature (U_0) would deem the two alternatives welfare equivalent.[14]

Economists often note the arbitrariness of using U_0 as a welfare criterion in the multi-selves model. It is not clear what hedonic utility calculations have led neuroeconomists to decide that U_0 represents the right trade-off among the hedonic utilities of the various selves. Our point is different: standard economics has neither need nor use for a welfare criterion that trades off utility among the various selves of a single individual. Such trade-offs can never play a role in explaining or understanding economic institutions. By definition, only behavior can influence economic data or institutions. Hence, beyond their effect on behavior, the various "selves" are irrelevant for the analysis. By contrast, neuroeconomists view the existence of multiple selves as both an opportunity and a rationale for activism. They wish to urge the individual to do a better job at accommodating the welfare of their future selves (i.e., resist $\beta < 1$ and other biases). Failing that, they would like to convince third parties to intervene on behalf of the agent's future selves. This therapeutic/paternalistic stance is similar to the position of medical professionals who attempt to cure a patient's addiction. By proposing a welfare criterion, the modeler is either urging the individual to reform his behavior or urging someone in a position of authority to force the individual to do so.

Identifying what makes people happy, defining criteria for trading off one person's (or selves) happiness against the happiness of another, and advocating social change in a manner that advances overall happiness by this criterion are tasks many neuroeconomists find more worthy than dealing with the more pedestrian questions of standard economics. However, the expression of this preference constitutes neither an empirical nor a methodological criticism of standard economics.

THE UNIFICATION OF ECONOMICS AND NEUROSCIENCE

Neuroeconomists often cite improvements in neuroscience, in particular, improvements in measurements, as a central reason for unifying the disciplines of economics, psychology, and brain science:

> Since feelings were meant to predict behavior, but could only be assessed from behavior, economists realized that without direct measurement, feelings were useless intervening constructs. In the 1940s, the concepts of ordinal utility and revealed preference eliminated the superfluous intermediate step of positing immeasurable feelings. Revealed preference theory simply equates unobserved preferences with observed choices. Circularity is avoided by assuming that people behave consistently, which makes the theory falsifiable; once they have revealed

that they prefer A to B, people should not subsequently choose B over A . . . . The "as if" approach made good sense, as long as the brain remained substantially a black box. The development of economics could not be held hostage to progress in other human sciences. But now neuroscience has proved Jevons' pessimistic prediction wrong; the study of the brain and nervous system is beginning to allow direct measurement of thoughts and feelings. [CLP, 2005: 10]

Thus, neuroeconomists view the revealed preference approach to be an outdated concession to technological limitations of the past.[15] Since the technology for distinguishing between "liking" (i.e., a criterion of substantive rationality) and "wanting" (i.e., choice) may soon be available, economics (and presumably other social sciences) should abandon the revealed preference methodology and adopt the methodology of psychology and neuroscience.

The dominant role of revealed preference analysis in economics has little to do with technology. Economic phenomena consist of individual choices and their aggregates and do not include hedonic values of utilities or feelings. Therefore, it is not relevant for an economic model to explore the feelings associated with economic choices. The point of revealed preference theory is to separate the theory of decision making from the analysis of emotional consequences of decisions. This separation is useful whether or not emotions can be measured simply because it facilitates specialization. Note that the more detailed and sophisticated the measurement, the greater is the potential benefit of specialization.

Brain imaging data are of a radically different form than are typical economic data. If the prediction of great advances in brain science turns out to be correct, they will certainly be accompanied by theoretical advances that address the particular data in that field. It is unreasonable to require those theories to be successful at addressing economic data, as well. By the same token, the requirement that economic theories simultaneously account for economic data and brain imaging data places an unreasonable burden on economic theories.

Note that the above does not say that psychological factors are irrelevant for economic decision making, nor does it say that economists should ignore psychological insights. Economists routinely take their inspiration from psychological data or theories. However, economic models are evaluated by their success at explaining economic phenomena. Since hedonic utility values and brain imaging data are not economic phenomena, economists should not feel constrained to choose models that succeed as models of the brain.

The arguments advanced by neuroeconomists in favor of unification often fail to distinguish between a novel philosophical position and a scientific breakthrough. Often, what neuroeconomists present as an empirical challenge to economics is best viewed as an invitation to an ethical debate. For example, Kahneman [1994: 21] writes: "The history of an individual through time can be described as a succession of separate selves. . . . Which one of these selves should be granted authority over outcomes in the future?" Hence, neuroeconomics interprets the individual as a flawed and inconsistent sequence of "pleasure machines" that need therapeutic and paternalistic assistance for assessing the right intertemporal trade-offs and making the right choices.

It is not clear what evidence neuroeconomics can offer to answer such questions as "should physicians increase the actual pain experienced by the patient in order to facilitate his memory and improve his decision making for the future?" [Kahneman, 1994: 32]. What is clear is that finding out how to trade off the welfare of one self against another or deciding "which one of these selves should be granted authority over outcomes in the future" is not an economic problem.

CLP [2004] suggest a more modest goal: that neuroscience may facilitate direct measurement of preference parameters by "asking the brain, not the person" [573]. The authors have no example of observing a choice parameter—such as the coefficient of relative risk aversion or the discount factor—through brain imaging, and no suggestions as to how such inference could be done. They offer no criteria for distinguishing a brain where $\delta = 0.97$ versus one where $\delta = 0.7$. They do not explain what language to use when "asking the brain, rather than the person" which language the brain will use to respond, or what to do when the brain's answer conflicts with the answer of the person.

In the end, scientific developments play a small role in the arguments of neuroeconomists: when it comes to substantiating the central philosophical position that there is a difference between what people want and what is good for them, subjective readings of the facial expressions of mice do just as well as anything that might be learned from fMRI readings.

CONCLUSION: WHY THE NEUROECONOMICS CRITIQUE FAILS

Kahneman [1994] notes the following two problems facing "a critic of the rationality assumption": "(i) a willingness of choice theorists to make the theory even more permissive, as needed to accommodate apparent violations of its requirements; (ii) a methodological position that treats rationality as a maintained hypothesis making it very difficult to disprove" [34]. Kahneman's observations make it clear that rationality is not an assumption in economics but a methodological stance. This stance reflects economists' decision to view the individual as the unit of agency and investigate the interaction of the purposeful behaviors of different individuals within various economic institutions. One can question the usefulness of this methodological stance by challenging individual economic models or the combined output of economics, but one cannot disprove it.

The difficulties that Kahneman observes for critics of the rationality assumption are no different than the difficulties that one would encounter when challenging the assumption that laboratory experiments on individual choice are useful for understanding real-life behavior. For example, a critic of such experiments may complain that real-life choice problems do not come with explicit probabilities. If successful, such a criticism will lead to a new class of experiments, ones that do not make explicit references to probabilities.[16] However, a critic cannot expect to disprove the usefulness of experimental methods for understanding choice behavior. Criticisms that aim to disprove a broad and flexible methodology as if it were a single falsifiable assumption are best viewed as demands for a shift in emphasis from questions that the critic considers uninteresting to ones that he finds more interesting.

This latter description fits our view of what CLP [2005], Rabin [1998], and Kahneman [1994] describe as the radical challenge to economics:

> The radical approach involves turning back the hands of time and asking how economics might have evolved differently if it had been informed from the start by insights and findings now available from neuroscience. Neuroscience, we will argue, points to an entirely new set of constructs to underlie economic decision making. The standard economic theory of constrained utility maximization is most naturally interpreted either as the result of learning based on consumption experiences (which is of little help when prices, income and opportunity sets change), or careful deliberation—a balancing of the costs and benefits of different options—as might characterize complex decisions like planning for retirement, buying a house, or hammering out a contract. Although economists may privately acknowledge that actual flesh-and-blood human beings often choose without much deliberation, the economic models as written invariably represent decisions in a "deliberative equilibrium." [CLP, 2005: 10]

Populating economic models with "flesh-and-blood human beings" was never the objective of economists. Constrained optimization, Bayes's law, and other economic abstractions do not represent the state-of-the-art psychology of an earlier era. Therefore, there is no reason to believe that making the state-of-the-art psychology of our time available earlier would have had such a profound effect on the development of economics.

Rabin [1998] argues that "it is sometimes misleading to conceptualize people as attempting to maximize a coherent, stable, and accurately perceived $U(x)$" [12]. Economists have at their disposal numerous devices to incorporate instability (or change) into individual preferences. They can assume that the decision maker's preferences depend on an exogenous state variable, on the information of her opponents, or on her own consumption history. The decision maker may be learning about a relevant preference parameter, over time. All this flexibility or permissiveness notwithstanding, it is likely that the economists' model of the individual is not suitable for psychologists' goals. It does not follow from this that economists should adopt both the goals and methods of psychology.

Regardless of the source of their inspiration, economic models can only be evaluated on their own terms, with respect to their own objectives and evidence. A revolution in economics has to yield great economic insights. The CLP and Rabin agendas seem far reaching only because they define the task of economics as continually importing psychology-neuroscience ideas. Similarly, all the challenges CLP [2005] identify for the emerging discipline of neuroeconomics resemble the current questions of psychology more than the current questions of economics.

A choice theory paper in economics must identify the revealed preference implications of the model presented and describe how revealed preference methods can be used to identify its parameters. Revealed preference earns such a central role in economics because this is the form of evidence that is available to economists—and not because of a philosophical stance against other forms of evidence.

Greater psychological realism is not an appropriate modeling criterion for economics, and therapeutic social activism is not its goal. Welfare analysis helps economists understand how things are by comparing the existing situation to how things might have been in a plausible alternative institutional setting; welfare theory is not a blueprint for a social movement.

We may be skeptical of neuroscientists' ability to come up with universal, physiologically grounded criteria for measuring happiness. We may also have doubts about the potential effectiveness of neuroeconomists at convincing individuals, or society as a whole, to adopt policies that increase "total happiness" by their measure. Our response to the neuroeconomics welfare theory is simpler: such a combination of moral philosophy and activism has never been the goal of economics; grounding this combination in biology is unlikely to make it so.

NOTES

This research was supported by grants from the National Science Foundation. We thank Drew Fudenberg and Philipp Sadowski for helpful comments and suggestions.

1. This description might overstate the therapist's discretion. Either a professional code or market forces may limit the extent to which she can pursue the patient's true happiness. Hence, the two philosophical questions above may or may not have some relevance to the therapist. Our contention is that they have none for economists.

2. The welfare statement is made relative to the constraints the agent faces. For example, the agent may be imperfectly informed of the consequences of his actions. In that case, the choice of x is welfare maximizing given the agent's information. If the agent had better information, he might choose y, and hence y is the welfare-maximizing choice for a better informed agent. See our discussion of mistakes.

3. This line of inquiry is often referred to as behavioral economics. We have avoided using this term, in order to distinguish it from standard economics models that deal with similar behavioral issues.

4. The agent frequently consumed the drug at a particular location and—as a result of this consumption history—being in that location triggers a craving for drugs. Similarly, the agent frequently smoked a cigarette while drinking coffee in the past. This—perhaps incidental—pairing of consumption goods in the past implies that coffee consumption triggers a craving for cigarettes.

5. The relationship between anxiety and preference for early or late resolution of uncertainty is explored and further developed in the work of Caplin and Leahy [2001].

6. For example, the Kreps-Porteus independence axiom may not be appropriate in the case where the agent has a second decision to make, whereas the anxious patient might very well satisfy it.

7. A teacher in an intermediate microeconomics class might say something like, "The consumer equates the marginal utility of consuming the good to the marginal utility of the last dollar spent on the good," while explaining a first-order condition in a partial equilibrium model with separable preferences. This statement is meant to provide some intuition for the first-order condition, not as a description of the consumer's mental process: the marginal utilities in question depend on the particular utility function used to represent the preference and hence are, to some extent, arbitrary. There is no presumption that either these particular marginal utilities or the underlying calculus arguments are the actual currency of the consumer's reasoning.

8. See Gul and Pesendorfer [2006] for a precise statement and proof.

9. While in most applications it is appropriate to identify these dimensions with the physical consumption dimensions, with this approach our theory (or any theory) of reference dependence would in some cases make bad predictions. Köszegi and Rabin [2004] argue that gain-loss utility should be defined over "hedonic" dimensions of consumption that people experience as psychologically distinct; in some situations, judgment is needed to identify these dimensions. And as noted in part III, even more judgment is required in determining the moment of first focus [Köszegi-Rabin (2006), page 1156].

10. Presumably, psychologists interested in human physiology find it worthwhile to study rats because of the similarities in the neurological makeup of the two species. Apparently, the similarities between the economic institutions of the two species are not sufficient to generate interests in rats among economists.

11. See Loewenstein and Prelec [1992] for a recent survey of the experimental evidence. In the typical experiment, subjects choose between a smaller, date 2 reward and a larger, date 3 reward. If the choice is made at date 2, then the smaller, earlier reward is chosen. If the choice is made earlier (i.e., at date 1), then the larger, later reward is chosen. This phenomenon is sometimes referred to as dynamic inconsistency or a preference reversal.

12. Note that choosing between $\{(0,0,9)\}$ and C is not a feasible option in period 2. Therefore, revealed preference experiments cannot uncover whether or not in period 2, the individual has a preference (or distaste) for commitment.

13. See, for example, O'Donoghue and Rabin [2003].

14. In standard analysis, this issue does not arise because the same utility function (U_1) is used to describe behavior (and welfare) at each decision date. In period 2, period 1 consumption cannot be altered, and therefore, the additively separable form of the utility function allows us to drop the first term as a simplification without affecting optimal choices.

15. For Kahneman [1994], the rejection of hedonic utility as the basis for economic analysis of decisions has less to do with technology than the adherence to an outdated philosophy of science. Rabin [1998] seems to view a doctrinaire obstinacy as the only explanation for the persistence of economists' "habitual" assumptions.

16. Compare, e.g., earlier experiments on the Allais Paradox and the common ratio effect with later experiments on framing and reference points.

REFERENCES

Bernheim, B. Douglas, and Antonio Rangel. 2004. Addiction and Cue-Conditioned Cognitive Processes. *American Economic Review* 94(5): 1558–1590.

Blakeslee, Sandra. "Brain Experts Now Follow the Money," *New York Times*, June 17, 2003.

Camerer, Colin F. 2005. *What Is Neuroeconomics?* Available: http://www.hss.caltech.edu/camerer/web_material/n.html.

Camerer, Colin, Samuel Issacharoff, George Loewenstein, Ted O'Donoghue, and Matthew Rabin. 2003. Regulation for Conservatives: Behavioral Economics and the Case for "Asymmetric Paternalism." *University of Pennsylvania Law Review* 151: 1211–1254.

Camerer, Colin F., George Loewenstein, and Drazen Prelec. 2004. Neuroeconomics: Why Economics Needs Brains. *Scandinavian Journal of Economics* 106(3): 555–579.

————. 2005. Neuroeconomics: How Neuroscience Can Inform Economics. *Journal of Economic Literature* 34(1): 9–64.

Caplin, Andrew, and John Leahy. 2001. Psychological Expected Utility Theory and Anticipatory Feelings. *Quarterly Journal of Economics* 116: 55–79.

Epstein, Larry G., and Stanley Zin. 1989. Substitution, Risk Aversion, and the Temporal Behavior of Consumption and Asset Returns: A Theoretical Framework. *Econometrica* 57(4): 937–969.

————. 1991. Substitution, Risk Aversion, and the Temporal Behavior of Consumption and Asset Returns: An Empirical Analysis." *Journal of Political Economy* 99(2): 263–286.

Gintis, H. 2003. Towards the Unity of the Behavioral Sciences. http://www.unix.out.umass.edu/~gintis/.

Gul, Faruk, and Wolfgang Pesendorfer. 2001. Temptation and Self-Control. *Econometrica* 69(6): 1403–1436.

————. 2004. Self-Control and the Theory of Consumption. *Econometrica* 72(1): 119–158.

————. 2005. The Revealed Preference Theory of Changing Tastes. *Review of Economic Studies* 72(2): 429–448.

————. 2006. The Revealed Preference Implications of Reference Dependent Preferences. Mimeo, Princeton University.

Ingersoll, Jonathan E. 1987. *Theory of Financial Decision Making.* New York: Rowman and Littlefield.

Kahneman, Daniel. 1994. New Challenges to the Rationality Assumption. *Journal of Institutional and Theoretical Economics* 150: 18–36.

Köszegi, Botond. 2005. *Utility from Anticipation and Personal Equilibrium.* Available: http://elsa.berkeley.edu/~botond/feelingsnew.pdf.

Köszegi, Botond, and Matthew Rabin. 2004. A Model of Reference-Dependent Preferences. Working Paper, University of California–Berkeley.

————. 2006. A Model of Reference Dependent Preferences. *Quarterly Journal of Economics* 121: 1133–1164.

Kreps, David, and Evan L. Porteus. 1978. Temporal Resolution of Uncertainty and Dynamic Choice Theory. *Econometrica* 46(1): 185–200.

Loewenstein, George, and Drazen Prelec. 1992. Anomalies in Intertemporal Choice: Evidence and an Interpretation. *Quarterly Journal of Economics* 107(2): 573–597.

O'Donoghue, Ted, and Matthew Rabin. 2003. Studying Optimal Paternalism, Illustrated with a Model of Sin Taxes. *American Economic Review Papers and Proceedings* 93(2): 186–191.

Rabin, Matthew. 1998. Psychology and Economics. *Journal of Economic Literature* 36(1): 11–46.

Strotz, Robert H. 1955. Myopia and Inconsistency in Dynamic Utility Maximization. *Review of Economic Studies* 23(3): 165–180.

Thaler, Richard H. 1980. Towards a Positive Theory of Consumer Choice. *Journal of Economic Behavior and Organization* 1(1): 39–60.

Thaler, Richard H., and Cass R. Sunstein. 2003. Libertarian Paternalism. *American Economic Review (Papers and Proceedings)* 93(2): 175–179.

PART II

THE DEBATE

CHAPTER 2

THE CASE FOR MINDFUL ECONOMICS

COLIN CAMERER

> The besetting fallacy of writers on economic method has been justly said to be the fallacy of exclusiveness. A single aspect or department of economic study is alone kept in view, and the method appropriate thereto aggrandized, while other methods, of equal importance in their proper place, are neglected or even explicitly rejected. Hence, the disputants on both sides, while rightly positive, are wrong negatively. Their criticisms on rejected methods are, moreover, too often based on misapprehension or misrepresentation.
>
> John Neville Keynes

THIS chapter is about how ideas and measurements from psychology and neuroscience (behavioral economics and neuroeconomics, respectively) might be generally incorporated into theories of economic choice. I define economics as the study of the variables and institutions that influence "economic" choices, choices with important consequences for health, wealth, and material possession and other sources of happiness.

The term "mindful economics" (hereafter, neuroeconomics) serves as a counterpoint to the language of Gul and Pesendorfer in chapter 1 (hereafter GP), who call the revealed-preference, rational-choice approach "mindless economics." I encourage readers to read both their chapter and mine consecutively, in either order.

Neuroeconomics is a specialization of behavioral economics that plans to use neural data to create a mathematical and neurally disciplined approach to the microfoundation of economics. Data from brain imaging attract the most attention, but it is crucial to note that neuroscientists also use animal studies, behavior of patients with permanent lesions and temporary disruption or stimulation (Transeranial Magnetic Stimulation [TMS]), response times,[1] tracking eye movements to measure information acquisition, psychophysiological measures (skin conductance, pupil dilation, etc.), and computational modeling. The variety of complementary approaches usually means that an obvious limit of one method can be overcome by another method. So one should not be too quick to *criticize* the flaws of any single method without considering whether another method overcomes those flaws.

Note that the behavioral approach should ideally fully encompass rational-choice approaches as a special case. Keep in mind that behavioral economists do not doubt that incentives matter and do not believe that traditional analysis is useless. (As Spiegler argues eloquently in chapter 4, there will always be a role for careful grounding of functional forms in choice-theoretic axiomatization to reveal all the implications—including hidden predictions—of those functional forms.) Indeed, behavioral economics is meant to be a generalization of rational-choice theory that incorporates limits on rationality, will power, and self-interest in a formal way. These generalizations allow the possibility that conventional rationality is an adequate approximation, and often permit a parametric way to measure the "degree" of limitedly rational behavior and its economic impact.

This chapter develops my latest view about grounding economic choice in neural details. This perspective is developing rapidly. As a result, viewpoints expressed only a couple of years ago are updated and informed by the latest data and perspective on methods. Revision of viewpoints, particularly the details of language and its sweep, is common and desirable in empirical science as new data and methods arrive. Early neuroeconomics papers that describe ideas and potential discoveries [e.g., Camerer, Loewenstein, and Prelec, 2005] should therefore not be viewed as logical conclusions derived from mathematical analysis. These early neuroeconomics papers should be read as if they are speculative grant proposals that conjecture what might be learned from studies that take advantage of technological advances.

This chapter is also a positive rebuttal of the "case for mindless economics" in the form of the case for mindful economics (i.e., its potential). GP's paper consists primarily of two arguments. The first is simply a fundamentalist definition of economics that excludes nonchoice data and limits the role for psychological facts by appeal to the claim that there are differences in tastes and interests between the two fields. This argument is simply a *definition* of economics as inherently mindless, and there is no debating a definition. The definition simply draws a preferred boundary rather than makes an evidentiary "case" for mindless economics.

The second, much more interesting, argument is that rational choice theory is sufficiently flexible to explain behavioral anomalies using the conventional language of preferences, beliefs, and constraint. This second argument is worthy of discussion. Indeed, my view is that conventional economic language can indeed approximate a lot of neural phenomena (which, if true, undermines the argument that the two approaches are fundamentally incompatible). But at some point, it is more efficient to simply adopt constructs as they are defined and understood in other fields, because defining those constructs in economic language is clumsy.

The Case for Mindful Economics

Keep in mind while reading this chapter that my assumed goal is that economics should make predictions about important choices and say something disciplined about the welfare implications of policies.

One way to make predictions is to look at past choices and to use those data to specify functions that express an unobservable basis of choice (e.g., utilities and beliefs), in order to predict how choices might respond to changes in observable variables. "Mindless economics" (i.e., rational choice theory or revealed preference) relies solely on observed choice patterns and mathematical restrictions on what choice patterns imply about underlying functional representations that are predictively useful.

Neuroeconomics has the same aspirations. Neuroeconomics is not in opposition to rational choice theory, but sees potential in extending its scope by observing variables that are considered inherently unobservable in rational choice theory. As Glimcher and Rustichini [2004] put it, the goal of neuroeconomics is a "mathematical, behavioral, and mechanistic" account of choice. What their definition adds to rational choice theory is the mechanistic component. So the goals of neuroeconomics are not fundamentally different than those of rational choice theory, since neuroeconomics strives to link mathematical formalisms and observed behavior just as rational choice theory does. The central issue is therefore whether having a mechanistic basis will improve the capacity to understand and predict choice, while maintaining a mathematical discipline and use of behavioral (choice) data.

Inferring preferences from observed choices also has limits. For example, an important problem for companies and regulators is forecasting demand and welfare consequences of introducing new products. By definition, a rational choice theory that relies on previously observed choices of old products is limited in its capacity to forecast behavior toward new choices (particularly those that do not share a lot of attributes with previous products, e.g., some new gadgets, or genetically engineered foods). Policy makers who decide whether to permit a new product must also forecast how much consumers will buy and whether the product will work. They cannot rely on observed choice data. It is conceivable that a neuroeconomic model of preference could add to extrapolations from similar old products in forecasts of demand for new products.

One way to see the potential for neuroeconomics is by analogy to organizational economics [see Sanfey, Loewenstein, McClure, and Cohen, 2006]. Until the 1970s, the theory of the firm was a reduced-form model of how capital and labor are combined to create a production function. The idea that a firm just combines labor and capital is obviously a gross simplification—it neglects the details of principal–agent relations, gift exchange and efficiency wages, social networks and favor exchange in firms, substitution of authority for pricing, corporate culture, and so forth. But the gross simplification is useful for the purpose of building up an industry supply curve.

Later, contract theory opened up the black box of the firm and modeled the details of the nexus of contracts among shareholders, workers, and managers. The new theory of the firm replaces the (perennially useful) fiction of a profit-maximizing firm that has a single goal, with a more detailed account of how components of the firm—individuals, hierarchies, and networks—interact and communicate to determine firm behavior.

Neuroeconomics proposes to do the same by treating an individual economic agent like a firm. The last sentence in the preceding paragraph can be exactly rewritten to replace firms and individual agents, the components of firms, with individuals and neural components of individuals. Rewriting that sentence gives this one: The neuroeconomic theory of the individual replaces the (perennially useful) fiction of a utility-maximizing individual that has a single goal, with a more detailed account of how components of the individual—brain regions, cognitive control, and neural circuits—interact and communicate to determine individual behavior.

The case for the potential of mindful economics rests on several principles, which are each discussed in turn:

- The brain is the organ that makes choices.
- More will be known about the brain due to technological advances.
- Sciences should respond to technological advances.
- Neuroeconomics can use technological advances in understanding the choice-making organ (the brain) to find how nonprice neural and psychological variables predict and change economic choices.
- Rational choice theory can be enriched by new psychological constructs.
- Behavioral economics and neuroeconomics could lead to improvements in welfare economics.
- Drawing sharp boundaries between fields is difficult and, fortunately, is not necessary.

The Brain Is the Organ That Makes Choices

Every economic choice (even institutional choices) depends on an individual saying "Yes," nodding, handing something to a cashier, signing a contract, reaching into a wallet, clicking "submit" online, releasing an earnings announcement, or executing some other action that requires brain activity. In this sense, all economic activity flows through the brain at some point. Even economic institutions rely on expectations, sometimes mystical ones such as credibility of Federal Reserve Board governors or consumer confidence, which exist in the brain. So it is hard to imagine that understanding brain function could not be useful for understanding some aspects of economic choice and its aggregated consequences.

Of course, it is often useful to abstract from these details and posit a higher level abstraction (e.g., utility maximization) that is a reduced-form representation of some neural process. The value of such abstractions—which is beyond dispute—does not imply that unpacking the reduced form couldn't be valuable too.

Indeed, one argument for the use of neural data is that economic theorists are almost too good at rapidly producing sensible characterizations of simple behavioral regularities based on different axiomatic systems (the supply of theories outstrips the supply of diagnostic data). Experimental evidence of ambiguity aversion, for example (à la the Ellsberg paradox), has given rise to about a dozen different reduced-form theories. All these theories can explain the basic Ellsberg patterns. How do we choose among them? A bad way is by weighing informal opinions about plausibility or reasonableness of the underlying axioms. A slightly better way is a new wave of experimentation designed to distinguish among competing theories (which is laborious, but certainly useful [e.g., Halevy, 2007]). An even better way, which is even more laborious, is to apply these different theories to models of contracting, asset pricing, consumer choice, and so forth, and see which theories can best explain existing stylized facts and accurately predict surprising new patterns.

Another way is to assume that if two theories can both explain the Ellsberg paradox, and appear equally promising for explaining some pattern in, say asset prices, then if one of the theories also is neurally plausible, that theory should be taken more seriously. This criterion is a simple application of the idea that the theory that can explain the most data (especially data that discriminate theories strongly) wins incumbency. Essentially, neuroeconomists are betting that in some cases, neural tests[2] could winnow a crowded field of possible theories down to the more plausible theories, and that doing so economizes on the hard work of figuring out all the implications of the different theories for different domains, such as asset pricing, and testing them.

More Will Be Known about the Brain Due to Technological Advances

While journalists might inadvertently do so, it is hard to exaggerate the genuine scientific advances in understanding brain function in recent years. An important part of the advances is that many tools are developing at the same time. These include tools from several different disciplines, including genetics, psychology, biology, and computer science. For example, the ability to map animal and human genomes and correlate them with phenotypic behavior is enormous. Genes can be easily manipulated in mice, so we can "knock out" a gene and see exactly which tasks require that gene; this gives us an important clue about the gene's expression and function. fMRI brain imaging is only about 10–15 years old, and data are accumulating at a rapid pace. Diffusion tensor imaging (DTI) is showing more and more about connectivity of brain regions. MS and administration of drugs and synthetic hormones permit causal experiments in which brain areas or neurotransmitters are disrupted or stimulated. What happens when area X is disrupted, for example, can establish the necessity of X for various tasks.

In addition to technological advancements, simple methodological improvements have advanced our understanding of choice on a more basic level. This is particularly apparent in the study of childhood development, which is important to adult choice behavior because of the path dependence and irreversibility of development. Databases of patients with lesions in specific areas are also growing; their growth permits a jump from tiny to modest samples of patients with damage in specific areas. Just as with TMS and stimulation inference, what patients with damage in area X cannot do (compared to matched controls) tells us what area X is necessary for.

Sciences Should Respond to Technological Advances

Industries take advantage of new technologies and substitute resources into them and away from less relatively valuable technologies. Science is the same. The boundaries of biology, astronomy, and neuroscience were shifted and expanded by the microscope, telescope and satellites, and neuroscientific tools. If choice occurs in the brain, there should be some degree of substitution into tools that can understand the brain, to predict choice. The range of tools described above also implies that an interest in neuroeconomics is not a speculation about brain imaging or any other single tool since all tools are being explored, linked, and improved.

A milder way to put this argument, as one prominent economist put it, is that neuroeconomics has option value. The very fact that its potential payoff has variance increases option value.

Neuroeconomics Can Use Technological Advances in Understanding the Choice-Making Organ (the Brain) to Find How Nonprice Neural and Psychological Variables Predict and Change Economic Choices

The first three arguments above suggest it is conceivable that something could be learned about economic choices from recently developed neuroscientific measurements. In fact, there are already many examples of where psychological or neural measures either predict later choices or actually influence choices causally.

In their chapter GP write that Camerer, Loewenstein, and Prelec [2004] (hereafter, CLP) "have no example of observing a choice parameter—such as the coefficient of relative risk aversion or the discount factor—through brain imaging, and no suggestions as to how such inference could be done" [GP].

GP are simply wrong. CLP [2004] did cite a report containing an example[3], a paper by Hsu, Bhatt, Adolphs, Tranel, and Camerer [2005] that reported an inferential procedure (a clear "suggestion") and was already in press when GP's chapter was first circulated as a paper. In that study, a choice parameter expressing the degree of ambiguity aversion was inferred from subjects' choices for money. Those parameter estimates were correlated (across subjects) with activity in right orbitofrontal cortex (OFC) observed in fMRI brain imaging. That is, subjects with low parametric ambiguity aversion had less activity in the OFC. So GP's "no example" criterion was refuted in print just days after their paper was circulated. Furthermore, extrapolating the correlation between the choice parameter and brain imaging activity to patients with no activity in the relevant area (OFC) implied that patients with lesions in that area would behave as if they had a particular numerical parameter (0.85). Later experiments with those patients based on their choices yielded a numerical estimate of 0.82. So the fMRI measurement delivered a choice parameter value that actually predicted later choices of a separate group of subjects.

There are now several more studies linking choice parameters inferred from behavior with neural processes. Tom, Fox, Trepel, and Poldrack [2007] and Sokol-Hessner, Delgado, Hsu, Camerer, and Phelps [2007] infer loss aversion parametrically from actual choices and correlate the parameter value with fMRI signals and skin conductance, respectively. Plassman, O'Doherty, and Rangel [2007] correlate medial OFC activity with free bids for consumer goods. Kable and Glimcher [2007] correlate neural firing rates with discount rates inferred from choice. Hampton, Bossaerts, and O'Doherty [2006] correlate activity with inferred prior beliefs and outcomes in a model of learning about a Markov reward process. Knutson, Rick, Wimmer, Prelec, and Loewenstein [2007] find that neural activity helps predict actual purchases of consumer goods, beyond stated preferences and stated consumer surplus. Many more examples are emerging rapidly.

Listed below are some other examples of nonprice psychological and neural variables that affect choice. It is certainly true that many of these phenomena can be translated into conventional economic language. Indeed, a major contribution of neuroeconomics may be to provide a formal language for talking about these phenomena. As I argue below, however, other phenomena are more clearly understood by adopting new terms from psychology and neuroscience rather than struggling to fit the brain's complex activity awkwardly into the Procrustean bed of economic language.

It is useful to sort the examples into those that are close to how economists reason, and easily translated into economic language (the first three examples), those that illustrate how a psychological measure could improve upon theory testing (example 4), and several (examples 5–12) that show the causal effect of psychological or neural variables or treatments that appear to be distant from economic analysis and of special interest only to neuroscientists.

Examples that are easy to explain in economic terms include the following:

1. Gender of children influences parents' political preferences: Washington [2006] finds that parenting an additional daughter increases the likelihood that legislators will vote for reproductive rights. What makes this result interesting is that gender is largely exogenous (female-minded fathers cannot easily order up girl babies instead of boys). Of course, the fact that parents' preferences are influenced by their children is hardly surprising or uneconomic; however, the details of how that process works could be illuminated further by understanding the neurobiology of parent–child attachment.

2. Alcohol increases restaurant tipping: Using field data, Conlin, Lynn, and O'Donoghue [2003] found that consuming any alcohol at a restaurant increased the tip percentage by about 2 percentage points (e.g., tips go from 13% to 15% of the bill). The number of times the patron visits a particular restaurant (a crude measure of reputational effects) increased tipping by 0.2% per visit. Drinking alcohol has an effect equivalent to 10 trips per month (and the alcohol variable is also statistically more significant).

3. Verbal labeling of "mad cow disease" changes behavior: Eating meat from cows infected with "bovine spongiform encephalopathy" (BSE) appears to have caused a couple of hundred cases of a variant of Creutzfeldt-Jacob disease in humans. When media outlets began to describe the cows' disease as "mad cow disease," rather than as BSE, people began to eat less beef [Sinaceur and Heath, 2005]. Lab experiments also show stronger emotional reactions and less rational reaction than when the scientific BSE label was used.

These three examples are merely correlations between economic or political choices and interesting variables that are not obviously price, income, or information. However, it is easy to quickly describe these phenomena in the language of preferences, beliefs, and constraints. We could infer from the data, for example, that alcohol and tipping must be complements, that parent preferences depend on child characteristics, or that relabeling BSE as "mad cow disease" genuinely conveys new information (doubtful) or grabs attention and activates emotion (more likely).

The fourth example is:

4. Pupil dilation predicts deception in cheap-talk games: Wang, Spezio, and Camerer [2006] record increases in pupil diameter (pupil dilation) and attention in a sender–receiver game of strategic information transmission. Pupil dilation is correlated with the amount of deception (the difference between the sender's message and his or her privately known state). Pupil dilation and attention together have statistical value for predicting the state from the message.

This example is different from the previous three: it illustrates how a psychophysical measure might help differentiate theories. Pupil dilation is an involuntary (autonomic) response that is well known to be linked to cognitive difficulty and arousal. The advantage of an autonomic response is that it can be measured rapidly (many times per second), and it is more reliable than such measures as subjective reports. (People might, e.g., say they find a task easy or an image unarousing when their pupil dilation indicates otherwise.) For the purposes of studying strategic information transmission, measures such as these (ideally, in conjunction with eye tracking) might enable us to separate theories that are importantly different but have similar observable implications. For example, the experimental data suggest that subjects without much experience seem to transmit too much information compared to equilibrium predictions (i.e., they are too honest) [Radner and Schotter 1989; Valley, Thompson, Gibbons, and Bazerman 2002; Cai and Wang, 2006]. One explanation is rooted in social preference or social image (e.g., they feel guilty lying). Another is that figuring out how much to deceive is cognitively difficult. A combination of looking at the payoffs of others, and dilation of pupils upon deception is consistent with the guilt explanation. Pupil dilation without looking at how much other players get is more consistent with the cognitive difficulty explanation. Based on the data, Wang, Spezio, and Camerer [2006] endorse the cognitive difficulty explanation, but their conclusion is tentative.

Of course, a long string of careful experiments manipulating experimental displays and information treatments could also separate theories without using pupil dilation measures. But the marginal cost of eyetracking and pupil dilation measures is essentially zero. Recording pupil dilation can only speed up the process of inference from an experimental program, and could do so rapidly.

The next eight examples all involve causal influences on choices:

5. Childhood brain development creates adult human capital: Knudsen, Heckman, Cameron and Shonkoff [2006: F10155] write that:

> studies of human capital formation indicate that the quality of early childhood environment is a strong predictor of adult productivity and

that early enrichment for disadvantaged children increases the probability of later economic success. Although explanatory mechanisms for interpreting these correlations still are being developed, recent advances in neuroscience are illuminating because they demonstrate the extent to which experience influences the development of neural circuits that mediate cognitive, linguistic, emotional and social capacities.

6. Disruption of brain activity increases ultimatum-offer acceptance: Using fMRI, Sanfey, Rilling, Aronson, Nystrom, and Cohen [2003] found activity in the dorsolateral prefrontal cortex (DLPFC) associated with evaluation of unusually low offers in ultimatum games. Building on this observation, Wout, Kahn, Sanfey, and Aleman [2005] and Knoch, Pascual-Leone, Meyer, Treyer, and Fehr [2006] used repetitive TMS (magnetic stimulation that temporarily disrupts brain activity) to deactivate the DLPFC when people received offers. Disrupting the DLPFC increased acceptances of low offers. A key point here is that you would not know which area to disrupt, in order to increase acceptances, without the geographical specificity of brain activity that comes from fMRI.

7. Cognitive load reduces resistance of temptation: Shiv and Fedorikhin [2002] find that when subjects are under cognitive load (having to remember a seven-digit number rather than a two-digit one), their ability to resist a tempting snack falls.

8. "Cognitive reappraisal" of gamble outcomes reduces parametric loss aversion: Sokol-Hessner, Delgado, Hsu, Camerer, and Phelps [2007] instructed subjects to "cognitively reappraise" gamble choices (by imagining they are traders making choices for others, and that they make choices often). During reappraisal, the degree of loss aversion inferred parametrically from actual choices for money drops. Changes in skin conductance are correlated with changes in inferred loss aversion.

9. Subconscious exposure to happy and angry faces influences demand for liquid: Hundreds of studies show that "priming" (subconscious exposure of subjects to semantic or visual stimuli) can change behavior in remarkable ways. Niedenthal, Barsalou, Winkielman, Krauth-Gruber, and Ric [2005] found that showing angry versus happy faces increased the amount thirsty subjects would pay to drink a small amount of liquid.

10. Identity priming affects test scores: A large, fast-growing body of research shows that "priming" behavior by exposing people to words and images can affect later behavior. For example, asking questions related to an Asian female's ethnic background before a math test increases her actual test scores; asking gender-related questions decreases test scores [Shih, Pittinsky, and Ambady, 1999].[4]

11. Disgust erases and sadness reverses buying–selling price gaps: Lerner, Small, and Loewenstein [2004] showed subjects four-minute film clips that reliably induce sadness, disgust, or neither emotion. Disgust erases the typical gap between buying and selling prices for goods (a highlighter set), and sadness reverses it (buying prices go up, à la "retail therapy").

12. Oxytocin causes trust: Oxytocin is a powerful hormone in social bonding. Kosfeld, Heinrichs, Zak, Fischbacher, and Fehr [2005] had subjects play a trust game in which one player could choose whether to invest money or keep it, and another player decided how much to repay from the tripled investment amount. Subjects who were given a synthetic dose of oxytocin trusted more (compared to a placebo control group and a random risky-choice control group).

Some of these effects are large, and some are small. Some represent a single intriguing finding (e.g., TMS disruption causes acceptance of low ultimatum offers), and others are examples of a well-established phenomenon that is related to economic choice (e.g., cognitive reappraisal). And this list is just the tip of a scientific iceberg, which is growing rather than melting. The point of the list is that the dependent variables are all either economic choices for money or goods, or other outcomes that economists study;[5] and the list is not short. All the examples also show causation of choices in neurally interpretable ways, with variables that are not prices, income, or information. This is challenging for the conventional view of stable preference. A narrow way out is to infer that the causal variables must be providing information, and then to invent exotic types of information to explain the causal effects.[6]

Some of these phenomena can certainly be understood by economic theories that stretch the language only a little. For example, the effect of identity priming on test scores can be expressed in a model where the priming influences belief of success and where people have a preference to behave consistently with that belief. That is roughly how the psychologists characterize the phenomenon, too, and is similar in structure to Benabou and Tirole's [2003] model of crowding out of intrinsic motivation [and see Benabou and Tirole, 2006].

Other phenomena are sensibly described as expressions of state-dependent preferences, where states include "states of mind" influenced by hormones, cognitive disruption, cortical damage, induced emotions, and other forces. This interpretation raises the question of which state variables matter, and whether states can be self-produced, overridden, and so forth. If we are to make progress in understanding the nature of state dependence, it is hard to imagine we can do so without knowing some facts and ideas from psychology, evolutionary modeling, and neuroscience.

Even the examples that seem to interest neuroscientists only narrowly are tools for creating neuroeconomic theory that should eventually have broader implications. Consider the causal influence of oxytocin on trust. Many observable social behaviors (e.g., touch) can generate oxytocin. It could be, for example, that business practices that emphasize socializing and getting to know one another before deal making have to do with production of oxytocin or some other biochemical process that genuinely increases trust. Hormones such as oxytocin often operate differently across people and across the life cycle. For example, testosterone (T) drops with age. If T is linked to an economic behavior (e.g., violence), and the behavior is correlated with an observable such as age, then understanding T unpacks the reduced-form model of age correlating with violence. Put differently, if one could measure T and include it in regressions predicting violence, it might be that age effects disappear and are shown to be driven by T.

Similarly, the studies of subconscious face priming and sadness and disgust effects on prices (examples 9 and 11) are simply illustrations of how emotional state variables can influence choice subconsciously. The subconscious influence is a reminder that decisions may be influenced by exogenous nonprice variables we are not aware of (or variables we are aware of, but whose effects we believe we overcome). In thinking about field phenomena, the analogue to a study such as the sadness–disgust study is to find some observable event or variable that is likely to induce emotion reliably and study its effects (e.g., Hirshleifer and Shumway [2003] find that sunshine is correlated with stock returns).

Rational Choice Theory Can Be Enriched by New Psychological Constructs

The most useful debate between the rational-choice mindless approach and the mindful approach is how sensibly psychological and neural phenomena can be characterized by the language of preferences, beliefs (especially information imperfections), and constraints. GP argue that "the methods of standard economics are much more flexible than assumed in the neuroeconomics critique and [we] illustrate this with examples of how standard economics deals with inconsistent preferences, mistakes, and biases." First, as a description of how neuroeconomists think, they are wrong. It is impossible to have an economics or business Ph.D. from the University of Chicago (as I do) and not know the rational model is flexible.[7] Behavioral economists are also reminded of its flexibility constantly in referee reports and seminar comments. The issue is whether there are any phenomena that are better described by simply importing language and constructs from other disciplines as needed rather than mixing and matching familiar language. After all, economics doesn't have a name for everything in the world. And we have adopted other language when it is useful to do so (e.g., "laissez faire" or "tâttonnement").

Furthermore, if it is true that the language of preference, belief, information, and constraint can characterize "inconsistent preferences, mistakes, and biases," then this is great news for psychology and neuroscience. It means there is some prospect for an increase in common language despite GP's insistence (discussed further below) that the tastes and motives in disciplines are fundamentally different.

Besides the examples in the preceding section, below I discuss three phenomena —cues, Stroop mistakes, and emotional regulation—and suggest the mixture of rational-choice language and new language that best describes them.

Cues

In the addiction literature, a "cue" is a sensory stimulus that triggers a drug craving because the cue was learned to be associated with drug use in the past (e.g., walking past a neighborhood where a recovering junkie shot up heroin; the neighborhood is the cue). GP state that, "For economists, the notion of a cue is not useful because it lumps together two distinct economic phenomena." I think the opposite is true— precisely because there is no special word in economics language for a good or state variable that is both complementary and (potentially) external. It might be useful to have such a word, if the goal is to predict addict behavior and also think about policy. Furthermore, cues have other properties: Typically, cue effects can be extinguished with repeated exposure (this is a common basis of therapies) but can also be rapidly reinstated. Cues also are typically asymmetric—that is, seeing *Scarface* might increase demand for cocaine, but ingesting cocaine does not create demand for seeing *Scarface*. So we could adapt the language of economics to describe "cues" as "dynamically adaptive, rapidly reinstatable asymmetric complements to consumption." Or we can just learn a new vocabulary word—"cue," which summarizes certain kinds of complements.

Stroop Mistakes

Take the example of American tourists crossing the street in London, who often look in the wrong direction, to the left (the direction familiar from American driving, in which cars drive on the right-hand side of the road), which leads to pedestrian accidents. GP explain this in the language of standard economics by saying that "[T]he strategy 'only cross the street when no car is approaching' may be unavailable in the sense that it violates a *subjective constraint* on the set of *feasible* strategies" [emphasis added].

This explanation puts a strain on such words as "constraint" and "feasible." A dictionary definition of feasible closest to what GP seem to have in mind is "feasible: capable of being accomplished or brought about; possible."[8] Is looking to the right really impossible? If the visiting American wore a neck brace (from an injury) that made it excruciatingly painful to look to the right, then a term like "feasible" or "constraint" would be appropriate. But is looking to the right really not "feasible" (not in the choice set)?

Psychology has an ideal term for precisely this kind of mistake—a "Stroop mistake." In 1935 John Stroop created a task to measure mental flexibility.[9] He asked subjects to rapidly name the color of ink a word is printed in. When the word "green" is printed in black ink, for example, many subjects rapidly say "green" and then correct themselves and say "black."

"Stroop task" is now a generic term for any choice in which there is an automatic, highly practiced response that is incorrect and that must be inhibited or controlled by a slower deliberative process. (Another famous example is the game "Simon says," in which people must perform physical actions only if the commands are preceded by the phrase "Simon says.") Americans looking for cars in London are performing a Stroop task.

To an economist, a natural way to describe a Stroop task is that one element in the choice set is chosen automatically unless some scarce cognitive resources are expended to override it. A model like Samuelson's [2001] model of overadaptation to familiar tasks, or a variant of Fudenberg and Levine's [2006] planner–doer model in which the planner must incur utility costs to restrain the doer, are probably the right sorts of models. GP's use of the phrase "subjective constraint" is on the right track—except the subjectivity can be fully understood only by thinking about the psychology and doing experiments.

The reason that I am resisting language like "feasible strategy" to explain Stroop mistakes is that experimental data suggest some other interesting regularities that are hard to accommodate in an explanation grounded purely in feasibility. For example, when subjects do Stroop tasks over and over, they get better at them (essentially, the correct response becomes more automatic). A process of learning the correct default (or the state of nature that makes one response optimal) is needed to explain this, so you need a learning component that, in the translated language, makes strategies more feasible or less subjectively constrained.

Another fact is that Stroop mistakes are sensitive to cognitive overload, fatigue, and other variables. For example, mountain climbers at high altitude probably make more Stroop-like mistakes, often leading to death.[10] A full model would therefore include such biological variables as oxygen and visceral states (e.g., in a Fudenberg-Levine type model, the planner needs oxygen to restrain the doer).

Based on the effect of cognitive load (illustrated by the Shiv-Fedhorikhin [2002] study in the last section's long list), we could predict that Americans talking on their cell phones in the United Kingdom are more likely to fail to look in the correct direction and more likely to be injured. Any other variables that increase cognitive load would increase mistakes, too. It is hard to see how to make sense of all these facts without concepts of learning-by-doing in the brain (the right choice becomes more automatic) and scarce cognitive resources that are required to make the right choice.

Emotional Regulation

In the study by Sokol-Hessner, Delgado, Hsu, Camerer, and Phelps [2007] described in the preceding section, subjects made a series of choices between certain amounts and 50–50 gain–loss gambles. They were instructed at the start that any gambles they choose would be immediately played out and generate gains or losses, which would accumulate across the task and pay at the end. They were trained to turn on and off a "cognitive reappraisal," in blocks of 10 trials, which is intended to control their emotions and influence choice. The instructions were as follows:

> One way to think of this instruction is to imagine yourself a trader. You take risks with money every day, for a living. Imagine that this is your job, and that the money at stake is not yours—it's someone else's. Of course, you still want to do well (your job depends on it). You've done this for a long time, though, and will continue to. All that matters is that you come out on top in the end—a loss here or there won't matter. In other words, you win some and you lose some.

Their choice behavior is measurably different when they are thinking this way, compared to the control condition. Loss aversion parameters estimated from a standard maximum likelihood logit model are lower when they are doing the cognitive reappraisal, and their palms sweat less (a standard measure of arousal, used in lie detectors, e.g.).

How do we explain this in standard economic language? Keep in mind that the subjects know that in every trial they are winning or losing money. So while they are simulating the idea that it is "not yours—it's someone else's," they also "know" that it is their money. The handiest conventional language explanation is that they misinterpret the instruction to mean that they won't be paid on those trials (i.e., the instruction changes their belief about payment). But they do know they will be paid (and tell us so).

The psychological explanation is the following: People have the capacity to imagine how they would feel and behave in different states. When they imagine these states, neural activity (and skin conductance) actually changes, and so does behavior. Another way to think of it in Sokol-Hessner et al.'s [2007] experiment is that subjects know they will be paid, but in the cognitive reappraisal they also "know" (i.e., simulate the state of knowing) that they won't be paid. Attention to the simulated state crowds out attention to the true state, that changes behavior.

In fact, this sort of imagination is used routinely in life and in economics. One approach to acting is to imagine previous experiences that produce the emotion that is desired. For example, if you imagine how you would feel if a beloved pet died, you might feel genuine sadness. This doesn't mean that you "think" your pet is dead; it just means you have the capacity to do counterfactual reasoning, and that reasoning can produce powerful emotions and can change behavior.

In economics, the ability to imagine what you might do in another state is essentially assumed in game theory when there are information asymmetries (e.g., bidders must imagine what bidders with a different value than their own will do, in an auction, unless they learned an equilibrium bidding function over time). So in economic language, we could translate the psychological concept of emotional regulation into "the use of scarce cognitive resources to self-create alternative states." Or we can just learn some new vocabulary—cognitive reappraisal.

Behavioral Economics and Neuroeconomics Could Lead to Improvements in Welfare Economics

Behavioral economics and neuroeconomics present a challenge to the conventional view that choices reveal unobservable preferences and should be the basis for welfare economics. This is an important challenge for behavioral economics, but is not one I have much to say about.[11]

It is true that the revealed preference approach kills two birds with one stone: by using observed choices to infer unobserved underlying preferences, and by using those choices as evidence of what people truly prefer. Behavioral economists who think choices and preferences are not always the same now must supply a theory of when they are different, and what governments should do (if anything).

The sensible route is to list defensible cases in which choices are mistakes, explain why those choices are mistakes (preferably basing the judgment that they are mistakes on a person's own choices; see, e.g., Köszegi and Rabin, chapter 8), then explain how mistakes might be identified and avoided in a way that political and professional organizations would accept. This is where behavioral economics is likely to make some inroads (see Bernheim and Rangel, chapter 7, and Loewenstein and Haisley, chapter 9).

The solution will not be as elegant and simple as the conventional view, of course. The revealed preference approach solves the problem of figuring out when choices betray true preferences by assuming it never happens. This is like an ostrich solving the problem of escaping danger by sticking its head in the sand.

Furthermore, societies already have a fabric of paternalistic interventions that reveal an implicit theory about situations in which people make bad choices that must be restricted. In most societies, those subject to paternalism include minors, the mentally ill, and, in many countries, women or ethnic minorities. Behavioral economics might provide a language or characterize the preference for these paternalistic restrictions and, most pass important, judgment on which ones make economic sense. For example, in most American states the age of sexual consent is around 16, the voting age is 18, and the drinking age is 21. Either this composite policy arises from idiosyncraties of historical practice, interest group pressures, or local moral norms, or it reflects a coherent legal concept of human nature and the development of that nature during adolescence. It is hard to believe that adolescents are able to wisely make choices about whether to have sex (which may lead to child-bearing) several years before they can decide whether to have a single beer. If there is no coherent legal concept, behavioral economics might provide an improvement in coherence.

Drawing Sharp Boundaries between Fields Is Difficult and, Fortunately, Is Not Necessary

The least interesting part of this debate is what "is economics" and "isn't economics." Much of GP's chapter is linguistic gerrymandering by defining economics as the revealed-preference approach and then constantly reminding the reader that anything else is, by their definition, not economics.

Drawing sharp boundaries between academic disciplines, like other complex categories, is notoriously difficult. Precise definitions are necessary in mathematics, and the invention of abstract symbolic systems permits them. In virtually all other domains, the more important a concept is, the less simple it is to define it precisely. Is Marcel Duchamps's notorious sculpture Foundation "art"? (It's just a toilet.) Is a blog "journalism"? Is the Unification Church a "religion"?

Happily, it is not necessary to have sharp categorical boundaries to answer these questions. If it is necessary to divide objects into categories for practical purposes—as a museum curator, White House credential-giver, and taxation agency must—then institutions generally develop vague categorical boundaries and decide what is in the category and what is not on a case-by-case basis. The result is not like separating a set A into disjoint subsets, because there is no clear separation. The result is more like dividing objects into two sets with a fuzzy boundary and then debating cases that are close to the boundary to clarify the boundary. As Justice Potter Stewart put it, avoiding a precise definition of obscene material: "I know it when I see it."

It is clearly true that researchers in different disciplines often use different tools, pose questions at different levels of analysis, and are interested in different applications. There is no doubt about this. There is also no doubt that some of what scientists do in different fields overlaps. The synthesis of neuroscientific facts and methods and economic tasks and analysis in neuroeconomics is not meant to unify the fields, but rather to improve both fields on their own terms. At the same time, our view is that some degree of shared language can't hurt and might help. In CLP [2004: 573–573] we wrote: "It is possible that a biological basis for behavior in neuroscience, perhaps combined with all purpose tools like learning models or game theory, could provide some unification across the social sciences [cf. Gintis, 2007]."

GP disagree; they write, "Far from being an all-purpose tool, game theory is a formalism for stripping away all strategically irrelevant details of the context, details that Gintis describes as central for psychologists."

The mild point we were trying to make is perhaps expressed better by the game theorists Sergiu Hart and Robert Aumann. In an interview Hart notes that: "This is a good point to discuss the universality of game theory. In the preface to the first volume of the *Handbook of Game Theory* [iv] we wrote that game theory may be viewed as a sort of umbrella or unified field theory" [Hart, 2006].

Aumann then adds, "It's a way of talking about many sciences, many disparate disciplines."

To illustrate their belief in a strict disciplinary division of labor, GP also offer an example of how different fields use different models:

> [A] learning model in economics is *different than* a learning model in psychology. For an economist, a theory of learning might be a process of Bayesian inference in a multiarmed bandit model. This theory of learning is useful for addressing economic phenomena such as patent races but *may be inappropriate* for cognitive psychologists. [emphasis added]

Just after the GP paper was circulated, neuroscientists [Daw, O'Doherty, Dayan, Seymour, and Dolan, 2006] immediately proved GP wrong, by publishing a paper about neural circuitry that implements components of multiarmed bandit optimal search. So the claim that learning is modeled differently in economics and psychology is false. Similarly, reinforcement models originating in behaviorist psychology have been widely applied in economics [e.g., Erev and Roth, 1998].

CONCLUSION

This chapter is intended as part of a conversation about how psychological and neural measurement might inform economic theory and analysis in the long run. From papers by myself, Loewenstein and Prelec, and others, GP infer something about the beliefs and interests of neuroeconomists and compare those inferred beliefs to "economics," by which they mean the traditional revealed preference approach and accompanying tools and applications. Their paper does not argue against the potential of learning something from neural data, and admits to no understanding or interest in details of those data, but nonetheless quickly rules out such data as noneconomic as a matter of definition.

I define economics more broadly, as the study of the variables and institutions that influence "economic" (large, consequential) choices. This definition allows Jim Heckman to take neuroscientific data seriously in an attempt to explain the importance of early childhood development for human capital formation and labor economics outcomes. It also allows Vince Crawford (chapter 10) to measure attention directly in order to infer algorithms used when people choose strategies in games. The broader definition also includes Princeton colleagues Alan Blinder and Alan Krueger, who have both worked with nonchoice data,[12] to be considered economists. To reiterate my initial points above, another argument for paying some attention to psychological and neural data is technological substitution and option value. Advances in neuroscience make it possible to measure and causally manipulate many processes and quantities that were not imaginable a hundred years ago when the foundation of neoclassical economics was being laid. Quantities that were previously considered unobservable are now partially observable. (As Gabaix and Laibson note in chapter 12, science has often progressed by being able to observe smaller and smaller units of analysis that were invisible to earlier generations.) To ignore these developments entirely is bad scientific economizing. Can you imagine an astronomy profession that spent centuries making inferences by peering through increasingly sophisticated telescopes refusing to send up planetary probes or send people to the moon because "that's not astronomy"?

Along these lines, a heuristic way to think of the potential of neuroeconomics is this: Economic discussions sometimes refer to "unobservables" such as beliefs and emotions, and vague concepts such as confusion (a common "explanation" for experimental results that contradict theory). The presumption in neuroeconomics is that many "unobservables" are observable, in the usual sense (i.e., that strong correlates of the unobservables can be observed). That is, every time the term "unobservable" pops up, one should ponder whether that variable is truly unobservable.

For example, how might we measure confusion (rather than simply infering it from surprising behavior)? Confused subjects should take longer (or perhaps answer too rapidly) to respond. They may exhibit correlates of anxiety and cognitive difficulty, such as skin conductance or pupil dilation or (in fMRI) cingulate activity. Eye tracking could be used to measure whether subjects actually read the instructions (or at least looked at them). These kinds of measures are easiest to collect in lab experimentation, but even in field settings one might be able to measure quite a lot. Lo, Repin, and Steenbarger [2005] collected daily emotion surveys of day traders. Lo and Repin [2002] recording psychophysiological responses of foreign exchange traders. Coval and Shumway [2001] recorded the noise level in the Chicago Board of Trade pit and found that it correlated with price volatility and other trading measures. Surveyors who collect important large-scale surveys such as the Panel Study of Income Dynamics could, in principle, use computerized surveys with eye tracking, and recordings of response time as correlates of confusion.

Another argument sometimes raised about measuring quantities other than choices is that the conclusions we will reach from these studies could have been reached by other studies that observed only choice. This might be true, but using only choices will typically be inefficient since we have other tools.

For example, in the 1980s experiments with bargaining choices showed that in alternating-offer games, opening offers typically lie somewhere between an equal split and the subgame perfect prediction (assuming mutual knowledge of self-interest). One view, consistent with choices in the clever experiments by Neelin, Sonnenschein, and Spiegel [1988] varying the number of bargaining rounds, was that people do not look ahead and use backward induction. Another view is that people are looking ahead and making subgame perfect equilibrium choices, but care about other players' payoffs (or believe others have such social preferences).

It would certainly be possible to distinguish between these two views with more experiments observing only choices.[13] But since the key distinction between these two theories is what people are looking at, measuring what people are looking at is the most efficient way to make progress.

Similarly, somebody could have conjectured that damage to the OFC would change preferences over ambiguous money gambles (à la Knight and Ellsberg) and then done an experiment to test that conjecture by comparing choices of people with OFC damage with choices by control subjects. But in the long history of study of ambiguity, nobody ever made that conjecture. It came only because Hsu, Bhatt, Adolphs, Tranel, and Camerer [2005] could see, using fMRI, that there was activity in the OFC.[14]

One more small issue is worth addressing before ending this conclusion. I have heard several people say that neuroeconomics is interesting but is too expensive. This is a dangerous myth. First, whether it is too expensive is an empirical question, and one that should be judged by whomever is paying for the research. Second, it is true that fMRI is expensive at the margin, but other neuroscientific techniques are not. For example, experiments with small samples of lesion patients are cheap at the margin, and good attention-measurement software is free (see, e.g., mouse-labweb.org). Third, while the activity being measured is sometimes physically small (e.g., pupil dilation), measures can be so accurate that very strong inference emerges from small sample sizes, which keeps costs down. (I.e., don't mistake our inability to measure with the naked eye with the ability of a specialized instrument to measure something that we cannot see very accurately.) Fourth, virtually none of the funding sources for this research (mostly private foundations and NIH, in the United States) is shifting grants away from other kinds of economics research.[15] So even if neuroeconomics funding were shut down, it would not produce an increase in funding for other economics research. Fifth, if neuroeconomics is judged expensive, then all types of economic research should be judged by the same standard, Researchers should be forced to substitute into lower cost alternatives when feasible (e.g., experimental economists should have to do most of their experiments in poor, literate countries). Judgment of expense also needs to include a calculation of expected benefit. Research that is cheap but that does not produce measurable expected benefit would become endangered.

Where do we go from here? A debate about the merits of "mindless" and "mindful" economics cannot possibly be won or lost in the short run. Behavioral economics drawing heavily on psychology has already "won" because it has proved to be useful and popular. And the case for mindful neuroeconomics cannot lose in the short run because it is mostly based on promise. It cannot lose until enough time has passed to declare its promise unfulfilled.

Perhaps the debate is moot, because we don't have to choose between the approaches: economists can do both, and should. The proliferation of dual-process models, informed by psychological and neural evidence to various degrees [see, e.g., chapters 7 and 14, and Fudenberg and Levine, 2006], shows the potential of using familiar pieces of economic modeling to explain psychologically and neurally grounded facts and develop new predictions.

Indeed, the difference between the latter models and the mindless style is mostly a matter of how much psychological detail is used to motivate the modeling. GP concede that psychology can be "inspirational" but it is not essential to invent good mathematical models. In contrast, the dual-process chapters mentioned in the preceding paragraph are full of thoughtful distillations of large psychological and biological literatures. These facts constrain modeling choices by forcing the model to explain a lot of related phenomena, rather than one small piece of a literature. In contrast, the philosophy GP espouse suggests that knowing a lot about actual human behavior, as established by psychology and neuroscience, is a waste of time in improving economic models of decision making. It is ironic that mindless economists prefer less knowledge to more, since preferring more to less is such a fundamental premise in economics. And sciences that have found new tools have always become more productive by using them.

Appendix: The Style and Rhetoric of "The Case for Mindless Economics"

I find it necessary to comment about the rhetorical style of the GP chapter. The style of their chapter is sweeping and therefore technically incorrect. This material is deliberately placed here in an appendix since it would interrupt the narrative flow of the text of my chapter, and it isn't really important for explaining what neuroeconomics is trying to do; it is important only for readers new to the debate to judge whether GP have characterized neuroeconomics sensibly, in the course of articulating their arguments for mindless economics.

Readers who are familiar with the background debates in behavioral economics and neuroeconomics that are summarized in GP's chapter will recognize that their summaries are either overgeneralized or wrong in almost every sentence, if their sentences are read literally as a claim about what other social scientists think or do. As a result, any reader who is learning about what behavioral economists or neuroeconomists have discovered, learn, think, theorize, or plan to do from the GP chapter ends up at least somewhat misled.

One problem is that the field is moving rapidly. Perspectives expressed a couple of years ago may be replaced by more thoughtful ones. Furthermore, there are a lot of data emerging rapidly, so it is difficult to keep on top of the field and describe it accurately. For example, as noted in the text of this chapter, GP make two concrete claims that were already wrong at the time their working paper was first circulated (viz., that neuroeconomists have never linked brain activity to choice parameters—many have[16]—and that learning models in psychology and economics are different). Indeed, readers would be surprised at how rapidly the choice-parameter approach is spreading throughout cognitive neuroscience; by the time you read this, there may be dozens of such examples.

However, the central semantic problem is that GP typically use broad generalizations without qualifiers. Neuroeconomics and behavioral economics are deliberately grouped together. Broad grouping is a confusing mistake and is misleading because there is much disagreement among those researchers about basic facts and the value of different methods. (Many behavioral economists—perhaps most—are skeptical that we need to know much about brain detail.)

Several examples illustrate how misleading the inclusive rhetorical style is. At various points GP state that neuroeconomists or neuroeconomics

- "proposes radical changes in the methods of economics." This is wrong. CLP [2005] clearly distinguish between incremental and radical changes; an incremental approach "add[s] variables to conventional account of decision makings" (p.10) and is not at all radical.
- "import the questions and abstractions of psychology and reinterpret economic models as if their purpose were to address those questions." We can search for neural firing rates correlated with utility numbers inferred from choices and still understand that utility theory was not developed with that purpose in mind.
- "insist on a new notion of welfare based on these answers [to age-old philosophical questions]." We don't insist; we suggest exploring the possibility.
- "plan to enlist the support of the state—a stand-in for a benign therapist—who may, on occasion, conceal facts and make decisions on behalf of the individual's future selves." If behavioral economics can document systematic mistakes, it may have something to say about paternalism (or may not), and at some point should meet the challenge of doing so. This doesn't imply "enlist[ing] the support of the state" or "conceal[ing] facts."
- "The central questions of neuroeconomists are: How do individuals make their choices? How effective are they making the choices that increase their own well-being?" The second question is not central for most neuroeconomists.
- "argue that the time is ripe for the methodology of economics to be brought in line with the methods and ideas of psychology and neuroscience." The idea is simply to see whether psychology and neuroscience can help economics on its own terms.
- "begins with the implicit or explicit assumption that economics, psychology, and possibly other social sciences all address the same set of questions and

differ only with respect to the answers they provide." The explicit assumption is that in some cases any one discipline can learn something about how to answer the question its discipline poses from facts and ideas in other disciplines.

Why is there so much deliberate overstatement in the language of their chapter? Perhaps it is just a colorful style[17] or is designed to sharpen the point or provoke a debate ... which it certainly has. This thoughtful volume shows that the debate is a useful one because it forces mindful economists to articulate more carefully what they are trying to do and, how new methods might achieve their goals.

NOTES

Thanks to Meghana Bhatt, Alex Brown, Min Jeong Kang, and Joseph Wang for editorial help; to Andrew Caplin and especially Doug Bernheim and George Loewenstein for helpful discussion; and to Ernst Fehr, Paul Glimcher, Read Montague, Antonio Rangel, my lab group members, and many others for useful conversations.

1. Economists also use response times, e.g., to infer the depth of strategic thinking [Rubinstein, 2007].

2. Keep in mind that I am not referring to fMRI alone, which is admittedly noisy and still developing rapidly (it is only a little more than 10 years old), but instead to the combination of complementary methods including fMRI, lesion patient tests, eye tracking, and causal manipulations, e.g., priming and TMS.

3. It is true, however, that CLP [2004] did not specifically discuss the choice parameter/imaging link in their brief passage, but they did describe a paper containing such an example.

4. These priming effects do tend to wear off rapidly and have not yet been shown experimentally to cause very consequential behavior, although my sense is that most researchers in the field are optimistic that they can do so.

5. E.g., labor economists are interested in test scores and human capital, and public health economists are interested in smoking choices.

6. This strategy is what doomed the behaviorist emphasis on reinforcement as an all-purpose theory of complex human behavior. Evidence emerged that rewarding behaviors emerge spontaneously without any reinforcement (e.g., children learn to utter phrases without being directly reinforced). So behaviorists would infer that a condition must be a reinforcer if its presence predicted behavior (e.g., children are reinforced for imitating parental speech, and imitation leads to their own accurate speech). The business of inferring what must have been reinforcing after observing the behavior became more and more contrived and was gradually supplanted by the cognitive processing paradigm and later waves that were more fruitful and disciplined.

7. As a graduate student, I recall overhearing a late-night conversation in the library between an enthusiastic student and his apparent girlfriend. He explained that he loved her because their utility functions were interdependent. Using the flexible rational model, I inferred from her subsequent choice that she preferred hearing more poetic language.

8. From www.bartleby.com/61/8/F0060800.html.

9. See www.snre.umich.edu/eplab/demos/sto/stroopdesc.html#The%20 Neurophysiology.

10. See, e.g., www.pbs.org/wgbh/nova/everest/exposure/braintest.html.

11. A popular view is that behavioral economists are eager to regulate based on what we learn about human behavior. This view is mistaken. First, it is clearly not necessarily true that more mistakes should lead to more regulation, as Camerer, Issacharoff, Loewenstein, O'Donoghue, and Rabin [2003] pointed out and Glaeser [2006] showed more generally. Mistakes that are easily remedied by market-supplied restraint or advice might imply less regulation. Second, my own limited writing on behavioral economics and paternalism is not motivated by a desire to parent; it is motivated purely by the demand for such thinking and a feeling that it is an important professional challenge to the field (much as engineering presents the challenge of putting science to work). It is striking how interest in paternalism and regulation is described. For example, GP state that "neuroeconomists plan to enlist the support of the state—a stand-in for a benign therapist—who may, on occasion, conceal facts and make decisions on behalf of the individual's future selves." This is simply false (particularly the charge that facts should be concealed). Indeed, the Federal Trade Commission invited several behavioral economists to an April 2007 conference on how behavioral economics might inform regulation. The "state" was trying to enlist my "support" (or at least, was interested in my ideas) rather than vice versa.

12. Blinder, Canetti, Lebow, and Rudd [1998] is a survey of reasons for sticky pricing, and Kahneman, Krueger, Schkade, Schwarz, and Stone [2004] used survey data on subjective well-being.

13. In chapter 3, Schotter describes clever experiments with Partow on equilibrium refinements. These experiments compare behavior in two conditions: In one, the players know each other's payoffs; in the other, they do not. The difference in behavior between the two conditions tells us whether attention to the information that is present influences behavior. With modern eye tracking, the same experiment could be done more efficiently with half the sample size, by presenting the payoff information to all subjects and measuring how much people attend to it. The subjects' attention then self-sorts them into low- and high-information treatments (and also provides finer grained measurements than are available by simply varying the amount of information presented, without measuring attention to that information).

14. Of course, economists are not keenly interested in the OFC per se. As with many neuroscience studies, the reason that identifying specific regions is important is to understand individual differences and differential development in the life cycle (including childhood, adolescence, and aging), constrain evolutionary theorizing, and guide choice of economic institutions. Different regions can also be stimulated and disrupted with drugs, deep-brain stimulation, and other methods in different ways to cause behavior, if we know what those regions are.

15. E.g., most of my own research in fMRI and eye tracking so far has been supported by universities and the private Moore Foundation. The Moore Foundation grant is explicitly aimed at high-risk research that the National Science Foundation will not support.

16. At a summer 2006 meeting, John O'Doherty suggested that the model of correlating behaviorally derived parameters, often trial by trial, with brain activity might rapidly become the dominant statistical style in neuroeconomics.

17. The conservative author Ann Coulter wrote: "Liberals hate America, they hate 'flag-wavers,' they hate abortion opponents, they hate all religions except Islam (post 9/11). Even Islamic terrorists don't hate America like liberals do. They don't have that much energy. If they had that much energy, they'd have indoor plumbing by now." Interviewed on the TV show *Hardball* by Mike Barnicle, Coulter was asked whether she really believed what she had written. Coulter replied, "I think I write in a colorful style."

REFERENCES

Benabou, Roland, and Jean Tirole. 2003. Intrinsic and Extrinsic Motivation. *Review of Economic Studies* 7: 489–520.

———. 2006. Identity, Dignity, and Taboos: Beliefs as Assets. Mimeo. Princeton University.

Blinder, A. S., E. Canetti, D. E. Lebow, and J. B. Rudd. 1998. *Asking about Prices: A New Approach to Understanding Price Stickiness.* New York: Russell Sage Foundation.

Cai, Hongbin, and Joseph Tao-Yi Wang. 2006. Overcommunication in Strategic Information Transmission Games. *Games and Economic Behavior* 56: 7–36.

Camerer, C., S. Issacharoff, G. Loewenstein, T. O'Donoghue, and M. Rabin. 2003. Regulation for Conservatives: Behavioral Economics and the Case For "Asymmetric Paternalism." *University of Pennsylvania Law Review* 151: 1211–1254.

Camerer, C., G. Loewenstein, and D. Prelec. 2004. Neuroeconomics: Why Economics Needs Brains. *Scandinavian Journal of Economics* 106: 555–579.

———. 2005. Neuroeconomics: How Neuroscience Can Inform Economics. *Journal of Economic Literature* 43: 9–64.

Conlin, Michael, Michael Lynn, and Ted O'Donoghue. 2003. The Norm of Restaurant Tipping. *Journal of Economic Behavior and Organization* 52: 297–321.

Coval, Joshua, and Tyler Shumway. 2001. Is Sound Just Noise? *Journal of Finance* 60: 1887–1910.

Daw, Nathaniel D., John P. O'Doherty, Peter Dayan, Ben Seymour, and Raymond J. Dolan. 2006. Cortical Substrates for Exploratory Decisions in Humans. *Nature* 441: 876–879.

Erev, Ido, and Alvin E. Roth. 1998. Predicting How People Play Games: Reinforcement Learning in Experimental Games with Unique, Mixed Strategy Equilibria. *American Economic Review* 88: 848–881.

Fudenberg, Drew, and David Levine. 2006. A Dual Self Model of Impulse Control. *American Economic Review* 95: 1449–1476.

Gintis, Herbert. 2007. A Framework for the Unification of the Behavioral Sciences. *Behavioral and Brain Sciences* 30: 1–16.

Glaeser, E. 2006. Paternalism and Psychology. *University of Chicago Law Review* 73: 133–156.

Glimcher, Paul W., and Aldo Rustichini. 2004. Neuroeconomics: The Consilience of Brain and Decision. *Science* 306: 447.

Halevy, Yoram. 2007. Ellsberg Revisited: An Experimental Study. *Econometrica* 75: 503–536.

Hampton, Alan, Peter Bossaerts, and John O'Doherty. 2006. The Role of the Ventromedial Prefrontal Cortex in Abstract State-Based Inference During Decision Making in Humans. *Journal of Neuroscience* 26: 8360–8367.

Hart, sergiu, 2006. An Interview with Rebort Aumanne. In P. Samuelson and William Barnett (Eds.), *Inside the Economist's Mind*. New York, Wiley.

Hirshleifer, David, and Tyler Shumway. 2003. Good Day Sunshine: Stock Returns and the Weather. *Journal of Finance* 58: 1009–1032.

Hsu, Ming, Meghana Bhatt, Ralph Adolphs, Daniel Tranel, and Colin F. Camerer. 2005. Neural Systems Responding to Degrees of Uncertainty in Human Decision-Making. *Science* 310: 1680–1683.

Kable, Joseph W., and Paul W. Glimcher, 2007. The neural correlates of subjective value during intertemperal choice. *Natural Neuroscience* (online Nov. 4).

Kahneman, Daniel, Alan B. Krueger, David A. Schkade, Norbert Schwarz, and Arthur A. Stone. 2004. A Survey Method for Characterizing Daily Life Experience: The Day Reconstruction Method. *Science* 306: 1776.

———. Knoch, Daria, Alvaro Pascual-Leone, Kaspar Meyer, Valerie Treyer, and Ernst Fehr. 2006. Diminishing Reciprocal Fairness by Disrupting the Right Prefrontal Cortex. *Science* 314: 829–832.

Knudsen, Eric I., James J. Heckman, Judy L. Cameron, and Jack P. Shonkoff. 2006. Economic, Neurobiological, and Behavioral Perspectives on Building America's Future Workforce. *Proceedings of the National Academy of Sciences of the USA* 103: 10155–10162.

Knutson, Brian, Scott Rick, G. Elliott Wimmer, Drazen Prelec, and George Loewenstein. 2007. Neural Predictors of Purchases. *Neuron* 53: 147–156.

Kosfeld, Michael, Markus Heinrichs, Paul J. Zak, Urs Fischbacher, and Ernst Fehr. 2005. Oxytocin Increases Trust in Humans. *Nature* 435: 673–676.

Lerner, Jennifer, Deborah A. Small, and George Loewenstein. 2004. Heart Strings and Purse Strings: Carryover Effects of Emotions on Economic Decisions. *Psychological Science* 15 (May): 337–341.

Lo, Andrew, and Dmitry Repin. 2002. The Psychophysiology of Real-Time Financial Risk Processing. *Journal of Cognitive Neuroscience* 14: 323–339.

Lo, Andrew, Dmitry Repin, and Brett Steenbarger. 2005. Fear and Greed in Financial Markets: A Clinical Study of Day-Traders. *American Economic Review* 95: 352–359.

Neelin, Janet, Hugo Sonnenschein, and Matthew Spiegel. 1988. A Further Test of Noncooperative Bargaining Theory: Comment. *American Economic Review* 78: 824–836.

Niedenthal, Paula M., Lawrence W. Barsalou, Piotr Winkielman, Silvia Krauth-Gruber, and Francois Ric. 2005. Embodiment in Attitudes, Social Perception, and Emotion. *Personality and Social Psychology Review* 9: 184–211.

Plassman, Hilke, John O'Doherty, and Antonio Rangel. 2007. Orbitofrontal Cortex Encodes Willingness-to-Pay in Everyday Economic Transactions. Working paper, California Institute of Technology.

Radner, Roy, and Andrew Schotter. 1989. The Sealed-Bid Mechanism: An Experimental Study. *Journal of Economic Theory* 48: 179–220.

Rubinstein, Ariel. 2007. Instinctive and Cognitive Reasoning: A Study of Response Times. *Economic Journal* 117: 1243–1259.

Samuelson, Larry. 2001. Analogies, Adaptation, and Anomalies. *Journal of Economic Theory* 97: 320–366.

Sanfey, Alan G., George Loewenstein, Samuel M. McClure, and Jonathan D. Cohen. 2006. Neuroeconomics: Cross-Currents in Research on Decision-Making. *Trends in Cognitive Sciences* 10: 108–116.

Sanfey, Alan G., James K. Rilling, Jessica A. Aronson, Leigh E. Nystrom, and Jonathan D. Cohen. 2003. The Neural Basis of Economic Decision-Making in the Ultimatum Game. *Science* 300: 1755–1758.

Shih, Margaret, Todd Pittinsky, and Nalini Ambady. 1999. Stereotype Susceptibility: Identity Salience and Shifts in Quantitative Performance. *Psychological Science* 10: 80–83.

Shiv, B., and A. Fedorikhin. 2002. Spontaneous Versus Controlled Influences of Stimulus-Based Affect on Choice Behavior. *Organizational Behavior and Human Decision Processes* 87: 342–370.

Sinaceur, Marwan, and Chip Heath. 2005. Emotional and Deliberative Reactions to a Public Crisis: Mad Cow Disease in France. *Psychological Science* 16: 247–254.

Sokol-Hessner, Peter, Mauricio Delgado, Ming Hsu, Colin Camerer, and Elizabeth Phelps. 2007. Thinking Like a Trader: Cognitive-Reappraisal and Loss-Aversion in Gamble Choice. Mimeo, New York University.

Tom, Sabrina M., Craig R. Fox, Christopher Trepel, and Russell A. Poldrack. 2007. The Neural Basis of Loss Aversion in Decision-Making under Risk. *Science* 315: 515–518.

Valley, K., L. Thompson, R. Gibbons, and M. H. Bazerman. 2002. How Communication Improves Efficiency in Bargaining Games. *Games and Economic Behavior* 38: 127–155.

Wang, Joseph Tao-yi, Michael Spezio, and Colin F. Camerer. 2006. Pinocchio's Pupil: Using Eyetracking and Pupil Dilation to Understand Truth-Telling and Deception in Biased Transmission Games. Mimeo, California Institute of Technology.

Washington, Ebonya. 2006. Female Socialization: How Daughters Affect Their Legislator Fathers' Voting on Women's Issues. NBER Working Paper 11924. National Bureau of Economic Research.

Wout, Mascha van 't, Rene S. Kahn, Alan G. Sanfey, and Andre Aleman. 2005. Repetitive Transcranial Magnetic Stimulation over the Right Dorsolateral Prefrontal Cortex Affects Strategic Decision-Making. *Neuroreport* 16: 1849–1852.

CHAPTER 3

....

WHAT'S SO INFORMATIVE ABOUT CHOICE?

....

ANDREW SCHOTTER

Those who can do science; those who can't prattle about its methodology.

—Paul Samuelson

INTRODUCTION

....

THIS is a chapter on economic methodology written by someone who, I hope, contradicts Samuelson's dictum. It is hard to discuss scientific methods without first agreeing on the purpose of our science. It is my claim here that the goal of economics, like the goal of any science, is to explain phenomena. As Milton Friedman [1953: 7] suggested, "The ultimate goal of a positive science is the development of a 'theory' or 'hypothesis' that yields valid and meaningful (i.e., not truistic) predictions about phenomena not yet observed."

Note that Friedman expects us to make "predictions about phenomena not yet observed," so our theories should be predictive ex ante and not simply ex post rationalizations of events we know the outcome of. While he certainly permits us to look back in history and explain the past, he states that "predictions" by which the validity of a hypothesis is tested need not be about phenomena that have not yet occurred, that is, need not be forecasts of future events; they may be about phenomena that have occurred but observations on which have yet to be made or are not known to the person making the prediction. [7]

Being an experimentalist, my objective is to test theory by matching the predictions it makes with choices made in the lab, so to some extent, much of what I say here I comes off sounding like old-style positivism, but I think my position is far more nuanced (or perhaps confused) than that. In fact, I am a very reluctant positivist, my position being more like that of Clark Glymour [1980: ix]: "If it is true that there are but two kinds of people in the world—the logical positivists and the god-damned English professors—then I suppose I am a logical positivist."

Like other sciences, the process of discovery used to explain phenomena is first to construct a theory, then to test it empirically (experimentally), and finally to modify it in the light of empirical (experimental) evidence.

A question has been raised recently about what types of data are admissible in this scientific quest. For conventional theory, choices and their direct observable consequences, such as prices, are considered the only truly reliable types of data. While choices give us insights into the preferences of individuals, prices give us insights into the allocative properties of institutions (mostly markets). Variables such as beliefs, emotions, intentions, verbal reports, and mental states are suspect because only in making choices are people "putting their money where their mouth is." Only choices are reliable data in this operationalist view of science. This is what economics is all about. Faruk Gul and Wolfgang Pesendorfer (chapter 1) put it this way:

> Standard economics focuses on revealed preference because economic data come in this form. . . . The standard approach provides no methods for utilizing nonchoice data to calibrate preference parameters. The individual's coefficient of risk aversion, for example, cannot be identified through a physiological examination; it can only be revealed through choice behavior. . . . In standard economics, the testable implications of a theory are its content; once they are identified, the nonchoice evidence that motivated a novel theory becomes irrelevant.

If our goal is theory falsification and prediction, however, it is not clear that we would want to limit ourselves only to choice variables. We should be able to use whatever helps us in that task. If a variable is useful in testing theory or in prediction, why not use it?

In this chapter, I discuss the consequences of placing choices and only choices on such a pedestal. While I certainly do not question their usefulness (no one trained as an economist could) or even their primacy, I do ask why choices alone should be placed in such an exalted position and why they are considered to be reliable indicators of such things as preferences.

I explain my position in five sections. In each section I rely on experimental evidence to make my point. I tend to use experiments that I have done simply because I am most familiar with them and know how they can be used to make my point. My argument can be summarized by the following five points, which are discussed in the remaining sections of this chapter:

Point 1: Making a Virtue out of a Constraint

Sanctifying choices confuses a constraint with a virtue—we rely on choices because the variables we are most interested in many times are unobservable non-choice variables (preferences, costs, beliefs, etc.), and we use choice to infer them. We use choices, therefore, because we are constrained to and not because proper science dictates that we must. But using choice data as a proxy for unobservables involves the creation of a theory linking observable choice data to the unobservable variables we are interested in. If that theory is faulty, the choice data used are suspect, and nonchoice variables may be as (or even more) reliable. Think of the structural empirical literature on auctions. The object of analysis is the underlying distribution of costs (or values), and this is identified by assuming all bidders use a Nash bid function and inverting to find the revealed costs associated with the observed bids. What we'd like to know directly is what costs or values are, but that is not available, so we are forced to use bids (choices). Using bid data is therefore a solution to a constraint and not a free choice.

Point 2: Knowing Why Instead of Knowing That

Theory cannot be confirmed by merely observing *that* a choice has been made that is consistent with it. We must know *why* it was made and verify it was made for the reasons stipulated by the theory. It is only when choice is consistent not only with the predictions of a theory but also with the reasons stipulated for that choice that we can be confident that the predictions of the theory will remain valid when the parameters of the model change. In other words, we need to know why a choice was made, and not just that it was made, in order to explain the comparative statics of the theory. Knowing why a choice was made may require data other than choices. This may require us knowing something more deeply psychological about the person making the choice, about his or her mental states, wants, needs, thought process, desires, and so on. It is here that a door is opened for neuroscience.

Point 3: Incomplete Real-World Data

We must decide what subset of available choice data we will restrict ourselves to. Real-world choice data are incomplete and therefore cannot be used alone to test theory. The world offers us data that have not been generated to test our theories, so inferences from real-world choices to the validity of a theory are incomplete and therefore unreliable. Improper inferences about the validity of a theory can be made if the data used do not span the relevant sets of treatments that one would need in order to (tentatively) validate a theory. This suggests that controlled experiments are required, but if they are not feasible, we may need to supplement our available choice data with other types.

Friedman agrees with this point, or at least laments the fact that economists cannot perform controlled experiments. His famous 1953 essay "The Methodology of Positive Economics," however, was written before the advent of experimental economics. "Unfortunately, we can seldom test particular predictions in the social sciences by experiments explicitly designed to eliminate what are judged to be the most important disturbing influences. Generally we must rely on evidence cast up by 'experiments' that happen to occur."

Point 4: Framing and the Reliability of Choices

There has been a long and robust literature documenting the fact that how one frames a choice problem to a person can change the way that person makes his or her choice. The problem we face as social scientists is that when we observe choice data we do not always observe the frame used to elicit it. If that is the case, then the inferences we can make from these choices are very likely to be limited and unreliable unless we are able to observe the actual frame used.

Point 5: Institutional Design Using Neuro Data

While much has been made about the usefulness of neuroscience (mental state) data and their failure to be of interest to economic theory and of use in designing institutions, I present experimental evidence that such information can, in fact, be useful in that enterprise. That is, fMRI data can be used to design revenue-enhancing auction institutions and can do so by capitalizing on knowledge of the mental states bidders experience when they contemplate winning and losing.

GETTING BIBLICAL: MAKING A VIRTUE OUT OF A CONSTRAINT

Let me start with a biblical reference. When God kicked Adam and Eve out of the Garden of Eden, the punishment he placed on Adam was to force him to earn his living by the sweat of his brow (perhaps the birth of labor economics). Eve's punishment was to give birth in pain (certainly the beginning of labor economics).

Finally, the punishment that He placed on the serpent was forbidding him the ability to walk upright.

If economists had also been living in the Garden of Eden and had been kicked out, their punishment would have been to force them to make indirect inferences using only those variables that they could observe, namely, choices. In response, economists would need to infer what they could not see. The entire corpus of econometrics is involved in this enterprise, and the theory of revealed preference is another exquisite response to this constraint.

But our use of choices and only choices is merely a response to a constraint, and the fact that we as a profession have been so clever in constructing theories that explain the world, despite the paucity of the data available, does not mean that we should not search to expand the list of variables of interest and perhaps admit the use of what are presently unobservable but may, in the future, via new technologies, become observable. Stating, as Gul and Pesendorfer do, that "standard economics focuses on revealed preference because economic data come in this form" is equivalent to cursing the darkness rather than lighting a match.

In an influential article on the use of experiments in economics, Vernon Smith [1982: 929] writes, "Over twenty five years ago Guy Orcutt characterized the econometrician as being in the same predicament as that of an electrical engineer who has been charged with the task of deducing the laws of electricity by listening to the radio play." For many years, I failed to understand the significance of this quote, until I had to sit down and write this chapter. It then struck me that Orcutt is saying exactly what I am trying to say here—that the challenge of most sciences is precisely the fact that the world does not offer us data in the form we would like it to be, and the scientific process is therefore forced to be an inferential one, much like being constrained to try to understand the laws of electricity through inferences made only by listening to the radio.

The beauty of economics is how well we have done in the face of this constraint, but we should not conclude that that is our destiny. Obviously, Orcutt would have loved to have had more, better, and different types of data. If they were available, I would suspect that he would embrace them. No good applied economist throws away useful data of any type.

For example, what about such nonobservables as beliefs, intentions, and emotions? Clearly they affect behavior but are not directly observable and are not choice based. Are they ruled out as being useless to our scientific enterprise? To answer this question, let me talk about beliefs and learning.

Consider the theory of learning. Much of what is done in the lab is the comparison of various learning models, since one focus of attention in experimental economics is not only theory falsification but also theory comparison: which theory predicts better. When comparing theories or models, however, one must make sure that the data used for the comparisons are comparable. More precisely, every model has an ideal data set that, if available, would allow it to perform at its peak efficiency. When such a data set is not available, one is forced to use proxies for those variables that are unobservable, and one must provide a theory linking these proxies to the behavior of the unobservable variable that one is interested in. For example, take two models, A and B, and assume that the ideal data set for model A is observable to the analyst while this is not the case for model B. If we were then to compare the performance of these two models and conclude that model A was better, we would face the problem of not knowing how much of its performance to impute to the model and how much to impute to the fact that it had its ideal data set available while model B did not and had to use proxies. First-best comparisons of two models occur only when each has its ideal data set available.

The consequences of these ideas for the comparison of learning models are numerous and significant. For example, reinforcement models of learning are fortunate in often being able to have their ideal data sets observable. This is so because they typically rely only on the observable outcomes of play (actions and payoffs) as inputs into their models. In other words, in order to calculate a player's propensity to choose a given strategy, all that is needed is a time series of that player's own payoffs from all previous plays of the game. The Experience Weighted Attraction (EWA) model, as written, is a model where how attractive a strategy is depends on how it has been reinforced in the past when it was used and counterfactually when it was not. It also has its ideal data set available since it posits a model in which strategies are chosen in accordance with their attractions that, as defined by Camerer and Ho [1999] are functions of past observable outcomes.[1] In general, ideal data sets for belief learning models are not available since their basic components, beliefs, are private and hence not observable. To rectify this, experimentalists and theorists have used history-based proxies as substitutes for these beliefs, but as Nyarko and Schotter [2002] have demonstrated, these proxies are inadequate. Using a proper scoring rule to elicit truthful beliefs about the actions of their opponents, Nyarko and Schotter [2002] found that belief learning models that use elicited beliefs outperform all other belief learning models that employ historical proxies for their belief estimates.

To explain, consider a "belief learning" model such as fictitious play, where at every point in time people form beliefs about their opponent based on the observable frequency of his or her actions in the past. Once these beliefs are formed, agents best respond to these beliefs either deterministically or stochastically.

Note that if we are only allowed to use observables in our models, then their predictive value will only be as good as the theories we create connecting these observables to the unobservable variables we are most interested in. For example, fictitious play presents us with a rather rudimentary model connecting past choices with beliefs. If this model is faulty, which it most certainly is (see Nyarko and Schotter [2002] and Ehrblatt, Hyndman, Ozbay, and Schotter [2007] for two examples), then the predictions of the theory will fail. But if we could find ways to directly measure beliefs, then we may be able to produce a more reliable theory. Let me explain.

The model of fictitious play as specified is a fully complete model based only on observables—in fact, choices. Choices are the basis of beliefs, and beliefs are the basis of choice. Note that beliefs do not depend on the payoffs that one's opponent receives, just his or her choices in the past. Hence, in this theory, one does not need to even know the payoffs of the game to one's opponent, much less his or her unobservable utility function. If one fears that the fictitious play belief model is too primitive, one can improve it by adding a more flexible form belief equation such as that of Cheung and Friedman [1997], where past choices by one's opponent are geometrically discounted. Still, restricting us to using only choices as inputs ties the reliability of the theory to the theory relating previous choices to beliefs.

Under the constraint that beliefs are unobservable, these models, or models like them, might be all we could do. But what if we could observe beliefs or make them observable? Would the resulting model explain behavior better, and if so, might we be missing something by limiting our models only to data that are choice based?

Nyarko and Schotter [2002] and others [Huck and Weizsäcker, 2002; Costa-Gomes and Weizacker, 2006] have tested belief learning models using beliefs elicited with a proper scoring rule. In other words, people are paid for their beliefs in such a way that revealing one's true belief is a dominant strategy. This is one technology that laboratory experiments have provided us for making unobservables observable. Of course, one could say that since people are paid for their beliefs, this elicits choice data and hence its use does not violate the constraint, but we could have alternatively simply asked people to reveal to us their beliefs and use them, or waited until fMRI technology is developed to a point where it can locate where beliefs are created in the brain and use them. The relevant question is which learning models are better predictors of behavior: choice-based belief or elicited (fMRI measured or self-reported) belief learning models?

So ultimately, if we do better by simply asking people what they believe than by relying on historical models, then that is legitimate, especially if our goal is prediction. Why restrict our data to those that are choice based?

Nyarko and Schotter [2002] come to the conclusion that belief learning models based on elicited beliefs (using a proper scoring rule) do a far better job of describing behavior than do those based only on historical choice. While this is not the place to go into detail, let me provide two pieces of evidence to support their position. First, one could ask if the time series of beliefs for fictitious play and elicited beliefs are similar for individuals. In other words, do historical-choice-based fictitious-play beliefs look like elicited beliefs? The answer here is a resounding no. To understand why, consider figure 3.1, which shows a striking difference in two belief series: while the elicited belief series is very volatile and indicates that beliefs can take on very extreme values, as expected, the fictitious play beliefs are very stable and more centered. Obviously, this must be true by construction, so elicited beliefs look nothing like fictitious-play, choice-based beliefs.

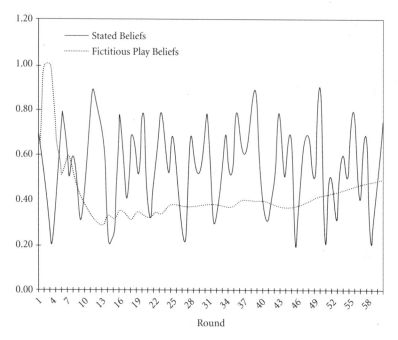

Figure 3.1. Time series of elicited beliefs and fictitious play beliefs of a subject who played the 2 × 2 constant sum games shown in table 3.1 repeatedly with the same partner for 60 periods. From Nyarko and Schotter [2002, figure 2].

Table 3.1. Payoff Matrix for Nyarko and Schotter [2002]

Strategy	Green	Red
Green	6, 2	3, 5
Red	3, 5	5, 3

Rows indicate strategy for player 1; columns, strategy for player 2. Cells show the payoff for player 1 followed by the payoff for player 2.

But the proof of the pudding is in the eating. Which predicts choices better? In other words, which type of beliefs, when used in the logit choice model

$$\text{Probability of Red in period } t = \frac{e^{\beta_0 + \beta_1 \left[E(\pi_t^d) \right]}}{1 + e^{\beta_0 + \beta_1 \left[E(\pi_t^d) \right]}}, \tag{3.1}$$

$$\text{Probability of Green in period } t = 1 - \frac{e^{\beta_0 + \beta_1 \left[E(\pi_t^d) \right]}}{1 + e^{\beta_0 + \beta_1 \left[E(\pi_t^d) \right]}},$$

where $E(\pi_t^d)$ is the expected payoff difference to be derived from using the Red strategy instead of the Green strategy in period t given the beliefs that the subjects hold at that time, best fits the actual choices made by the subjects?

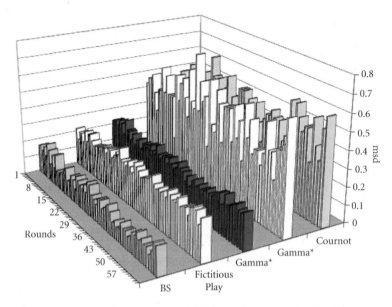

Figure 3.2. Mean cross-subject mean standard deviation scores for five different methods of belief estimation. From Nyarko and Schotter [2002].

To answer this question, Nyarko and Schotter [2002] constructed the following goodness-of-fit measure. For each individual and for each of our logit models (i.e., stated or elicited, fictitious play), we have an estimated β_0 and β_1 coefficient. Hence, for any round, if we were to plug one of our belief measures into the logit equation, we would get a predicted probability of Red (and Green) for that round. This predicted probability vector can be compared to the actual $\{0, 1\}$ choice vector made in that round to generate a standard deviation (SD) score for that subject in that round. If in any round we average these scores across the K subjects in the experiment, we get a mean cross-subject MSD score (MCSMSD) for round t defined as follows:

$$\text{MCSMSD}_t = \frac{1}{K} \sum_{i=1}^{K} (p_t^i - a_t^i)^2,$$

where p_t^i is the predicted probability of choosing Red for subject i in round t, and a_t^i is i's actual choice (equal to 1 if Red is chosen and 0 if Green is chosen). For any model, we estimated we can define 60 such MCSMSDs, one for each round of the experiment.

Figure 3.2 presents these scores for experiment 1. Our stated belief model clearly outperforms the fictitious play model. This is seen by comparison of the MCSMSD measure for the BS model using elicited beliefs and the fictitious play model. The MCSMSD is smaller for BS than for fictitious play in every round, suggesting clearly that elicited beliefs are better proxies for "true beliefs" or those beliefs that seem to be used to make decisions.

So what does this all mean? To my mind, it means that we can make good use in economics of unobservable nonchoice variables if we can find a reliable way to discover them. This may be done in several ways. First, it can be done by inferring them from choices. In Nyarko and Schotter [2002], it was done using a proper scoring rule. But the same exercise they did could be done by merely asking people their beliefs or running the experiment in an fMRI machine if the science progresses far enough to discover where in the brain beliefs are processed. Restricting ourselves to choice-based belief models such as fictitious play makes sense only if we are confident that the theory of belief formation we use, which relies only on previous historical choices, is more reliable in predicting beliefs than are similar theories we could construct that would relate beliefs to brain scans or verbal reports. This is an empirical question, not a matter of economic methodology or theology.

KNOWING "WHY" INSTEAD OF KNOWING "THAT"

To return to the theme I started with, if our objective is to test theory, then we must ask what constitutes a proper test. According to standard economic theory, proof is finding choices that are consistent with predictions, so choices validate theory (or falsify it). But can we stop there? Don't we, perhaps, need to know that the choices are made for the reasons stipulated by the theory? This is important for a number of obvious reasons, but mostly because it is only when we know that a theory works for the right reasons that we can be confident that it will continue to work when the parameters of the world it is applied to change, that is, only then will we have confidence in the theory's comparative statistics.

This fact has been demonstrated in a very clever way by Holt and Goeree [2001]. They present subjects with a number of games that they play once and only once. The clever thing they do, however, is to present them with several versions of the same game, one of which they call a "treasure" treatment, since it is their expectation that in that treatment the Nash predictions will hold. In the other versions, they change one of the parameters defining the game and investigate whether, when they change this parameter, they will be able to predict behavior.

For example, consider the 2 × 2 matching pennies game in table 3.2. When this game is offered to subjects, they choose top left 48% of the time and bottom right 52% of the time. Since the Nash prediction is 50–50, this appears to be strong support for the theory. But the theory suggests that these choices are being made in an effort to make one's opponent indifferent to his or her choice and hence are invariant to changes in one's own payoff. Hence, when the payoff of 80 is changed to 320 in the

Table 3.2. Payoff Matrix for Symmetric Matching Pennies

Strategy	Left	Right
Top	80, 40	40, 80
Bottom	40, 80	80, 40

Rows indicate strategy for player 1; columns, strategy for player 2. Cells show the payoff for player 1, followed by the payoff for player 2.

Table 3.3. Payoff Matrix for Strongly Asymmetric Matching Pennies

Strategy	Left	Right
Top	320, 40	40, 80
Bottom	40, 80	80, 40

Rows indicate strategy for player 1; columns, strategy for player 2. Cells show the payoff for player 1 followed by the payoff for player 2.

top left cell, as is true in table 3.3, Nash predicts that this will not change the behavior of the row chooser at all. This is far from the truth. When that payoff is changed, row players choose top 96% of the time, in strong contradiction to the predictions of the theory. The choices made in the symmetric game were not sufficient to confirm the theory. While choices were theoretically consistent, the motives behind them were not—the subjects were not making Nash choices for Nash reasons. So while choices are our bread and butter, they alone are not sufficient confirmatory data for theory. We need to know why, and finding out why cannot easily be done by simply looking at choices. In this case, one might as well ask subjects what they were doing, and while such data is not on par with choices, it certainly could come in handy if subjects offered a coherent heuristic that explained their behavior.

This sentiment is common among experimentalists. For example, Johnson, Camerer, Sen, and Rymon [2002] use Mouselab in an experiment about backward induction to try to infer the thought processes that subjects went through in order to assess whether they were using backward induction, one of the cornerstones of game-theoretic logic. Broseta, Costa-Gomes, and Crawford [2001] used similar techniques in trying to assess how subjects reasoned in normal form games. In a paper dealing with signaling games, Partow and Schotter [1993] (henceforth PS) investigate whether subjects choose to behave according to various refinements of Nash equilibrium for the reasons stipulated by the theory.

To understand what they did, consider the signaling game described in table 3.4, first used by Banks, Camerer, and Porter [1994] (henceforth BCP) and Brandts and Holt [1993] (henceforth BH). In this game, there are two players, a sender, player S, and a receiver, player R. The sender can be of two types, type H and type L, which is

Table 3.4. Payoff Matrix for Signaling Game 2 of Brandts and Holt [1993]

Type	Message N			Message S		
	C	D[a]	E	C[b]	D	E
H	15, 30	30, 30	0, 45	45, 15	0, 0	30, 15
L	30, 30	15, 60	45, 30	30, 30	0, 0	30, 15

Columns show the message of the sender and the strategy of receiver. Rows show different types for the sender. Cells show the payoff for the sender followed by the payoff for the receiver.
[a] Message N and strategy D form the nonsequential Nash equilibrium.
[b] Message S and strategy C form the sequential equilibrium.

chosen with equal probability before the game starts. The type is revealed to player S but not player R, although player R knows the probability distribution determining types. Once player S knows his type he must send a message of either N or S. The message determines which of the two payoff matrices shown above is relevant for the game. At this point it is player R's turn to move, and she chooses an action of C, D, or E. Payoffs are then determined by the message sent by S, the action chosen by R, and the partially known type of player S.

In this game, there are two Nash equilibria or two Bayesian-Nash equilibria, only one of which is sequential. In the nonsequential equilibrium player S sends message N no matter which type he is, while the receiver takes action D no matter what message is sent. In the sequential equilibrium, player S sends message S no matter what type she is, and a message of S is responded to by action C while a message N is responded to by action D. This game, therefore, has two equilibria, one of which is more refined than the other.

Let us then see how the refinement literature expects us to rule out the nonsequential Nash equilibrium from consideration. Consider either type of subject at the Nash equilibrium. Note that if player S is of type H, she will receive a payoff of 30 at the equilibrium, while if she is of type L she will get 15. According to the equilibrium, if the out-of-equilibrium message S is ever sent, it should be met with a reply of D leading to a payoff of 0 for each player. However, such a response on the part of player R is irrational since it requires that he would choose his dominated strategy D instead of his weakly dominant strategy C, leading to a payoff of 45 for type H and 30 for type L. As a result, both types have an incentive to deviate from the Nash equilibrium and can be expected to do so. It is this process that game theory expects subjects to work their way through.

Clearly, this is a very complex thought process, one that might well exceed the reasoning capabilities of mere mortals. In fact, it is this complexity that has led us to question whether game-theoretic logic could be responsible for the observed behavior of subjects in the laboratory experiments run on such games even when that behavior is consistent with the predictions of the theory.

In response to the same set of concerns, BH posit the following naive decision model to explain people's behavior in such games. Assume that player S thinks of his opponent not as a player but as a naive decision machine that chooses actions C, D, and E with equal probabilities. In such a case, when player S is of type H he will find it beneficial to choose message S since that message will maximize his expected utility. If player S is of type L, message N will be sent. Likewise, if player R believes that messages N and S are equally likely to be sent by either type, she will choose action C when S is sent and D when N is sent. Hence, these choices may be what we expect in the early rounds of the experiments. As time goes on, however, type L subjects will have an incentive to deviate since they are better off sending message S if player R is going to choose action C than they are sending message N and having D chosen. As a result, the play of the game converges to sequential equilibrium but for a very different reason than suggested by the refinement literature.

Now consider game 2, described in table 3.5. This game has exactly the same equilibria as does game 1 except that here, because of the payoff changes, the BH heuristic does not select the sequential equilibrium but rather the Nash equilibrium. So if choices converge to the sequential equilibrium in game 1 but the Nash equilibrium in game 2, such convergence cannot be the result of game-theoretic logic since in both cases the refinement predicts the sequential equilibrium.

PS replicate the BH experiment with one significant difference: subjects were only allowed to see their own and not their opponent's payoffs. If this is the case, then game-theoretic logic is ruled out since such logic is impossible without knowledge of one's opponent's payoffs. Hence, if we see behavior or choices that are identical to those predicted by the theory, it is evidence that such behavior is not occurring because of the theory and that something else is underlying it. More important, if behavior changes in a manner that is consistent with the BH heuristic when we move from game 1 to game 2, then that indicates that their heuristic is a better approximation to the thinking process of subjects than that of the Nash refinements. So again, simply seeing choices consistent with Nash in game 1 is not a good confirmation of the theory—we need to know why.

Table 3.5. Payoff Matrix for Signaling Game 2 of Brandts and Holt [1993]

	Message N			Message S		
Type	C	D[a]	E	C[b]	D	E
H	75, 30	45, 30	75, 45	60, 15	0, 0	0, 45
L	75, 30	15, 75	75, 30	45, 60	0, 0	45, 15

Columns show message of the sender and strategy of the receiver. Rows show different types for the sender. Cells show the payoff for the sender followed by the payoff for the receiver.
[a] Message N and strategy D form the nonsequential Nash equilibrium.
[b] Message S and strategy C form the sequential equilibrium.

Table 3.6. Proportion of Outcomes by Refinement

Game	Nonequilibrium	Nash equilibrium	Sequential equilibrium	Sample size
1[a]	.25	.12	.63	60
1[b]	.10	.32	.58	72
1[c]	.05	.31	.64	71
2[b]	.28	.50	.22	72
2[c]	.22	.68	.13	72

[a] Results from Banks, Camerer, and Porter [1994] in the first five rounds.
[b] Results from Brandts and Holt [1993] for the first six periods of their experiment.
[c] Results from Partow and Schotter [1993].

The results obtained by PS, as well as those reported in BH and BCP, are summarized in table 3.6. This table presents the results of the PS game 1 and game 2 experiments along with the results of BH and BCP, who ran identical games. Note that in the PS version of game 1, only 5% of the outcomes were nonequilibrium (vs. 10% found by BH and 25% for BCP), while 64% were sequential (vs. 58% for BH and 63% for BCP). In game 2, 22% of the PS outcomes are nonequilibrium (vs. 28% in BH); PS also found a bigger shift toward the Nash outcome and away from the sequential outcome as the payoff structure was modified.

We consider the data presented in table 3.6 to support for our hypothesis that game-theoretic logic is not the determinant of the results obtained by either BCP or BH. Hence, merely observing that strategic choices are consistent with a theoretical refinement, as was true in BCP, is not sufficient grounds to conclude that a theory is supported—one needs to know why.

INCOMPLETE REAL-WORLD DATA

If we are to restrict ourselves to choice data in testing theory, the question becomes whether or not the choice data existing in the world present a sufficiently rich environment upon which to test theory. More precisely, to fully put a theory through its paces, we need to see it function in a variety of parametric situations. If the world presents us only with data taken from a small subset of the potential parameter space upon which the theory is defined, then even if the choices observed are consistent with the predictions of the theory, we have no idea if the theory would continue to be supported if the world changed sufficiently to present another part of the parameter space. As a result, if the choice data we face are not sufficiently rich to fully test a theory, then supplementing the data we look at with nonchoice data may be advisable.

Let me explain this point by referring to an experiment conducted by Kfir Eliaz and myself [Eliaz and Schotter, 2006]. In this experiment, subjects were faced with the following simple decision problem: A monetary prize X is hidden in one of two boxes, labeled A and B: The probability that each box contains the prize depends on the state of nature. There are two possible states: high and low. The probability that box A contains the prize is h in the high state and $l < h$ in the low state, where h and l are both strictly above $1/2$. The subject's task is to choose a box. If she chooses correctly, she wins the prize. Before she makes her choice, the subject can pay a fee to learn the state of nature. If she chooses not to pay, the subject then must choose a box without knowing the state of nature. Whether or not the subject pays the fee, she receives a payment immediately after she makes his choice. Since a choice of A first-order stochastically dominates a choice of B, knowing the state of nature should not affect one's choice. This is true under any model of decision making under risk that respects first-order stochastic dominance. It is also independent of the subject's attitude toward risk. Thus, a subject who pays the fee exhibits an intrinsic preference for noninstrumental information.

In this experiment, we ran three treatments, a baseline and two variants, although I only discuss two of them here: the baseline and treatment 2. In the baseline, subjects are first asked if they want to pay a fee to learn the state of nature *before* making their choice. If they answer yes, they are shown the true state and are then asked to choose a box. If they answer no, they are asked to choose a box without any further information. In treatment 2, subjects are first asked to choose a box without knowing the state of nature. After they make their choice, but before being paid, they are given the opportunity to pay a fee to learn the state of nature.

In Eliaz and Schotter [2006] we posited two theories that would explain that despite the fact that the information offered had no instrumental value, subjects overwhelmingly were willing to pay for it. One is the theory of Kreps and Porteus [1978], which indicates that subjects are willing to pay the fee because they have a preference for the early resolution of uncertainty. The other is a hypothesis that indicates that people pay the fee because they get utility from being confident about the decisions they make at the time they are making them and are willing to pay just to feel good about their choices. We call this effect the "confidence effect" since we posit that people are willing to pay a fee in order to be confident that what they are doing is correct.

Note that these two explanations have very different implications for choice in the baseline and treatment 2. According to the Kreps-Porteus theory, if a subject is willing to pay a fee in the baseline, he should be willing to also pay it in treatment 2 since both situations offer him identical date 1 lotteries over lotteries at date 2 (see Eliaz and Schotter [2006] for a demonstration of this point). In contrast, the confidence effect predicts that subjects should be willing to pay for noninstrumental information only before they make their decision (as in the baseline) but not in treatment 2 since there the decision has already been made and the information comes too late to make them feel confident while they make their decision.

Table 3.7. Choice Situations—Baseline and Treatment 2

Situation	α	β	Fee ($)
3	1.0	0.60	0.50
6	1.0	0.51	2.00
12	1.0	0.51	0.50

This table refers to experiments in Eliaz and Schotter [2006]. α is the probability that box A contains $20 in the high treatment, while β is the probability that A contains $20 in the low treatment.

Table 3.8. Fraction of Subjects Paying Fee [Eliaz and Schotter, 2006]

Situation	Baseline	Treatment 2
3	0.783	0.063
6	0.565	0.125
12	0.739	0.125

To make a long story short, we found a stunning rejection of the Kreps-Porteus explanation and strong support for the confidence effect. More precisely, consider three situations (called situations 3, 6, and 12 in Eliaz and Schotter [2006]) presented in table 3.7. In these situations, the probability that box A contains the $20 in the high state, h, is α, the probability that box A contains the $20 in the low state is β, and f is the fee that needs to be paid in order to find out what the state is.

Subjects in the baseline and in treatment 2 were asked if they would be willing to pay the fee in one of these situations. The results are shown in table 3.8. Note that these data are a stunning disconfirmation of the Kreps-Porteus theory in this particular instance. While the fraction of subjects willing to pay for noninstrumental information is extremely high in the baseline, in treatment 2, where the propositions should be the same according to Kreps-Porteus, it is dramatically lower. In other words, after a choice has been made (as in treatment 2) subjects are no longer willing to pay a fee to reveal the state.

My point here is not to refute the Kreps-Porteus theory since this experiment falls far short of a general refutation. Rather, it is to demonstrate that if we relied on real-world choice data and the world was arranged such that people were never put in a position where they were asked to pay a fee for information after they had made a decision, then we would never have been able discover the weakness in the Kreps-Porteus theory for this particular choice situation. In other words, say the world was never in treatment 2 but always existed in the baseline condition. If that were the case, then by observing choices, we would infer strong support for behavior consistent with Kreps-Porteus, yet that inference might be wrong specifically because the world was not constructed to test that theory. Observed real-world choices alone seem inadequate to confirm a theory when naturally occurring data do not offer the proper tests.

Clearly, this is the justification for experimental economics in general, but if such experiments are not feasible, it still might be beneficial to simply ask people why they are doing what they are doing. If they say, "I am choosing to pay the fee because I prefer to get information earlier rather than later," then such statements support the Kreps-Porteus theory. If they say, as one of our subjects did, "I did understand the chance that the money was in box A was greater than 50%; however, I wanted to be positive of my choice," then they are refuting it. If they say nonsense, then who knows. Still, choices alone are inadequate to separate our conflicting explanations.

FRAMING AND THE RELIABILITY OF CHOICES

As stated in the introduction to this chapter, it is well known that the framing of problems can affect the choices made when those problems are presented to people. The question here is how this fact impinges on the reliability of choice data. The answer is not at all, if we as scientists know the frame used to generate the data we are using. But in many situations, this is not known. All we have are problems described by feasible sets, actions, and consequences and must infer some unobservable (preferences or risk attitudes) from the choice data we have. To illustrate how this may lead us astray, consider the famous framing example of Kahneman and Tversky [1984], modified here to represent a choice between pure money gambles (as opposed to choices about policy measures that would save or cost lives).

Consider the following two problems:

Problem 3.1: Imagine that you are about to lose $600 unless you take an action (choose a risky gamble) to prevent it. If gamble A is chosen, $200 of your $600 loss will be saved for sure. If gamble B is chosen, there is a one-third probability that all $600 will be saved and a two-thirds probability that you will not save any of the $600. Which of the two action would you favor?

Problem 3.2: Imagine that you are about to lose $600 unless you take an action (choose a risky gamble) to prevent it. If gamble A is chosen, you will wind up losing $400 for sure. If gamble B is chosen, there is a one-third probability that nothing will be lost and a two-thirds probability that you will lose the entire $600.

As we know, people when confronted with these two problems typically choose the risky action when the problem is framed negatively (stressing losses) as in problem 3.2. When the problem is framed positively (money saved), just the opposite is the case. Now say that your task was to estimate the risk aversion of people using the choices they made but you know only that they faced a problem where they could choose one gamble {1, −$400} that would give them a sure loss of $400 and another {1/3, $0; 2/3, −$600} that gave them a lottery with a 1/3 chance of losing nothing and a 2/3 chance if losing $600 (both problems present these identical lotteries, just framed differently), but you do not know the frame. Obviously, if the frame of problem 3.1 is used we will get a very different answer than if the frame of problem 3.2 were used. So any inference we make is inherently unreliable. Of course we might try to infer what the frame was or, if we suspect different frames were used for different people, what the distributions of frames were, but this is making the situation worse, not easier. In other words, the reliability of choice data is suspect if such choices are not robust to such things as framing or other possible interferences, such as emotional states.

INSTITUTIONAL DESIGN USING NEUROSCIENCE DATA

Two claims have been made to discount the use of neuroscience data in economics. The first is that, while neuroscience data may be of interest to neuroscientists, it is of no interest or use to economists since we simply don't care why people do what they do as long as we can predict that they do it—the "who cares what's under the hood" argument. The second is that since we care about designing the proper set of institutions for use in society, neuroscience can hardly be expected to be of use in that endeavor since we do not care where a person's preferences come from. This argument is summarized by Gul and Pesendorfer in chapter 1 as follows: "The purpose of economics is to analyze institutions, such as trading mechanisms and organization structures, and to ask how those institutions mediate the interests of different economic agents. This analysis is useful irrespective of the causes of individuals' preferences." In this chapter I hope to demonstrate how these claims may be misguided. In other words, neuroscience data may be of use in the design of economic institutions precisely because it gives us insights into mental states that affect behavior.

To explain all of this, consider the experimental literature on auctions. There is an often perceived experimental regularity that laboratory subjects bidding in first-price sealed-bid auctions tend to bid above the risk-neutral Nash equilibrium bid function (see, e.g., Cox, Robertson, and Smith [1982]). One of the standard explanations of this phenomenon is risk aversion, since in these auctions risk aversion increases bids. But those same authors who suggest risk aversion invariably make reference to another explanation that they call the "joy of winning." Under this explanation, there is something inherently satisfying about winning that makes it worth bidding above one's Nash bid simply to experience the satisfaction of winning. Winning represents a positive utility shock—an enjoyable mental state that people are willing to pay for.

If choice data were all we could use in disentangling these two influences, then we might proceed as Cox et al. [1982] and Goeree, Holt, and Palfrey [2002] and try to infer from bid data whether a "joy of winning" parameter can be estimated and can have a significant and positive sign. This is indeed what Goeree et al. [2002] did.

In their study, they presented subjects with an auction where there are a finite (in fact six) values that a subject could have for the good being sold and only seven bids allowable to be made. They posit that subjects make "noisy" bids for any value they receive as dictated by the following power function:

$$P(b \mid v) = \frac{U^e(b \mid v)^{\frac{1}{\mu}}}{\sum_{b'=0}^{v-1} U^e(b' \mid v)^{\frac{1}{\mu}}}, \quad b = 0, 1, 2, \ldots v,$$

where $U^e(b \mid v)$ is the expected payoff of a subject given her conjecture about the probabilities that her opponent will make each of their bids. Using a constant relative risk aversion utility function of the form $U(b \mid v) = \frac{(v-b)^{1-r}}{1-r}$, Goeree et al. [2002] estimate μ and r after solving for the fixed point, implied by the quantal response equilibrium.

To investigate the "joy of winning," they modified their original utility function to include a joy of winning term as follows: $U(b \mid v) = (\frac{(v-b)^{1-r}}{1-r} + w)$. They then recalculated their estimation and compared the results. They concluded that there is little support for the joy of winning:

> The coefficient on the joy of winning is low in magnitude and has the wrong sign. The constrained model ($w = 0$) cannot be rejected since the inclusion of w adds little to the likelihood. Moreover, the estimates of μ and r are unaffected by the inclusion of w. Thus the "joy of winning" at least as we have formulated it here, does not add anything to the explanation of overbidding. [266]

Similar conclusions had previously been reached by most investigators (see Cox et al. [1982]).

Now the question whether we can do better than this by supplementing bid data with fMRI data and, more important, whether we can use these data to help us design better first-price auctions.

Delgado, Ozbay, Schotter, and Phelps [2007] tried to do exactly this: subjects bid while we observed brain activity using fMRI. As with Goeree et al. [2002], subjects could only receive a finite number of values (in our case, one of four values) in each round {12, 10, 8, 6} and make only one of four bids {8, 7, 5, 2}. The symmetric risk-neutral Nash equilibrium is for subjects to bid 8, 7, 5, and 2 for values 12, 10, 8, and 6, respectively. Brain responses were observed both while a subject was contemplating his bid and also when he received feedback as to whether he had won or lost in a given round.

What we found is that the striatum, a region of the brain that is known to be involved in processing reward, showed a differential response when subjects won or lost. Activation in this region increased, relative to a resting baseline, when subjects were informed that they won the auction and decreased when subjects were informed that they lost. An exploration of the relation of this brain signal to the bid placed by the subject revealed that only the loss signal significantly correlated with the bid amount, suggesting that subjects' anticipated "fear of losing" may be more strongly linked with an increase of their bids in a given round. In other words, instead of an anticipated "joy of winning" affecting bidding behavior, we seem to have uncovered a significant impact of the anticipated "fear of losing" (see Delgado et al. [2007] for details).

This result is established as follows. For each subject, we have data on the bid she made given the value she received in each round. We also have data on the strength of the striatal signal when the subject was told that she either won or lost a given profit (or profit opportunity). This strength of signal is measured by the blood oxygenation-dependent (BOLD) response, represented as a β, which assesses the hemodynamic changes in the striatum when the subject is informed of a win or loss. This allows us to run two separate regressions of the following type, one for win situations and one for loss situations:

$$\text{bid}^{j} = \alpha + b_1 \text{ value} + b_2(\beta) + \varepsilon,$$

$$j = \text{win, lose,}$$

where ε is a normally distributed error term. Our results are presented in tables 3.9 and 3.10. While the striatal signal in loss situations is significantly related in a positive way to bids, the same is not true for striatal signals in win situations. We interpret this to mean that when subjects anticipate winning and losing before they make their bids, it is the anticipated fear of losing that has a significant impact on the

Table 3.9. Relationship Between Bid, Value, and Striatum Signal for Losses [Delgado et al., 2007]

Variable	Coefficient	Standard error	Probability = 0
β	0.509	0.1599	0.002
Value	0.307	0.0587	0.000
Constant	3.04	0.4574	0.000

$N = 163, R^2 = .166, F(2.160) = 15.98, \text{Prob} > F = 0.0000.$

Table 3.10. Relationship Between Bid, Value, and Striatum Signal for Wins [Delgado et al., 2007]

Variable	Coefficient	Standard error	Probability $= 0$
β	0.116	0.1256	0.357
Value	0.508	0.0438	0.000
Constant	1.75	0.4583	0.000

$N = 166, R^2 = .14527, F(2.163) = 67.40, \text{Prob} > F = 0.00000.$

bids that are made and not the anticipated joy of winning. This is true despite the fact that the activation in the striatum is significantly different from the baseline (at rest) activation for both win and loss situations.

Taking this result as informative led Delgado et al. [2007] to run a behavioral experiment to see if this hypothesis, derived from brain imaging, could be exploited by a mechanism designer in his design of an auction. More precisely, if the fMRI data implied that subjects' anticipated fear of losing caused them to increase their bid in order to avoid that unpleasant state, then that result implies that if we were to take a first-price auction and in one experiment make the losing state more unpleasant while in another make winning more enjoyable (while still keeping the equilibrium bids of subjects in these two auctions equal), we would expect, if our inference is correct, that the loss-emphasized auction would not only increase bids conditional on value, but also raise more revenue than either the control auction, where there was no manipulation of the win or loss outcome, or the treatment where the benefits of winning were enhanced.

To do this, Delgado et al. [2007] ran three first-price auctions, which can be called here the baseline, "win-frame," and "loss-frame" auctions. In each experiment, subjects engaged in a two-bidder auction with a random opponent for 30 rounds.

The baseline was a typical first-price auction where subjects were given values drawn uniformly from the interval [0, 100] and made bids accordingly. The loss-frame auction was identical to the baseline except that subjects were told the following:

At the beginning of each round you will be given a sum of 15 experimental dollars, which are yours to keep if you win the auction. This will be your "initial endowment." If you lose the auction, you will have to give this initial endowment of experimental dollars back. Only the person who wins will be able to keep them. In other words, your payoff in this auction will be equal to your value minus your bid plus your initial endowment of 15 experimental dollars if you win the auction and zero if you lose, since by losing you must give back your initial endowment.

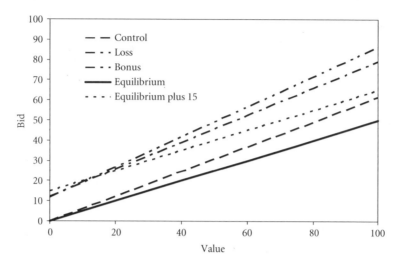

Figure 3.3. Estimated value functions for five different experimental conditions. See text for details.

The win-frame auction was again identical to the baseline except they were told that "the payoffs for the auction you engage in will differ slightly from what is described above since in addition to receiving your value minus your bid if you win, you will also be given an additional sum of 15 experimental dollars. Only the winner will receive this sum so if you lose your payoff is still zero."

Note that while the risk neutral Nash equilibrium of the two nonbaseline auctions are identical, subjects should bid what they bid in the baseline plus 15 experimental dollars, and that risk aversion affects these bid functions identically, so there should be no difference in the bids made in each auction no matter how it is framed. Our fMRI data suggest that because we have highlighted losing in the loss-frame auction, we should observe higher bids there than in the win-frame auction.

Our fMRI conjectures were supported by the data of our behavioral experiment, as shown in figure 3.3 and tables 3.11 and 3.12, both of which report the results of our estimation of the bid functions of subjects (a quadratic specification was rejected in preference to a linear one). Note in figure 3.3 that the bid function for the loss-frame treatment is almost everywhere above that of all other treatments. This is true despite the fact that both the win- and loss-frame treatments have identical equilibrium bid functions.

In terms of expected revenue, we can calculate what the expected revenue to the auctioneer would be if subjects bid as they did in our three treatments and received values drawn from a uniform distribution defined over [0, 100]. Given our regression results, we found that the expected revenue from our auctions were 46.70, 41.89, and 40.67 for our loss-frame, win-frame, and baseline treatments,

Table 3.11. Estimated Bid Function for Loss Frame [Delgado et al., 2007]

Variable	Coefficient	Standard error	Probability $= 0$
Value	0.748	0.0136	0.000
Constant	11.70	2.130	0.000

$N = 540$, $R^2 = .765$.

Table 3.12. Estimated Bid Function for Bonus Frame [Delgado et al., 2007]

Variable	Coefficient	Standard error	Probability $= 0$
Value	0.671	0.0142	0.000
Constant	12.08	2.130	0.000

$N = 660$, $R^2 = .805$.

respectively, and 33.33 for the risk-neutral prediction. In other words, we have been able to leverage a neuroeconomic finding into a result that allows us to increase the expected revenue received from a first-price auction.

The point I am making here is that it may be of use for us as economists to know the "causes of individuals' preferences," or at least what motivates people, since that may make a difference in how we design auctions. In addition, it is unlikely that we could have designed our loss-frame experiment without the aid of some nonchoice data. Knowing why our subjects bid above Nash equilibrium was important to our ultimate mechanism design, and while this insight might have been arrived at in other ways, we have at least demonstrated that it may be possible to arrive at it using fMRI data. Finally note that risk aversion cannot explain our results here since no matter what the level of a bidder's risk aversion, his behavior is expected to be the same in both the loss-frame and the win-frame treatments. In short, it appears as if nonchoice data may be useful for mechanism design.

CONCLUSION

In this chapter I question why we, as a profession, are so reluctant to allow data other than choice data into our analysis. My point is that if the object of our enterprise is to test the properties and accuracy of our theories, then choices alone are many times not sufficient. This is true for several reasons. First, the use of choices as proxies for unobservables is only as good as the theory we have relating those choices to what we would like to observe. Second, to fully test theory, we need to know why choices are made, and this might require nonchoice data. Third, real-world data are incomplete and therefore cannot alone be used to test theory. If a laboratory experiment cannot be run to fill in the missing observations, then we may need to rely on nonchoice data. Finally, nonchoice neuroscience data may give us insights useful for intelligent mechanism design.

NOTES

1. The fact that Camerer and Ho [1999] suggest that EWA nests belief learning models is more a matter of interpretation and not essence. The two types of models are quite different in spirit, and EWA only nests belief learning models of a particular fictitious-play-like type. Other belief learning models that define beliefs differently are not nested in this model.

REFERENCES

Banks, J., Colin F. Camerer, and D. Porter. 1994. Experimental Tests of Nash Refinements in Signaling Games. *Games and Economic Behavior* 6: 1–31.

Brandts, J., and Charles Holt. 1993. Adjustment Patterns and Equilibrium Selection in Experimental Signaling Games. *International Journal of Game Theory* 22: 279–302.

Broseta, B., Miguel Costa-Gomes, and Vincent Crawford. 2001. Cognition and Behavior in Normal-Form Games: An Experimental Study. *Econometrica* 69: 1193–1235.

Camerer, C., and Teck H. Ho. 1999. Experience-Weighted Attraction Learning in Normal Form Games. *Econometrica* 67(4): 827–874.

Cheung, Y.-W., and Daniel Friedman. 1997. Individual Learning in Normal Form Games. *Games and Economic Behavior* 19: 46–76.

Costa-Gomes, M., and Georg Weizsäcker. 2006. Stated Beliefs and Play in Normal-Form Games. Mimeo, London School of Economics.

Cox, J. C., Bruce Robertson, and Vernon L. Smith. 1982. Theory and Behavior of Single Price Auctions. In *Research in Experimental Economics*, ed. Vernon L. Smith, 1–43. Greenwich, CT: JAI Press.

Delgado, M., Erkut Ozbay, Andrew Schotter, and Elizabeth Phelps. 2007. The Neuroeconomics of Overbidding: The Neural Circuitry of Losses and Gains in Auctions. Unpublished manuscript. 2007.

Ehrblatt, W., Kyle Hyndman, Erkut Ozbay, and Andrew Schotter. 2007. Convergence: An Experimental Study of Teaching and Learning in Repeated Games. Mimeo, New York University.

Eliaz, K., and Andrew Schotter. Paying for Confidence: An Experimental Study of the Demand for non-Instrumental Information. Mimeo, New York University, June 2007.

Friedman, M. 1953. *Essays in Positive Economics*. Chicago: University of Chicago Press.

Glymour, Clark. 1980. *Theory and Evidence*. Princeton, NJ: Princeton University Press.

Goeree, J., Charles Holt, and Thomas Palfrey. 2002. Quantal Response Equilibrium and Overbidding in Private-Value Auctions. *Journal of Economic Theory* 104(1): 247–272.

Holt, C., and Jacob Goeree. 2001. Ten Little Treasures of Game Theory, and Ten Intuitive Contradictions. *American Economic Review December* 91(5): 1402–1422.

Huck, S., and Georg Weizsäcker. 2002. Do Players Correctly Estimate What Others Do? Evidence of Conservatism in Beliefs. *Journal of Economic Behavior and Organization* 47(1): 71–85.

Johnson, E., Colin Camerer, Sankar Sen, and Talia Rymon. 2002. Detecting Failures of Backward Induction: Monitoring Information Search in Sequential Bargaining. *Journal of Economic Theory* 104(1): 16–47.

Kahneman, D., and Amos Tversky, A. 1984. Choices, Values and Frames. *American Psychologist* 39: 341–350.

Kreps, D., and E. Porteus. 1978. Temporal Resolution of Uncertainty and Dynamic Choice Theory. *Econometrica* 46: 185–200.

Nyarko, Y., and Andrew Schotter. 2002. An Experimental Study of Belief Learning Using Elicited Beliefs. *Econometrica* 70: 971–1005.

Partow, Z., and Andrew Schotter. 1993. Does Game Theory Predict Well for the Wrong Reasons? An Experimental Investigation. *Working Paper* 93–46, New York University.

Smith, Vernon. 1982. Microeconomic Systems as an Experimental Science. *American Economic Review* 72(5): 923–955.

CHAPTER 4

....

ON TWO POINTS OF VIEW REGARDING REVEALED PREFERENCE AND BEHAVIORAL ECONOMICS

....

RAN SPIEGLER

THE concept of revealed preferences surfaces quite often in methodological debates over behavioral economics. There seems to be a close linkage between economists' attitudes to the revealed preference principle and the opinions that they hold regarding paternalistic policies, or their relative evaluation of decision models. This chapter is an attempt to clarify several aspects of this linkage.

The revealed preference principle is part of a philosophical tradition that places restrictions on professional discourse, by judging parts of it to be "meaningless." It was originally formulated at a time when economic models involved little more than static choice of a consumption bundle from a budget set. In this simple consumer-theoretic environment, a single "mental construct" is attributed to the decision maker, namely, a utility function $u : X \rightarrow R$. The revealed preference principle then means that any property of u is meaningful only if it can be defined in terms of a preference relation $R \subseteq X \times X$, which in turn can be elicited from choice experiments whose outcomes are summarized by a choice correspondence c, where $c(A) \subseteq A$ for every nonempty $A \subseteq X$. To quote Gul and Pesendorfer (chapter 1):

> In the standard approach, the terms "utility maximization" and "choice" are
> synonymous. A utility function is always an ordinal index that describes how the

individual ranks various outcomes and how he behaves (chooses) given his constraints (available options). The relevant data are revealed preference data, that is, consumption choices given the individual's constraints.

To illustrate the principle in action, consider an economist who discusses a policy issue and employs the "mental construct" of utility for this purpose. For whatever reason, the economist's policy analysis hinges on whether an agent's utility function is concave or convex. The revealed preference principle implies that the economist's distinction is meaningful only if concave and convex utility functions are distinguishable on the basis of the agent's observable choices in the domain of choice problems that are relevant for the policy issue. If they are not, then an adherent of the revealed preference principle would dismiss the economist's conclusions from the policy analysis.

As decision models became more complex, additional "mental constructs" entered economic analysis. For instance, subjective expected utility theory involves *two* mental constructs: utility rankings and subjective probability. It has been pointed out [see Karni, 2005] that in subjective expected utility theory, subjective probability and state-dependent utility cannot be distinguished behaviorally. Thus, even when we remain safely within the boundaries of what Gul and Pesendorfer call "mindless economics," the "revealed preference justification" for the concept of utility is more nuanced than in the basic consumer-theoretic environment.

When we reach the "nonstandard" decision models that appear in the bounded rationality and behavioral economics literatures, the tension with the revealed preference principle becomes much stronger. Here are a few examples of such models:

- A choice procedure that selects the median alternative from each choice set, according to a linear ordering of the grand set of alternatives
- A utility maximization model, in which the sole carrier of utility is the decision maker's subjective belief
- A multi-selves model, in which an extensive form decision problem is modeled as an intrapersonal game, and the decision maker's choice is the outcome of subgame perfect equilibrium in that game

In all three cases, the primitives of the decision model contain a preference relation or a utility function. However, it is not true that "'utility maximization' and 'choice' are synonymous." In the first example, the "median" procedure (which captures the "compromise effect" discussed by psychologists—see Simonson [1989]) induces a choice correspondence that violates the Weak Axiom of Revealed Preferences. In the second example, a utility ranking between two subjective beliefs cannot be revealed by an observable act of choice. In the third example, the decision maker's choice is the outcome of an algorithm that involves a collection of utility functions, but not by way of maximizing any of them. Thus, any economic analysis—especially one that involves welfare judgments—that makes use of the concept of utility inherent in these models is inconsistent with the revealed preference principle in its narrow formulation, which finds expression in the statement that "'utility maximization' and 'choice' are synonymous."

One possible response to this state of affairs is that the concept of revealed preferences was invented when economists lacked tools for direct measurement of mental constructs such as utility. Nowadays we have better tools. If, thanks to these tools, a theorist puts a lot of faith in a nonstandard decision model, she can discard the revealed preference principle altogether. In particular, she should not allow the principle to interfere with a potentially useful welfare analysis, which happens to be based on a concept of utility that appears in the description of the model yet fails to be synonymous with observable choices.

Another possible response is to discredit the nonstandard models. According to this point of view, since utility maximization and observed choice are not synonymous in these models, an economic analysis (especially one that involves welfare judgments) that relies on the concept of utility inherent in these models is inadmissible. Either economists give up the ambition to incorporate the psychological factors that these models purport to capture, or they substitute these decision models with alternative models for which "'utility maximization' and 'choice' are synonymous."

I believe that many economists would associate the first point of view with the behavioral economics approach and the second point of view with the decision-theoretic approach to "psychology and economics"—especially with the "mindless economics" vision portrayed in Gul and Pesendorfer. In this chapter, I address these two viewpoints, and the bigger question that they reflect: What is the role of the revealed preference principle in nonstandard decision models that incorporate novel psychological factors? My approach is to examine more specific, concrete claims, which I perceive as being representative of the two respective viewpoints.

Claim 4.1.

Behavioral economists can "safely" express decision models in the language of utilities, without trying to characterize them in terms of general properties of their induced choice correspondences. This "revealed preference exercise" can be left entirely for specialized decision theorists.

This claim is implicit in the modeling practice of behavioral economics. Rarely do we see a paper that can be identified as a "behavioral economics" paper, in which a choice-theoretic characterization exercise, however rudimentary, is carried out. This avoidance may be a by-product of a rejection of the status of the revealed preference principle as a philosophical foundation for decision models.

However, the explanation may also be "cultural": in its style and rhetoric, behavioral economics is closer to "applied theory" than to "pure theory" and, as such, perpetuates the traditional division of labor between applied theorists and decision theorists.

Let us turn to the second claim. In a series of articles, Gul and Pesendorfer [2001, 2004, 2005a] present a modeling approach to dynamic decision making in the presence of self-control problems, and contrast it with the multi-selves approach. In particular—and this is most relevant for the present discussion—they argue that the former approach is consistent with the revealed preference principle, whereas the latter approach is not. Gul and Pesendorfer's claim can be summarized as follows:

Claim 4.2.

Multi-selves models of dynamic decision making are inconsistent with the revealed preference principle. Moreover, they can and should be reformulated as (or substituted by) decision models for which utility maximization and choice are synonymous.

This essay is critical of both claims. Contrary to claim 4.1, I argue that a rudimentary revealed preference exercise is a highly useful "diagnostic" tool for economists who develop nonstandard, "behavioral" decision models, independently of their attitude to the principle of revealed preferences as a philosophical foundation for decision models. And contrary to claim 4.2, I argue that the narrow version of the revealed preference principle has limitations as a theory-selection criterion in the development of decision models with a "rich" psychology.

The rest of this chapter is structured as follows: First I present a critical discussion of claim 4.1. In order to make the analysis as concrete as possible, I use the literature on "utility from beliefs," which has received wide attention in recent literature, as a test case. Then I discuss claim 4.2, in the context of Gul and Pesendorfer's model of self-control preferences. Last, I summarize my "lessons" from these analyses.

Revealed Preferences as a "Diagnostic Tool": The Case of "Utility from Beliefs"

When theorists embed a decision model in a larger model of an economic environment, they typically express the decision model in the language of utilities, without bothering to characterize it first in terms of general properties of its induced choice correspondence. This modeling practice is very efficient. However, it tends to make it difficult to perceive general properties of the behavior implied by the decision model. Partly because of this difficulty, there is a specialized branch of economic theory, namely, decision theory, whose job is to clarify, via "representation theorems," how properties of a utility function are defined in terms of revealed preferences. When an applied theorist writes down a model in the language of utilities, he is typically "reassured" that a decision-theoretic analysis that "permits" him to use the model has already been carried out.

In behavioral economics, the difficulty is intensified for several reasons. First, "behavioral" models sometimes retain the concept of utility yet abandon utility maximization, which makes it harder to grasp the relation between choice behavior and the shape of the utility function, Second, even when utility maximization is retained, the domain over which utility is defined is often unusual and complicated. Finally, the behavioral economist typically writes down the decision model before the "reassuring" decision-theoretic exercise has been conducted.

This certainly does not lead me to conclude that proposing a "behavioral" model must be accompanied by a standard decision-theoretic exercise, which most conspicuously includes axiomatization. However, in this section I argue that a rudimentary revealed preference exercise is *heuristically valuable* for the behavioral economist. The reason is that it may serve as a safeguard against misleading interpretation of the model's assumptions, domain of applicability, and conclusions.

To substantiate this claim, I discuss it in the context of the literature on "utility from beliefs," which has received wide attention recently. The basic idea underlying this literature is that people's well-being is often directly affected by their beliefs. For example, a decision maker may derive direct satisfaction from anticipation of high material payoffs; or, she may suffer a disutility (called "cognitive dissonance") if her belief fails to rationalize her actions. In games, a player's sense of disappointment at his opponent's lack of generosity often depends on how he expected the opponent to behave in the first place.

Models with utility from beliefs provide an ideal test case for claim 4.1. On one hand, the idea that beliefs directly affect our sense of well-being is highly intuitive. This intuition is supported by a rich psychology literature that documents the emotional effects of beliefs and how they sometimes lead decision makers to self-serving distortion of their beliefs. On the other hand, the idea of "utility from beliefs" obviously runs counter to the narrow version of the revealed preference principle, since no choice experiment can directly reveal the utility ranking between two subjective beliefs.

For an adherent of the narrow version of revealed preferences, economic analysis that is based on a utility-from-beliefs model (especially welfare analysis) is inadmissible. But does it follow that if one does not share this dismissive attitude to the concept of utility from beliefs, one can entirely dispense with the revealed preference exercise when analyzing a utility-from-beliefs model? In this section I describe a number of recently proposed utility-from-beliefs models and show how the notion of revealed preferences has value as a "diagnostic tool," which is independent of one's opinion regarding the principle's status as a philosophical foundation for decision models.

Self-Deception

I begin by examining the model of "optimal expectations" due to Brunnermeier and Parker [2005] (henceforth BP). This is a model of self-deception, according to which subjective belief is a *choice variable*. When people choose how much to distort their beliefs, they trade off the anticipatory gains from holding an overoptimistic belief against the material loss that results from making a decision that is based on an incorrect belief.[1]

Whereas BP analyze a rather complicated model with a long horizon, here I examine a stripped-down, two-period version of their model. Let $\Omega = \{\omega_1, \ldots, \omega_n\}$ be a set of states of nature where $n \geq 2$, and let A be a set of feasible actions. Let $u(a, \omega)$ be the material payoff that the decision maker (henceforth DM) derives from action a in state ω. Let $q(\omega)$ be the objective probability of ω. Finally, let $\alpha \in (0, 1)$.

The DM's decision rule is to choose a belief p and an action a to maximize the following expression:

$$\alpha \cdot \sum_{\omega \in \Omega} p(\omega) \cdot u(a, \omega) + (1 - \alpha) \cdot \sum_{\omega \in \Omega} q(\omega) \cdot u(a, \omega) \tag{4.1}$$

where a maximizes $\sum_{\omega \in \Omega} p(\omega) \cdot u(a', \omega)$, and the support of p is contained in the support of q. Let c_{BP} denote the choice correspondence induced by the BP decision rule.

The BP model is inconsistent with the narrow version of the revealed preference principle. Expression 4.1, which is intended to represent the DM's "well-being," is defined over a subset of $A \times \Delta(\Omega)$. However, the DM's act of choosing the subjective belief $p \in \Delta(\Omega)$ is unobservable. Note that we could interpret the BP model as if it describes the following two-stage game, in which a "preacher" manipulates a gullible "student" into holding any belief. The reason the preacher can do that is that the student believes that the preacher is absolutely truthful, whereas in fact the preacher conveys information selectively. The preacher moves first by choosing p, and the student moves second by choosing a. The preacher's objective is to maximize expression 4.1, whereas the student's objective is to maximize $\sum_{\omega \in \Omega} p(\omega) \cdot u(a, \omega)$. In this case, the preacher's choice of p corresponds to an observable, selective transmission of information. Under this interpretation, the model is consistent with revealed preferences, but it ceases to be a model of self-deception.

BP's first application of the model concerns risk attitudes. They examine the DM's choice between *two* actions: a safe action and a risky action. In terms of our specification of the model, let $A = \{a_s, a_r\}$, let $u(a_s, \omega) = 0$ for every $\omega \in \Omega$, and suppose that $\sum_\omega q(\omega) u(a_r, \omega) < 0$, yet $\max_\omega u(a_r, \omega) > 0$. Denote $\omega^* \in$ arg $\max_\omega u(a_r, \omega)$.

A standard DM who maximizes expected material payoffs without trying to deceive himself would play safe (a_s). In contrast, it is easy to see that there exists $\alpha^* \in (0, 1)$, such that for every $\alpha > \alpha^*$, the DM prefers to believe $p(\omega^*) = 1$ and play a_r. Under this belief–action pair, expression (4.1) is reduced to $\alpha \cdot 1 \cdot u(a_r, \omega^*) + (1 - \alpha) \cdot \sum_\omega q(\omega) u(a_r, \omega)$, which is strictly positive if α is sufficiently close to one.

BP conclude that their model implies excessive risk taking. Indeed, some features of this effect appear attractive. People often like to gamble when the maximal loss is very low but the maximal gain is very high, and the explanation may well be that they enjoy the pure anticipation of a large gain. However, recall that BP's conclusion relies on choice problems that involve two actions. What happens when we add a third action to the choice set?

Proposition 4.1.

Fix q and α. Let a_s be a safe action; that is, $u(a_s, \omega) = 0$ for every $\omega \in \Omega$. Then, there exist a material payoff function u and a pair of actions a_r, a_r', such that $a_r \in c_{BP}\{a_s, a_r\}$ and $c_{BP}\{a_s, a_r, a_r'\} = \{a_s\}$.

Proof

Construct the following payoff function u:

action/state	ω_1	ω_2	$\cdots$	ω_n
a_s	0	0	$\cdots$	0
a_r	1	$-k$	$\cdots$	$-k$
a_r'	m	$-n$	$\cdots$	$-n$

where $k, m, n > 0$, $m > 1$, and k satisfies

$$\alpha + (1 - \alpha) \cdot [q(\omega_1) - k(1 - q(\omega_1))] = 0.$$

Under this specification, $c_{BP}\{a_s, a_r\} = \{a_s, a_r\}$. To see why, note that when the DM chooses to believe $p(\omega_1) = 1$, the only action in the choice set $\{a_s, a_r\}$ that is compatible with this belief is a_r. But under this belief–action pair, the DM's payoff, given by expression 4.1, attains a value of 0. Clearly, every other belief that is compatible with a_r yields a payoff below 0. Therefore, the only belief that justifies playing a_r is $p(\omega_1) = 1$.

Now suppose that the choice set is $\{a_s, a_r, a_r'\}$. If the DM chooses to believe $p(\omega_1) = 1$, then since $m > 1$, the only action that is compatible with this belief is a'_r. The DM's payoff under this belief–action pair is

$$\alpha m + (1 - \alpha) \cdot [mq(\omega_1) - n(1 - q(\omega_1))],$$

which is strictly negative if n is sufficiently large. For every other belief that is compatible with a'_r, the DM's payoff will be even lower. Thus, as long as n is sufficiently large, the DM necessarily chooses the action a_s together with any belief that is compatible with it (e.g., $p = q$). ■

Thus, the choice correspondence implied by the BP model violates Independence of Irrelevant Alternatives (IIA). For every objective probability distribution over Ω and for every α, one can construct a material payoff function such that the DM's tendency to choose a (materially inferior) risky action can be undone by adding another risky action to the choice set.[2]

The intuition for this IIA violation is interesting. In the two-alternative choice problem, when the DM chooses the risky action a_r, she might as well deceive herself into thinking that $p(\omega^*) = 1$. This huge overoptimism justifies taking the risky action, because the material decision loss is outweighed by the large anticipatory gain. However, when the risky action a'_r is added to the feasible set, excessive optimism would cause the DM to choose a'_r. Given q and u, the expected material loss from a'_r is so big that it outweighs the anticipatory gain. Thus, in order to induce a_r, the DM must restrain her overoptimism, but this means that the anticipatory gain is not high enough to justify this action anymore. Therefore, the DM ends up choosing the safe action.

I find this quite insightful and certainly worthy of further study. It may well turn out to shed light on how decision makers' propensity for self-deception varies with their set of options. At any rate, the result greatly qualifies BP's claims regarding the risk attitudes implied by their model. The finding that the DM's risk attitudes vary with the choice set is clearly more fundamental than the finding that the DM displays excessive risk seeking in some choice problems with a safe asset and a risky asset.

Had BP approached the issue a bit more like choice theorists, they would have attached greater importance to checking whether c_{BP} satisfies IIA:

- If IIA is satisfied, then the model is behaviorally indistinguishable from a standard model in which the DM maximizes a utility function over actions. This raises an interesting question: Suppose that two decision models account for the same behavior in a prespecified domain of choice problems, yet only one of them is consistent with the narrow version of the revealed preference principle (in the sense that utility maximization is synonymous with observed choice). How should we respond to such behavioral equivalence?

- If IIA is violated, then any statement about the DM's choice under uncertainty has to be qualified because adding an "irrelevant alternative" may reverse the DM's choices between risky and safe actions.

In this case, it appears that a rudimentary revealed preference exercise is valuable, even if the ultimate goal is to develop an "applied" model. I do not think that this little exercise should be left for some future decision theorist who may take it upon himself to axiomatize the BP model. Instead, it should accompany the original development of the model. The question of whether the choice correspondence induced by a decision model satisfies IIA is so basic that readers of an article that presents the model for the first time would probably like to know about it.

This example illustrates that thinking in terms of revealed preferences is "diagnostically" valuable for the development of a "behavioral" decision model. In particular, reexpressing the model in the language of choice correspondences brings to the fore key behavioral properties, which are known to be insightfully linked to properties of utility, and yet are sometimes obscured by the utility language.

Information Acquisition

The primitives of a "revealed preference" model are choice correspondences or preference relations, and the modeler's problem is to relate properties of these objects to properties of the utility representation she is interested in. This encourages the researcher to search for choice problems that seem most likely a priori to elicit the psychological factors under study. For instance, choices between insurance policies are intuitively a good place to look for elicitation of risk aversion; choices between menus are a good place to look for elicitation of a DM's awareness of his self-control problems. Thus, thinking in terms of revealed preferences about a decision model involves looking for domains of choice problems that are promising in the sense that they intuitively seem capable of eliciting the psychology captured by the model.

The BP utility-from-beliefs model is meant to be about self-deception—namely, about the way people manipulate their own beliefs. Although the model assumes that the DM directly chooses what to believe, people can also distort their beliefs indirectly, through their choice of information sources. Indeed, introspection and casual observation suggest that the phenomenon of self-deception has a lot to do with aversion to potentially unpleasant information. People who try to deceive themselves are also likely to hire "yes men" as advisors, flip TV channels in order to avoid disturbing news, and keep "dangerous" books out of their home. In particular, there is a strong intuition that people's choice of a biased information source over another (e.g., watching Fox News rather than BBC News) is often indicative of the kind of self-serving distortion of beliefs they are trying to attain. Finally, this way of influencing one's beliefs is observable in principle.

Thus, according to the prescription given at the top of this subsection, we should be interested in examining how a DM who derives direct utility from anticipated payoffs chooses information sources. BP leave information acquisition outside their model. In order to extend the model to this domain, we need to add a preliminary stage to the decision process, in which the DM chooses a signal from a set of feasible signals S. Given the realization of the chosen signal, the DM chooses a belief and an action as in the original BP model, so as to maximize expression 4.1.

This description is incomplete, because it does not tell us how the DM updates her beliefs, or how the updating process interacts with the DM's direct choice of beliefs. I cannot think of any assumption that would not sound artificial in this context. However, the most standard assumption would be that the DM updates her beliefs according to Bayes's rule upon the realization of a signal, so that the subjective belief p is chosen given the updated objective probability distribution.

Proposition 4.2.

Fix A, and suppose that S consists of signals that never rule out any state with certainty. Then, the DM's behavior throughout the two-stage decision problem—and particularly his choices between signals in the first stage—is indistinguishable from those of a standard DM who tries to maximize the expectation of some utility function $v(a, \omega)$.[3]

Proof

Given a, let P_a be the set of subjective beliefs p for which

$$a \in \arg\max_{a' \in A} \sum_{\omega \in \Omega} p(\omega) u(a, \omega).$$

Let $p_a^* = \arg\max_{p \in P_a} \sum_{\omega \in \Omega} p(\omega) u(a, \omega)$. Define

$$v(a, \omega) = (1 - \alpha) \cdot u(a, \omega) + \alpha \cdot \sum_{\omega \in \Omega} p_a^*(\omega) u(a, \omega).$$

Note that the second term in this expression is a function of a only. Thus, in the second stage of the two-stage decision problem, a DM who chooses p and a according to the BP decision rule behaves as if she chooses a to maximize the expectation of v.

Let us turn to the first stage. Recall that we restrict attention to signals that never rule out any state with certainty. Therefore, the set of feasible subjective beliefs p in the second stage remains the set of probability distributions over Ω whose support is weakly contained in the support of q. Therefore, the DM chooses signals in the first stage as if his objective is to maximize the indirect utility function induced by the maximization of the expectation of v in the second stage. ∎

This result means that under a slight restriction of the domain of feasible signals, the DM is never averse to information.[4] But if the most standard extension of the BP model cannot capture preference for biased information sources, which intuitively seem to originate from a desire to attain self-serving beliefs, what does it mean for the self-deception interpretation of the BP model? In particular, how should we regard the theory that a financial investor's excessive risk taking is due to self-deception, when we know that according to the same theory, she never rejects potentially unpleasant information?

Note that under the "indoctrination" interpretation suggested in the preceding subsection, there is nothing strange about the observation that the preacher is never averse to information. Of course, the economic situations that fit the "indoctrination" interpretation are quite different from those that fit the "self-deception" interpretation.

As in the preceding subsection, a "revealed preference approach" has value as a diagnostic tool. Specifically, looking at choices of signals—a domain of choice problems that seems capable of exposing the psychology of self-deception—may lead us to question the original interpretation of the model and its domain of applicability.

Other Utility-from-Beliefs Models

In the extended BP model of the preceding subsection, the DM distorts his beliefs both through self-deception and through choice of signals. In another class of utility-from-beliefs model [e.g., Caplin and Leahy, 2004; Köszegi, 2003, 2006], the DM's belief enters as an argument in his utility function, but he does not get to choose what to believe. The only way he can affect his beliefs is through information.

The decision process that is embedded in these models consists of two stages. In the first stage, the DM chooses a signal and updates her beliefs according to the signal's realization, via Bayes's rule. In the second stage, the DM chooses an action a, given her updated belief. A common application of the model involves a patient who faces a choice between diagnostic tests having different probabilities of a false positive and a false negative. Another application may involve a media consumer who chooses a TV news channel in order to be informed about the latest Middle East crisis.

In these models, the DM's objective function typically takes the following form:

$$M(p) + \sum_{\omega \in \Omega} p(\omega) \cdot u(a, \omega), \tag{4.2}$$

where u is a material payoff function and $p \in \Delta(\Omega)$ is the DM's posterior belief, arrived at from the prior q and the observed signal, via Bayesian updating. The second term in the DM's objective function represents his expected material payoff. The term $M(p)$ is a continuous function, which is meant to represent the "anticipatory payoff" associated with a posterior belief p (details of u may enter the specification of M). Depending on the shape of M, the DM may display aversion to information in the first stage.

The DM's indirect expected utility conditional on the posterior belief p can be written as follows:

$$U(p) = M(p) + \max_{a \in A} \sum_{\omega \in \Omega} p(\omega) \cdot u(a, \omega)$$

Thus, as long as we are only interested in the DM's first-stage behavior, we may adopt a reduced-form model, according to which the DM chooses a signal that maximizes the expectation of $U(p)$, given her prior q, knowing that she will update q according to Bayes's rule.[5]

Eliaz and Spiegler [2006] carry out a rudimentary revealed preference analysis of this reduced form model. Note that the DM's first-stage choices between signals are *indexed* by the parameter q. If the DM's choices of signals are rational, the first-stage "choice data" can be represented by a profile of preference relations $(\succsim_q)_{q \in \Delta(\Omega)}$ over the set of signals S. The problem is to account for the choice data by the reduced-form model.

Eliaz and Spiegler [2006] point out several difficulties with this model. First, if U accounts for the choice data, then so does the function $V(p) = U(p) - pc^T$, where $c = (c_1, \ldots, c_n)$ is a vector of real numbers. In particular, we can choose c such that there will be two beliefs, p and p', for which $U(p) > U(p')$ and $V(p) < V(p')$. In some special cases, we can choose c such that U and V will induce opposite rankings for *any* pair of beliefs.

Why does this little result pose an interpretational difficulty? In their article on economic implications of cognitive dissonance, Akerlof and Dickens [1982: 307] state: "[P]ersons ... manipulate their own beliefs by selecting sources of information likely to confirm "'desired beliefs.'" Bénabou and Tirole [2002: 906] write in a similar vein: "[P]eople just like to think of themselves as good, able, generous, attractive, and conversely find it painful to contemplate their failures and shortcomings." Indeed, there is an intuition that people's preference for information sources having a particular bias is related to their perception of what constitutes a desired belief.

For instance, we may expect that when a media consumer chooses whether to be informed about the latest Middle East conflict by watching Fox News or BBC News, his decision will be linked to the kind of narrative he wants to believe in (which of the parties to the conflict is to blame, or which party won). The fact that U and

V may represent the same choices between signals implies that two different media consumers, having diametrically opposed views as to what constitutes a desired narrative, could end up watching the same channel. Thus, contrary to the intuition articulated by Akerlof and Dickens [1982], the distinction between "desired" and "undesired" beliefs may be irrelevant to the DM's choice of information sources, according to the above utility-from-beliefs model.

Comment

Caplin and Leahy [2004] make essentially the same observation, but they do not seem to share my view that it is a cause for concern. Instead, they highlight a different implication. Suppose that the DM is the receiver in a communication game, in which the sender is a "concerned expert" whose objective is to maximize the receiver's expected utility from beliefs. A "signal" in this model represents the sender's information transmission strategy. In this environment, *U* and *V* may be distinguished behaviorally, because they imply different disclosure incentives for the sender, and therefore may induce different equilibrium outcomes. I agree with this claim, but find it independent of the above interpretational difficulty.

Another difficulty pointed out by Eliaz and Spiegler [2006] is that the model fails to account for a variety of realistic prior-dependent attitudes to information, which intuitively seem to originate from anticipatory feelings. For instance, suppose that the DM ranks the fully informative signal above all other signals when $q(\omega_1)$ is close to 1. Then, according to the model, this ranking must hold for all priors. It follows that the model cannot capture the behavior of a patient who wants to have full knowledge of her medical condition when she is quite sure that she is in good health, yet does not want to know the whole truth when she is not so sure.

Both difficulties raise doubts regarding the model's ability to explain anomalous attitudes to information, despite the intuition that such attitudes sometimes originate from the direct effect of beliefs on the DM's well-being. It should be emphasized that these difficulties can be discovered without abandoning the "applied theory" manner of expressing models purely in the language of utilities. Nevertheless, a rudimentary revealed preference exercise makes it easier to notice them. One ingredient of this exercise is to check whether the utility representation is unique with respect to certain transformations. This makes the first difficulty easy to discover. In addition, once the "choice data" are written down systematically, it becomes obvious that the DM's choices over signals are indexed by the prior q, whereas the%enlargethispage11pt utility function *U* is not indexed by q. This observation makes it more urgent for the theorist to seek connections between the DM's choices of signals at different priors, which makes the second difficulty easy to discover.

Summary

The point of this section is simple. Even if one rejects the revealed preference principle as a criterion for determining the admissibility of "behavioral" decision models, the principle still has value in the development of such models. A rudimentary revealed preference exercise helps clarifying general aspects of the behavior induced by the model. The clarification obtained in this way is so basic that it cannot be left for a future decision theorist. Instead, it should be part of the behavioral theorist's bag of tools.

Rubinstein and Salant (chapter 5) make a related comment. They argue that although certain choice procedures cannot be described as the outcome of utility maximization, they can be characterized and differentiated from one another by properties of their induced choice correspondence. Thus, a revealed preference exercise is instrumental in characterizing "nonstandard" decision models that incorporate novel psychological factors.

REVEALED PREFERENCES AS A THEORY-SELECTION CRITERION: THE CASE OF SELF-CONTROL PREFERENCES

In the preceding section I argue in favor of a modeling approach that borrows the "diagnostic" aspect of the revealed preference principle. Claim 4.2 described in the introduction enunciates a more ambitious view of the role of the revealed preference principle in behavioral economics. According to this claim, if a decision model fails to satisfy the property that "'utility maximization' and 'choice' are synonymous," then it is an inferior model, in the sense that it cannot provide a basis for welfare analysis that is consistent with the revealed preference principle. Therefore, the model should be reformulated as, or substituted by, a model for which utility maximization and choice are synonymous.

This position has been articulated most insistently by Faruk Gul and Wolfgang Pesendorfer (GP henceforth) in a series of papers. For instance, in GP [2005b], they propose a theory of social preferences, in which a player's preferences over strategy profiles in a game depend on his and his opponent's types, where a player's type represents his "personality." GP pit this theory against models of social preferences based on the formalism of psychological games (due to Geanakopolos, Pearce, and Stachetti [1989]), in which players' payoffs are also a function of their hierarchy of beliefs regarding the strategy profile. The two theories are meant to cover the same terrain (social preferences), yet one is a "revealed preference theory," whereas the other is not.

Such comparisons have received the widest attention in the context of GP's highly original decision-theoretic modeling approach to changing tastes and self-control (which builds on foundations laid by Kreps [1979], Dekel, Lipman, and Rustichini [2001], and Kreps and Porteus [1978]). GP compare this approach to the multi-selves approach. In GP [2005a: 430], they argue: "The advantage of our approach is that preferences over decision problems are—at least in principle—observable. Rather than speculate about the appropriate model of expectation formation, we offer choice experiments that identify Strotz's model of behavior." Epstein [2006: 4] endorses this view:

> Gul and Pesendorfer [2005a] describe advantages of their approach. One is that the axiomatic method permits identification of the exhaustive empirical content of the model, expressed through restrictions on in principle observable behavior at a fixed time 0. In contrast, Strotz's multi-selves interpretation involves hypotheses not only about time 0 behavior, but also about expectations of future behavior.

Thus, GP's position seems to be as follows: The decision-theoretic modeling approach is consistent with the revealed preference principle, in the sense that all relevant "mental constructs" (not only utility rankings, but also the DM's expectations of future behavior) are revealed by observable choices. In contrast, the multi-selves approach is inconsistent with the revealed preference principle, in the sense that it relies on a priori assumptions regarding the DM's formation of expectations of future behavior. In this section I discuss the GP modeling approach in light of these claims. In particular, I ask whether it jibes with the revealed preference principle in a way that the multi-selves approach fails to.

In the simplest form of the GP model of self-control preferences [GP 2001], the DM goes through a two-period decision process. In the first period, she chooses a menu of lotteries. In the second period, she selects a lottery from the chosen menu. GP assume that the DM has complete, transitive preferences over menus, which can be represented by the following utility function:

$$U(A) = \max_{x \in A}[u(x) + v(x)] - \max_{y \in A} v(y),$$

where u and v are expected utility functions. As far as first-period behavior is concerned, the GP model definitely meets the requirement that "'utility maximization' and 'choices' are synonymous."

But the interest in the GP model lies precisely in the interpretation of the menu as a choice set, and of the function U as an indirect utility. In particular, one of the components in the utility representation, namely, $\arg\max_{x \in A}[u(x) + v(x)]$, is interpreted as the lottery that the DM expects to choose in the second period. Moreover, when applying this model, GP and other practitioners assume that these expectations are correct. This interpretation is crucial for the applications of the model. Yet, it is *external* to the revealed preference exercise. We could just as well assume that the DM's expectations are systematically incorrect, without changing anything in the analysis of "time 0" preferences over menus.

GP [2005a] appear to be saying the same thing, in reference to their "revealed preference theory of changing tastes" (which, in its two-period version, is essentially an axiomatization of the first-period behavior implied by the two-period Strotzian model):

> As in standard models of dynamic choice we view the decision maker as expressing a preference at one point in time (period 0). The representation of these preferences suggests behavior in future periods that can be interpreted as the agent's implicit expectations. Whether these expectations are correct or not (that is, whether the agent is sophisticated or not) can be treated as a separate question. That is, the representation is a valid description of period 0 behavior whether or not the agent has correct expectations, as long as the axioms are satisfied. [432]

The same words could apply to the GP model of self-control preferences. Yet, in light of this statement, the decision-theoretic and multi-selves approaches appear to have the same justification for their assumptions on the DM's first-period expectations of future behavior. Of course, there is a methodological difference between the two modeling practices. The multi-selves approach views as primitive the two selves' preferences over terminal histories of the two-period decision problem (i.e., decision paths) and make explicit assumptions regarding the solution concept that is applied to the extensive decision problem. One can then derive from these assumptions an induced first-period preference relation over menus. The GP modeling practice takes this preference relation as primitive.

But this simply means that the two approaches complement each other. In particular, in line with my claim above, GP's revealed-preference exercise enables a deeper understanding of the decision model. This is quite distinct from claiming that one modeling approach is philosophically more appealing than another because it is consistent with the revealed preference principle in a way that the other approach fails to be. The revealed preference principle cannot be used as a criterion for selecting between the two modeling approaches.[6]

Preferences over Decision Paths

GP [2001] propose an alternative approach to modeling two-period dynamic decision making. The DM is now assumed to have stable *extended* preferences over *decision paths*, instead of first-period menus. Let us denote a decision path by a pair (A, x), where A is a menu and $x \in A$ is a lottery. Let $c(A)$ represent the set of lotteries which the DM actually chooses in the second period, conditional on facing the menu A. GP impose axioms on the DM's preferences over decision paths, which imply the same choice behavior as their original formulation.

In standard models, we do not distinguish between two decision paths with the same chosen elements, (B, x) and (A, x), because we assume that the chosen element is all that matters to the DM. However, when self-control issues are relevant, the decision paths $(\{x, y\}, x)$ and $(\{x\}, x)$ are not necessarily equivalent, because choosing x over y may require the DM to exercise self-control, whereas self-control is not called for when x is the only feasible element.

If we insist on the requirement that "'utility maximization' and 'choice' are synonymous," we must define the DM's preferences over decision paths entirely in terms of choice experiments that directly reveal these preferences.[7] Yet, what *is* the choice experiment that directly reveals the ranking $(A, x) \succ (B, y)$ when $x \notin c(A)$—that is, when the DM never chooses x from A out of his own free will? The only choice experiment that can directly reveal such a ranking involves a choice between *committing* to the decision path (A, x) and *committing* to the decision path (B, y). However, if the DM is able to commit to a path, then the interpretation of A and B as choice sets disappears, and self-control considerations become irrelevant. Consequently, a decision model that incorporates self-control issues cannot be revealed by such choices.[8]

We see that the alternative decision-theoretic approach to self-control is inconsistent with the narrow version of the revealed preference principle, in the sense that some of the utility rankings assumed by the model are not synonymous with observable choices. I do not think that this failure is specific to the GP model. Rather, it seems that the very nature of self-control considerations makes it difficult to provide a complete revealed-preference justification for a model of self-control that assumes a utility ranking over decision paths.

Comment: Game-Theoretic Applicability of the Extended GP Model

The question of what it means for the DM to rank (A, x) over (B, y) when $x \notin c(A)$ is especially important if we wish to embed the extended GP model in *game-theoretic* environments. Consider the following scenario: In the beginning, player 1 is on a diet, with only broccoli at her disposal. She is offered a gift consisting of a cash-equivalent voucher as well as a piece of tempting chocolate. She chooses whether to accept this gift. If she does, then she later has to choose whether to eat the chocolate or exercise self-control and have broccoli. Player 2 has the power to veto a decision to eat chocolate. He chooses whether to exercise his veto power, *after* player 1's first action and *before* his second action. However, player 1 does not observe player 2's decision. Figure 4.1 shows the extensive form of this game.

If we wish to apply the extended GP self-control preferences, then the description of a consequence for player 1 is as written under the terminal nodes of the extensive game. Suppose that player 1 expects player 2 not to exercise his veto power. In this case, player 1 thinks that she has real choice between chocolate and broccoli when she accepts the gift. The feasible consequences for her are $(\{b\}, b)$ (in case

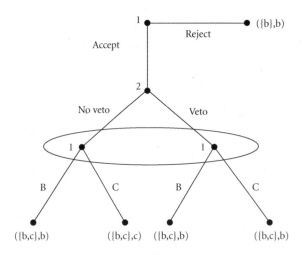

Figure 4.1. A self-control game

she rejects the gift), $(\{b, c\}, b)$ (in case she accepts the gift and eats broccoli), and $(\{b, c, \}, c)$ (in case she accepts the gift and eats the chocolate). Assume that given her expectations, player 1 chooses to accept the gift and plans to eat the chocolate. If this plan is carried out, it reveals the rankings $(\{b, c\}, c) \succ (\{b\}, b)$ and $(\{b, c\}, c) \succ (\{b, c\}, b)$.

However, suppose that player 2 surprises player 1 by deviating and exercising his veto power. Then, the consequence of this game is now $(\{b, c\}, b)$. The alternative b is not chosen from the set $\{b, c\}$, but follows from player 2's surprise deviation. Is player 1 better or worse off than if she had rejected the gift in the first place? This question is essential to the welfare analysis of this game—and also to the positive analysis, if player 2's objective is to maximize player 1's utility—yet the answer to this question cannot be given by player 1's revealed preferences.

[Alternatively, suppose that player 1 expected player 2 to exercise his veto power in the first place. Would it be appropriate to describe the outcome of accepting the gift and having broccoli as $(\{b, c\}, b)$? Or, would it be more apt in this case to describe it as $(\{b\}, b)$, given that player 1 *perceives* that she has no real freedom to choose chocolate? More generally, in the description of a consequence, is a "menu" the set of alternatives that the player *perceives* as feasible, given his expectation of the opponent's behavior, or is it the set of alternatives that are *truly* feasible given the opponent's actual behavior?]

One could argue that the above description of a consequence does not fit the scenario, because it treats two different experiences of player 1 as if they are equivalent: eating broccoli from the menu $\{b, c\}$ as a result of a personal choice, and eating broccoli from the same menu against personal choice, as a result of player 2's surprise deviation. If we accept this argument, the implication seems to be that the GP model is inapplicable to this game. What does this mean for the applicability of the GP model, or any other model of self-control for that matter, in game-theoretic contexts? I leave these questions for future inquiry.

Summary

In this section I examined two decision-theoretic approaches to modeling self-control preferences, proposed by GP. One approach assumes utility maximization over decision problems, while another approach assumes utility maximization over decision paths. We first saw that the first approach is no more consistent with the revealed preference principle than the multi-selves approach, as far as the treatment of expectations is concerned. Next, we saw that the second approach cannot be reconciled with the narrow version of the revealed preference principle. This raises doubts regarding the claim that the principle can be used as a criterion for selecting between different decision models that incorporate "nonstandard" psychological motives such as self-control.

CONCLUSION

"Revealed preferences" are first and foremost a way of getting a systematic, abstract understanding of decision models, most notably utility-maximization models. A revealed preference exercise allows us to realize which aspects of a mental construct that appears in a model are relevant for behavior in a variety of domains of choice problems. Such a systematic understanding is useful as a safeguard against blind spots that working purely with utility functions often creates.

I have argued that this "diagnostic" value of thinking in terms of revealed preferences is especially high in the case of "behavioral" models, and demonstrated this claim with a discussion of several recent utility-from-beliefs models. In my opinion, a philosophical stance that rejects revealed preferences as a justification for decision models does not mean that the behavioral theorist should discard the revealed preference exercise altogether. A rudimentary revealed preference analysis is a very useful member in the theorist's bag of tools as he develops a nonstandard, "behavioral" decision model.

At the same time, I have argued against what I perceive as an attempt to use the narrow version of the revealed preference principle as a theory-selection criterion in the development of decision models with a "rich" psychology. In the case of models of self-control, I showed that it is hard to discriminate between the multi-selves approach and the decision-theoretic approach on this basis. If we wish to continue relying on some notion of revealed preferences as a basis for welfare analysis, and at the same time admit novel psychological phenomena such as self-control or self-deception into our models, then we face the challenge of redefining the concept

of revealed preferences. This challenge may originate from the psychological phenomena themselves, rather than from any particular model that purports to capture
them, or from the kind of data that the economist can observe.

NOTES

This chapter is based on a talk I gave at the Methodologies of Modern Economics
conference that took place at NYU in July 2006. I am grateful to the organizers of this
conference. I also thank Eddie Dekel, Kfir Eliaz, Barton Lipman, and Ariel Rubinstein for
numerous conversations that made this chapter possible. I also thank Andy Schotter for
useful comments.

1. Other models in which decision makers directly choose their beliefs are due to
Akerlof and Dickens [1982], Eyster [2002], and Yariv [2002].

2. The proposition assumes that both a_s and a_r are chosen from $\{a_s, a_r\}$, in order to
facilitate the proof. One could construct a payoff function u for which $C_{BP}\{a_s, a_r\} = \{a_r\}$
and $C_{BP}\{a_s, a_r, a'_r\} = \{a_s\}$, but the proof would be more tedious.

3. There is no contradiction between this result and proposition 4.1, since here A is
held fixed.

4. BP seem to acknowledge this: "However, without relaxing the assumptions of
expected utility theory and Bayesian updating, agents would not choose that uncertainty be
resolved later because agents take their beliefs as given" [1109].

5. Of course, U may be induced by other functional forms than the one given by
expression (4.2).

6. There is an important *economic* difference between the GP model of self-control
preferences and the typical Strotzian model. The latter assumes that the domain of
first-period and second-period preferences can be restricted to the set of chosen
alternatives, whereas the former allows unchosen alternatives to affect preference rankings.
This is indeed one of the important contributions of the GP model. However, it does not
engender a fundamental methodological distinction between the two approaches.

7. Some of these rankings can be deduced by using the transitive closure of other,
directly observed rankings. However, such deduced rankings are based on introspection
rather than observable choices and therefore cannot be viewed as revealed preferences.

8. GP [2001: 1415] partially acknowledge this incompleteness of revealed preferences in
this model: "For example, if (A, x) is strictly preferred to (A, y) and (A, z), there is no
experiment that can determine the agent's ranking of (A, y) and (A, z)."

REFERENCES

Akerlof, George, and William Dickens. 1982. The Economic Consequences of Cognitive
    Dissonance. *American Economic Review* 72: 307–319.
Bénabou, Roland, and Jean Tirole. 2002. Self-Confidence and Personal Motivation.
    Quarterly Journal of Economics 470: 871–915.

Brunnermeier, Markus, and Jonathan Parker. 2005. Optimal Expectations. *American Economic Review* 95: 1092–1118.

Caplin, Andrew, and John Leahy. 2004. The Supply of Information by a Concerned Expert. *Economic Journal* 114: 487–505.

Dekel, Eddie, Barton Lipman, and Aldo Rustichini. 2001. A Unique Subjective State Space for Unforeseen Contingencies. *Econometrica* 69: 891–934.

Eliaz, Kfir, and Ran Spiegler. 2006. Can Anticipatory Feelings Explain Anomalous Choices of Information Sources? *Games and Economic Behavior* 56: 87–104.

Epstein, Larry. 2006. Living with Risk. Mimeo, University of Rochester.

Eyster, Erik. 2002. Rationalizing the Past. Mimeo, Nuffield College.

Geanakopolos, John, David Pearce, and Ennio Stachetti. 1989. Psychological Games and Sequential Rationality. *Games and Economic Behavior* 1: 60–79.

Gul, Faruk, and Wolfgang Pesendorfer. 2001. Temptation and Self-Control. *Econometrica* 69: 1403–1436.

———. 2004. Self-Control and the Theory of Consumption. *Econometrica* 72: 119–158.

———. 2005a. The Revealed Preference Theory of Changing Tastes. *Review of Economic Studies* 72: 429–448.

———. 2005b. The Canonical Type Space for Interdependent Preferences. Mimeo, Princeton University.

Karni, Edi. 2005. State-Dependent Preferences. In *The New Palgrave: A Dictionary of Economic Theory and Doctrine,* ed. John Eatwell, Murray Milgate, and Peter Newman. London: Macmillan.

Köszegi, Botond. 2003. Health Anxiety and Patient Behavior. *Journal of Health Economics* 22: 1073–1084.

———. 2006. Emotional Agency. *Quarterly Journal of Economics* 121: 121–156.

Kreps, David. 1979. A Representation Theorem for "Preference for Flexibility". *Econometrica* 47: 565–576.

Kreps, David, and Evan Porteus. 1978. Temporal Resolution of Uncertainty and Dynamic Choice Theory. *Econometrica* 46: 185–200.

Simonson, Itamar. 1989. Choice Based on Reasons: The Case of Attraction and Compromise Effects. *Journal of Consumer Research* 16: 158–174.

Yariv, Leeat. 2002. I'll See It When I Believe It—A Simple Model of Cognitive Consistency. Mimeo, Yale University.

CHAPTER 5

....

SOME THOUGHTS ON THE PRINCIPLE OF REVEALED PREFERENCE

....

ARIEL RUBINSTEIN AND YUVAL SALANT

ECONOMIC theorists characterize an individual decision maker using three basic concepts:

1. *A collection of objects:* The manner in which a decision maker perceives an object does not have to be objective. For example, one decision maker might think about a red triangle as a triangle while another might think about it as a red object.

2. *Mental preferences:* These describe the mental attitude of an individual toward the objects. They can be defined in contexts that do not involve actual choice. In particular, preferences can describe tastes (e.g., a preference for one season over another) or can refer to situations that are only hypothetical (e.g., the possible courses of action available to an individual were he to become emperor of Rome) or that the individual does not fully control (e.g., a game situation in which a player has preferences over the entire set of outcomes).

3. *Choice:* It is customary to describe a choice situation using a set of objects the individual can choose from. A choice function spells out how the individual will respond to any choice situation he might face.

The standard economic approach assumes that a decision maker is rational in the sense that (i) in any choice situation within the domain of his choice function he objectively identifies the set of objects, (ii) his choice function is consistent with maximization of some preference relation that we will refer to as the *behavioral preferences*, and (iii) the behavioral preferences are identical to the mental preferences.

The Principle of Revealed Preference, as we understand it, is a methodological paradigm that follows the standard economic approach, whereby observed choices are used only to reveal the mental preferences of the individual over the set of objects as perceived by the modeler.

In this short chapter we wish to make three statements about the way that economists view this principle as a modeling guide:

Statement 1. There is no escape from including mental entities, such as the way in which an individual perceives the objects and his mental preferences, in economic models.

Statement 2. Economists should be also looking at models in which the observed choice leads to conclusions other than that the chosen element is always mentally preferred to the other elements in the set.

Statement 3. There is room for models in which the observable information about a choice situation is richer than just the set of available alternatives and the alternative chosen.

Before proceeding, we introduce some standard notation and definitions. Let X be a finite set of alternatives. A choice problem is a nonempty subset of X. Let D be the collection of all choice problems. A choice function c attaches to every choice problem $A \in D$ a single element $c(A) \in A$. A choice function informs us that the individual chooses the element $c(A)$ when facing the choice problem A. A choice correspondence C attaches to every $A \in D$ a nonempty subset $C(A) \subseteq A$. The interpretation of a choice correspondence is more subtle than that of a choice function. We follow the approach whereby $C(A)$ is the set of alternatives that are chosen from the choice problem A under certain circumstances that are not part of the model.

A choice function c satisfies the property of Independence of Irrelevant Alternatives (IIA) if $c(B) \in A \subseteq B$ implies that $c(A) = c(B)$. A choice correspondence C satisfies the Weak Axiom of Revealed Preference (WA) if $a, b \in A \cap B$, $a \in C(A)$, and $b \in C(B)$ imply that $a \in C(B)$. When $C(A)$ is always a singleton, WA is equivalent to IIA.

We say that a choice function c [correspondence C] is rationalizable if there exists a preference relation $\succsim$ such that $c(A)$ is the $\succsim$-maximal element in A [$C(A)$ is the set of all $\succsim$-maximal elements in A] for every $A \in D$. A choice function [correspondence] is rationalizable if and only if it satisfies IIA [WA].

STATEMENT 1

There is no escape from including mental entities, such as the way in which an individual perceives the objects and his mental preferences, in economic models.

If the individual in an economic model were treated as a robot who receives a description of a choice problem as input and produces a chosen element as output, then the assumption that his behavior is rationalizable would have only a procedural rather than a mental meaning. In particular, when IIA is violated, the order in which the decision maker makes his choices becomes crucial in describing his behavior. For example, if an individual chooses a from $\{a, b, c\}$ and b from $\{a, b\}$, then his response to the task "choose from a, b, and c" differs from his response to a two-stage task in which he first has the option of choosing c and, if he does not, he must then choose between a and b.

However, as economists, we are interested not just in describing the behavior of individuals but also their well-being. When we analyze social mechanisms and make welfare statements, we have in mind the individual's mental preferences, which reflect his well-being. We cannot find any a priori reason to assume that an individual's behavioral preferences, which describe his choices, fully represent or convey his mental preferences. On the contrary, there are reasons to assume that they don't. [See also Sen (1973) for a related discussion.]

First, there is often no objective specification of the outcome space. A decision maker may have in mind a description of the alternatives that differs from that of the modeler [see Rubinstein, 1991].

Example 5.1.

Assume that a decision maker receives a pair of files of candidates A and B piled alphabetically and chooses A. An observer might conclude that the decision maker prefers candidate A to candidate B. However, assume that unlike the observer, the decision maker ignores the content of the files and pays attention only to the location of each file in the pile. He simply prefers the top location in the pile to the bottom location. In this case, the observer's interpretation that the individual has chosen the "best" candidate is incorrect.

Second, the decision maker might be operating in a very systematic way but not according to his mental preferences. Following is an extreme example [see Rubinstein, 2006]:

Example 5.2.

An individual has in mind a clear notion of utility that expresses his desires. Imagine that we are even able to measure his utility using an "ultimate happiness measure." However, the individual behaves in a way that is consistent with minimizing this measure of utility. This might be due to a mistake in his "operating system," due to some mental problem or simply because he applies a rule of thumb that has nothing to do with his mental preferences. Of course, in this case the individual's choice function is rationalizable; that is, there exists a preference relation whose maximization describes the individual's behavior. However, this preference relation is clearly the opposite of the individual's mental preferences, and it would be absurd to consider his behavioral preferences, as an indication of his well-being.

The importance of referring to mental preferences is revealed when we consider the basic welfare concept of Pareto efficiency. Pareto efficiency is an intuitively appealing concept because everybody can be made better off by moving from a Pareto-dominated outcome to a Pareto-dominant one. However, this intuition is often based on viewing preferences as mental.

One could argue that the meaning of a Pareto-inefficient outcome is that it is unstable even when defined with respect to behavioral preferences. According to this interpretation, an inefficient outcome is unstable since every individual will choose to support a move to the Pareto-dominant outcome. However, note that an individual's preference for a Pareto-dominant outcome over a Pareto-dominated one usually involves a change in the behavior of other individuals and therefore may not be observable in any choice situation.

Example 5.3.

Consider a 2 × 2 coordination game with two actions {a, b} available to each player. Assume that both players have the same mental preferences over the outcomes of the game: $(a, a) \succ (b, b) \succ (a, b) \sim (b, a)$. Thus, (a, a) and (b, b) are the two pure strategy equilibria of the game and (a, a) is Pareto-superior to (b, b). The rankings $(a, a) \succ (b, a)$ and $(b, b) \succ (a, b)$ are revealed by the actions of player 1. However, the ranking between (a, a) and (b, b) is not revealed in any choice situation associated with the game since player 1 does not control player 2's actions. Thus, the statement "(b, b) is an undesirable equilibrium and (a, a) is a desirable one" is based on each player's preference for (a, a) over (b, b), a preference that is not revealed by the choices of the players in the game.

Thus, even the basic welfare criterion of Pareto efficiency cannot be based solely on behavioral preferences without referring also to mental preferences.

STATEMENT 2

....

> Economists should be also looking at models in which the observed choice leads to conclusions other than that the chosen element is always mentally preferred to the other elements in the set.

Some choice procedures violate the weak axiom of revealed preference (or the IIA property) and thus are not consistent with maximizing a preference relation. In such cases, there is no basis to conclude from an observed choice that the chosen element is always preferred to the other elements in the set. Nevertheless, other conclusions about the properties of a choice procedure can be drawn. This is in fact the objective of axiomatic analysis of a choice procedure.

To demonstrate this point, consider the Post-Dominance Rationality (PDR) choice procedure analyzed in Manzini and Mariotti [2007]. In what follows, we provide a different axiomatization of this procedure [for a discussion of additional interesting procedures, see Masatlioglu and Ok (2005, 2006)].

According to the PDR procedure, the decision maker first simplifies a given choice problem by eliminating any alternative that he feels is dominated in some sense by another alternative in the set. He then chooses the best alternative among those that remain. For example, consider an individual who chooses among hotel resorts in the following manner: He first eliminates any resort for which there is another with more stars and a lower per night price. He then applies a complicated rule to choose from among the remaining resorts. Formally, the decision maker's choice procedure is characterized by two binary relations:

1. A dominance relation R that is acyclic.
2. A post-dominance relation $\succ$ that is complete and transitive whenever restricted to sets of elements that do not dominate one another.

When facing a choice problem A, the decision maker first identifies the set of non-dominated elements according to R and then chooses the $\succ$-maximal element from among them.

Obviously, this choice procedure generates choices that may violate IIA. For example, let $X = \{a, b, c\}$, bRc, and $a \succ b \succ c \succ a$. The PDR procedure based on these parameters violates IIA since a is chosen from $\{a, b, c\}$ but c is chosen from $\{a, c\}$.

The following behavioral property characterizes a choice function c induced by a PDR procedure: If adding an element a to a choice problem A implies that neither the previously chosen element $c(A)$ nor the new element a is chosen from the new set, then $c(A)$ is never chosen from a choice problem that includes a. Formally, a choice function c satisfies *exclusion consistency* if for every set A and for every $a \in X$, if $c(A \cup \{a\}) \notin \{c(A), a\}$, then there is no set A' that contains a such that $c(A') = c(A)$.

It is straightforward to verify that a PDR choice procedure induces a choice function that satisfies exclusion consistency. Indeed, consider a PDR choice procedure based on a dominance relation R and a post-dominance relation $\succ$. Then the chosen element from a set A is the $\succ$-maximal element among the R-maximal elements in A. We need to show that the induced choice function c satisfies exclusion consistency. Assume that the element a is chosen from the choice problem A and that the element $a' \notin \{a, b\}$ is chosen from $A \cup \{b\}$. It must be that bRa. Otherwise, the element a continues to be non-dominated in $A \cup \{b\}$ and the only (possibly) new non-dominated element is b, which means that either a or b is chosen from $A \cup \{b\}$. By the definition of PDR, since b dominates a, the element a is never chosen from sets in which b appears.

One can also show that a choice function that satisfies exclusion consistency can be represented as a PDR choice procedure. The proof of this statement is important to our argument since it contains a construction of a dominance relation and a post-dominance relation based only on the choices of the individual. Thus, assume c satisfies exclusion consistency. We define the two binary relations R and $\succ$ as follows:

1. aRb if there is a set A such that $c(A) = b$ and $c(A \cup \{a\}) \notin \{a, b\}$.
2. $a \succ b$ if $c(\{a, b\}) = a$.

The relation R is acyclic. If there were a cycle then by Exclusion Consistency no element could be chosen from the set of all elements in the cycle. The relation $\succ$ is asymmetric and complete. The relation $\succ$ is transitive when restricted to sets of elements that are not related to one another by R. Otherwise, assume that $a \succ b$, $b \succ c$, and $c \succ a$ and that a, b, and c are not related by R. Without loss of generality, assume that $c(\{a, b, c\}) = b$. Then, since $c(\{a, b\}) = a$, we should have cRa, which is a contradiction.

Since R is acyclic and $\succ$ is complete and transitive when restricted to sets of elements that do not dominate one another, the PDR procedure based on R and $\succ$ chooses exactly one element from every set A. It is not difficult to complete the proof and show that the element chosen by the procedure is identical to $c(A)$.

To conclude, an essential component of the principle of revealed preference is that one should be able to deduce the parameters of the choice procedure from behavior. With the rational man's choice procedure in mind, we elicit a single preference relation from a choice function by the inference that choosing a when b is available means that a is at least as good as b. Analogously, with the PDR choice procedure in mind, we elicit a dominance relation and a post-dominance relation. Of course, different "deduction rules" should be applied to different choice procedures.

But, nonetheless, economic analysis based on observables can accommodate choice procedures other than the rational man's, in which the parameters of the procedure are elicited from observable information as in the case of the rational man.

STATEMENT 3

There is room for models in which the observable information about a choice situation is richer than just the set of available alternatives and the alternative chosen.

Classical choice theory usually assumes that a researcher observes a pair (A, a) with the interpretation that the decision maker chooses the alternative a from the choice set A. However, in many cases, additional information relevant to choice is available in the same sense that the set of alternatives and the chosen alternative are available. Accepting the idea that the analysis of the decision maker's behavior should depend on observables implies that we should use a model of choice that takes this information into account rather than a model that ignores it.

Consider, for example, the model of order-dependent choice in which the alternatives are presented to the decision maker in the form of a list of distinct elements of X. It is actually quite common that a choice problem is presented as a *list* rather than as a *set*. For example, when purchasing a product online, the alternatives are positioned in some order, or when looking for a job, offers are received sequentially. A decision maker who uses a systematic method to choose from lists may choose differently from two different lists that induce the same set of alternatives.

In Rubinstein and Salant [2006] we investigate some properties of choice functions from lists that assign a chosen element to every list. In particular, we analyze the following property:

Partition Independence (PI): Dividing a list arbitrarily into several sublists, choosing an element from each, and then choosing from the list of chosen elements yields the same result as choosing from the original list.

PI is satisfied by the rational procedure as well as by the satisficing procedure [Simon, 1955]. According to the satisficing procedure, the decision maker classifies each element as either satisfactory or nonsatisfactory and chooses the first satisfactory element from each list (if no such element exists, we assume that he chooses the last element in the list). In fact, we show that PI characterizes a larger class of choice functions from lists. In this class, each function is parameterized by a preference relation $\succsim$ over X and a labeling of every $\succsim$-indifference set by "first" or "last." Given a list, the decision maker first identifies the set of $\succsim$-maximal elements within that list. He then chooses the first or the last element among them according to the label of the $\succsim$-indifference set they belong to. For example, in the satisficing procedure, there are two indifference classes of the preference relation: the class of satisfactory elements labeled "first" and the class of nonsatisfactory elements labeled "last." The family of functions satisfying PI naturally generalizes the class of preference-maximizing procedures in the context of standard choice functions.

We then relate the notion of a choice function from lists to the standard notion of a choice correspondence by assigning to every set all the elements chosen for *some* listing of that set. For example, a satisficing procedure induces a choice correspondence that chooses all the satisfactory elements from every set; if there are none, the correspondence chooses the entire set. We show that a choice function from lists satisfying PI induces a choice correspondence satisfying WA. Conversely, if a choice correspondence satisfies WA, it can be "explained" by a choice function from lists satisfying PI.

One might therefore argue that there is no need to study choice from lists since the outcome (in terms of choice correspondences) is indistinguishable from that of a correspondence satisfying WA. In Salant and Rubenstein [forthcoming] we argue that this is not the case. The two terms are indistinguishable only if we choose to ignore the additional information that is often observable (especially when the list is generated by an exogenous mechanism, as in the case of entrees listed on a menu or products listed in a sales brochure). In such cases, the notion of a choice function from lists is typically richer than a standard choice correspondence and provides a more accurate description of behavior. So why should we ignore this additional information? As we remarked above, an essential component of the principle of revealed preference is that one should be able to deduce the parameters of the choice procedure based on behavior. But there is no reason to adopt a position that restricts the scope of the observable information to the set of alternatives and the actual choice.

NOTES

We thank Douglas Gale, Andy Schotter, and Rani Spiegler for most helpful comments.

REFERENCES

Manzini, Paola, and Marco Mariotti. 2007. Sequentially Rationalizable Choice. *American Economic Review*, 97(5): 1824–1839.

Masatlioglu, Yusufcan, and Efe Ok. 2005. Rational Choice with Status Quo Bias. *Journal of Economic Theory* 121(1): 1–29.

———. 2006. Reference-Dependent Procedural Decision Making. Mimeo, New York University.

Rubinstein, Ariel. 1991. Comments on the Interpretation of Game Theory. *Econometrica* 59(4): 909–924.

———. 2006. Comments on Behavioral Economics. In *Advances in Economic Theory* (2005 World Congress of the Econometric Society), ed. by R. Blundell, W. K. Newey, and T. Persson, 2: 246–254. Cambridge: Cambridge University Press.

Rubinstein, Ariel, and Yuva, Salant. 2006. A Model of Choice from Lists. *Theoretical Economics* 1(1): 3–17.

Salant, Yuva, and Ariel Rubinstein. Forthcoming. (A,f): Choice with Frames. *Review of Economic Studies.*

Simon, Herbert. 1955. A Behavioral Model of Rational Choice. *Quarterly Journal of Economics* 69(1): 99–118.

Sen, Amartya. 1973. Behavior and the Concept of Preference. *Econimca,* New Series 40 (159): 241–259.

CHAPTER 6

MINDLESS OR MINDFUL ECONOMICS: A METHODOLOGICAL EVALUATION

DANIEL HAUSMAN

In chapter 1 Faruk Gul and Wolfgang Pesendorfer lay out the case against the relevance of neurological and psychological theory and data to the concerns of positive and normative economics. I conjecture that many members of the profession are in sympathy with Gul and Pesendorfer's attitude and arguments. If this conjecture is correct, it is particularly important to scrutinize their case.

In addition to presenting their own methodological position, Gul and Pesendorfer criticize grandiose methodological claims of experimental, behavioral, and neuroeconomists and their fellow travelers. I do not discuss these criticisms, some of which are well taken. It is not my objective to argue that economists are in the midst of a revolution, nor even that behavioral and neuroeconomics will make valuable contributions to economics. How much behavioral and neuroeconomics will contribute to economics is an empirical question, which has not yet been answered. As Gul and Pesendorfer correctly insist, the facts that psychology establishes about what goes on in people's minds when they make choices and that neurology establishes about what goes on in the brain do not automatically enhance economics. The questions economists ask are not the same as the questions that psychologists and neurologists ask, and good answers to the questions psychologists and neurologists ask may be bad answers to the questions economists ask. But I argue that

Gul and Pesendorfer are mistaken to infer from the fact that economists are interested in market behavior, rather than what goes in people's heads, that behavioral and neuroeconomics have little to contribute to economics.

Accordingly, the object of this chapter is Gul and Pesendorfer's argument that— regardless of their empirical successes or failures—behavioral and neuroeconomics cannot provide evidence to support or reject models in positive economics and that the concepts of welfare employed by behavioral and neuroeconomics render their findings irrelevant to normative economics. So as not to keep repeating "behavioral and neuroeconomics," I shall sometimes speak of one and sometimes of the other as seems most appropriate, unless I want to emphasize that the points under discussion are relevant to both. Gul and Pesendorfer choose instead to use the term "neuro-economists" to refer both to those who regard brain imaging data and neurological theory as potentially relevant to economics and to those who regard psychological data and theory as possessing the same sort of relevance. As Gul and Pesendorfer point out, those who do economic experiments do not automatically count as "neuroeconomists" in their expansive sense. The defining feature of those whom Gul and Pesendorfer call "neuroeconomists" is that they seek to employ psychological and neurological data and theory to appraise economic models.

In the sections below, I lay out the structure of Gul and Pesendorfer's case for the irrelevance of behavioral and neurological findings to positive economics. I argue that it turns on a claim, which I call the "relevance thesis," that only data concerning choices are relevant to the assessment of economic models. I next discuss three related arguments that Gul and Pesendorfer sketch in defense of the relevance thesis, and then focus on the misleading invocation of revealed preference theory by Gul and Pesendorfer and others. In the final section, I dispute their characterization of standard normative economics and argue that although Gul and Pesendorfer are right to object to the welfare pronouncements of some prominent psychologists and behavioral economists, they mistake what is objectionable about these pronouncements. In my view, the problem with these claims concerning welfare lies in identifying welfare and pleasure, not, as Gul and Pesendorfer argue, in distinguishing welfare and choice.

GUL AND PESENDORFER'S ARGUMENTS THAT PSYCHOLOGICAL AND NEUROLOGICAL DATA ARE IRRELEVANT TO POSITIVE ECONOMICS

Gul and Pesendorfer's case against the relevance of neuroeconomic data to positive economics rests on one central proposition:

Proposition 6.1 (The Relevance Thesis).

Only data concerning choices and the consequences of choices, particularly for market quantities, are relevant to the acceptance or rejection of economic models.

Given the relevance thesis and the premise that data about feelings or brain physiology do not constitute or imply data concerning agents' choices or the implications of choices, it follows trivially that data about brain physiology or feelings are not relevant to the acceptance or rejection of economic models.

Gul and Pesendorfer do not state the argument precisely this way. But they do make claims such as the following three:

"Economic models make no predictions or assumptions about body temperature, blood sugar levels, or other physiological data, and therefore, such data cannot refute economic models."

"Since expected utility theory makes predictions only about choice behavior, its validity can be assessed only through choice evidence."

"Our central argument is simple: neuroscience evidence cannot refute economic models because the latter make no assumptions or draw no conclusions about physiology of the brain."

The additional premise (that data about feelings or brain functioning are distinct from data concerning agent's choices or the implications of choices) raises questions concerning what counts as an agent and what counts as a choice. If one takes agents to be individual people, this premise is plausible, and in order to focus on the central issues, let us grant it.

The relevance thesis is controversial and seems—at least initially—to be obviously false. Economic models contain many propositions, which apparently have diverse observable implications. Some models state that there are an uncountable infinity of traders, while others assert there is just one representative agent. The use of the calculus in consumer choice theory implies that commodities are infinitely divisible. Data concerning how many traders there are apparently bear on the observable implications of many models, as do data about the divisibility of commodities, and, as good empiricists, economists should regard evidence that bears on the observable implications of models as relevant to their assessment.

Gul and Pesendorfer do not merely assert the relevance thesis—they argue for it. They have three main arguments, which I'll call the "Samuelson argument," the "revealed preference argument," and the "Friedman argument." These arguments are closely related, and they might be regarded as variations on a single argument, but it is helpful to distinguish these variants.

THE SAMUELSON ARGUMENT

The Samuelson argument equates the content of a model with its relevant predictive consequences. I call it the "Samuelson argument" because it is reminiscent of an argument that Paul Samuelson makes in commenting on Friedman's methodological views. Samuelson writes:

1. Define a "theory" (call it B) as a set of axioms, postulates or hypotheses that stipulate something about observable reality. . . .
5. If C is the complete set of consequences of B, it is identical with B. B implies itself and all the things that itself implies. . . . The minimal set of assumptions that give rise to B are identical with B, and if A is given this interpretation, its realism cannot differ from that of the theory B and the consequences C. [Samuelson, 1963: 233–234]

Samuelson goes on to argue that if some set of assumptions, $A+$, of which A is a subset, implies some falsehoods in addition to implying B and C, then this is a fault and $A+$ should be pared down to A. In addition, if only some subset $C-$ of C is correct, then C should be trimmed to $C-$, and both B and A should be trimmed so that they imply no more than $C-$. The bottom line for Samuelson is that the content of economic theory should consist of the true observable consequences of the theory and nothing more. Andrew Caplin (chapter 15) describes Samuelson's view this way: "If observations are ultimately limited to choices alone, what is the point in theorizing about inner comparisons?" Theory is only a compact way of stating observable consequences.

As shown in the above quotations, Gul and Pesendorfer repeatedly deny that economic models make predictions concerning anything other than choice behavior and its implications. Taken literally, this is false. Whether a model (plus a specification of initial conditions) makes a prediction concerning X is a logical, not a methodological, question. Whether X is of interest or is an intended application is irrelevant. For example, models that assume that commodities are infinitely divisible or that all futures markets exist or that all individuals live for exactly three periods make predictions about the divisibility of commodities, the existence of futures markets, and whether anybody dies young, regardless of whether economists have any interest in these implications. Rather than denying these logical truths, I conjecture that Gul and Pesendorfer are, like Samuelson, assuming that economic models can be pared down so that their content will be limited to some set of their predictions—in Gul and Pesendorfer's case, these are their predictions concerning choice behavior and its consequences. Gul and Pesendorfer maintain, for example, "In standard economics, the testable implications of a theory are its content; once they are identified, the nonchoice evidence that motivated a novel theory becomes irrelevant." The apparent nonchoice content should be regarded merely as an heuristic shortcut, not part of the model proper.

One might then attribute to Gul and Pesendorfer the following argument:

The Samuelson Argument

1. The significant implications of economic models—the implications that matter to economists—concern choices and implications of choices (e.g., market prices and quantities). (premise)
2. The content of good models consists of the set of their significant implications and nothing more. (premise)
3. The content of good economic models concerns choices and the implications of choices (e.g., market prices and quantities) and nothing more (from 1 and 2).
4. Only data concerning the content of models bears on their acceptance or rejection. (premise)
5. Only data concerning agent's choices and the implications of choices (e.g., market prices and quantities) bear on the acceptance of good economic models. (from 3, 4)

I mention this argument because of Gul and Pesendorfer's repeated insistence that the reason that neurological and psychological data are irrelevant is that economic models have no implications concerning nonchoice phenomena. Caplin (chapter 15) also attributes to them something like this argument: "Surveying the scene with their eyes fixed on observables, Gul and Pesendorfer (chapter 1) posed anew the question of Samuelson. If two distinct psychological theories produce the same implications for choice in all situations, are they really different in a way that matters to economists?"

Whether or not Gul and Pesendorfer intend to make this argument, it is unsound. There is no justification for the claim that theories should be trimmed down to their (significant) implications, which is, in any case, rarely possible. For example, many of the most important theories in physics make claims about entities that cannot be observed. Though physicists judge whether neutrinos exist by checking whether the implications of models that refer to neutrinos are confirmed by the data, the claim "Neutrinos exist" is not equivalent to any set of claims about data sets.

This is not just a fact about physics, but an important element in scientific progress. Although, as Samuelson points out, the observable implications of the claim that planets move in elliptical orbits are identical to the observable implications of the claim that planets move on epicycles of just the right kind, only elliptical orbits can be explained by an inverse square central force. In Samuelson's view, "Post-Copernicans were also wrong to go to the stake for the belief that Keplerian ellipses, B, were a more correct theory than epicycles, B*. Relativism should have told both sides that this was a nonsense issue [since both imply the same orbits]" [Samuelson, 1963: 236]. Adopting such an antitheoretical stance would hobble science. Taking seriously claims about the orbits of planets generates demands to explain those orbits, which leads to theoretical progress. Even if one does not care about theoretical progress for its own sake, such progress may lead to better empirical representations of orbits. In just the same way, it is possible (though not guaranteed) that taking seriously the implicit mechanics of economic models of decision making and testing them against neurological and psychological data can lead to theoretical progress and, indirectly, to economic models that better fit the data that economists care about. Both Colin Camerer (chapter 2) and Andrew Schotter (chapter 15) provide examples that illustrate such possibilities.

The Revealed Preference Argument

I have called Gul and Pesendorfer's second argument for the relevance thesis the "revealed preference" argument. This argument is implicit in the following two quotations from Gul and Pesendorfer:

> The relevant data are revealed preference data, that is, consumption choices given the individual's constraints. These data are used to calibrate the model, . . . and the resulting calibrated models are used to predict future choices and perhaps equilibrium variables such as prices. Hence, standard (positive) theory identifies choice parameters from past behavior and relates these parameters to future behavior and equilibrium variables.
>
> Standard economics focuses on revealed preference because economic data come in this form. . . . The standard approach provides no methods for utilizing nonchoice data to calibrate preference parameters.
>
> A choice theory paper in economics must identify the revealed preference implications of the model presented and describe how revealed preference methods can be used to identify its parameters. Revealed preferences earns such a central role in economics because this is the form of evidence that is available to economists—and not because of a philosophical stance against other forms of evidence.

One way to formulate the argument that these quotations suggest is as follows:

Revealed Preference Argument (version 1)

1. The only data economists possess are data concerning agent's choices and the implications of their choices. (premise)
2. Only the data that economists possess are relevant to the acceptance or rejection of economic models. (premise)
3. Only data concerning agent's choices and the implications of their choices are relevant to the acceptance or rejection of economic models. (from 1 and 2)

This argument is valid but unsound, because premise 1 is false. Countless data of many varieties are readily available to economists and, indeed, to anybody with an Internet connection.[1] The question is not what data economists have access to, but what data are relevant. In addition, premise 2 seems to beg the question. If, as Gul and Pesendorfer apparently assert, data concerning brain processes are not available to economists, then premise 2 simply assumes that such data do not bear on the acceptance or rejection of economic models.

An alternative formulation suggested by the comments Gul and Pesendorfer make concerning the importance of revealed preference implications is as follows:

Revealed Preference Argument (version 2)

1. Data are relevant to the acceptance or rejection of economic models if and only if they bear on the calibration of preference parameters. (premise)
2. Only revealed preference data—data concerning choices and the implications of choices (e.g., market prices and quantities) bear on the calibration of preference parameters. (premise)
3. Only data about agent's choices and the implications of choices (e.g., market prices and quantities) are relevant to the acceptance or rejection of economic models.

The premises here seem as questionable as the conclusion. Whether sound or not, this argument will not persuade anyone who does not already accept its conclusion. With respect to premise 1, exactly what count as "preference parameters"? Do data concerning the production possibilities available to firms in a particular industry (which are relevant to the economic predictions of some models) bear on preference parameters? With respect to premise 2, why couldn't neurological data bear on the calibration of preference parameters? For that matter, why is it impossible to get information about preference parameters simply by asking people what they prefer and conversely, how much revealed preference data is available?

Gul and Pesendorfer's claim that "[r]evealed preferences earns such a central role in economics because this is the form of evidence that is available to economists—and not because of a philosophical stance against other forms of evidence" is dubious. Data of many other forms are available to economists. Why don't data of other forms ever constitute evidence? The invocation of revealed preference seems not to advance Gul and Pesendorfer's case.

AGAINST REVEALED PREFERENCE

Before turning to Gul and Pesendorfer's last argument for the relevance thesis, I would like to say a few words about revealed preference theory, since invocations of revealed preferences play such a large role in discussions of behavioral economics. Indeed, the phrase "revealed preference" shows up again and again in the chapters in this volume. These references to revealed preferences can be confusing, because the phrase refers to several different things. For example, Ran Spiegler, in chapter 3, focuses critically on a narrow interpretation according to which utility maximization and choice are synonymous, and Andrew Caplin, in chapter 15, maintains that "The revealed preference approach to choice theory ... fully identifies theories with their behavioral implications." On the other hand, in chapter 8, Botond Köszegi and Matthew Rabin do not interpret the "revelation" of preferences and beliefs by choices to be a matter of synonymy or identity. They take beliefs to be "revealed" by choices, if they can be deduced from choices given assumptions about preferences. Once the different interpretations of revealed preference are distinguished from one another, it becomes clear— indeed, obvious—that economics cannot function without a subjective notion of preference, which does not and cannot stand in any one-to-one relationship with choices.[2] Once economists are convinced of this conclusion, they will have no reason to speak of "revealed preference" and excellent reason to avoid this misleading terminology.

I distinguish three views that might be called "revealed preference theory: (1) actual revealed preference theory, (2) hypothetical revealed preference theory, and (3) conditional revealed preference theory. Further distinctions could be drawn, but these will suffice for my purposes.

Actual Revealed Preferences

Actual revealed preference theory is an interpretation of formal results explored initially by Paul Samuelson [1938], [1947], generalized and developed by many others (especially Houtthakker [1950]), and elegantly summarized a generation ago by Arrow [1959], Richter [1966], and Sen [1971]. Actual revealed preference theory identifies utility maximization and choice. Many economists have drawn the mistaken conclusion that the literature on revealed preferences proves that choice reveals preference. Thus, for example, Henderson and Quandt [1980] take it as proven that "the existence and nature of her [an agent's] utility function can be deduced from her observed choices among commodity bundles" [45], and Gravelle and Rees [1981] take it as demonstrable that "the utility maximizing theory of the consumer and the revealed preference theory are equivalent" [115]. When Gul and Pesendorfer write, "In the standard approach, the term's utility maximization' and 'choice' are synonymous," or "To say that a decision maker prefers x to y is to say that he never chooses y when x is also available, nothing more," they are espousing actual revealed preference theory. But as documented below, other passages in their essay are inconsistent with these quotations and count against attributing to them a commitment to actual revealed preference theory.

Here is a simple version of the fundamental technical result: Let X be a nonempty finite set, S a subset of X, and K the set of all nonempty subsets of X. Let C be a set-valued function from each $S \in K$ to a nonempty subset $C(S)$ of S. Define a two-place relation R as xRy if and only if there exists S such that $x, y \in S$ and $x \in C(S)$. Define $C^R(S)$ as $\{x \in S$ such that $\forall y \in S, xRy\}$. One axiom is needed, the so-called "weak axiom of revealed preference" (WARP): if there exists $S \in K$ such that $x \in C(S)$ and $y \in S$ but $y \notin C(S)$, then there is no $S \in K$ such that x and $y \in S$ and $y \in C(S)$. Given the definition of R, WARP may be restated: if there exists $S \in K$ such that $x \in C(S)$ and $y \in S$ but $y \notin C(S)$, then it is not the case that yRx. WARP implies that R is complete and transitive and that $C^R(S) = C(S)$. Call this theorem the "revelation theorem." Its proof can be sketched simply. Since for all $x, y, C(\{x, y\})$ is not empty, R is complete. Suppose that R were not transitive and that xRy, yRz, but not xRz. Then by WARP $C(\{x, y, z\})$ would have to be empty, so R must be transitive. Thus, for all S, if $x \in C(S)$, then for all $y \in S, xRy$, and so $x \in C^R(S)$. Conversely, if for any $S, x \notin C(S)$, then for some $y \in S, yRx$ and it is not the case that xRy, and so $x \in C^R(S)$. (For elaborations and proofs, see Sen [1971].)

Since the revelation theorem really is a theorem, it is easy to see why many economists take it as demonstrating that preferences can be defined in terms of choices. But matters are more complicated, and one needs to distinguish carefully between the theorem and its interpretations. The intended interpretation is of course that $C(S)$ consists of the alternatives an agent chooses from S. Even though R is defined in terms of choice, "xRy" is supposed to be read as "x is weakly preferred to y." But whether this definition of "preference" captures what economists mean by "preference" is not settled by the theorem. If one rejects the interpretation of "xRy" as "x is weakly preferred to y," then the revelation theorem shows only that when WARP is satisfied, then there is some complete and transitive relationship R defined in terms of choice. Only if one is willing to interpret $C(S)$ as the choice set and R as weak preference will the revelation theorem show that if an agent's choices satisfy WARP, then the agent's preference relation can be deduced from the agent's choices.

Actual revealed preference theory consists of the revelation theorem plus these interpretations of $C(S)$ and xRy. Since R is defined in terms of choice, these interpretations imply that an agent's preferences among alternatives among which they do not choose are undefined. Some economists have interpreted the revelation theorem as showing that it is possible for economists to dispense with the notion of preference altogether. They have concluded that there is nothing to be said employing the notion of preference that cannot be said employing only the language of choice. In this way, economists with strict empiricist scruples, such as Samuelson or Little [1949], defended the scientific credentials of economics. But this is not the only possible moral of the story. Rather than taking the one-to-one correspondence between preferences and choices as showing that talk of subjective preferences is dispensable, other economists regard the correspondence between choice and preference as legitimating talk of subjective states. In Sen's [1973] words, "The rationale of the revealed preference approach lies in the assumption of revelation and not in doing away with the notion of underlying preferences" [244].

Actual revealed preference theory allows belief no role in linking preference and choice:

> In the pure example of this [revealed preference] method a decision maker is presented with choices among acts. An act describes the consequence that the decision maker will obtain for every realization of a state of nature. A theory of choice is a complete list of what the decision maker will choose for any possible option that he is facing. [Benhabib and Bisin, chapter 14]

If preference can be defined in terms of choice among such acts, then belief has no role to play. But preference cannot be defined in terms of behavior, regardless of belief. What agents choose is not necessarily what they prefer, because agents may make mistakes and because agents may act when they cannot rank some of the alternatives. Moreover, the actions among which people choose are mappings from states of nature to the consequences that the agent believes (with some probability) will obtain. To describe people's actions, one needs to know how they individuate the alternatives. As Rubinstein and Salant note in chapter 5, "[T]here is often no objective specification of the outcome space. A decision maker may have in mind a description of the alternatives that differs from that of the modeler." In addition, the preferences of agents not only in fact extend over many alternatives among which they have no choice, but on pain of trivializing economics, they must so extend. If all economists had to say about choice is that the item chosen was among the top-ranked feasible alternatives, their consulting fees would not be high.

It is false to maintain that if B prefers x to y, then B will never choose y when x is available. B may prefer x to y, yet choose y because B falsely believes that x is not available.[3] A revealed preference theorist might reply that it does not matter whether B "really prefers" x to y and fails to choose y because of mistaken beliefs. The choice of y is sufficient to show that either B does not prefer x to y or that B violates WARP. This response would disqualify WARP as a principle of rationality, and it would prevent economists from basing predictions concerning B's behavior on the reasons why B fails to choose x.

Some comments Gul and Pesendorfer make concerning welfare suggest a different tack. They argue that A's choice of x over y maximizes A's welfare relative to the various constraints A faces, which include informational constraints. So one might attribute to Gul and Pesendorfer the view that preference is a three-place relation: A prefers x to y relative to constraints C. One can then say that the choice of y over x reveals that B prefers y to x given the constraint consisting of B's false belief that x is not available. As I argue below, adding this third place transforms actual revealed preference theory into what I am calling "conditional revealed preference theory," which is a version of revealed preference theory in name only.

According to "folk psychology" (the theory people employ in everyday life to predict and explain actions), an agent's desires or preferences, like an agent's beliefs and expectations, are mental states that cause their actions. This is a claim about a theory, not about the dictionary meanings of the words "prefers" and "preference." Beliefs and preferences, unlike actions, are subjective, and they are distinct from the actions they give rise to, explain, and justify. Within folk psychology, one cannot infer preferences from choices alone, because choices depend on both belief and preference. Consider, for example, a pared-down ultimatum game experiment, in which the proposer can choose to offer an even division of $10 or a $9–$1 split. To predict whether experimental subjects will offer an equal or unequal division of $10, one needs to know not only whether they care about fairness or want only to maximize their own payoff, but also whether they believe that the other player will accept or reject an uneven offer. The inverse inference from choice to preference depends equally on premises concerning beliefs. Observing an offer of an equal division, one can infer that either the experimental subject blundered, or that the subject preferred to make an equal offer. But the choice doesn't tell us whether the agent values fairness or whether the agent is self-interested and believed that the unequal offer would be rejected. And knowing why the agent acts as she does bears on what one would predict the agent would do in other circumstances. Drastically different preferences can lead to the same action, depending on what the agent believes. Even though preferences cause choices, they do not cause choices all by themselves. Choice could not by itself reveal preference, because, given the right set of beliefs, any set of choices is consistent with any set of preferences. Neither beliefs nor preferences can be identified from choice data without assumptions about the other.

How, then, can a folk psychologist (i.e., each of us) determine the beliefs and preferences of others? Since one cannot infer beliefs or preferences from actions alone, and actions (including speech) are virtually the only source of evidence,[4] it would seem that one could never reach any conclusions about beliefs or preferences. This conundrum is resolved by "bootstrapping." By assuming one knows some beliefs and preferences, one can make inferences from actions about other beliefs and preferences. (This is what Köszegi and Rabin rely on in chapter 8). When people run screaming from burning buildings, we rely on our presumption that people don't generally want to be burned alive to infer that they believe there is a fire. Since initial assumptions can lead to trouble later, this bootstrapping is subject to empirical control. When economists observe people's purchases at the grocery store or their actions in a laboratory for experimental economics, they assume that the subjects they observe share the economists' understanding of the alternatives, that the subjects are not attempting to make fools of the observers or experimenters, and so forth. Against a background of shared beliefs and shared preferences, people can discover details of the idiosyncratic beliefs and preferences of others.

Gul and Pesendorfer are, of course, well aware of the truism that choice depends on both belief and preference. When American tourists walk in front of cars in London, they are not revealing a preference for being run over. Their action depends on their false beliefs about the direction of traffic as well as their preferences. Gul and Pesendorfer do not, however, use this terminology or conclude that choice fails to reveal preference. They talk instead of "subjective constraints on the feasible strategies." Choice cannot reveal preference, since one cannot infer preferences from choices without premises concerning beliefs.[5]

Actual revealed preference theorists have attempted to evade this simple problem in three ways. One is to focus on preferences over the immediate objects of choice. But this trivializes economics and, in any case, fails, since people can have mistaken beliefs about which alternatives are available for choice. A second way has been to focus on circumstances of perfect knowledge, in which beliefs can be equated with the facts and disappear from the models. But one cannot in this way make beliefs irrelevant in reality. A third way, which Gul and Pesendorfer endorse, it to embed the dependency on belief in the utility functions (which, of course, represent preferences). Gul and Pesendorfer note that economists can model preferences as depending "on an exogenous state variable, on the information of her opponents, or her own consumption history. The decision maker may be learning about a relevant preference parameter, over time." So preferences can be revealed by choice plus circumstance, information, or history. If beliefs were facts about choices or choice situations, one could in this way preserve the link between choice and preference that Samuelson and Little sought. But beliefs are subjective states, and as functions from beliefs to choices, preferences must be subjective states, too.

Before showing that actual revealed preferences cannot serve the purposes of economists, let me turn to hypothetical revealed preferences, since the inadequacy of actual and hypothetical revealed preferences are similar.

Hypothetical Revealed Preferences

Although Gul and Pesendorfer maintain that "[t]o say that a decision maker prefers x to y is to say that he never chooses y when x is also available, nothing more," this is not really their view. Later they write, "Welfare-improving changes to an economic institution are defined to be changes to which the individual(s) would agree. Policy x is deemed better than policy y for an individual if and only if, given the opportunity, the individual would choose x over y." Although this quotation does not specifically mention "preference," Gul and Pesendorfer identify what increases an individual's welfare with what an individual prefers. So here they equate preference with what an individual would choose, given the opportunity, rather than with what an individual does choose. Among the many who would prefer to be offered a raise, very few can choose to offer one to themselves. Preferences range much more widely than actual choices. If they are to be identified with choices, it seems they must be identified with hypothetical choices.

If the objects over which preferences are defined could be limited to the objects of hypothetical choice, then one could define preferences in terms of hypothetical choices (though one would still have problems with mistakes and false beliefs). But it is unclear what such a reduction of preference to hypothetical choice would accomplish. In switching from actual to hypothetical choice, one has abandoned the empiricist ideal of avoiding references to and reliance on anything that is not observable. How Ted Kennedy would choose to set the minimum wage in the hypothetical circumstances (whatever they might be) in which he all by himself gets to choose what the minimum wage should be is not something that can be read off his choice behavior. (And it is not obvious why only facts about his actual choices, as opposed to anything behavioral economists might discover, would bear on claims about his hypothetical choices.)

Furthermore, economists cannot limit the objects over which preferences are defined to objects of hypothetical choice. Can one coherently describe a hypothetical situation in which the United States continues to have representative institutions and Pat Robertson gets to choose all by himself whether gay marriage will be legal? If not, does that mean that Pat Robertson has no preferences concerning whether to legalize gay marriage in the United States? Or consider a simple game in which player 1 can choose whether or not to make a marriage proposal to player 2, who then has a choice of accepting or rejecting the proposal. In order for this to be a well-defined game of perfect information, both players must have preferences over the three terminal nodes (no proposal made, proposal made and accepted, proposal made and rejected). The state of affairs in which player 1 makes the proposal and player 2 accepts cannot be equated with any hypothetical choice of a single agent.[6] It is not identical to player 1 making a proposal and then hypothetically accepting his own offer. Nor is it identical to player 1 making an offer and then performing some action that causes his offer to be accepted. In the case of a marriage proposal, it matters crucially that the other person does the deciding. Preferences range far more widely than even hypothetical choices and so cannot be defined in terms of choices. (And even if they could be defined in terms of choices, choices themselves cannot be defined without reference to the individual's subjective identification of the alternatives.) The relation R defined in the revelation theorem cannot sensibly be interpreted as "prefers."

Furthermore, limiting preferences to the objects of choice and defining preferences in terms of choices would trivialize economics. One standard explanatory and predictive strategy in economics is to deduce what people will choose from their preferences over the possible consequences of the choices and their beliefs about the probability of the states in which the actions lead to those consequences. Consider a simple example that Gul and Pesendorfer give, a "prize ($100) is placed either in a red or a blue box, and the agent knows that there is a 60% chance that the money is in the red box. Confronted with a choice between the two boxes, the agent chooses the red box." Economists would predict or explain this action in terms of the agent's preference for $100 over nothing and the agent's belief that Pr($100/red) > Pr($100/blue) (and the agent's belief that no other significant consequence follows from choosing red rather than blue). If economists limited the objects of preferences to the set of alternative objects of choice—that is, to the two-member set {red box, blue box}, with U(red box) > U(blue box)—they would have nothing to say here or elsewhere other than "among the feasible alternatives, the agent chose the one he or she preferred." What gives economics content is being able to explain or predict the choice [or, equivalently, why U(red box) > U(blue box)] in terms of the agent's beliefs and his or her underlying preference for more money rather than less. When economists employ this strategy, preferences over consequences must be given and preferences over alternative choices must remain to be predicted or explained. Similarly, one does not have a well-defined game until one has specified the player's preferences over the outcomes. But one has nothing to do if the player's preferences over the strategies are already known.

The bottom line is that economists generate predictions of choices and give explanations of choices by deriving choices (or preferences over the immediate objects of choice) from preferences and beliefs. Subjective preferences combine with beliefs to cause actions. Revealed preferences do not. Neither actual nor hypothetical revealed preferences will do the jobs that preferences do in economics.

Conditional Revealed Preferences

In some contemporary work such as Köszegi and Rabin's (see chapter 8) and at some points in Gul and Pesendorfer's argument (chapter 1), the term, "revealed preference" is used in a different way. When Köszegi and Rabin write in chapter 8, "Preferences are revealed in behavior, even if they are not implemented by behavior," they clearly do not mean that preferences can be defined by behavior. They propose instead to "make reasonable assumptions that render mistakes [beliefs] and preferences jointly observable from behavior." Green and Osbard [1991] and Border [1992] similarly take revealed preference theory to maintain that preferences can be inferred from choices given premises concerning belief. When Gul and Pesendorfer suggest that beliefs be treated as subjective constraints on choices, they are following the same path.[7]

There is no mistake in holding that once beliefs are fixed, preferences can be inferred from choices (and vice versa). The folk-psychological view of choices as determined jointly by beliefs and preferences lies at the foundation of economics. But economists should not conflate this view, which I am here calling "conditional revealed preference theory," with either hypothetical or actual revealed preference theory, because preferences as defined by conditional revealed preference theory are subjective states that cause choices, while preferences as defined by hypothetical or actual revealed preference theory are constructs defined in terms of actual or hypothetical choices.

The preferences economists work with are subjective states. They are rankings of alternatives in terms of all considerations that bear on choice behavior, but they are not definable in terms of actual or hypothetical choices, because they rank alternatives that are not objects of actual or hypothetical choice and because their connection to choice is mediated by belief. This understanding of preferences does not imply that neuroeconomics will have anything to teach us about preferences, but it does not rule out the possibility, either.

THE FRIEDMAN ARGUMENT THAT ONLY CHOICE DATA ARE RELEVANT

Above I argued that Gul and Pesendorfer's case against behavioral and neuroeconomics turned crucially on the relevance thesis: that only data about agent's choices and the implications of choices (e.g., market prices and quantities) are relevant to the acceptance or rejection of economic models. I then addressed the Samuelson argument and the revealed preference argument for the relevance thesis. The third argument, which I call the Friedman argument, is the subject of this section.

The context in which Milton Friedman wrote his renowned essay, "The Methodology of Positive Economics" [Friedman, 1953] is in important ways analogous to the context in which Gul and Pesendorfer are writing, and their central arguments in chapter 1 concerning positive economics are, I believe, similar to Friedman's. When Friedman wrote his essay, mainstream economics was under methodological attack. In 1939, R. L. Hall and C. J. Hitch published a paper reporting the results of a questionnaire they distributed to British firms, which apparently showed that the firms employed "full-cost" pricing rather than looking to marginal costs. In 1946, Richard Lester argued that survey results showed that firms do not maximize profits by equating marginal costs and marginal revenues.

The surveys done by Hall and Hitch [1939] and Lester [1946] were primitive and faulty and in no way comparable to the sophisticated work that contemporary neuroeconomists and experimental economists carry out. But their results were taken seriously nevertheless, since they merely made public what most economists already knew: economic models did not accurately portray business behavior. In the words of Fritz Machlup [1956], who was a staunch defender of the standard theory of the firm, "Surely, some businessmen do so [maximize profits] some of the time; probably, most businessmen do so most of the time. But we would certainly not find that all businessmen do so all of the time. Hence, the assumption of consistently profit-maximizing conduct is contrary to fact" [488]. Merely demonstrating the inadequacy of the particular surveys could not make the inconvenient truth disappear that "the assumption of consistently profit-maximizing conduct is contrary to fact." Nor could economists merely shrug their shoulders, for in the 1940s and 1950s, narrow empiricist views of theory appraisal dominated thinking in philosophy and the sciences, including the social sciences. Economists needed some way to defend what they were doing despite the fact that their basic principles appeared to be false.

Friedman offered economists what they wanted. Rather than presenting a complicated story whereby the basic generalizations of economics could be construed as inexact truths,[8] he argued that their truth or falsity was irrelevant. The only thing that mattered was the truth or falsity of the predictions of economic theories or, in more contemporary language, economic models. Merely saying this much does not help at all, because economic models of firms may make predictions about survey results as well as predictions about prices and quantities. So what Friedman [1953] does—though he is not very clear about this—is to argue that only the predictions of economic models concerning market data matter to their assessment. Consider the following three quotations from Friedman [1953]:

> Viewed as a body of substantive hypotheses, theory is to be judged by its predictive power for the class of phenomena which it is intended to "explain." [8–9]
> For this test [of predictions] to be relevant, the deduced facts must be about the class of phenomena the hypothesis is designed to explain. [12–13]
> The decisive test is whether the hypothesis works for the phenomena it purports to explain. [30]

Friedman is arguing that all that matters to economists is how successful models are in predicting what economists are interested in—that is, market phenomena. The fact that economic models may make mistaken predictions concerning surveys is irrelevant.[9]

Gul and Pesendorfer, like Friedman, argue that certain data that apparently bear on generalizations employed in economic models are in fact irrelevant to the acceptance or rejection of those models. These data come from experiments and neural imaging, and unlike the survey results reported by Hall and Hitch [1939] and Lester [1946], some of these data are surprising, precise, and solid. Rather than casting doubt on particular data, Gul and Pesendorfer argue that these data are not relevant. Only data about agents' choices and the implications of choices (such as market prices and quantities) are relevant. One way to defend this claim is, like Friedman, to argue that one's goals determine what evidence is relevant—that is, to argue that only data concerning choices and their consequences are relevant to the assessment of economic models because only the implications of economic models for choices and their consequences are of interest to economists.

The argument might be formulated as follows:

The Friedman Argument

1. The goal of constructing a model is to make correct predictions concerning the class of phenomena it is intended to explain or predict. (premise)
2. Economic models are intended to explain or predict choices and the consequences of choices, particularly for market quantities. (premise)
3. The only data that are relevant to the acceptance or rejection of a model concern the class of phenomena the model is intended to explain or predict. (invalidly from 1)
4. Only data concerning choices and the consequences of choices, particularly for market quantities, are relevant to the acceptance or rejection of economic models. (from 2 and 3)

Gul and Pesendorfer never formulate this argument explicitly, but it is implicit in several of their remarks. Consider the following three quotations:

> If an economist proposes a new theory based on nonchoice evidence, then either the new theory leads to novel behavioral predictions, in which case it can be tested with revealed preference evidence, or it does not, in which case the modification is vacuous.
>
> For economists, the physiological distinction between the two examples is unimportant. What matters is that demand for those goods responds in a similar way to price changes.
>
> The theory is successful if preference for early resolution of uncertainty turns out to be an empirically important phenomenon, that is, if models that incorporate it are successful at addressing economic behavior.

Gul and Pesendorfer do not maintain that psychological factors are unimportant. On the contrary, they write, "Note that the above does not say that psychological factors are irrelevant for economic decision making, nor does it say that economists should ignore psychological insights. Economists routinely take their inspiration from psychological data or theories." But for Gul and Pesendorfer, the fact that economists may take "inspiration" from psychological data changes nothing with respect to evaluation: "Regardless of the source of their inspiration, economic models can only be evaluated on their own terms, with respect to their own objectives and evidence."

The Friedman argument is invalid. The fact that economists care only about certain implications of a model does not imply that the model has no other implications or that only the implications economists care about are relevant to their assessment of the model. Suppose one grants Friedman's narrow instrumentalist view of economic models as tools for making predictions concerning market phenomena. Is it the case that tools that are designed for a particular purpose should be tested only by checking how well they fulfill that purpose? In an essay concerning this argument in Friedman's essay [Hausman, 1992b], I suggested the following analogy: A used car is also a tool. Suppose that all one wants of a used car is that it will drive safely, reliably, and economically. It does not, however, follow that the only relevant test is a road test. A mechanic who lifts the hood and examines the engine may have something useful to tell a prospective buyer. If one were clairvoyant and had already examined the future driving history of the car, then of course the mechanic's findings would be irrelevant. But a road test provides only a small sample of the car's performance under only some of the conditions in which the car will be driven. The mechanic can help one to judge whether the sampled performance is a good indicator of future performance and to predict how the car will perform in new conditions. The mechanic can also help diagnose the cause of breakdowns.

Similarly, if economists already know how well a model predicts the phenomena in which they are interested with respect to all its future applications, then there would be no predictive advantage to psychological and neurological probing of parts of the model. But all they know is how well the model has performed in a few past applications—and indeed, they often do not know even that much. (Econometric evaluation of models is hardly a simple, straightforward, and decisive matter!) Psychological and neurological data, even if they are of no interest themselves to economists, may provide evidence concerning whether the past is a good guide to the future and whether the model will perform well in new applications. In just the same way that information about a car's fuel injectors, even if of no interest itself to a driver, may help to predict the performance of the car in different circumstances and help to diagnose failures, so psychological and neurological data may help economists to diagnose failures and to judge when it is sensible to rely on particular models.

Nothing in my criticism of the relevance thesis and of the argument Gul and Pesendorfer make in its defense shows that neurological data or behavioral theories will actually help further the objectives of economists. But there is no methodological shortcut that establishes that nothing that psychologists or neurologists learn can support or refute economic models.

Behavioral Economics and Normative Economics

Gul and Pesendorfer deny that behavioral data and theories are relevant to the concerns of standard welfare economics by asserting a tendentious characterization of standard welfare economics, and they criticize behavioral economists for defending paternalistic views, which Gul and Pesendorfer regard as unjustified and destructive of economic science. In this section, I first dispute Gul and Pesendorfer's characterization of welfare economics. Then I turn to questions concerning paternalism where I distinguish between judging whether people sometimes choose what is worse for them and judging whether paternalistic policies are well advised. In noting that people sometimes choose what is worse for them, behavioral economists do not—or so I argue—make any mistake, and Gul and Pesendorfer are wrong to criticize them on these grounds. But even though Gul and Pesendorfer's condemnation is off the mark, there is a good deal to criticize, and I end this section by criticizing the account of well-being defended by some psychologists and behavioral economists.

Gul and Pesendorfer assert, "Standard welfare economics functions as a part of positive economics." In their view, welfare economics permits economists to explain why efficient institutions and policies persist, identifies puzzling cases of persistent inefficiencies, and assists in the design of institutions that meet specified requirements. They maintain that "welfare is defined to be synonymous with choice behavior"—which means, of course, that those who suggest that people sometimes choose what is worse for them are contradicting themselves or talking about something other than the subject matter of welfare economics. Gul and Pesendorfer focus on those behavioral economists who are hedonists and who criticize standard welfare economics on the ground that what people choose may fail to make them happy. Because alternatives that people do not choose sometimes would make them happier than the alternatives they do choose, these behavioral economists believe there is a role for economists in designing paternalistic policies that make people happier than letting them choose without interference. But what matters to welfare economics, as characterized by Gul and Pesendorfer, is what people choose, not what makes them happy nor what makes them truly better off. Gul and Pesendorfer conclude that when behavioral economists address normative questions, they fail to address the questions that characterize welfare economics, and rather than offering a competing view, they change the subject.

Gul and Pesendorfer's characterization of "standard welfare economics" is hard to accept. It implies that none of the arguments concerning the normative attractiveness of axioms of social choice theory or, indeed, of Pareto efficiency is a part of normative economics, nor are discussions of trade-offs between efficiency and equity, of ways in which to model freedom, of the normative attractions of measures of inequality, and so forth. Cost–benefit analyses are a part of welfare economics only insofar as they infer willingness to pay from demand behavior. As soon as cost-benefit analyses employ contingent valuation techniques (which rely on verbal reports of willingness to pay), they change the subject. Gul and Pesendorfer's account also makes it mysterious why the activities they describe should be called "welfare economics." If "better for A" is just synonym for "chosen by A," why use the language of "better," "benefit," "advantage," or "welfare" except to sow confusion? And why should anybody care about whether an institution is efficient or not? The answer presumably is that economists think that there is something good about people getting alternatives that rank higher in their preference rankings—where "good" means, of course, something other than "chosen." Gul and Pesendorfer themselves state, "Individuals sometimes make obviously bad decisions." They maintain that "an agent may make better decisions if he is given better information" and that "there are situations where an outsider could improve an individual's decisions." What is the meaning of "bad"? It cannot be "unchosen." Similarly, "better" and "improve" cannot be synonyms for "chosen." [10] Nor is it a matter of definition that poor information implies bad decisions while better information results in better or improved decisions. Learning new facts can easily lead to worse choices. The criterion for what is better for the individual cannot simply be what the individual chooses.

The underlying point is obvious. We all know of choices that others have made that we believe were bad for them and of choices we made in the past that we now believe were bad for us. And it is not impossible to choose knowingly to sacrifice one's own well-being to bring about something that one thinks more important. These beliefs about what would be good for others or ourselves might be mistaken, but they are not automatically mistaken merely in virtue of disagreeing with what is chosen. When a healthy and nonsuicidal American tourist named Ellen steps in front of a rapidly moving London taxi, what Ellen has "chosen" is worse for her than remaining on the curb.

Gul and Pesendorfer respond that the action of remaining on the curb was not part of a feasible strategy that Ellen would choose (ex ante) over the strategy that put Ellen in the morgue. So one has no counterexample here to the claim that what Ellen chose is what Ellen preferred. The objects of choice are strategies rather than outcomes, and given the constraints she faced, Ellen was better off with the strategy that she chose. It is not clear why we should believe this, but at least it is not as obviously false as the claim that Ellen was better off being hit by the cab.

This treatment of the case of the unfortunate pedestrian does nothing to shore up the claim that x is at least as good for A as y if and only if A chooses x from a set of feasible alternatives that includes y. Whatever the prospective benefits of the strategy that turned out so unfortunately for Ellen, the outcome was very bad for her.[11] Even if, as Gul and Pesendorfer implicitly assert, the strategies that would have prevented Ellen from being hit by the cab all had a lower expected utility than the one that got her run over, many of them (e.g., "Never walk in London" or "Don't visit England") would have turned out better. Whether or not it is true, as Gul and Pesendorfer assert, that the strategy Ellen employs is no worse (by their definition, since it is the strategy she chose), the outcome is bad for her. Someone who interfered with her choice and pulled her back when she started walking across the street would have benefited her. It is not the case that whatever someone chooses has better consequences than feasible but unchosen alternatives.[12]

Neither is it impossible to benefit someone by coercing someone against her will. Suppose that when Ellen sets out to cross the street a helpful bystander grabs her and pulls her back. After the initial shock of having been grabbed by a stranger, Ellen is grateful. But she was nevertheless coerced. The bystander's action is an example of a justified paternalistic action. Notice that paternalism is not the view that people sometimes make choices that are bad for them. This last view is a matter of fact accepted by both paternalists and antipaternalists such as John Stuart Mill. It is hard to see how there could be any reasonable disagreement about whether people sometimes choose what is bad for them, and I think that on a charitable interpretation of welfare economics, welfare economists grant this claim, too. Although Gul and Pesendorfer are correct that standard welfare economics measures well-being by preference satisfaction, the link economists draw between preference and welfare should be understood not as defining welfare but as maintaining (substantively) that people generally prefer what is good for them. This substantive claim may be a useful and sensible approximation in some contexts, even though it is clearly mistaken in others [Hausman and McPherson, 2006]. In this way, one can avoid attributing to economists the untenable view that people never prefer or choose what is worse for them over what is better, while leaving open the possibility that welfare economists have other reasons to reject paternalistic policies.

If one rejects the untenable claim that it is logically impossible to coerce people for their own benefit, then one must face the question of whether paternalistic policies should be endorsed or rejected. Some paternalistic actions, such as the action of the hypothetical bystander who pulls Ellen back, are clearly justified. Even John Stuart Mill in his classic critique of paternalism in *On Liberty* [1859] makes exceptions for cases such as this one.[13] In considering whether to support paternalistic policies, one must consider what their consequences will be in the light of more general moral principles. Although there is some controversy about the interpretation of Mill's argument, he maintains that his principle of liberty (which rules out almost all paternalism) follows from utilitarianism coupled with some general facts. Among these are the facts that people are typically better informed about their own circumstances than the government or society at large and that people typically are more strongly motivated to protect their own interests than are others. Also crucial to Mill's case against paternalism are his views about individuality: that individuality is a crucial ingredient in a good life, that individuality is essential to social progress, and that individuality thrives only in an atmosphere of individual liberty. Add to these considerations the dangers of intrusive government, and one has a principled utilitarian argument that society is better off letting individuals make their own choices, where their actions do not impinge on the rights of others, even when individuals choose badly.

The fact that behavioral economists recognize that it may be possible to design institutions and policies that make people better off by interfering with their choices is not grounds for criticism. This recognition does not automatically put one on the road toward embracing an intrusive "nanny state." I personally would not go as far as Mill in rejecting all paternalism, because I believe that some paternalistic policies, such as seat belt laws, have minimal effects on liberty and on the size of government, yet provide large benefits to individuals. There are, nevertheless, powerful reasons to be cautious about paternalism. The argument that by interfering with choices paternalistic policies automatically make people worse off is, however, not one of them.[14]

Though Gul and Pesendorfer are wrong to criticize behavioral economists on the grounds that their views may support paternalistic policies, there are nevertheless serious problems with the hedonistic views of welfare defended by prominent theorists such as Daniel Kahneman. Not all behavioral and neuroeconomists accept these views of welfare, and hedonism is not implicit in the project of attempting to inform economics through the study of psychology and neurology. I shall call defenders of these views of welfare "Kahneman et al." so as to avoid the implication that hedonistic views of welfare are accepted by all behavioral economists. For example, in their argument in chapter 9 in defense of "light paternalism," Loewenstein and Haisley explicitly repudiate any reliance on hedonistic views such as Kahneman's.

Kahneman et al. take well-being to be the sum of net momentary pleasures. This view is even more implausible than is the identification of well-being with preference or choice. It is a particularly narrow version of hedonism, the position that well-being consists in happiness or pleasure. Though the great nineteenth century utilitarians all took well-being to be some sort of mental state, Mill [1863] and Sidgwick [1907] emphatically rejected the view that well-being was identical to or could be measured by pleasure. Bentham [1789], on the other hand, did take well-being to be pleasure, although it is questionable whether even Bentham meant anything as narrow as Kahneman does [see Kahneman et al., 1997; Kahneman, 2000; Kahneman and Krueger, 2006]. Bentham's view that the ultimate good for human beings is pleasure has long been regarded as implausible and even degrading, and recent psychological studies that demonstrate that people are bad at anticipating and remembering pleasures and pains render the view even more implausible. Even if taking care of one's children is less pleasurable than watching television,[15] its contribution to what most people take to be a life worth living is far greater. The result of combining vulgar hedonism with paternalism justifies Gul and Pesendorfer's hostile reaction to the normative views of those they call "neuroeconomists." Designing social policies so as to maximize people's momentary pleasures, even at the cost of coercively preventing them from pursuing projects that they find valuable, is an unappealing prospect.

Kahneman et al. distinguish between what they call "decision utility" and "experience utility." Decision utility is utility as an index of preference, which many behavioral economists (like their critics) mistakenly take to be revealed preference.

"Experience utility" is pleasure, and Kahneman et al. argue that "pleasure" should be understood as a momentary state that is objectively detectable and perhaps even eventually measurable via brain scans. The dichotomy between decision utility and experience utility is, I believe, deeply flawed. First, Kahneman et al. assume that decision utility is based on an individual's expectations of experienced utility. Though this may sometimes be the case, as when I order an ice cream cone with expectations of gustatory gratification, it is implausible as an account of people's preferences in general. I am not writing this sentence because of any conscious expectation that doing so will bring me more pleasure than some feasible alternative. Perhaps Kahneman knows me better than I know myself and can demonstrate that all my choices are governed by unconscious expectations of pleasure, but clearly lots of argument is needed.

Second, the dichotomy between experience utility and decision utility fails to distinguish between utility as a measure of a subjective state that can be used to explain and predict choice behavior and utility as well-being, that is, what makes life good or bad for a person. Accepting a folk-psychological view in which preference (and belief) explains choice does not commit one to any theory of well-being. Indeed, the explanatory roles of decision utility and experience utility, unlike their normative roles, are not obviously incompatible. Furthermore, not distinguishing the predictive and normative roles of utility leads one to identify what makes people better off with what they aim for. But it is not self-contradictory to choose to sacrifice one's well-being to some cause to which one is committed.

Third, the dichotomy is false. There are other explanatory theories and, more important, lots of other views of well-being. Indeed, no contemporary philosopher who has written on well-being has adopted either of these two views. Although it is untenable to take well-being to be the satisfaction of preferences, it is more sensible to follow the course of standard welfare economics and take preference satisfaction as an indicator of well-being than to suppose that psychology or neurology can tell us what makes for a good life. Psychological and neurological research can tell us a good deal about what motivates people and what effects various activities and outcomes have on people's moods and brain states. This information is relevant to deciding what makes for a good life, but it does not answer the age-old question of how to live.

CONCLUSIONS

In the manifestos of behavioral economics and neuroeconomics, one finds some exaggerated optimism. This is unsurprising. and even unobjectionable. It takes optimism to motivate academics to leap into unknown territory with unknown rewards. It is also unsurprising that some exaggerations will be irksome to main-stream economists, who see these new activities as distractions from the serious problems they face. But there is no good argument against the possibility that psychological and neurological research may generate data that will be relevant to the acceptance or rejection of economic theory, and criticisms of the claims about welfare economics espoused by Kahneman et al. should be addressed to their inadequate views of well-being, not to the unobjectionable views that people can be wrong about what makes them better off and that they may be coerced to their own advantage.

NOTES

I thank Andrew Schotter and Philippe Mongin for criticisms of an earlier draft of this chapter.

1. It might seem uncharitable to attribute the premise to Gul and Pesendorfer, but I am not alone in reading them this way [see Caplin, chapter 15].

2. Although Ariel Rubinstein and Yuval Salant do not state their conclusions this strongly in chapter 5, their arguments lead to the same conclusion. See particularly their discussion of the interpretation of preferences in games.

3. How is such a case possible, given the revelation theorem? Either one can restrict revealed preference theory to the very special case in which individuals have no false beliefs, or one can interpret S as the set of alternatives that the agent believes to be available for choice. In that case, x will not be in S, and hence not in $C(S)$. But in that case, one is obviously no longer linking preference to behavior that is observable without reference to an agent's subjective states.

4. There are some other sources of evidence, e.g., facial gestures and, potentially, data from brain scans.

5. See Hausman [2000] and Rosenberg [1992: 123]. Sen's [1993: 501–502] discussion of the ways in which consistency of choice depends on how agents conceive of their choices makes essentially this point, although not in these terms. Ran Spiegler (chapter 4) cites a related claim of Edi Karni [2005].

6. Rubinstein and Salant (chapter 5) make the same point: "However, note that an individual's preference for a Pareto-dominant outcome over a Pareto-dominated one usually involves a change in the behavior of other individuals and therefore may not be observable in any choice situation. Thus, it must have an additional mental meaning."

7. Benhabib and Bisin offer a similar criticism of Gul and Pesendorfer in chapter 14: "We claim instead that a structural model of the choice process leading to such *mistakes* would constitute a better methodological practice. It would avoid adding a "subjective constraint" every time needed, and it could provide explanatory power to understand choice in several different interesting contexts in which attention control might be relevant."

8. This is the route I favor—see Hausman [1992a].

9. As argued above, whether or not a model has an empirical implication is a question about what can be deduced from it with the help of specifications of initial conditions. The fact that economists are not interested in survey results does not mean that economic theories do not make predictions about survey results.

10. In much the same spirit as Gul and Pesendorfer, Bernheim and Rangel write in chapter 7: "The standard approach to welfare analysis is based on choice, not on utility, preferences, or other ethical criteria. In its simplest form, it instructs the social planner to respect the choices an individual would make for himself." This is itself a normative claim, and except as a rough first approximation, it is indefensible. Indeed Bernheim and Rangel themselves note instances where this principle is unacceptable, although they describe these as cases where the "generalized choice situation" is "suspect" and actual choice a bad guide to what the individual would choose, rather than as cases where a planner should not mimic what the affected individual would choose. As Bernheim and Rangel note, this principle goes far beyond a rejection of paternalism. It implies not only that individuals should be free to act as they choose when they do not harm others, but that the planner should endeavor to choose for the individual as that individual would choose, no matter how harmful the result to that person. Adhering to the principle would imply not only that addicts should be permitted to purchase crack, but that planners should (other things being equal) attempt to make it available to them. In chapter 7, Bernheim and Rangel argue against adhering to the principle in cases like these.

11. The badness of being hit does not consist of something else being chosen over being hit, because, on Gul and Pesendorfer's account, being hit or not hit is not part of the choice set. If Ellen had had a choice of whether or not to be hit by the taxi, she would have chosen not to be hit, but this hypothetical does nothing to support the identification between welfare and actual choice. If what is better for her is what she would choose if she were better informed or free of certain constraints, and what she actually chooses is not what she would choose if she were better informed or less constrained, then actual choice and welfare come apart. She does not choose what is better for her.

12. As note 11 suggests, this does not imply that one has to give up all connection between preference and choice, on the one hand, and well-being, on the other. One might try, as many philosophers have done, to link well-being to what people would prefer (or choose) if they were calm, reflective, and well informed. Such informed preference theories of well-being do not, however, lend any support to the view that whatever people actually prefer or choose is better for them than what they did not choose.

13. Mill gives the example of preventing someone from walking across an unsafe bridge [1859: 95].

14. Like Gul and Pesendorfer, Bernheim and Rangel in chapter 7 are deeply concerned about encouraging government to act like an intrusive big brother that claims to know better than individuals do what is good or bad for them. They suggest that "political dangers" justify their insistence that the planners' choices should almost always match the actual choices of individuals (in suitable generalized choice situations). I maintain that the proper response to these political dangers should be to defend principled limits on what governments can do, not to distort welfare economics and pretend that government intrusions can never make people better off.

15. This is the result of a detailed and often cited survey involving 900 Texas women [Kahneman et al., 2004].

REFERENCES

Arrow, Kenneth. 1959. Rational Choice Functions and Ordering, *Economica, New series,* 26: 121–127.

Bentham, Jeremy. 1789. *The Principles of Morals and Legislation.* Reprint, Amherst, MA: Prometheus Books, 1988.

Border, Kim. 1992. Revealed Preference, Stochastic Dominance, and the Expected Utility Hypothesis. *Journal of Economic Theory* 56: 20–42.

Friedman, Milton. 1953. The Methodology of Positive Economics. In *Essays in Positive Economics, Ed,* 3–43. Chicago: University of Chicago Press.

Gravelle, Hugh, and Ray Rees. 1981. *Microeconomics.* London: Longman.

Green, Edward, and Kent Osbard. 1991. A Revealed Preference Theory for Expected Utility. *Review of Economic Studies* 58: 677–696.

Hall, R. L., and C. J. Hitch. 1939. Price Theory and Business Behaviour. *Oxford Economic Papers* 2: 12–45. Reprint, in T. Wilson and P. W. S. Andrews, (ed.) *Oxford Studies in the Price Mechanism.* Oxford: Clarendon Press, 1951.

Hausman, Daniel. 1992a. *The Inexact and Separate Science of Economics.* Cambridge: Cambridge University Press.

———. 1992b. Why Look Under the Hood? In *Essays on Philosophy and Economic Methodology,* 70–73. Cambridge: Cambridge University Press.

———. 2000. Revealed Preference and Game Theory. *Economics and Philosophy* 16: 99–115.

Hausman, Daniel, and Michael McPherson. 2006. *Economic Analysis, Moral Philosophy and Public Policy.* Cambridge: Cambridge University Press.

Henderson, James, and Richard Quandt. 1980. *Microeconomic Theory: A Mathematical Approach,* 3rd ed. New York: McGraw-Hill.

Houtthakker, H. S. 1950. Revealed Preference and the Utility Function. *Economica* 17: 159–174.

Kahneman, Daniel. 2000. Experienced Utility and Objective Happiness: A Moment-Based Approach. In *Choices, Values and Frames,* ed. Daniel Kahneman and Amos Tversky, 673–692. New York: Cambridge University Press.

Kahneman, Daniel, and Alan Krueger. 2006. Developments in the Measurement of Subjective Well-Being. *Journal of Economic Perspectives* 20: 3–24.

Kahneman, Daniel, Peter Wakker, and Rakesh Sarin. 1997. Back to Bentham? Explorations of Experienced Utility. *Quarterly Journal of Economics* 112: 375–405.

Kahneman, Daniel, Alan Krueger, David Schkade, Norbert Schwarz, and Arthur Stone. 2004. A Survey Method for Characterizing Daily Life Experience: The Day Reconstruction Method. *Science* 306(5702): 776–780.

Karni, Edi. 2005. State-Dependent Preferences. In *The New Palgrave: A Dictionary of Economic Theory and Doctrine,* ed. John Eatwell, Murray Milgate, and Peter Newman. London: Macmillan.

Lester, R. A. 1946. Shortcomings of Marginal Analysis for Wage-Unemployment Problems. *American Economic Review* 36: 63–82.

Little, I. M. D. 1949. A Reformulation of the Theory of Consumer's Behaviour. *Oxford Economic Papers* 1: 90–99.

Machlup, Fritz. 1956. Rejoinder to a Reluctant Ultra-empiricist. *Southern Economic Journal* 22: 483–493.

Mill, John Stuart. 1859. *On Liberty.* Reprint, Indianapolis: Hackett, 1978.

————. 1863. *Utilitarianism.* Reprint, 321–398, in Marshall Cohen, ed. *The Philosophy of John Stuart Mill.* New York: Modern Library, 1961.

Richter, Marcel. 1966. Revealed Preference Theory. *Econometrica* 34: 635–645.

Rosenberg, Alexander. 1992. *Economics: Mathematical Politics or Science of Diminishing Returns?* Chicago: University of Chicago Press.

Samuelson, P. 1938. A Note on the Pure Theory of Consumer's Behaviour. *Economica* 5: 61–71.

————. 1947. *The Foundations of Economic Analysis.* Cambridge, MA: Harvard University Press.

————. 1963. Problems of Methodology—Discussion. *American Economic Review* 53: 232–236.

Sen, Amartya. 1971. Choice Functions and Revealed Preference. *Review of Economic Studies* 38: 307–317.

————. 1973. Behaviour and the Concept of Preference. *Economica* 40: 241–259.

————. 1993. Internal Consistency of Choice. *Econometrica* 61: 495–521.

Sidgwick, Henry. 1907. *The Methods of Ethics,* 8th ed London: Macmillan.

PART III

NEW DIRECTIONS
FOR NORMATIVE
ECONOMICS

....

CHAPTER 7

CHOICE-THEORETIC FOUNDATIONS FOR BEHAVIORAL WELFARE ECONOMICS

B. DOUGLAS BERNHEIM AND ANTONIO RANGEL

....

INTEREST in behavioral economics has grown in recent years, stimulated largely by accumulating evidence that the standard model of consumer decision making provides an inadequate positive description of human behavior. Behavioral models are increasingly finding their way into policy evaluation, which inevitably involves welfare analysis. No consensus concerning the appropriate standards and criteria for behavioral welfare analysis has yet emerged.

One common strategy in behavioral economics is to add arguments to the utility function (including all of the conditions upon which choice seems to depend) in order to rationalize choices, and to treat the new arguments as welfare relevant. Unfortunately, such an approach is often problematic as a guide for normative analysis, and in some instances simply untenable. For example, if an individual's decision depends on whether he has first viewed the last two digits of his social security number (as the literature on anchoring suggests, e.g., Tversky and Kahneman [1974]), should a social planner attempt to determine whether the individual has recently seen those digits before making a choice on his behalf? Perhaps more important, in many cases the nature and significance of the condition under which the choice is made change when the choice is transferred to a social planner. Consider the example of time inconsistency: the individual chooses alternative x over alternative y at time t, and y over x at time $t - 1$. One could rationalize this behavior by inserting the time of the decision into the utility function, so that the individual pursues different objectives at $t - 1$ and t (quasi-hyperbolic discounting is an example, e.g., Laibson [1997]). But if a social planner must choose for the individual from the set $\{x, y\}$ at time t, which perspective should it adopt? One could argue that the planner should choose x, the same alternative that the individual would pick at time t. But one could also argue that the planner should mimic the choice of y at time $t - 1$, on the grounds that the planner's decision, like the individual's decision at time $t - 1$, is at "arms length" from the experience. Much of the literature on self-control takes this second view. However, neither answer is obviously superior.

The obvious problems with the normative methodology described in the preceding paragraph have led many behavioral economists to distinguish between "decision utility," which provides an "as if" representation of choices, possibly by invoking unconventional assumptions concerning preferences, and "true" or "experienced" utility, which is viewed as the proper measure of well-being. This approach forces one to take a stand on the nature of true utility. But the objective basis for making any assumptions about true utility is, at best, obscure.[1]

This chapter is a partial summary of Bernheim and Rangel [2007], which reflects our effort to develop a unified framework for behavioral welfare economics—one that can be viewed as a natural extension of standard welfare economics. (It is also related to work by Rubinstein and Salant [2007]; we explain the relations below.) The standard approach to welfare analysis is based on choice, not on utility, preferences, or other ethical criteria. In its simplest form, it instructs the social planner to respect the choices an individual would make for herself. The guiding normative principle is an extension of the libertarian deference to freedom of choice, which takes the view that it is better to give a person the thing she would choose for herself rather than something that someone else would choose for her. Thus, with respect to public policy decisions, the standard approach instructs the planner to mimic individual choices.

We show that it is possible to extend standard choice-theoretic welfare analysis to situations in which individuals make "anomalous" choices of the various types commonly identified in behavioral research. Indeed, standard welfare economics is a special case of the framework proposed here; specifically, it is a limiting case in the sense that our framework converges to the standard framework as behavioral anomalies become small. We also show that it is possible to generalize standard tools such as compensating and equivalent variations, consumer surplus, and Pareto optimality.

The chapter is organized as follows. First we review the perspective of standard welfare economics, and then present a general framework for describing choices.

Next we set forth choice-theoretic principles for evaluating individual welfare in the presence of choice anomalies. Then, after describing the generalizations of compensating variation and consumer surplus in this setting, we explain how we generalize the notion of Pareto optimality, and examine market efficiency as an application. Last, we set forth an agenda for refining our welfare criterion and explain the role of nonchoice evidence in behavioral welfare economics, followed by our conclusion.

A Review of the Foundations for Standard Welfare Economics

Standard welfare economics consists of two separate tasks. The first task involves an assessment of each individual's welfare; the second involves aggregation across individuals. Our object here is to develop a general framework for executing the first task—one that encompasses the various types of anomalous choices identified in the behavioral literature. As we discuss further below, aggregation can then proceed much as it does in standard welfare economics, at least with respect to common concepts such as Pareto efficiency. Consequently, our main objective here is to review the standard perspective on individual welfare.

Choices and Welfare

To summarize the standard perspective formally, we must introduce some notation. We will use $\mathbb{X}$ to denote the set of all possible choice objects. The standard framework allows for the possibility that choice objects are lotteries, and/or that they describe state-contingent outcomes with welfare-relevant states.[2] A *standard choice situation* (SCS) consists of a constraint set $X \subseteq \mathbb{X}$. When we say that the standard choice situation is X, we mean that, according to the objective information available to the individual, the alternatives are the elements of X. The choice situation thus depends implicitly both on the objects among which the individual is actually choosing, and on the information available to him concerning those objects.

The objective of standard welfare economics is to provide coherent criteria for making welfare judgments concerning possible selections from standard choice situations. We will use $\mathcal{X}$ to denote the domain of standard choice situations with which standard welfare economics is concerned. Usually, the standard framework takes $\mathcal{X}$ to include some reasonably exhaustive collection of compact sets. To minimize technical details, throughout this chapter assume that $\mathcal{X}$ includes all nonempty, finite subsets of $\mathbb{X}$; naturally, it may also include other subsets.

The choices that an individual would make are described by a correspondence $C : \mathcal{X} \Rightarrow \mathbb{X}$, with the property that $C(X) \subseteq X$ for all $X \in \mathcal{X}$. We interpret $x \in C(X)$ as an action that the individual is willing to choose when her choice set is X. Though we often speak as if choices are derived from preferences, the opposite is actually the case. Standard economics makes no assumption about how choices are actually made; preferences are merely constructs that summarize choices. Accordingly, meaningful assumptions pertain to choices, not to preferences.

The standard framework assumes that the choice correspondence satisfies a consistency property known as *weak congruence*, which generalizes the weak axiom of revealed preference (see Sen [1971]). According to the weak congruence axiom, if there exists some X containing x and y for which $x \in C(X)$, then $y \in C(X')$ implies $x \in C(X')$ for all X' containing x and y. In other words, if there is some set for which the individual is willing to choose x when y is present, then the individual is never willing to choose y but not x when both are present.

In the standard framework, welfare judgments are based on binary relationships R, P, and I defined over the choice objects in $\mathbb{X}$, which are derived from the choice correspondence in the following way:

$$xRy \text{ iff } x \in C(\{x, y\}) \tag{7.1}$$

$$xPy \text{ iff } xRy \text{ and } \sim yRx \tag{7.2}$$

$$xIy \text{ iff } xRy \text{ and } yRx \tag{7.3}$$

Under the weak congruence axiom, the relation R is an ordering, commonly interpreted as "revealed preference."[3] Though this terminology suggests a model of decision making in which preferences drive choices, it is important to remember that the standard framework does not embrace that suggestion; instead, R is simply a summary of what the individual chooses in a wide range of situations. Further technical assumptions allow us to represent R with a continuous utility function.

When we use the orderings R, P, and I to conduct welfare analysis, we are simply asking what an individual would choose. For example, for any set X, we can define an *individual welfare optimum* as the set of maximal elements in X according to the relation R—that is, $\{x \in X \mid xRy \text{ for all } y \in X\}$. Under the weak congruence axiom, this set coincides exactly with $C(X)$, the set of objects the individual is willing to select from X.

All of the tools of applied welfare economics are built from this choice-theoretic foundation. For example, the compensating variation associated with some change in the economic environment equals the smallest payment that would induce the individual to choose the change. A similar observation holds for the equivalent variation. The notion of consumer surplus is also entirely choice-theoretic because it measures the compensating variation of a price change. In settings with many individuals, Pareto efficiency is a choice-theoretic concept: an alternative x is Pareto efficient if there is no other alternative that everyone would voluntarily choose over x.

Positive versus Normative Analysis

Usually, choice data are not available for all elements of $\mathcal{X}$, but rather for elements of some restricted set $\mathcal{X}^D \subset \mathcal{X}$. The objective of positive economic analysis is to extend the choice correspondence C from observations on $\mathcal{X}^D$ to the entire set $\mathcal{X}$. This task is usually accomplished by defining a parametrized set of utility functions (preferences) defined over $\mathbb{X}$, estimating the utility parameters with choice data for the opportunity sets in $\mathcal{X}^D$, and using these estimated utility function to infer choices for opportunity sets in $\mathcal{X} \backslash \mathcal{X}^D$ (by maximizing that function for each $X \in \mathcal{X} \backslash \mathcal{X}^D$).

The objective of normative economic analysis is to identify desirable outcomes. In conducting standard choice-based welfare analysis, we take the product of positive analysis—the individual's extended choice correspondence, C, defined on $\mathcal{X}$ rather than $\mathcal{X}^D$—as an input, and then proceed as described in the preceding section.

Preferences and utility functions, which are constructs used to extend C from $\mathcal{X}^D$ to $\mathcal{X}$, are therefore positive tools, not normative tools. They simply reiterate the information contained in the extended choice function C. Beyond that reiteration, they add no new information that might pertain to welfare analysis.

A General Framework for Describing Choices

In behavioral economics as in standard economics, we are concerned with choices among objects drawn from some set $\mathbb{X}$. To accommodate certain types of behavioral anomalies, we introduce the notion of an *ancillary condition*, denoted d. An ancillary condition is a feature of the choice environment that may affect behavior, but that is not taken to be a welfare-relevant characteristic of the chosen object. Typical examples of ancillary conditions include the manner in which information is presented at the time of choice, or the presentation of a particular option as the "status quo." With respect to intertemporal choice, the ancillary condition is the particular decision tree used to choose from a fixed opportunity set (which includes the points in time at which the component choices are made, and the set of alternatives available at each decision node); hence this framework can accommodate dynamically inconsistent choices.

We define a *generalized choice situation* (GCS), G, as a standard choice situation, X, paired with an ancillary condition, d. Thus, $G = (X, d)$. We will use $\mathcal{G}$ to denote the set of generalized choice situations of potential interest. When $\mathcal{X}$ is the set of SCSs, for each $X \in \mathcal{X}$ there is at least one ancillary condition d such that $(X, d) \in \mathcal{G}$. Rubinstein and Salant (chapter 5) have independently formulated a similar framework for describing the impact of choice procedures on decisions; they refer to ancillary conditions as "frames."

The choices that an individual would make in each GCS are described by a correspondence $C : \mathcal{G} \Rightarrow \mathbb{X}$, with the property that $C(X, d) \subseteq X$ for all $(X, d) \in \mathcal{G}$. We interpret $x \in C(G)$ as an action that the individual is willing to choose when the generalized choice situation is G. We will assume throughout that $C(G)$ is nonempty for all $G \in \mathcal{G}$; in other words, faced with any set of alternatives, the individual can always make a choice.

What Are Ancillary Conditions?

As a general matter, it is difficult to draw a bright line between the characteristics of the objects in $\mathbb{X}$ and the ancillary conditions d. The difficulty, as described below, is that one could view virtually any ancillary condition as a characteristic of objects in the choice set. How, then, do we decide whether a feature of the choice environment is an ancillary condition?

In some cases, the nature and significance of a condition under which a choice is made change when the choice is delegated to a planner. It is then *inappropriate* to treat the condition as a characteristic of the objects among which the *planner* is choosing. Instead, it necessarily becomes an ancillary condition.

Consider the example of time inconsistency discussed in the introduction: the time at which a choice is made does not necessarily hold the same significance for the individual's welfare when a decision is delegated to a planner, as when the individual makes the decision himself. We can, of course, include the time of choice as a characteristic of the chosen object: when choosing between x and y at time t, the individual actually chooses between "x chosen by the individual at time t" and "y chosen by the individual at time t"; likewise, when choosing between x and y at time $t - 1$, the individual actually chooses between "x chosen by the individual at time $t - 1$" and "y chosen by the individual at time $t - 1$." With that formulation, we can then attribute the individual's apparently different choices at t and $t - 1$ to the fact that he is actually choosing from different sets of objects. But in that case, when the decision is delegated, we must describe the objects available to the planner at time t as follows: "x chosen by the planner at time t" and "y chosen by the planner at time t." Since this third set of options is entirely new, a strict interpretation of libertarianism implies that neither the individual's choices at time t nor his choice at time $t - 1$ provides us with any useful guidance. If we wish to construct a theory of welfare based on choice data alone, our only viable alternative is to treat x and y as the choice objects and to acknowledge that the individual's conflicting choices at t and $t - 1$ provide the planner with conflicting guidance. That is precisely what we accomplish by treating the time of the individual's choice as an ancillary condition.

The same reasoning applies to a wide range of conditions. Although we can in principle describe any condition that pertains to the individual as a characteristic of the available objects, we would typically have to describe that characteristic differently once the decision is delegated to the planner. So, for example, "x chosen by the individual after the individual sees the number 47" is different from "x chosen by the planner after the individual sees the number 47," as well as from "x chosen by the planner after the planner sees the number 47." Thus, we would necessarily treat "seeing the number 47" as an ancillary condition.

In some cases, the analyst may also wish to exercise judgment in distinguishing between ancillary conditions and objects' characteristics. Such judgments may be controversial in some situations but relatively uncontroversial in others. For example, there is arguably no plausible connection between certain types of conditions, such as seeing the number 47 immediately prior to choosing, and well-being. According to that judgment, seeing the number 47 is properly classified as an ancillary condition. Conceivably, in some cases the analyst's judgment could be informed by evidence from psychology or neuroscience, but the foundations for drawing pertinent inferences from such evidence remain unclear.

Within our framework, the exercise of judgment in drawing the line between ancillary conditions and objects' characteristics is analogous to the problem of identifying the arguments of an "experienced utility" function in the more standard approach to behavioral welfare analysis. Despite that similarity, there are some important differences between our framework and the experienced utility approach. First, within our framework, choice remains the preeminent guide to welfare; one is not free to invent an experienced utility function that is at odds with behavior. Second, our framework allows for ambiguous welfare comparisons where choice data conflict; in contrast, an experienced utility function admits no ambiguity. It is important to emphasize that the tools we develop here provide a coherent method for conducting choice-based welfare analysis no matter how one draws the line between ancillary conditions and objects' characteristics.

Sometimes, the appropriate definition of the ancillary conditions for a given choice problem can be rather subtle. Consider, for example, the hypothesis that hunger affects choices pertaining to future food consumption, even when the individual knows that her hunger won't persist (e.g., Read and van Leeuwen [1998]). To simplify this discussion, suppose that hunger is determined both by recent consumption and by randomly occurring, transient, and privately observed emotional states. In that case, each $x \in X$ would specify consumption for each emotional state and each point in time.

To capture the effect of hunger on future consumption choices, it may be tempting to think of either hunger, or the emotional states that drive it, as ancillary conditions. It is important to remember, however, that ancillary conditions must be observable in principle; otherwise, we would not be aware that a choice anomaly (i.e., the dependence of choice on the ancillary condition) exists in the first place. With current technology, we can observe *manifestations* of hunger and emotions, but we cannot observe them directly; when we say that someone is hungry, we are merely *interpreting* those manifestations.

To specify the ancillary conditions properly, it helps to think in terms of the experimental conditions that give rise to the choice anomaly. Read and van Leeuwen [1998], for example, presented subjects with different decision trees. For some, the decision tree required them to choose future consumption immediately after lunch; others made this choice in the late afternoon. Because the individual is more likely to be hungry in the late afternoon than immediately after lunch, they *interpret* their experiment as indicating that temporary hunger affects choices of future consumption. However, for our purposes, that interpretation is immaterial. The important point is that the individual can be induced to choose different objects from the same set by modifying the decision tree used to make the selection (in particular, by delaying one component decision, e.g., from 1 P.M. to 4 P.M.). Thus, the *decision tree* is the ancillary condition.

Scope of the Framework

Our framework can incorporate nonstandard behavioral patterns in four separate ways. First, as discussed above, it allows for the influence of ancillary conditions on choice. Standard economics proceeds from the assumption that choice is invariant with respect to ancillary conditions. Positive behavioral economics challenges this basic premise. Documentation of a behavioral anomaly usually involves identifying some SCS, X, along with two ancillary conditions, d' and d'', for which there is evidence that $C(X, d') \neq C(X, d'')$. This is sometimes called a *preference reversal*, but in the interests of greater precision we will call it a *choice reversal*.

Second, our framework does not impose any choice axiom analogous to weak congruence. Hence, it allows for choice reversals based on "irrelevant alternatives," as well as for intransitivities. For example, even when ancillary conditions are irrelevant, we might still have $C(\{x, y\}) = \{x\}$, $C(\{y, z\}) = \{y\}$, and $C(\{x, z\}) = \{z\}$.

Third, our framework subsumes the possibility that people can make choices from opportunity sets that are not compact. For example, suppose we ask an individual to choose a dollar prize from the interval $[0, 100)$. This set does not lie in the domain of a standard choice correspondence. And yet, one can easily imagine someone making a choice from this set; he might be willing to choose any element of [99.99, 100), on the grounds that any such payoff is good enough. In that case, we would have $C([0, 100)) = [99.99, 100)$.

Fourth, we can interpret a choice object $x \in \mathbb{X}$ more broadly than in the standard framework. For example, if x is a lottery, we might want to allow for the possibility that anticipation is welfare relevant. In that case, the description of x would include information concerning the point in time at which uncertainty is resolved, as in Caplin and Leahy [2001].

More on Positive Versus Normative Analysis

In this chapter, we are concerned with normative analysis. We draw the same distinction between positive and normative analysis discussed as above, in the context of the standard model. In particular, we assume that choice data are available for some subset of the environments of interest, $\mathcal{G}^D \subset \mathcal{G}$. The objective of positive economic analysis is to extend the choice correspondence C from observations on $\mathcal{G}^D$ to the entire set $\mathcal{G}$. As in standard economics, this may be accomplished by defining preferences over some appropriately defined set of objects, estimating these preferences using choice data drawn from sets in $\mathcal{G}^D$, and then using those estimated preferences to infer choices for GCSs in $\mathcal{G} \backslash \mathcal{G}^D$. However, a behavioral economist might also use other positive tools, such as models of choice algorithms, neural processes, or rules of thumb.

In conducting choice-based normative analysis, we take as given the individual's choice correspondence, C, defined on $\mathcal{G}$ rather than $\mathcal{G}^D$. The particular model used to extend C—whether it involves utility maximization or a decision algorithm—is irrelevant; for choice-based normative analysis, only C matters. Preferences and utility functions, which may (or may not) be used to extend the choice correspondence, are thus positive tools, not normative tools, just as in the standard framework. These constructs cannot meaningfully reconcile choice inconsistencies; they can only reiterate the information contained in the extended choice correspondence C (both the observed choices and the inferred choices). Thus, one cannot resolve normative puzzles by identifying classes of preferences that rationalize apparently inconsistent choices.[4]

Individual Welfare

In this section, we propose a general approach for extending standard choice-theoretic welfare analysis to situations in which individuals make "anomalous" choices of the various types commonly identified in behavioral research. We begin by introducing two closely related binary relations, which will provide the basis for evaluating an individual's welfare.

Individual Welfare Relations

Sometimes, welfare analysis involves the identification of an individual's "best" alternative (e.g., when solving an optimal tax problem with a representative consumer). More often, however, it requires us to judge whether one alternative represents an *improvement* over another, even when the new alternative is not necessarily the best one. Identifying improvements is central both to the measurement of changes in individual welfare and to welfare analysis in settings with many people (both discussed above). It is also equivalent to the construction of a binary relation, call it R, where xRy means that x improves upon y. Accordingly, behavioral welfare analysis requires a binary relation analogous to revealed preference.

What is the appropriate generalization of the standard welfare relation, R? While there is a tendency in standard economics to define R according to expression 7.1, that definition implicitly invokes the axiom of weak congruence, which assures that choices are consistent across different sets. To make the implications of that axiom explicit, it is useful to restate the standard definition of R as follows:

$$xRy \text{ iff, for all } X \in \mathcal{X} \text{ with } x, y \in X, y \in C(X) \text{ implies } x \in C(X) \tag{7.4}$$

Similarly, we can define P, the asymmetric component of R, as follows:

$$xPy \text{ iff, for all } X \in \mathcal{X} \text{ with } x, y \in X, \text{ we have } y \notin C(X) \tag{7.5}$$

These alternative definitions of weak and strict revealed preference immediately suggest two natural generalizations. The first involves a straightforward generalization of weak revealed preference, as defined in relation (7.4):

$$xR'y \text{ iff, for all } (X, d) \in \mathcal{G} \text{ such that } x, y \in X, y \in C(X, d) \text{ implies } x \in C(X, d)$$

In other words, for any $x, y \in \mathbb{X}$, we say that $xR'y$ if, whenever x and y are available, y is never chosen unless x is as well.

As usual, we can define the symmetric and asymmetric components of R'. We say that $xP'y$ if $xR'y$ and $\sim yR'x$. The statement "$xP'y$" means that, whenever x and y are available, sometimes x is chosen but not y, and otherwise either both or neither are chosen. Likewise, we can define $xI'y$ as $xR'y$ and $yR'x$. The statement "$xI'y$" means that, whenever x is chosen, so is y, and vice versa.

The relation P' generalizes the usual notion of strict revealed preference. However, within our framework, there is a more natural (and ultimately more useful) generalization of relation 7.5. Specifically:

xP^*y iff, for all $(X, d) \in \mathcal{G}$ such that $x, y \in X$, we have $y \notin C(X, d)$

In other words, for any $x, y \in \mathbb{X}$, we say that xP^*y iff, whenever x and y are available, y is never chosen. Corresponding to P^*, there is an alternative notion of weak revealed preference:

xR^*y iff, for some $(X, d) \in \mathcal{G}$ such that $x, y \in X$, we have $x \in C(X, d)$

The statement "xR^*y" means that, for any $x, y \in \mathbb{X}$, there is *some* GCS for which x and y are available and x is chosen. It is easy to check that P^* is the asymmetric component of R^*; that is, xR^*y and $\sim yR^*x$ imply xP^*y. Similarly, we can define the symmetric component of R^* as follows: xI^*y iff xR^*y and yR^*x. The statement "xI^*y" means that there is at least one GCS for which x and y are available for which x is chosen, and at least one such GCS for which y is chosen. We note that Rubinstein and Salant (chapter 5) have separately proposed a binary relation that is related to P' and P^*.[5]

How are R', P', and I' related to R^*, P^*, and I^*? We say that a binary relation A is *weakly coarser* than another relation B if xAy implies xBy. When A is weakly coarser than B, we say that B is *weakly finer* than A. It is easy to check that P^* is weakly coarser than P', that R' is weakly coarser than R^*, and that I' is weakly coarser than I^*.

R', P', and I' are more faithful to the standard notion of weak revealed preference, while R^*, P^*, and I^* are more faithful to the standard notion of strict revealed preference. Which of these two generalizations is most useful? Intuitively, since we are ultimately interested in identifying *improvements*, faithfulness to strict revealed preference may prove more important. However, the choice between these orderings should ultimately rest on their formal properties.

We begin with completeness. The relation R^* is obviously complete: for any $x, y \in \mathbb{X}$, we know that $\{x, y\} \in \mathcal{X}$, and the individual must choose either x or y from any $G = (\{x, y\}, d)$. In contrast, R' need not be complete, as illustrated by Example 7.1.

Example 7.1.

If $C(\{x, y\}, d') = \{x\}$ and $C(\{x, y\}, d'') = \{y\}$, then we have *neither $xR'y$ nor $yR'x$*, so R' is incomplete.

Without further structure, R', P', R^*, and P^* need not be transitive; example 7.2a shows shows that both P' and R' need not be transitive; example 7.2b makes the same point with respect to R^*. Example 7.3, presented later for another purpose, shows that transitivity can also fail for P^*.

Example 7.2a.

Suppose that $\mathcal{G} = \{X_1, X_2, X_3, X_4\}$ with $X_1 = \{a, b\}$, $X_2 = \{b, c\}$, $X_3 = \{a, c\}$, and $X_4 = \{a, b, c\}$ (there are no ancillary conditions). Suppose also that $C(\{a, b\}) = \{a\}$, $C(\{b, c\}) = \{b\}$, $C(\{a, c\}) = \{c\}$, and $C(\{a, b, c\}) = \{a, b, c\}$. Then $aP'bP'cP'a$. Thus, $aP'b$ and $bP'c$, but $\sim aR'c$.

Example 7.2b.

Suppose that $\mathcal{G} = \{X_1, X_2, X_3, X_4\}$ with $X_1 = \{a, b\}$, $X_2 = \{b, c\}$, $X_3 = \{a, c\}$, and $X_4 = \{a, b, c\}$ (there are no ancillary conditions). Suppose also that $C(\{a, b\}) = \{a\}$, $C(\{b, c\}) = \{b\}$, $C(\{a, c\}) = \{c\}$, and $C(\{a, b, c\}) = \{c\}$. Then aR^*b and bR^*c, but $\sim aR^*c$.

Fortunately, to conduct useful welfare analysis—in particular, to identify maximal elements of arbitrary sets, and to measure improvements—one does not necessarily require transitivity. Our first main result establishes that there cannot be a cycle involving R', the most natural generalization of weak revealed preferences, if even one of the links involves P^*, the most natural generalization of strict revealed preference. In other words, it generalizes the standard property that, if $x_1 R x_2 \ldots R x_N$ with $x_i P x_{i+1}$ for some i, then it is not the case that $x_N R x_1$.

Theorem 7.1.

Consider any $x_1, \ldots, x_N$ such that $x_i R' x_{i+1}$ for $i = 1, \ldots, N - 1$, with $x_k P^* x_{k+1}$ for some k. Then $\sim x_N R' x_1$.

This result has an immediate and important corollary:

Corollary 7.1.

P^* is acyclic. That is, for any $x_1, \ldots, x_N$ such that $x_i P^* x_{i+1}$ for $i = 1, \ldots, N - 1$, we have $\sim x_N P^* x_1$.

Acyclicity is weaker than transitivity, but in most contexts it suffices to guarantee the existence of maximal elements.

It is worth emphasizing that theorem 7.1 holds under extremely weak assumptions; we require only that choice is well defined for all finite sets of alternatives. Regardless of how poorly behaved the choice correspondence C might be, the binary relations R' and P^* are nevertheless well behaved in the sense of theorem 7.1.

Individual Welfare Optima

Both P' and P^* capture the notion of a welfare improvement, but P^* leads to a more demanding notion than P'. Accordingly, we will say that is possible to *strictly* *improve* upon a choice $x \in X$ if there exists $y \in X$ such that yP^*x; in other words, there is an alternative that is unambiguously chosen over x. We will say that it is possible to *weakly improve* upon a choice $x \in X$ if there exists $y \in X$ such that $yP'x$; in other words, there is an alternative that is sometimes chosen over x, and that x is never chosen over (except in the sense that both could be chosen).

Our two different notions of welfare improvements lead to two separate concepts of individual welfare optima. When a strict improvement is impossible, we say that x is a *weak individual welfare optimum*. In contrast, when a weak improvement is impossible, we say that x is a *strict individual welfare optimum*.

When is $x \in X$ an individual welfare optimum? The following simple observations address this question:

Observation 7.1.

If $x \in C(X, d)$ for some $(X, d) \in \mathcal{G}$, then x is a weak individual welfare optimum in X. If x is the unique element of $C(X, d)$, then x is a strict welfare optimum in X.

This first observation assures us that our notions of individual welfare optima respect the most obvious implication of libertarian deference to voluntary choice: any action voluntarily chosen from a set X under some ancillary condition is a weak individual welfare optimum within X. Moreover, any action that the individual uniquely chooses from X under some condition is a strict individual welfare optimum within X.

As a general matter, alternatives chosen from X need not be the only individual welfare optima within X. Observation 7.2 characterizes the set of individual welfare optima more precisely:

Observation 7.2.

An alternative x is a weak individual welfare optimum in X if and only if for each $y \in X$ (other than x), there is some GCS for which x is chosen with y available (y may be chosen as well). Moreover, x is a strict individual welfare optimum in X if and only if for each $y \in X$ (other than x), either x is chosen and y is not for some GCS with y available, or there is no GCS for which y is chosen and x is not with x available.

According to observation 7.2, some alternative x may be an individual welfare optimum for the set X even though there is no ancillary condition d under which $x \in C(X, d)$ (see example 7.5 below). Note, however, that this is still consistent with the spirit of the libertarian principle: x is chosen over every $y \in X$ in *some* circumstances, though not necessarily ones involving choices from X. In contrast, an alternative x that is *never* chosen over some alternative y in the set X cannot be an individual welfare optimum in X.

Example 7.3 below illustrates why it may be unreasonable to exclude the type of individual welfare optima described in the preceding paragraph. (See further below for another more formal argument.) Suppose a subject chooses a free sample of strawberry jam when only two other flavors are available, but feels overwhelmed and elects not to receive a free sample when 30 flavors (including strawberry) are available. Since the individual might not want the planner to act overwhelmed when choosing on her behalf, it is important to allow for the possibility that the planner should pick strawberry jam on her behalf even when 30 alternatives are available. Similar concerns would arise whenever thinking about X causes the individual to experience feelings (e.g., temptation) that affect her choice from X, and that vanish when the decision is delegated to a planner. Since we are confining ourselves at this juncture to choice evidence, we do not take a position as to whether these considerations are present; rather, we avoid adopting a notion of individual welfare optima that assumes away such possibilities.

Notice that observation 7.1 guarantees the existence of weak welfare optima (but not of strict welfare optima). Thus, the existence of a solution to the planner's policy problem is guaranteed even in situations where the individuals make conflicting choices across ancillary conditions.

The fact that we have established existence without making any additional assumptions, for example, related to continuity and compactness, may at first seem confusing, but this is simply a matter of how we have posed the question. Here, we have *assumed* that the choice function is well defined over the set $\mathcal{G}$—this is treated as data. Standard existence issues arise when the choice function is built up from other components. The following two examples clarify these issues.

Example 7.3.

Suppose that $\mathcal{G} = \{X_1, X_2, X_3, X_4\}$ with $X_1 = \{a, b\}$, $X_2 = \{b, c\}$, $X_3 = \{a, c\}$, and $X_4 = \{a, b, c\}$ (there are no ancillary conditions). Imagine that the individual chooses a from X_1, b from X_2, c from X_3, and a from X_4. In this case, we have aP^*b and bP^*c; in contrast, we can only say that aI^*c. So, despite the intransitivity of choice between the sets X_1, X_2, and X_3, the option a is nevertheless a strict welfare optimum in X_4, and neither b nor c is a weak welfare optimum. Note that a is also a strict welfare optimum in X_1 (b is not a weak optimum), b is a strict welfare optimum in X_2 (c is not a weak optimum), and both a and c are strict welfare optima in X_3 (a survives because it is chosen over c in X_4, which makes a and c not comparable under P^*).

Example 7.4.

Consider the same choice data as in example 7.3, but suppose we limit attention to $\mathcal{G}' = \{X_1, X_2, X_3\}$. In this case we have that $aP^*bP^*cP^*a$. Here, the intransitivity is apparent; P^* is cyclic because the assumption leading to Theorem 1 is violated ($\mathcal{G}'$ does not contain all finite sets). Even so, individual welfare optima exist within every set that falls within the restricted domain: a is a strict welfare optimum in X_1, b is a strict welfare optimum in X_2, and c is a strict welfare optimum in X_3. Naturally, if we are interested in creating a preference or utility representation based on the data contained in $\mathcal{G}'$ in order to project the individual's choice from X_4, the intransitivity would pose a difficulty. And if we try to make a welfare judgement concerning X_4 without knowing (either directly or through a positive model) what the individual would choose in X_4, we encounter the same problem—a, b, and c are all strictly improvable, so there is no welfare optimum. But once we know what the individual would do in X_4 (either directly or by extrapolating from a reliable positive model), the existence problem for X_4 vanishes. It is therefore important to emphasize again that our interest here is in forming welfare judgements from individual choices, not in the problem of representing or extending those choices to unobserved domains. We are in effect assuming that an adequate positive model of behavior already exists, and we are asking how normative analysis should proceed.

Depending on the nature and extent of choice conflicts, the welfare criteria proposed here may not be particularly discerning. Example 7.5 provides an illustration:

Example 7.5.

Suppose that $\mathcal{X} = \{X_1, X_2, X_3, X_4\}$ (defined in example 7.4), and that $\mathcal{G} = \mathcal{X} \times \{d, d'\}$. Suppose that, with ancillary condition d, b is never chosen when a is available, and c is never chosen. However, with ancillary condition d', b is never chosen with c available, and a is never chosen. Then no alternatives are comparable with P' or P^*, and the set of individual welfare optima (weak and strict) in X_i is simply X_i, for $i = 1, 2, 3, 4$.

In Example 7.5, two ancillary conditions produce diametrically opposed choice patterns. In most practical situations, the amount of choice conflict, and hence the sets of individual welfare optima, will be smaller. Generally, with greater choice conflict, it becomes more difficult to identify alternatives that constitute unambiguous welfare improvements, so the set of individual welfare optima expands.

Why This Approach?

It is natural to wonder whether there is some other, potentially more attractive approach to formulating a choice-theoretic foundation for behavioral welfare analysis. In this section, we provide further formal justifications for our approach.

Consider the following natural alternative to our approach: classify x as an individual welfare optimum for X iff there is some ancillary condition for which the individual is willing to choose x from X. This alternative approach would appear to adhere more closely to the libertarian principle than does our approach. However, it does not allow us to determine whether a change from one element of X to another is an *improvement*, except in cases where either the initial or final element in the comparison is one that the individual would choose from X. As explained at the outset of this section, for that purpose we require a binary relation that identifies improvements. Accordingly, our object in this section is determine whether there exists a general method of constructing an asymmetric binary welfare relation, Q, that is more faithful to the libertarian principle than the relations proposed above.

We will say that Q is an *inclusive libertarian relation* for a choice correspondence C if, for all X, the maximal elements under Q include all of the elements the individual would choose from X for some ancillary condition. We will say that Q is an *exclusive libertarian relation* for a choice correspondence C if, for all X, the maximal elements under Q are contained in the set of elements the individual would choose from X for some ancillary condition. Finally, we will say that Q is a *libertarian relation* for C if it is both inclusive and exclusive—that is, if the maximal elements under Q always coincide exactly with the set of elements the individual would choose from X for some ancillary condition.[6]

We have already demonstrated that P^* is always an inclusive libertarian relation (observation 7.1). We have also argued, by way of example, that there are good reasons to treat the "extra" maximal elements under P^*—the ones not chosen from the set of interest for any ancillary condition—as individual welfare optima. However, the following result shows that there is an even more compelling reason not to search for a general procedure that generates either a libertarian relation, or an exclusive libertarian relation, for all choice correspondences: none exists.

Theorem 7.2.

For some choice correspondences, exclusive libertarian relations do not exist.

Theorem 7.2 implies that, if we want to derive a completely general procedure for expressing libertarianism, we must confine attention to inclusive libertarian relations. There are, of course, inclusive libertarian relations other than P^*. For example, the null relation, R^{Null} ($\sim xR^{\text{Null}}y$ for all $x, y \in \mathbb{X}$), falls into this category; for any set X, the maximal elements under R^{Null} consist of X, which of course includes all of the chosen elements. Yet R^{Null} is far less discerning, and further from the libertarian principle, than P^*. In fact, one can prove the following result:

Theorem 7.3.

Consider any choice correspondence C, and any inclusive libertarian relation
$Q \neq P^*$. *Then P^* is finer than Q.*

It follows that for all choice correspondences C and choice sets X, the set of maximal elements in X under P^* is (weakly) smaller than the maximal elements in X under Q. Thus, P^* is *always* the most discriminating inclusive libertarian relation.

Relation to Multi-Self Pareto Optima

Our notion of an individual welfare optimum is related to the idea of a multi-self Pareto optimum, which has been used as a welfare criterion in a number of behavioral studies [see, e.g., Laibson, Repetto, and Tobacman, 1998; Bhattacharya and Lakdawalla, 2004]. Suppose in particular that the set of GCSs is the Cartesian product of the set of SCSs and a set of ancillary conditions (i.e., $\mathcal{G} = \mathcal{X} \times D$, where $d \in D$); in that case, we say that $\mathcal{G}$ is *rectangular*. Imagine also that, for each $d \in D$, the choice correspondence is consistent with the maximization of a well-behaved preference ranking R_d. If one imagines that each ancillary condition activates a different "self," then one can conduct welfare analysis by examining multi-self Pareto optima.

Observation 7.3.

Under the stated conditions, a weak multi-self Pareto optimum corresponds to a weak individual welfare optimum (as we have defined it), and a strict multi-self Pareto optimum corresponds to a strict individual welfare optimum.

The multi-self Pareto criterion has been used primarily in the literature on quasi-hyperbolic discounting, where it is applied to an individual's many time-dated "selves" (as in the studies identified above). Ironically, our framework does *not* justify the multi-self Pareto criterion for quasi-hyperbolic consumers, because $\mathcal{G}$ is not rectangular (see below).

In contrast, our framework does justify the use of the multi-self Pareto criterion for cases of "coherent arbitrariness," such as those studied by Ariely, Loewenstein, and Prelec [2003]. In that context, d is some psychological anchor. Although the anchor affects behavior, the individual conforms to standard consumer theory for any fixed anchor. To our knowledge, the multi-self Pareto criterion has not been proposed as a natural welfare standard in the presence of coherent arbitrariness.

For the narrow settings that are consistent with the assumptions described at the beginning of this section, one can view our approach as a way to justify the multi-self Pareto criterion without relying on untested and questionable psychological assumptions. Note, however, that while our framework justifies the application of the multi-self Pareto criterion in such contexts, the justification is choice-theoretic, not psychological. Furthermore, our approach is more general in that it does not require the GCS to be rectangular, nor the choice correspondence within each ancillary condition to be well behaved.

Some Applications

In this section, we examine the implications of our framework for some particular behavioral anomalies.

Coherent Arbitrariness

Let's consider a case in which an individual consumes two goods, y and z. Suppose that positive analysis delivers the following utility representation:

$$U(y, z \mid d) = u(y) + dv(z),$$

with u and v strictly increasing, differentiable, and strictly concave. Notice that the ancillary condition, $d \in [d_L, d_H]$, which we interpret here as an irrelevant signal, simply shifts the weight on "utility" from z to y. Given any particular signal, the individual behaves coherently, but his behavior is arbitrary in the sense that it depends on the signal. This type of behavior (coherent arbitrariness) has been documented by Ariely, Loewenstein, and Prelec [2003] and has led some to question the practice of basing welfare judgments on revealed preference.

Our normative framework easily accommodates this positive model of behavior. In fact, since $\mathcal{G}$ is rectangular, our welfare criterion is equivalent to the multi-self Pareto criterion, where each d indexes a different "self."

We know that, if $u(y') + dv(z') \geq u(y'') + dv(z'')$ for all $d \in [d_L, d_H]$, then the individual will never be willing to choose (y'', z'') without also being willing to choose (y', z') when both are available. We can rewrite that inequality as follows:

$$u(y') - u(y'') \geq d[v(z'') - v(z')] \tag{7.6}$$

Notice that, if relation 7.6 holds for d_L and d_H, then it holds for all $d \in [d_L, d_H]$. Therefore,

$$(y', z')R'(y'', z'') \text{ iff } u(y') + dv(z') \geq u(y'') + dv(z'') \text{ for all } d \in \{d_L, d_H\} \tag{7.7}$$

Replacing the weak inequality with a strict inequality, we obtain the definition of both P' and P^*. Replacing "for all" with "for any," we obtain the definition of R^*.

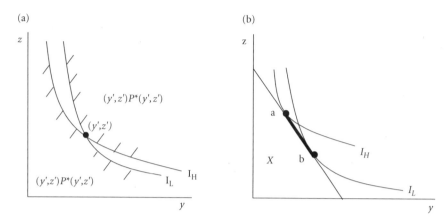

Figure 7.1. Coherent arbitrariness

For a graphical illustration, see figure 7.1(a). We have drawn two "indifference curves" through the bundle (y', z'), one for d_L (labelled I_L) and one for d_H (labeled I_H). For all bundles (y'', z'') lying below both indifference curves, we have $(y', z')P^*(y'', z'')$; this is the analog of a lower contour set. Conversely, for all bundles (y'', z'') lying above both indifference curves, we have $(y'', z'')P^*(y', z')$; this is the analog of an upper contour set. For all bundles (y'', z'') lying between the two indifference curves, we have *neither* $(y', z')R'(y'', z'')$ nor $(y'', z'')R'(y', z')$; however, $(y', z')I^*(y'', z'')$.

Now consider a standard budget constraint, $X = \{(y, z) \mid y + pz \leq M\}$, where y is the numeraire, p is the price of z, and M is income. The set X corresponds to the triangle in figure 7.1(b). The individual's choice from this set clearly depends on the ancillary condition d. In particular, she chooses bundle a when the ancillary condition is d_H, and bundle b when the ancillary condition is d_L. Each of the points on the darkened segment of the budget line between bundles a and b is uniquely chosen for some $d \in [d_L, d_H]$, so all of these bundles are strict individual welfare optima. In this case, there are no other welfare optima, weak or strict. Consider any other bundle (y', z') on or below the budget line; if it lies to the northwest of a, then $aP^*(y', z')$; if it lies to the southwest of b, then $bP^*(y', z')$; and if it lies anywhere else below the budget line, then $xP^*(y', z')$ for some x containing more of both goods than (y', z').

Dynamic Inconsistency

The β, δ model of hyperbolic discounting popularized by Laibson [1997] and O'Donoghue and Rabin [1999] has come into widespread use among economists. When our framework is applied to this positive model, what welfare criterion emerges? Here we focus on decisions involving the allocation of consumption over three periods; see Bernheim and Rangel [2007] for an analysis of the general multiperiod case.

The consumer's task is to choose a consumption vector, $c = (c_1, c_2, c_3)$, where c_t denotes the level of consumption at time t. The positive model functions as follows. At $t = 1$, all discretion is resolved to maximize the function

$$U_1(c) = u(c_1) + \beta[\delta u(c_2) + \delta^2 u(c_3)],$$

assuming perfect foresight with respect to continuation decisions (if any). At $t = 2$, all remaining discretion is resolved to maximize the function

$$U_2(c) = u(c_2) + \beta \delta u(c_3),$$

again assuming perfect foresight with respect to continuation decisions (if any). Finally, at $t = 3$, all remaining discretion is resolved to maximize the function

$$U_3(c) = u(c_3).$$

We assume that $0 < \beta \leq 1$ and $0 < \delta \leq 1$. We also assume that $u(0)$ is finite [and, for convenience, we normalize $u(0) = 0$].[7]

To conduct normative analysis, we must recast this positive model as a correspondence from GCSs into consumption vectors. Here, $\mathbb{X}$ is a set of intertemporal consumption bundles; an intertemporal budget constraint gives rise to a particular $X \subset \mathbb{X}$. An ancillary condition describes the decision tree used to choose the consumption vector. Clearly, c_1 must be chosen at $t = 1$. However, a decision at $t = 1$ may determine the constraint set encountered at $t = 2$. Likewise, any remaining discretion concerning c_2 must be resolved at $t = 2$; in addition, a decision at $t = 2$ may determine the constraint set encountered at $t = 3$. Finally, any remaining discretion concerning c_3 must be resolved at $t = 3$. We allow for all conceivable decision trees. Note that, in this instance, $\mathcal{G}$ is not rectangular.

Next we define the function

$$W(c) = u(c_1) + \beta \delta u(c_2) + (\beta \delta)^2 u(c_3).$$

This represents lifetime discounted utility using $\beta \delta$ as the time-consistent discount factor. Given our normalization $[u(0) = 0]$, it follows immediately that $W(c) < U_1(c)$ iff $c_3 > 0$, and $W(c) = U_1(c)$ iff $c_3 = 0$. In particular, it is never the case that $W(c) > U_1(c)$.

For this simple model, to determine whether c is unambiguously chosen over c' (and hence whether the welfare relation ranks c above c'), we compare the lifetime discounted utility associated with c using $\beta \delta$ as a time-consistent discount factor, with the "decision utility" associated with c' at $t = 1$. Formally:

Theorem 7.4.

   (i) $cR'c'$ *iff* $W(c) \geq U_1(c')$,

   (ii) cR^*c' *iff* $U_1(c) \geq W(c')$,

   (iii) cP^*c' *iff* $W(c) > U_1(c')$,

   (iv) For c, c' *with* c_3; $c_3' > 0$, $cP'c'$ *iff* $cR'c'$,

   (v) R', P', *and* P^* *are transitive.*

Using this result, we can easily characterize the set of individual welfare optima within X. For any X, let

$$W^*(X) = \max_{c \in X} W(c).$$

Then c is a weak individual welfare optimum in X iff $U_1(c) \geq W^*(X)$—in other words, if the "decision utility" that c provides at $t = 1$ is at least as large as the highest available discounted utility, using $\beta\delta$ as a time-consistent discount factor. Given that $W(c) \leq U_1(c)$ for all c, we know that $W^*(c) \leq \max_{c \in X} U_1(c)$, so the set of weak individual welfare optima is plainly nonempty (as we already knew it must be).

Notice that, for all c, we have $\lim_{\beta \to 1}[W(c) - U_1(c)] = 0$. Accordingly, as the degree of dynamic inconsistency shrinks, our welfare criterion converges to the standard criterion. In contrast, the same statement does *not* hold for the multi-self Pareto criterion, as that criterion is usually formulated. The reason is that, regardless of β, each "self" is assumed to care only about current and future consumption. Thus, consuming everything in the final period is always a multi-self Pareto optimum, even when $\beta = 1$.

The Standard Framework as a Limiting Case

Clearly, our framework for welfare analysis subsumes the standard framework; when the choice correspondence satisfies standard axioms, the generalized individual welfare relations coincide with revealed preference. Our framework is a natural generalization of the standard welfare framework in another important sense: when behavioral departures from the standard model are small, our welfare criterion is close to the standard criterion. This conclusion, which plainly holds in the applications considered above, is proven with generality in Bernheim and Rangel [2007].

The preceding conclusion is important for two reasons. First, it offers a formal justification for using the standard welfare framework (as an approximation) when choice anomalies are known to be small. Many economists currently adopt the premise that anomalies are small when using the standard framework; they view this as a justification both for standard positive analysis and for standard normative analysis. In the case of positive analysis, their justification is clear: if we compare the actual choices to predictions generated from a standard positive model and discover that they are close to each other, we can conclude that the model involves little error. However, in the case of normative analysis, their justification for the standard approach is problematic. To conclude that the standard normative criterion is roughly correct in a setting with choice anomalies, we would need to compare it to the correct criterion. But if we don't know the correct criteria for such settings, then we have no benchmark against which to gauge the performance of the standard criterion. As a result, we cannot measure the distance between the standard normative criterion and the correct criterion, even when choice anomalies are tiny. Our framework overcomes this problem by providing welfare criteria for all situations, including those with choice anomalies. One can then ask whether the criterion changes much if one ignores the anomalies. In this way, our analysis formalizes the intuition that a little bit of positive falsification is unimportant from a *normative* perspective.

Second, our limiting results imply that the debate over the significance of choice anomalies need not be resolved prior to adopting a framework for welfare analysis. If our framework is adopted and the anomalies ultimately prove to be small, one will obtain virtually the same answer as with the standard framework. (For the reasons described above, the same statement does not hold for the multi-self Pareto criterion.)

Tools for Applied Welfare Analysis

The concepts of compensating variation and equivalent variation are central to applied welfare economics. In this section we show that they have natural counterparts within our framework. Here, we focus on compensating variation; the treatment of equivalent variation is analogous. We illustrate how, under more restrictive assumptions, the compensating variation of a price change corresponds to an analog of consumer surplus.

Compensating Variation

Let's assume that the individual's SCS, $X(\alpha, m)$, depends on a vector of environmental parameters, α, and a monetary transfer, m. Let α_0 be the initial parameter vector, d_0 the initial ancillary conditions, and $(X(\alpha_0, 0), d_0)$ the initial GCS. We will consider a change in parameters to α_1, coupled with a change in ancillary conditions to d_1, as well as a monetary transfer m. We write the new GCS as $(X(\alpha_1, m), d_1)$. This setting will allow us to evaluate compensating variations for fixed changes in prices, ancillary conditions, or both.[8]

Within the standard economic framework, the compensating variation is the smallest value of m such that for any $x \in C[X(\alpha_0, 0)]$ and $y \in C[X(\alpha_1, m)]$, the individual would be willing to choose y in a binary comparison with x [i.e., $y \in C(\{x, y\})$, or equivalently, yRx].

In extending this definition to our framework, we encounter three ambiguities. The first arises when the individual is willing to choose more than one alternative in either the initial GCS $[X(\alpha_0, 0), d_0]$ or in the final GCS $[X(\alpha_1, m), d_1]$. In the standard framework, this causes no difficulty because the individual must be indifferent among all alternatives chosen from the same set. However, within our framework, these alternatives may fare differently in comparison to other alternatives. Here, we handle this ambiguity by insisting that compensation is adequate for all pairs of outcomes that might be chosen voluntarily from the initial and final sets.

The second dimension of ambiguity arises from the possibility that additional compensation could in principle reduce an individual's welfare. In the standard framework, if the payment m is adequate to compensate an individual for some change, then any $m' > m$ is also adequate. Without further assumptions, that property need not hold in our framework. Here, we will simplify matters by assuming that it does hold; see Bernheim and Rangel [2007] for an analysis of the more general case.

The third dimension of ambiguity concerns the standard of compensation: do we consider compensation sufficient when the new situation (with the compensation) is unambiguously chosen over the old one, or when the old situation is not unambiguously chosen over the new one? This ambiguity is an essential feature of welfare evaluations with inconsistent choice (see example 7.6, below). Accordingly, we define two notions of compensating variation:

Definition 7.1.

CV-A is the level of compensation m^A that solves

$$\inf \left\{ m \mid yP^*x \text{ for all } x \in C[X(\alpha_0, 0), d_0] \text{ and } y \in C[X(\alpha_1, m), d_1] \right\}$$

Definition 7.2.

CV-B is the level of compensation m^B that solves

$$\sup \left\{ m \mid xP^*y \text{ for all } x \in C[X(\alpha_0, 0), d_0] \text{ and } y \in C[X(\alpha_1, m), d_1] \right\}$$

In other words, a level of compensation slightly greater than CV-A guarantees that any alternative selected in the new choice situation (with the compensation) is unambiguously chosen over any alternative selected in the initial situation. Similarly, a level of compensation slightly smaller than CV-B guarantees that any alternative selected in the initial situation is unambiguously chosen over any alternative selected in the new situation (with the compensation).

CV-A and CV-B are well-behaved measures of compensating variation in the following sense: If the individual experiences a sequence of changes, and is adequately compensated for each of these changes in the sense of CV-A, no alternative that he would select from the initial set is unambiguously chosen over any alternative that he would select from the final set.[9] Similarly, if he experiences a sequence of changes and is not adequately compensated for any of them in the sense of CV-B, no alternative that he would select from the final set is unambiguously chosen over any alternative that he would select from the initial set. Both of these conclusions are corollaries of theorem 7.1. However, in contrast to the standard framework, the compensating variations (either CV-As or CV-Bs) associated with each step in a sequence of changes need not be additive.[10] This is not necessarily a serious problem; see Bernheim and Rangel [2007] for further discussion.

Example 7.6.

Let's revisit the application discussed above regarding coherent arbitrariness. Suppose the individual is offered the following degenerate opportunity sets: $X(0, 0) = \{(y_0, z_0)\}$, and $X(1, m) = \{(y_1 + m, z_1)\}$. In other words, changing the environmental parameter α from 0 to 1 shifts the individual from (y_0, z_0) to (y_1, z_1), and compensation is paid in the form of the good y. Figure 7.2 depicts the bundles (y_0, z_0) and (y_1, z_1), as well as the CV-A and CV-B for this change. CV-A is given by the horizontal distance (y_1, z_1) and point a, because

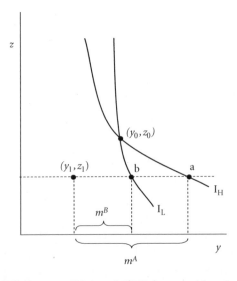

Figure 7.2. CV-A and CV-B for example 7.6

$(y_1 + m^A + \varepsilon, z_1)$ is chosen over (x_0, m_0) for all ancillary conditions and $\varepsilon > 0$. CV-B is given by the horizontal distance between (y_1, z_1) and point b, because (y_0, z_0) is chosen over $(y_1 + m_B - \varepsilon, z_1)$ for all ancillary conditions and $\varepsilon > 0$. Note, however, that for intermediate levels of compensation, $(y_1 + m, z_1)$ is chosen under some ancillary conditions, and (y_0, z_0) is chosen under others. Finally, note that as d_H converges to d_L, both notions of compensating variation converge to the standard notion.

Consumer Surplus

Next we illustrate how, under more restrictive assumptions, the compensating variation of a price change corresponds to an analog of consumer surplus. We continue to study the environment introduced above and revisited in example 7.6. However, we will assume here that positive analysis delivers the following more restrictive utility representation (which involves no income effects, so that Marshallian consumer surplus would be valid in the standard framework):

$$U(y, z \mid d) = y + dv(z)$$

Thus, for any given d, the inverse demand curve for z is given by $p = dv'(z)$, where p is the relative price of z.

Let M denote the consumer's initial income. Consider an increase in the price of z from p_0 to p_1 while holding the ancillary conditions constant, $d_0 = d_1$. Let z_0 denote the amount of z purchased at price p_0, and let z_1 denote the amount purchased at price p_1; given our assumptions, $z_0 > z_1$. Since there are no income effects, z_1 will not change as the individual is compensated (holding the ancillary condition fixed).

Through straightforward calculations, one can obtain the following expression for CV-A:

$$m^A = [p_1 - p_0]z_1 + \int_{z_1}^{z_0} [d_H v'(z) - p_0] dz$$

The first term measures the extra amount the consumer ends up paying for the first z_1 units. The second term is the area under the demand curve and above a horizontal line at p_0, when d_H is the ancillary condition. Figure 7.3(a) provides a graphical representation of CV-A, analogous to the one found in most microeconomics textbooks: it is the sum of the areas labeled A, B, and C.

Similarly, it is easily shown that CV-B is given by

$$m^B = [p_1 - p_0]z_1 + \int_{z_1}^{z_0} [d_L v'(z) - p_0] dz.$$

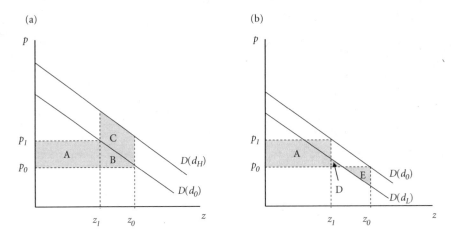

Figure 7.3. CV-A and CV-B for a price change

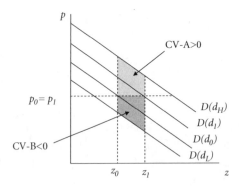

Figure 7.4. CV-A and CV-B for a change in an ancillary condition

Notice that this is the same as the expression for CV-A, except that we use the area under the demand curve associated with d_L, rather than the one associated with d_H. Figure 7.3(b) provides a graphical representation of CV-B: it is the sum of the areas labeled A and D, minus the areas labeled E.

As figure 7.3 illustrates, CV-A and CV-B bracket the conventional measure of consumer surplus that one would obtain using the demand curve associated with the ancillary condition d_0. In addition, as the range of possible ancillary conditions narrows, CV-A and CV-B both converge to standard consumer surplus. This underscores the fact that the standard framework is a special case of the framework considered here. Moreover, it also implies that, when inconsistencies are minor (i.e., $d_H - d_L$ is small), the ambiguity in welfare, as measured by the difference between CV-A and CV-B, is small.

The compensating variation associated with a change in ancillary conditions, from d_0 to $d_1 \neq d_0$, with fixed prices, is calculated in a similar way. For the purpose of illustration, assume that $z_1 > z_0$. Figure 7.4 shows CV-A and CV-B graphically. CV-A, the light gray area between the demand curve for the ancillary condition d_H and a horizontal line drawn at the price of z, is strictly positive. In contrast, CV-B, the dark gray area between a horizontal line drawn at the price of z and the demand curve for the ancillary condition d_L, is strictly negative. Once more, the ambiguity in welfare is minor when the behavioral inconsistencies between d_H and d_L are small.

Welfare Analysis Involving More Than One Individual

In settings with more than one individual, welfare analysis often focuses on the concept of Pareto optimality. In the standard framework, we say that a social alternative $x \in X$ is a Pareto optimum in X if there is no other alternative that all individuals would choose over x. In this section we describe a natural generalization of this concept to settings with behavioral anomalies, and we illustrate its use in establishing the efficiency of competitive market equilibria. For a more comprehensive discussion of these concepts, see Bernheim and Rangel [2007].

Generalized Pareto Optima

Suppose there are N individuals indexed $i = 1, \ldots, N$. Let $\mathbb{X}$ denote the set of all conceivable social choice objects, and let X denote the set of feasible objects. Let C_i be the choice function for individual i, defined over $\mathcal{G}_i$ (where the subscript reflects the possibility that the set of ancillary conditions may differ from individual to individual). These choice functions induce the relations R_i' and P_i^* over $\mathbb{X}$.

We say that x is a *weak generalized Pareto optimum* in X if there exists no $y \in X$ with yP_i^*x for all i. We say that x is a *strict generalized Pareto optimum* in X if there exists no $y \in X$ with $yR_i'x$ for all i, and yP_i^*x for some i.[11]

Since strict individual welfare optima do not always exist, we cannot guarantee the existence of strict generalized Pareto optima with a high degree of generality. However, we can trivially guarantee the existence of a weak generalized Pareto optimum for any set X: simply choose $x \in C_i(X, d)$ for some i and $(X, d) \in \mathcal{G}$ (in which case we have $\sim[yP_i^*x$ for all $y \in X]$).

In the standard framework, there is typically a continuum of Pareto optima that spans the gap between the extreme cases in which the chosen alternative is optimal for some individual. We often represent this continuum by drawing a utility possibility frontier or, in the case of a two-person exchange economy, a contract

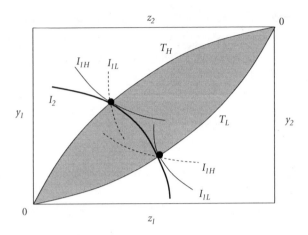

Figure 7.5. The generalized contract curve

curve. Is there also usually a continuum of generalized Pareto optima spanning the gap between the extreme cases described in the preceding paragraph? Example 7.7 answers this question in the context of a two-person exchange economy.

Example 7.7.

Consider a two-person exchange economy involving two goods, y and z. Suppose the choices of consumer 1 are described by the positive model set forth in the discussion above concerning coherent arbitrariness, while consumer 2's choices respect standard axioms. In figure 7.5, the area between the curves labeled T_H (formed by the tangencies between the consumer's indifference curves when consumer 1 faces ancillary condition d_H) and T_L (formed by the tangencies when consumer 1 faces ancillary condition d_L) is the analog of the standard contract curve; it contains all of the weak generalized Pareto optimal allocations. The ambiguities in consumer 1's choices *expand* the set of Pareto optima, which is why the generalized contract curve is thick. Like a standard contract curve, the generalized contract curve runs between the southwest and northeast corners of the Edgeworth box, so there are many intermediate Pareto optima. If the behavioral effects of the ancillary conditions were smaller, the generalized contract curve would be thinner; in the limit, it would converge to a standard contract curve. Thus, the standard framework once again emerges as a limiting case of our framework, in which behavioral anomalies become vanishingly small.

More generally, in standard settings (with continuous preferences and a compact set of social alternatives X), one can start with *any* alternative $x \in X$ and find a

Pareto optimum in $\{y \mid yR_i x$ for all $i\}$—for example, by identifying some individual's most preferred alternative within that set. Indeed, by doing so for all $x \in X$, one generates the contract curve. Our next theorem establishes an analogous result for weak generalized Pareto optima.

Theorem 7.5.

For every $x \in X$, the nonempty set $\{y \in X \mid \forall i, \, \sim xP_i^* y\}$ includes at least one weak generalized Pareto optimum in X.

Notice that theorem 7.5 does not require additional assumptions concerning compactness or continuity. Rather, existence follows from the fundamental assumption that the choice correspondence is nonempty over its domain.[12]

The Efficiency of Competitive Equilibria

To illustrate the usefulness of these concepts, in Bernheim and Rangel [2007] we provide a generalization of the First Welfare Theorem. Specifically, we consider a production economy consisting of N consumers, F firms, and K goods. The economy is standard in all respects, except that consumer i's behavior is governed by a general choice correspondence mapping budget sets and ancillary conditions into sets of consumption vectors. We make one simple assumption (akin to nonsatiation) with respect to consumer behavior: if $x^n > w^n$ (where $>$ indicates a strict inequality for every good), then consumer n never chooses w^n when x^n is available.

A *behavioral competitive equilibrium* involves a price vector, $\widehat{\pi} = (\widehat{\pi}^1, \ldots, \widehat{\pi}^K)$, along with a vector of ancillary conditions $\widehat{d} = (\widehat{d}^1, \ldots, \widehat{d}^N)$, that clear all markets. Although behavioral competitive equilibria may not exist, those that do exist are necessarily efficient:

Theorem 7.6.

The allocation in any behavioral competitive equilibrium is a strict generalized Pareto optimum.

It is worth emphasizing that a perfectly competitive equilibrium may be inefficient when judged by a refined welfare relation, after officiating choice conflicts, as described in the next section. This observation alerts us to the fact that, in behavioral economics, choice inconsistencies lead to a new class of potential market failures. It is also possible to demonstrate the inefficiency of market equilibria according to the welfare relations we have proposed in the presence of sufficiently severe but otherwise standard market failures, such as externalities [see Bernheim and Rangel, 2007].

Refining the Welfare Criterion Using Nonchoice Data

We have shown that the individual welfare orderings R', P', R^*, and P^* may not be very discerning in the sense that many alternatives may not be comparable and the set of individual welfare optima may be large. This tends to occur when there are significant conflicts between the choices made under different ancillary conditions.

In this section we consider the possibility that one might refine these relations by altering the data used to construct them, either by adding new choice data, or by deleting data. We also discuss the types of evidence that could be useful in making this type of refinement.

Refinement Strategies

The following simple observation indicates how the addition or deletion of data affects the coarseness of the welfare relation.

> *Observation 7.4.*
>
> Fix $\mathbb{X}$. Consider two generalized choice domains $\mathcal{G}_1$ and $\mathcal{G}_2$ with $\mathcal{G}_1 \subset \mathcal{G}_2$, where $\mathcal{X}_1$ includes all pairs $\{a, b\}$ with $a, b \in \mathbb{X}$. Also consider two associated choice functions C_1 defined on $\mathcal{G}_1$, and C_2 defined on $\mathcal{G}_2$, with $C_1(G) = C_2(G)$ for all $G \in \mathcal{G}_1$. The welfare relations R'_2 and P^*_2 obtained from $(\mathcal{G}_2, C_2)$ are weakly coarser than the welfare relations R'_1 and P^*_1 obtained from $(\mathcal{G}_1, C_1)$.

It follows that the addition of data (i.e., the expansion of $\mathcal{G}$) makes R' and P^* weakly coarser, while the elimination of data (i.e., the reduction of $\mathcal{G}$) makes R' and P^* weakly finer. Intuitively, if choices between two alternatives, x and y, are unambiguous over some domain, they are also unambiguous over a smaller domain. Notice, however, the same principle does not hold for P' or R^*.[13]

The following simple observation indicates how the addition or deletion of data affects the set of individual welfare optima.

> *Observation 7.5.*
>
> Fix $\mathbb{X}$. Consider two generalized choice domains $\mathcal{G}_1$ and $\mathcal{G}_2$ with $\mathcal{G}_1 \subset \mathcal{G}_2$, where $\mathcal{X}_1$ includes all pairs $\{a, b\}$ with $a, b \in \mathbb{X}$. Also consider two associated

choice functions C_1 defined on $\mathcal{G}_1$, and C_2 defined on $\mathcal{G}_2$, with $C_1(G) = C_2(G)$ for all $G \in \mathcal{G}_1$. Consider any $X \in \mathcal{X}_1$.

(a) If $x \in X$ is a weak welfare optimum for X based on $(\mathcal{G}_1, C_1)$, it is also a weak welfare optimum for X based on $(\mathcal{G}_2, C_2)$.

(b) Suppose that $x \in X$ is a strict welfare optimum for X based on $(\mathcal{G}_1, C_1)$, and that there is no $y \in X$ such that xI_1y. Then x is also a strict welfare optimum for X based on $(\mathcal{G}_2, C_2)$.

It follows that the addition of data cannot shrink the set of weak individual welfare optima and can only shrink the set of strict individual welfare optima in very special cases.

Observations 7.4 and 7.5 motivate an agenda involving refinements of the welfare relations considered in this chapter. Our goal is to make our proposed welfare relations more discerning while maintaining libertarian deference to individual choice by *officiating* between apparent choice conflicts. In other words, if there are some GCSs in which x is chosen over y, and some other GCSs in which y is chosen over x, we can look for *objective* criteria that might allow us to disregard some of these GCSs, and thereby refine the initial welfare relations. We can then construct new welfare relations based on the pruned data, which will be weakly finer than the initial ones, and which may contain fewer welfare optima.

Notably, observations 7.4 and 7.5 rule out the possibility of self-officiating—that is, discriminating between apparently conflicting behaviors through "meta-choices." As an illustration, assume there are two GCSs, G_1, $G_2 \in \mathcal{G}$ with $G_1 = (X, d_1)$ and $G_2 = (X, d_2)$, such that the individual chooses x from G_1 and y from G_2. Our object is to determine which behavior the planner should mimic when choosing from X. Instead of letting the planner resolve this based on external criteria, why not let the individual herself resolve it? Suppose we know that the individual, if given a choice between the two choice situations G_1 and G_2, would choose G_1. Doesn't this mean that G_1 provides a better guide for the planner (in which case the planner should select x)? Not necessarily. The choice between G_1 and G_2 is simply another GSC, call it $G_3 = (X, d_3)$, where d_3 indicates that component choices are made in a particular sequence, and under particular conditions. If the individual selects x in G_3, all we have learned is that there is one more ancillary condition, d_3, in which he would choose x. Since choices between generalized choice situations simply create new generalized choice situations, and since the addition of data on decisions in new generalized choice situations does not usefully refine the primary welfare relation, P^*, or the sets of welfare optima, it does not help us resolve the normative ambiguity associated with choice conflicts.

Refinements Based on Imperfect Information Processing

When we say that an individual's standard choice situation is X, we mean that, based on all of the objective information that is available to him, he is actually choosing among elements of X. In standard economics, we use this objective information to reconstruct X, and then infer that he prefers his chosen element to all the unchosen elements of X. But what if he fails to use all of the information available to him, or uses it incorrectly? What if the objective information available to him implies that he is actually choosing from the set X, while in fact he believes he is choosing from some other set, Y? In that case, should a planner nevertheless mimic his choice when evaluating objects from X? Not in our view.

Why would the individual believe himself to be choosing from some set, Y, when in fact, according to the available objective information, he is choosing from the set X? There are many possible reasons. His attention may focus on some small subset of X. His memory may fail to call up facts that relate choices to consequences. He may forecast the consequences of his choices incorrectly. He may have learned from his past experiences more slowly than the objective information would permit.

In principle, if we understand the individual's cognitive processes sufficiently well, we may be able identify his perceived choice set Y and reinterpret the choice as pertaining to the set Y rather than to the set X. We refer to this process as "deconstructing choices." While it may be possible to accomplish this in some instances (see, e.g., Köszegi and Rabin, chapter 8), we suspect that, in most cases, this is beyond the current capabilities of economics, neuroscience, and psychology.

We nevertheless submit that there are circumstances in which nonchoice evidence can reliably establish the existence of a significant discrepancy between the actual choice set, X, and the perceived choice set, Y. This occurs, for example, in circumstances where it is known that attention wanders, memory fails, forecasting is naive, and/or learning is inexplicably slow. In these instances, we say that the GCS is suspect.

We propose using nonchoice evidence to officiate between conflicting choice data by deleting suspect GCSs. Thus, for example, if someone chooses x from X under condition d' where she is likely to be distracted, and chooses y from X under condition d'' where she is likely to be focused, we would delete the data associated with (X, d') before constructing the welfare relations. In effect, we take the position that (X, d'') is a better guide for the planner than (X, d'). Even with the deletion of choice data, these welfare relations may remain ambiguous in many cases due to other unresolved choice conflicts, but R' and P^* nevertheless become (weakly) finer, and the sets of weak individual welfare optima grow (weakly) smaller.

Note that this refinement agenda entails only a mild modification of the core libertarian principles that underlie the standard choice-theoretic approach to welfare economics. Significantly, we do not propose *substituting* nonchoice data, or any external judgment, for choice data. Rather, we adhere to the principle that the social planner's objective should be to select an alternative that the individual would select for herself in *some* generalized choice situation.

The Role of Neuroscience, Psychology, and Neuroeconomics

What types of nonchoice evidence might one use to determine the circumstances in which internal information processing systems work well, and the circumstances in which they work poorly? Evidence from neuroscience, psychology, and neuroeconomics concerning the functioning of various cognitive processes can potentially shed light on the operation of processes governing attention, memory, forecasting, and learning. This evidence can provide an objective basis for determining whether a particular choice situation is suspect. For example, if memory is shown to function poorly under certain environmental conditions, GSCs that are associated with those conditions, and that require factual recall, are suspect. Our work on addiction [Bernheim and Rangel, 2004] provides an illustration. Citing evidence from neuroscience, we argue that the repeated use of addictive substances causes specific information processing systems to malfunction under identifiable ancillary conditions. The choices made in these circumstances are therefore suspect, and welfare evaluations should be guided by choices made in other ancillary conditions.

For those who question the use of evidence from neuroscience, we offer the following motivating example. An individual is offered a choice between alternative *x* and alternative *y*. When the alternatives are described verbally, the individual chooses *x*. When the alternatives are described partly verbally and partly in writing, the individual chooses *y*. Which choice is the best guide for public policy? Based on the information provided, the answer is unclear. But suppose we learn in addition that the information was provided in a dark room. In that case, we would be inclined to respect the choice of *x*, rather than the choice of *y*. We would reach the same conclusion if an ophthalmologist certified that the individual was blind. More interestingly, we submit that the same conclusion would follow if a brain scan revealed that the individual's visual processing was neurologically impaired. In all of these cases, nonchoice evidence sheds light on the likelihood that the individual successfully processed information that was in principle available to him, and thus was able to properly characterize the choice set *X*.

The relevance of evidence from neuroscience and neuroeconomics may not be confined to problems with information processing. Pertinent considerations would also include impairments that prevent people from implementing desired courses of action. Furthermore, in many situations, simpler forms of evidence may suffice. If an individual characterizes a choice as a mistake on the grounds that he neglected or misunderstood information, this may provide a compelling basis for declaring the choice suspect. Other considerations, such as the complexity of a GCS, could also come into play.

What Is a Mistake?

In our work on addiction, we have characterized certain types of choices as *mistakes*. This has led to considerable confusion, particular among those who regard the notion of a mistake as meaningless (or even self-contradictory) within the context of sensible choice-theoretic welfare economics. This is simply a matter of terminology. We use the word *"mistake"* to describe a choice made in a suspect GCS that is contradicted by choices in nonsuspect GCSs. In other words, if the individual chooses $x \in X$ in one GCS where she properly understands that the choice set is X at the moment of choice, and chooses $y \in X$ in another GCS where she misconstrues the choice set as Y, we say that the choice of $y \in X$ is a mistake. We recognize, of course, that the choice she believes she makes is, by definition, not a mistake given the set from which she believes she is choosing.

In Bernheim and Rangel [2007], we provide the following example of a mistake:

> American visitors to the UK suffer numerous injuries and fatalities because they often look only to the left before stepping into streets, even though they know traffic approaches from the right. One cannot reasonably attribute this to the pleasure of looking left or to masochistic preferences. The pedestrian's objectives—to cross the street safely—are clear, and the decision is plainly a mistake [32]

We know that the pedestrian in London is not attending to pertinent information and/or options, and that this leads to consequences that he would otherwise wish to avoid. Accordingly, we simply disregard this GCS on the grounds that behavior is mistaken (in the sense defined above), and instead examine choice situations for which there is nonchoice evidence that the pedestrian attends to traffic patterns.

DISCUSSION

In this chapter, we have proposed a choice-theoretic framework for behavioral welfare economics—one that can be viewed as a natural extension of standard welfare economics. We have shown that the application of libertarian welfare principles does not require all choices to be consistent, in the classic sense. Though the guidance provided by choice data may be ambiguous in some circumstances, it may nevertheless be unambiguous in others. This partially ambiguous guidance provides sufficient information for rigorous welfare analysis. Moreover, we have shown that one can carry out this analysis using straightforward generalizations of standard tools, such as compensating and equivalent variation, consumer surplus, and Pareto optima.

The framework for welfare analysis proposed here is a natural generalization of the standard welfare framework in two separate respects. First, it nests the standard framework as a special case. Second, when behavioral departures from the standard model are small, our welfare criterion is close to the standard criterion.

Finally, we have proposed an agenda for refining our welfare criterion. This agenda necessarily relies on the circumscribed but systematic use of nonchoice data. Significantly, we do not propose *substituting* nonchoice data, or any external judgment, for choice data. Rather, we adhere to the principle that the social planner's objective should be to select an alternative that the individual would select for herself *under some circumstances*. Nonchoice data are potentially valuable because they may provide important information concerning *which* choice circumstances are most relevant for welfare and policy analysis.

The approach that we have proposed has some important additional advantages. First, it allows economists to conduct welfare analysis in environments where individuals make conflicting choices, without having to take a stand on whether individuals have "true utility functions," or on how well-being might be measured. Second, the analyst is free to use a wide range of positive models, including those that do not entail the maximization of an underlying utility function, without sacrificing the ability to evaluate welfare.

The approach that we have proposed also has some limitations. First, in some applications, our welfare criteria may not be particularly discriminating. In such cases, the refinement agenda discussed above is particularly critical. Second, it is likely that, in some extreme cases, there will be an objective basis for classifying all or most of an individual's potential GCSs as suspect, leaving an insufficient basis for welfare analysis. Individuals suffering from Alzheimer's disease, other forms of dementia, or severe injuries to the brain's decision-making circuitry might fall into this category. Decisions by children might also be regarded as inherently suspect. Thus, our framework also carves out a role for paternalism.

Where will the refinements agenda ultimately take us? The two authors of this chapter hold somewhat different views on this subject. Rangel's view is that in the coming decades neuroeconomics will generate insights and tools that will allow us to objectively officiate between conflicting choice situations to the point where many inconsistencies can be eliminated. Bernheim sees the potential for neuroeconomics to provide a basis for officiating between conflicting choices, specifically insofar as it sheds light on information processing malfunctions or on functional impairments. However, he conjectures that the effects of many ancillary conditions will not fall unambiguously within those categories, and he anticipates that other types of evidence concerning brain processes will be susceptible to a variety of normative interpretations.

NOTES

We thank Colin Camerer, Andrew Caplin, Vincent Crawford, Robert Hall, Peter Hammond, Botond Köszegi, Preston McAfee, and seminar participants at Stanford University, the 2006 NYU Methodologies Conference, the summer 2006 Econometric Society meetings, at the winter 2007 American Economic Association meetings, and the 2007 conference on Frontiers in Environmental Economics sponsored by Resources for the Future, for useful comments. B. Douglas Bernheim gratefully acknowledges financial support from the National Science Foundation (SES-0452300). Antonio Rangel gratefully acknowledges financial support from the National Science Foundation (SES-0134618) and the Moore Foundation.

1. Evidence of incoherent choice patterns, coupled with the absence of a scientific foundation for assessing true utility, has led some to conclude that behavioral economics should embrace fundamentally different normative principles than standard economics (see, e.g., Sugden [2004]).

2. In the latter case, the states may not be observable to the planner. Instead, they may reflect the individual's private information. With respect to privately observed states, it makes little difference whether the state reflects an event that is external to the individual, or internal (e.g., a randomly occurring mood). Thus, the standard framework subsumes cases where states are internal; see, e.g., Gul and Pesendorfer [2006].

3. According to the definition proposed by Arrow [1959], x is revealed preferred to y if there is some $X \in \mathcal{X}$ for which $x \in C(X)$ and $y \notin C(X)$. Under the weak congruence axiom, that definition is equivalent to the statement that xPy, where P is defined as in the text [Sen, 1971].

4. One can illustrate this point with reference to "temptation preference" as formulated by Gul and Pesendorfer [2001]. Though the Gul-Pesendorfer analysis may appear to resolve normative ambiguities arising from time-inconsistent choices by virtue of establishing the uniqueness of a utility representation, the apparent resolution is illusory. For a related point, see Köszegi and Rabin (chapter 8), who argue that, as a general matter, utility is fundamentally unidentified in the absence of assumptions unsupported by choice data.

5. The following is a description Rubinstein and Salant's(chapter 5) binary relation, using our notation. Assume that C is always single valued. Then $x \succ y$ iff $C(\{x, y\}, d) = x$ for all d such that $(\{x, y\}, d) \in \mathcal{G}$. The relation $\succ$ is defined for choice functions satisfying a condition related to weak congruence and thus—in contrast to P' or P^*—depends only on binary comparisons. Rubinstein and Salant [2006] proposed a special case of the relation $\succ$, without reference to welfare.

6. When there are no ancillary conditions and the revealed preference relation is a libertarian relation for C, then C is called a *normal* choice correspondence [Sen 1971].

7. This is a natural assumption if we take the time periods to be short. It is possible, e.g., to compensate an individual fully for one day of fasting, but presumably not for one year of fasting, since that would be fatal.

8. This formulation of compensating variation assumes that $\mathcal{G}$ is rectangular. If $\mathcal{G}$ is not rectangular, then as a general matter we would need to write the final GCS as $(X(\alpha_1, m), d_1(m))$ and specify the manner in which d_1 varies with m.

9. For example, if m_1^A is the CV-A for a change from $(X(\alpha_0, 0), d_0)$ to $(X(\alpha_1, m), d_1)$, and if m_2^A is the CV-A for a change from $(X(\alpha_1, m_1^A), d_1)$ to $(X(\alpha_2, m_1^A + m), d_2)$, then nothing that the individual would choose from $(X(\alpha_0, 0), d_0)$ is unambiguously chosen over anything that he would choose from $(X(\alpha_2, m_1^A + m_2^A), d_2)$.

10. In the standard framework, if m_1 is the CV for a change from $X(\alpha_0, 0)$ to $X(\alpha_1, m)$, and if m_2 is the CV for a change from $X(\alpha_1, m_1)$ to $X(\alpha_2, m_1 + m)$, then $m_1 + m_2$ is the CV for a change from $X(\alpha_0, 0)$ to $X(\alpha_2, m)$. The same statement does not necessarily hold within our framework.

11. In Bernheim and Rangel [2007], we consider some other possible generalizations of Pareto efficiency.

12. The proof of theorem 7.5 is more subtle than one might expect; in particular, there is no guarantee that any individual's welfare optimum within the set $\left\{y \in X \mid \forall i, \sim xP_i^* y\right\}$ is a generalized Pareto optimum within X.

13. Suppose, e.g., that $xI_1' y$ given $(\mathcal{G}_1, C_1)$, so that $\sim xP_1' y$. Then, with the addition of a GCS for which x is chosen but y is not with both available, we would have $xP_2' y$; in other words, the relation P' would become finer. Similarly, suppose that $xP_1^* y$ given $(\mathcal{G}_1, C_1)$, so that $\sim yR_1^* x$. Then, with the addition of GCS for which y is chosen when x is available, we would have $yR_2^* x$; in other words, the relation R^* would become finer.

REFERENCES

Ariely, Dan, George Loewenstein, and Drazen Prelec. 2003. Coherent Arbitrariness: Stable Demand Curves Without Stable Preferences. *Quarterly Journal of Economics* 118(1): 73–105.

Arrow, Kenneth J. 1959. Rational Choice Functions and Orderings. *Economics* 26(102): 121–127.

Bernheim, B. Douglas, and Antonio Rangel. 2004. Addiction and Cue-Triggered Decision Processes. *American Economic Review* 94(5): 1558–1590.

———. 2007. Beyond Revealed Preference: Choice-Theoretic Foundations for Behavioral Welfare Economics. Stanford University, mimeo.

Bhattacharya, Jay, and Darius Lakdawalla. 2004. Time-Inconsistency and Welfare. NBER Working Paper No. 10345. Cambridge, MA: National Bureau of Economic Research.

Caplin, Andrew, and John Leahy. 2001. Psychological Expected Utility Theory and Anticipatory Feelings. *Quarterly Journal of Economics* 116(1): 55–79.

Gul, Faruk, and Wolfgang Pesendorfer. 2001. Temptation and Self-Control. *Econometrica* 69(6): 1403–1435.

———. 2006. Random Expected Utility. *Econometrica* 74(1): 121–146.

Laibson, David. 1997. Golden Eggs and Hyperbolic Discounting. *Quarterly Journal of Economics* 112(2): 443–477.

Laibson, David, Andrea Repetto, and Jeremy Tobacman. 1998. Self-Control and Saving for Retirement. *Brookings Papers on Economic Activity* 1: 91–172.

O'Donoghue, Ted, and Matthew Rabin. 1999. Doing It Now or Later. *American Economic Review* 89(1): 103–124.

Read, Daniel, and Barbara van Leeuwen. 1998. Predicting Hunger: The Effects of Appetite and Delay on Choice. *Organizational Behavior and Human Decision Processes* 76(2): 189–205.

Rubinstein, Ariel, and Yuval Salant. 2006. A model of choice from lists. *Theoretical Economics* 1: 3–17.

Sen, Amartya K. 1971. Choice Functions and Revealed Preference. *Review of Economic Studies* 38(3): 307–317.

Sugden, Robert. 2004. The Opportunity Criterion: Consumer Sovereignty Without the Assumption of Coherent Preferences. *American Economic Review* 94(4): 1014–1033.

Tversky, Amos, and Daniel Kahneman. 1974. Judgment under Uncertainty: Heuristics and Biase. *Science* 185: 1124–1131.

CHAPTER 8

··

REVEALED MISTAKES AND REVEALED PREFERENCES

··

BOTOND KÖSZEGI AND MATTHEW RABIN

PEOPLE often depart from the narrowest sense of rationality traditionally assumed in economics: they take actions that they would not take could they fully assess the distribution of all relevant consequences of those actions. We cannot rule out that such mistakes are common in domains of activity that economists care about, and if they are, this would obviously have many important implications. To design policy with regard to harmful and addictive substances, for instance, a planner should ideally know whether 18-year-olds who launch into a lifelong addiction are doing so as a well-calibrated accomplishment of maximizing their expected lifetime well-being. Hence, it would be useful to study mistakes until we either learn that they are not very common, or understand them and can incorporate them into our models and policy prescriptions.

Yet incorporating mistakes into economic models raises the methodological concern that research loses touch with behavioral data of economic interest. On the positive side, the fear is that mistakes are difficult or impossible to observe in economic data, so they become a free parameter to fit any situation. On the normative side, the fear is that if economists allow for mistakes, they lose the ability to employ the revealed-preference approach to extract welfare measures from behavior, and have to (paternalistically) impose a welfare measure themselves. Some researchers consider these concerns prohibitive enough to justify ignoring mistakes altogether.

In this chapter, we propose general methods to deal with these concerns and illustrate our methods through a number of examples. Our view is simple: despite mistakes, human behavior is not random. The mistakes people make are systematic, and often they can be easily identified in behavior. And most important, there is a strong association between what people do and what they intend to accomplish. So if we understand how people intend to accomplish their goals, including understanding their mistakes, we can identify their goals from behavior. Preferences are revealed in behavior, even if they are not implemented by behavior.

We begin with recalling that all economic theories, including standard theories, must make some assumptions to gain traction. Consider, for instance, the central question of welfare analysis—what policies a planner should choose on behalf of individuals to maximize their well-being. The classical revealed-preference approach proposes a simple answer: whatever a person would choose for herself. This approach is usually justified by assuming that people choose correctly. Yet even taking such rationality as given, "action-unobservable" assumptions are always necessary to make sure the proposed choice reflects the welfare question we are interested in.[1] As an extreme example, assuming only rationality, behavioral evidence cannot reject the hypothesis that imposing painful death on a person is the best policy. Even if she always chooses to avoid painful death when given a choice, her very favorite alternative could be painful death being imposed *without* a choice.

Recognizing that all theories make action-unobservable assumptions to connect preferences to behavior, we outline our proposal to follow this tradition: make reasonable assumptions that render mistakes and preferences jointly observable from behavior. In many situations, very minimal assumptions on preferences ensure that explicit or implicit "bets" on an event reveal a person's beliefs about the likelihood of the event. These beliefs may be found to be objectively incorrect. Much like we write theories to explain other types of behavior, the goal is then to look for a theory of behavior incorporating the systematic mistakes. This theory can and should tie preferences closely to behavior.

We next illustrate how our approach can be used to study mistakes about exogenous events such as a statistical process, the stock market, or a natural phenomenon. Suppose that when observing a series of coin flips, a person bets on (i.e., accepts a lower payoff contingent on) the event that the next flip will be different from recent ones. Under the painfully reasonable assumption that her preference for money is independent of coin flips, this means that she is making a mistake. We could try to maintain rationality and explain his behavior as a preference to bet on changes in coin flips, but the much more plausible theory is that she suffers from the gambler's fallacy: she believes that if the same side of the coin has come up a number of times, the other one is "due." Not only is this theory a natural and parsimonious explanation of the facts, but it helps make sense of behavior in other contexts, including using the behavior to identify the person's goals. That is, it facilitates application of the revealed-preference method. Suppose, for example, that after observing six flips of heads in a row, the person chooses to get blueberries if tails comes up next and huckleberries if heads comes up next—rather than vice versa—and she has the opposite preference after observing six flips of tails in a row. With a theory based on the gambler's fallacy, we can conclude that she likes blueberries more than huckleberries. With a theory based on a preference to bet money on changes in coin flips, we would be able to make no meaningful inference from this behavior.

Following this, we consider beliefs about one's own future behavior. For a given future choice set X from which an individual will choose, we can ask her to bet on her choice—to identify an option in X and be paid a small amount if and only if she chooses that option later. As long as the monetary payment does not change what she will actually choose, under minimal assumptions her bet on an option reveals a belief that she will choose that option. Consider, for instance, a person's future choice between an appetizer and a full entree. She may be hungry or satiated in the future, and independently of this state she may be hungry or satiated today. For simplicity, posit that these states are observable or can be induced. Suppose that if she is hungry today, she bets that she will choose the full course, and if she is satiated today, she bets she will choose the appetizer. Yet independently of the current state, she ends up choosing the entree if she is hungry in the future and the appetizer if she is satiated in the future. Under the excruciatingly reasonable assumption that she prefers to receive money with a chosen option rather than an unchosen option, this means that she has incorrect beliefs about future behavior whenever the future state is different from the current state. A parsimonious and portable theory that explains the mistake is that the person suffers from *projection* bias: she underestimates how changes in her state will change her preferences. And as with the gambler's fallacy, we show below how such a theory can be used to identify the person's preferences, even though she herself may not act in accord with those preferences.

Our approach to revealed preference is inconsistent with some—in our opinion, extreme—views of the role of normative analysis in economics. In one view, the role of normative analysis is to analyze what institutions might emerge if people are to agree to those institutions. Welfare analysis is then a part of positive analysis, addressing what institutions are stable. Theorizing about preferences hidden by mistakes may very well be useless in this analysis, because such preferences will never be expressed in the process of institutional design. In contrast, we feel (and believe most economists feel) that some social planners might be motivated at least in part to design institutions that are sensitive to people's values, even if people do not always choose according to those values. Researchers helping such planners can use our methods to identify preferences that are hidden by mistakes, and hence help in making sure the preferences *are* expressed in the process of institutional design.[2]

Within this view, our approach is a direct answer to the concern that normative analysis based on goals other than what people would choose for themselves necessarily involves the researcher (or policy maker) imposing her own values.[3] Since we propose to derive a person's preferences from her own behavior, any normative conclusions we draw respect the person's values—even if they do not coincide with her choices. Indeed, in most of our examples, our approach does not a priori rule out any option in the person's choice set, and could (depending on the person's behavior) lead a planner to prefer that option.

THE IMPOSSIBILITY OF SKINNERIAN WELFARE ECONOMICS

Because our approach relies on some action-unobservable assumptions and this may give it the appearance of inferiority relative to the revealed-preference method, we begin with some simple examples to illustrate that even classical theories make crucial action-unobservable assumptions beyond rationality.[4] We do not claim that the assumptions made in standard theories are unreasonable (we believe they are often *very* reasonable), only that they are there, and there is no logical or methodological reason why they could not in some cases be fruitfully replaced by other reasonable assumptions.

A textbook illustration of welfare conclusions derived from revealed preference is based on a choice between two simple consumption goods. If we observe, say, a person choosing blueberries over huckleberries, we can conclude that she likes blueberries more than huckleberries. This leads to the positive prediction that the person will choose blueberries over huckleberries in a similar situation, and to the normative implication that if someone else must make the choice on the person's behalf, the welfare-maximizing policy is to choose blueberries. While the positive prediction "merely" leaves it completely unspecified what constitutes a similar situation, the welfare conclusion also relies on an important implicit assumption: it requires that having to make the choice herself (rather than having someone else make it) does not affect the person's ranking between the two options. Much psychology indicates, and models such as Gul and Pesendorfer [2001] predict, that often this is an unreasonable assumption.

An extreme example clearly illustrates this point. Even supposing rational utility maximization, without further assumptions behavioral evidence cannot reject the hypothesis that a person is happier having painful death rather than a cake imposed on her. Her preferences could be such that she likes painful death if it is imposed on her without choice, but not if she has any choice, so observing that she never chooses painful death is not evidence that she does not like it. To see this, suppose that a person's utility is defined over the choice set she faces and the choice from it. In particular, for any decision problem she is facing—including arbitrarily complicated, dynamic decision problems—her preferences are over the set of final outcomes available and the outcome ultimately chosen. If the person's utility function satisfies $u(\text{death}|\{\text{death}\}) > u(\text{cake}|\{\text{cake}\})$, and $u(\text{cake}|\{\text{cake}, \text{death}\}) > u(\text{death}|\{\text{cake}, \text{death}\})$, she will choose cake whenever given the opportunity, but the welfare-maximizing policy is to impose death on her. More generally, the relationship between $u(\text{cake}|\{\text{cake,death}\})$ and $u(\text{death}|\{\text{cake, death}\})$ places no restriction on the relationship between $u(\text{cake}|\{\text{cake}\})$ and $u(\text{death}|\{\text{death}\})$, so observed behavior tells us nothing about the welfare-maximizing option.

It may appear that asking the person to make a decision over choice sets rather than final outcomes gets around this problem, because she can reveal whether she likes the singleton choice set {death} or the singleton choice set {cake}. But if the person's preferences are over available final outcomes as we assumed—a perfectly consistent set of preferences—such a choice is meaningless, because her choice set over ultimate outcomes includes both options.

REVEALED MISTAKES AND REVEALED (BUT UNIMPLEMENTED) PREFERENCES

The starting position of this chapter is that some deviations from patterns of behavior that would be expected based on standard models are due to mistakes in implementing preferences rather than due to unexplored types of preferences. Yet we do not want to abandon the idea that behavior reveals many economically important characteristics of a person, including her preferences as well as her mistakes. In this section, we outline our unsurprising proposal for how to proceed: to make assumptions so that preferences and mistakes become jointly action-observable. Because we do not impose rationality, we need alternative assumptions that are not necessary in the standard revealed preference setting. Our assumptions are often action-unobservable—but as we discussed in the preceding section, so are crucial assumptions underlying standard analysis.

Although this is not strictly necessary for our approach, we will interpret beliefs as a way of summarizing what a person thinks about the likelihood of events, and utility as a way of summarizing her experience with outcomes. This means that beliefs and utility are not solely abstractions that represent behavior, but rather abstractions that capture real mental states and experiences. Our interpretation seems natural, and simplifies many of our discussions and statements.

Our framework is designed for situations where mistakes about *measurable* variables—both exogenous events and one's own behavior—are possible. The first step is to make minimal assumptions about preferences so that a set of observable choices—essentially, a set of explicit or implicit bets on an event—reveals beliefs about the relevant variable. This often involves little more than assuming in some form that the person strictly prefers more money to less. The second step is to compare the beliefs elicited from behavior to objective probabilities. If the two are different, there are exactly two ways to explain the behavior. One can either abandon even the minimal assumptions on preferences that were used to infer beliefs, or one can accept the logical conclusion that the person has revealed a mistaken belief. Because the former option often leads the researcher into wacky theories, in many situations the latter option will be the more fruitful way to proceed. The third step, therefore, is to write a generally applicable theory of preferences and mistakes that explains the behavior in this as well as the largest possible number of other settings, and that ties welfare to behavior. An important component of such a theory will often be a set of assumptions about circumstances where mistakes do *not* happen, because these circumstances provide the most direct way to elicit preferences in the face of mistakes.

The usefulness of this general approach depends on its workability in specific settings. In the following sections, we demonstrate how the framework can help deliver essentially smoking-gun evidence for mistakes in a few types of settings, and how this understanding can help motivate a theory of preferences and mistakes.

MISTAKEN BELIEFS ABOUT EXOGENOUS OBJECTIVE EVENTS

In this section we provide a simple way to elicit what can naturally be interpreted as mistaken beliefs about objective events, and give examples of how a theory of mistakes can be integrated into a coherent theory of preferences and behavior. Our arguments follow the logic of the framework for integrating mistakes into economic models that we have proposed above: (i) make minimal assumptions about preferences so that mistaken beliefs can be detected for any decision maker with preferences in this class; (ii) compare beliefs to objective probabilities; and (iii) if the two are different, write a theory of preferences and mistakes that explains the behavior. A lot of the ideas here for eliciting beliefs have been around in the literature on eliciting subjective beliefs in expected utility theory. Our contribution is only in observing that many of the same ideas work for a much broader class of preferences, and that they can be used to spot mistakes regarding *objective* uncertainty.

As a simple illustration, suppose a person may have observed some flips of a fair coin, and we now offer her the following option to "bet" on the next flip of the coin. If she bets on tails (T) and T comes up, she wins $1 with probability 0.45; and if she bets on heads (H) and H comes up, she wins $1 with probability 0.55. To avoid complications regarding compound lottery reduction, all uncertainty is resolved at the same time as the coin flip. If the decision maker chooses to bet on T despite the lower probability payoff, that strongly suggests she believes T is more likely. More precisely, if her preferences are independent of the coin flip as well as the random process generating the above probabilities, and she prefers to win $1 with a higher rather than lower overall probability, then betting on T reveals a belief that T is more likely.

In general, we can elicit a person's precise beliefs regarding the probability of the event E using a variation of the Becker-DeGroot-Marschak procedure [Becker, DeGroot, and Marschak, 1964]. We inform the person that a "relative price" $r \in [0, 1]$ for E will be drawn randomly, and ask her to indicate a maximum price, q, for which she is willing to bet on E. If $r < q$, she wins $1 with probability $(1 - r)$ if event E occurs, and nothing if $\neg E$ occurs. If $r \geq q$, she wins $1 with probability r if event $\neg E$ occurs, and nothing if E occurs. All uncertainty is resolved at the same time. Intuitively, for each r the person is choosing whether to place a $(1 - r)$ bet on E or an r bet on $\neg E$. The cutoff value of r for which she switches her bet, q, is an indication of her beliefs about E. Specifically, if her preference for money is independent of E and the random process generating the probabilities r and $1 - r$, and she prefers to win money with higher probability, q is exactly the subjective probability she places on E.

Example: Gambler's Fallacy

To continue with our example, let E be the event that T comes up on the next flip. Suppose we find the following pattern in the person's betting behavior:

> Fact 1: If she has observed no flips, she chooses $q = 0.5$.
> Fact 2: If she has observed the sequence of flips HHHHHH, she chooses
> $q = 0.55$.
> Fact 3: If she has observed the sequence of flips TTTTT, she chooses $q = 0.45$.

Confronted with this empirical pattern, we have two options: we either have to conclude that the person incorrectly believes that the likelihood of T depends on previous flips, or we have to abandon even the minimal assumptions on preferences that allow us to interpret bets as reflections of beliefs. This is a case where the former seems to be a much more fruitful way to proceed. In order to explain all these facts in terms of preferences, an economist would have to assume that the person likes betting on T after HHHHHH, that she likes betting on H after TTTTTT, and that she is indifferent if she has observed no previous flips. This would be a wacky set of preferences indeed. When a preference-based methodology leads down on such a silly path, and when an intuitive mistake-based explanation is available, we are dumbfounded why economists should still restrict themselves to investigating and theorizing about only the preference-based alternative.

Indeed, to explain the same pattern of behavior in terms of mistakes, we can maintain the assumption that the decision maker's preferences are independent of the next flip, but also suppose that she believes in the "gambler's fallacy": she thinks that if H has come up a number of times, T is "due." Not only does this theory intuitively and parsimoniously explain the empirical facts, and is a theory that carries easily across contexts, but it also improves one's ability to make conclusions about preferences from behavioral data—that is, it increases the power of revealed preference.[5] For example, suppose we observe that after HHHHHH, the person strictly prefers to get blueberries if T comes up and huckleberries if H comes up, rather than vice versa, that he has the opposite preference after TTTTTT, and that she is indifferent if she has observed no flips. Having made the assumption that the decision maker believes in the gambler's fallacy and her preferences are independent of the coin flip, we can conclude that she likes blueberries more than huckleberries. Under the assumption that preferences are state dependent, we would be able to make no meaningful inference from this behavior.

As an economically more important domain of choice than blueberries and huckleberries, suppose that we observe a series of choices by both Fiona and Giles about whether they would rather have (x_h, x_t) if the next coin flip is heads or tails, or (y_h, y_t). Independently of the coin flips he has seen, Giles chooses (x_h, x_t) over (y_h, y_t) whenever $.5\sqrt{x_h} + .5\sqrt{x_t} > .5\sqrt{y_h} + .5\sqrt{y_t}$. Fiona's choices are more complicated:

1. If she has observed no flips, she chooses (x_h, x_t) over (y_h, y_t) whenever $.5\sqrt{x_h} + .5\sqrt{x_t} > .5\sqrt{y_h} + .5\sqrt{y_t}$.

2. If she has observed HHHHHH, she chooses (x_h, x_t) over (y_h, y_t) whenever $.45\sqrt{x_h} + .55\sqrt{x_t} > .45\sqrt{y_h} + .55\sqrt{y_t}$.

3. If she has observed TTTTTT, she chooses (x_h, x_t) over (y_h, y_t) whenever $.55\sqrt{x_h} + .45\sqrt{x_t} > .55\sqrt{y_h} + .45\sqrt{y_t}$.

How do we interpret this pattern of choices? The answer seems (to us) obvious: Giles does not succumb to the gambler's fallacy, and Fiona does. Through her pattern of choices, Fiona has made implicit bets that T is more likely than H to follow the sequence HHHHHH and H is more likely than T to follow the sequence TTTTTT. We are inclined to interpret this as a mistaken view about the way the world works, rather than a preference for betting (and losing money) on changes in coin flips.

But our point is not simply that we think it is useful to identify Fiona as making a mistake. It is also that we think we can use this understanding to identify Fiona's preferences. Indeed, we can identify her preferences as firmly as Giles's preferences: both are expected-utility maximizers representable with square root utility (at least over binary choices). We admit to not really understanding why we would at all be inclined to ban the study of Fiona from economics departments, but we are especially chagrined at that prospect in light of the fact that we can use the same powerful tools of economics to study Fiona as Giles in this case. Fiona has well-ordered and coherent preferences. She is making an error in statistical reasoning. The two can be jointly identified. It is useful to do so.

If one insists on the bad-psychology assumption that people of economic interest do not succumb to the gambler's fallacy, one is apt to misidentify and certainly underestimate the coherence of Fiona's preferences. To the anti-psychological-insight eye, Fiona's preferences may look a bit random, or stochastic; for instance, sometimes Fiona prefers less money to more [e.g., $(x_h, x_t) = (9, 11)$ to $(y_h, y_t) = (11, 10)$]. Abandoning our natural capacity to identify errors in this case means diminishing our capacity to apply the tools of revealed preference.

Is This Economically Important?

Our example of betting on coin flips is admittedly of little or no immediate economic relevance. It is intended not as an economically important setting, but rather as a clean platform to bring out and discuss some of our ideas and objections to them. Guessing that many researchers have tried to talk friends or relatives out of the gambler's fallacy, we hope that most will agree with the points we have made in this context. Yet many will disagree that economists should worry about mistakes in what they study. The extent of the disagreement may be that some believe mistakes—although they can be studied with economic tools—are empirically unimportant to actually engage. In that case, we are partly happy, and although we worry somewhat about a possible doctrinaire stand that maintains the lack of mistakes as a null hypothesis, we look forward to research and arguments to see who is right. But partly we find it painfully obvious that in some situations mistakes are so plausible that they should be considered carefully by any economist studying the question. We give an example that is closely related to betting on coin flips, but is economically more important.

Consider the empirical regularity that Odean [1999] and Barber and Odean [2001] documented and interpreted as overtrading: small investors pay substantial transaction costs—and thereby substantially decrease their returns—to keep moving their money between investments. That is, if they made similar trades but did so less frequently, their return would be much higher. In order to explain this behavior, we must either assume that investors are making a mistake, or assume that their investment behavior is motivated by something other than financial gain. As a plausible preference-based explanation, we may conjecture that they enjoy the process of trading and are willing to give up a large part of their financial return to be able to do it. In order to test this conjecture, we could (now hypothetically, since the above authors' data sets do not have this information) use our belief-elicitation method to see what investors seem to believe about the return of stocks in their portfolios. Suppose we find that investors tend to bet that the stocks they purchase will outperform other stocks. While one could maintain that investors have a preference to bet on these stocks (but will like to bet on other stocks soon), this finding would strongly suggest that they are misassessing the profitability of these stocks and are buying them for that reason. This possibility is sufficiently plausible empirically, and its implication that investors retire tens of thousands of dollars poorer sufficiently important economically, to warrant the time of economists to investigate. Perhaps it is very difficult to find data analogous to our betting experiment, but if so, economists should find the best data and methods to test between the different plausible theories.

In addition, we completely disagree with researchers who, rightly claiming that mistakes easily observed in the lab are often difficult or impossible to observe in economic data, propose to ignore them from the analysis altogether on the grounds that they constitute a free parameter to fit any situation. It is logical nonsense to respond to the difficulty of action-observing mistakes by making the very strong (as a corollary, action-unobservable) assumption that they do not exist, especially if they have been demonstrated robustly in other settings. We, of course, fully agree that economists should aim to write generally applicable models with few free parameters, but do not see why a model that incorporates a theory of mistakes cannot have that property.

MISTAKEN BELIEFS ABOUT FUTURE BEHAVIOR

If a person cannot predict what she will do in the future, she may make wrong decisions today. Hence, an important class of mistakes is about one's own future behavior. For instance, a teenager might falsely believe that she will end a possible period of experimentation with cigarettes by quitting, and so start smoking too easily. In this section we provide a (partial) way to elicit beliefs about future behavior, and again provide examples of how an understanding of mistakes can be incorporated into a theory of mistakes and preferences.

To elicit a person's beliefs about what she will choose at a given future date from the finite choice set X—and to see whether these beliefs are correct—we ask her to wager on her future choice. More precisely, we offer her a choice between the different choice sets $X_x = \{x + \$\epsilon\} \cup (X \backslash x)$ generated by all elements $x \in X$. That is, the decision maker can choose which option to attach a small monetary payment to, in essence placing a bet on one of the choices. If the following two conditions are satisfied, the person will select the decision set X_x if and only if she believes she would choose x from X:

(i) $\$\epsilon$ does not change the most preferred option in X.
(ii) It is better to choose $x + \$\epsilon$ from X_x than to choose x from any of the choice sets X_y for $y \in X, y \neq x$.

Condition (i), which is action-testable, ensures that the person cannot use the betting situation to provide herself incentives. If the bet was large enough to change her behavior, and she did not like how she thought she would behave, she might choose to wager on an option not because she thought she would choose it but to give herself a reason to choose it. Condition (i) is satisfied for a sufficiently small ϵ whenever the person does not believe she will be indifferent between any two options in X. Even if indifferences are possible, as long as condition (ii) holds, letting $\epsilon \to 0$ in the limit reveals an option the person believes she would not refuse to choose from X.

Condition (ii) says that the person prefers to attach money to a chosen option rather than an unchosen option. This condition is satisfied for all types of preferences with which we are familiar, including possibly time-inconsistent consequentialist preferences, and preferences that may depend on the choice set, such as temptation disutility.[6]

Example I: Naivete about Self-Control

Our approach can help identify an important class of mistaken beliefs, those about one's own future self-control. Suppose a person always commits a particular type of revealed mistake: she bets that she will choose exercise from the choice set {exercise, television}, but then she always chooses television. Furthermore, when asked ex ante whether to have the singleton choice set {exercise} or the singleton choice set {television} in the future—that is, when asked which option to commit to— she prefers {exercise}. A parsimonious explanation for this set of observations can be based either on models of hyperbolic discounting such as Laibson [1997] and O'Donoghue and Rabin [1999], or on models of temptation disutility by Gul and Pesendorfer [2001]: the person would like herself to exercise in the future, but may not have enough self-control to actually do so. In addition, her mistake is in overestimating her self-control, either because she underestimates her future short-term impatience or because she underestimates the strength of temptation disutility.

An important issue with our framework arises when the decision maker's eventual choice is not perfectly predictable, for instance, because random events affecting her valuation for different options are realized before she makes her choice. In this case, a bet on an option does not necessarily reflect a belief that that option is most likely. To continue with our example, suppose that 75% of the time the person chooses television from the choice set {exercise, television}, yet she bets on exercise. While she loses money with this bet, it is not necessarily a mistake. The bet can serve as an incentive to exercise, and under a time-inconsistent taste for immediate gratification, such an incentive is valuable. And under temptation disutility, the bet can decrease the temptation to watch television, increasing utility in states when exercise is chosen.

Example II: Projection Bias

As another example of mistaken beliefs about future behavior, consider a person's choice between an appetizer and a full entree at some given future date. She may be hungry or satiated in the future, and independently of this state she may be hungry or satiated today. Posit for now that these states are known to the observer of the person's behavior (or can be induced); below we turn to situations where the state is unknown to the observer. Suppose that if the person is hungry today, she bets that she will choose the full course, and if she is satiated today, she bets she will choose the appetizer. Yet independently of the current state, she ends up choosing the entree if she is hungry in the future and the appetizer if she is satiated in the future. Hence, she has revealed a mistaken belief about future behavior in situations where the future state is different from the current state.

A parsimonious and intuitive theory that explains the mistakes combines state-dependent utility with a partial inability to predict that utility. Denote the decision maker's hunger state by s, and consumption by c. Her utility can then be written as $u(c, s)$. Presumably, she has higher marginal utility for food when she is hungry, and that is why she selects the entree when hungry and the appetizer when satiated. But in addition to this, she suffers from projection bias as summarized and modeled in Loewenstein, O'Donoghue, and Rabin [2003]: she underestimates how changes in her hunger state will change her preferences. In its most extreme form, projection bias means that if the person is currently in state s, she believes her preferences in the future will be given by $u(c, s)$, even when she knows her future state will be different from her current one.

Unlike with the systematic misprediction of self-control above, in this example it is very hard to interpret the bets purely in terms of self-imposed incentives, even when the person's choice is not perfectly predictable. There does not seem to be a form of self-control problem such that the behavior the person would like to commit herself to depends on the current state but not on the future state. Hence, some misprediction must be going on.

In addition to being easy to spot when states are known, projection bias is sometimes apparent even when states are unknown. Suppose that based on observing the behavior of a large number of people, we establish the following empirical patterns:

1. When people make choices from the large finite choice set X, we observe an empirical distribution of choices $f(x)$, where each $f(x)$ is very small.
2. When people can choose ex ante whether to face the same choice set X or the choice set $X_x \equiv (x + \$\epsilon) \cup \{y - \$\epsilon\}_{y \in X}$ for some $x \in X$ of their choosing, they all select an $X(x)$ for some $x \in X$, and choice set X_x is chosen with probability $f(x)$. But independent of these ex ante choices, for each X_x the population chooses $x + \$\epsilon \in X_x$ with probability $f(x)$ and $y - \$\epsilon \in X_x$ with probability $f(y)$.

Selecting the set X_x ex ante is only beneficial if the person chooses $x + \$\epsilon$ ex post. Hence, this choice reveals a person's confident belief that she will prefer x. But people typically make a different choice ex post, so their belief is revealed to be incorrect. Projection bias provides an explanation: because people think their current preferences are indicative of their future preferences, they think they know what they will prefer in the future. But because their future state and preferences are random, their beliefs have little predictive power.

Eliciting State-Contingent Utility

When a person has mistaken beliefs about a relevant random variable or fails to correctly predict her own behavior, her behavior generally does not correspond to the strategy that maximizes her expected well-being. Hence, the standard revealed-preference methodology for assessing welfare must be modified. In this section we propose a simple and intuitive methodology to measure welfare for a particular class of preferences—time-consistent state-contingent utility—when a person may make systematic mistakes in assessing that utility. Our example is motivated by projection bias but works for other kinds of biases, as well.

Our method for eliciting a person's state-contingent preferences $u(c, s)$ relies partly on finding circumstances in which mistakes are unlikely. More precisely, one of our key assumptions is that for any state s, there is a state s' such that in state s', the decision maker correctly understands her preferences in contingency s. In the projection-bias example, $s = s'$ seems like a reasonable assumption: when hungry, a person accurately perceives the value of eating on an empty stomach; and when satiated, the person understands what it is like to eat on a full stomach. In other situations—for example, with impulsive consumption—it may be easier to accurately perceive one's preferences in a state when not in that state. Nevertheless, for notational simplicity we shall assume that when in state s, the person understands her utility in state s. This implies that it is easy to recover each of the cardinal preferences $u(\cdot, s)$ up to an affine transformation using standard revealed-preference techniques.

This, however, will not be sufficient if we also want to ask questions about trade-offs between states. For example, suppose we want to know whether to give a person an entree when she is not very hungry or an appetizer when she is hungry. That is, for some c, c', c'', c''' and s, s', we want to know the ranking of $u(c', s) - u(c, s)$ and $u(c''', s') - u(c'', s')$. If the person suffers from projection bias, we cannot rely on her own choice in the trade-off to make this judgment. When she is hungry, she does not appreciate that food will feel less good once she is less hungry, and hence she may incorrectly choose the entree. And when she is not so hungry, she does not appreciate how much better food will feel once she is hungry, and she may again incorrectly choose the entree.

To gain additional leverage, we assume that there is a "numeraire" good with state-independent value. In the projection-bias example, this could be retirement savings or another form of generic consumption far removed from the current state. We can then value the willingness to pay to move from c to c' in state s, and the willingness to pay to move from c'' to c''' in state s', in terms of the numeraire, and get a comparison of true utilities. Comparisons such as this will be sufficient to make all trade-offs whenever states are determined exogenously.

This method for eliciting true preferences in the face of mistakes requires some assumptions that are not necessary in the standard revealed preference framework. Crucially, however, the reason we need more assumptions is that we have dropped the key assumption of the standard method, that choices always correspond to welfare.

CAVEATS, DISCUSSION, AND CONCLUSION

While we believe our framework helps start incorporating theories of mistakes systematically into economic analysis—and bring those theories in line with standard economics methodology—several important issues remain unresolved. A major problem is that there may be situations where behavior clearly reveals a mistake, but the source of that mistake is unclear. That is, there may be multiple natural theories of preferences and mistakes that can explain a person's revealed mistakes. Yet the welfare implications of an observed mistake could depend fundamentally on its source.[7] The following example is based on our discussions of self-control problems and projection bias above. Suppose a pregnant woman predicts that she will give birth without anesthetics, and that if she could choose now, she would also make that choice. Yet when the time comes, she actually decides to give birth with anesthetics. One theory that explains this revealed mistake is projection bias: when not experiencing the pains of labor, it is difficult to appreciate just how bad it is. Another explanation is self-control problems: the mother would like herself to give birth naturally, but when confronted with the immediate pain of doing so, she cannot carry this through. The two theories give diametrically opposed welfare implications: projection bias says that the woman's later preference to give birth with anesthetics maximizes welfare, whereas hyperbolic discounting and temptation disutility say that the optimal policy is to commit to her early choice.

While this problem should be taken very seriously in any particular instance, we feel it is not a fundamentally new problem or one economists have no tools to deal with. Similarly to how economists attempt to distinguish theories in the standard framework, one can look for predictions that distinguish the two theories of mistakes in behavior.

Furthermore, our approach for eliciting mistakes in beliefs works only in certain circumstances. The method above for eliciting beliefs about exogenous events, for instance, assumes that utility for money is independent of the realization of uncertainty in question. As recognized by researchers such as Kadane and Winkler [1988] and Karni [1999], situations where a person already has "stakes" in the random process do not satisfy this assumption. For example, if an investor has money in the stock market, she will be poorer if the stock market does badly, and presumably have more value for money in that case. Hence, her bets regarding stock market returns reflect not just her beliefs about the stock market, but also her need for money in different contingencies.

NOTES

We thank Andrew Caplin for many fascinating conversations and helpful suggestions.

1. To clarify what we mean and to highlight that we believe nonbehavioral evidence is also important, throughout this chapter we use the term "action-observable" for assumptions or predictions that can be linked directly to choice. By dint of calling such assumptions simply "observable," standard economics suggests either that nothing else is observable, or (more likely) that such observations are unimportant for economics. Oral and written statements about beliefs, serotonin and dopamine levels, smiles, and brain activity are observable, often much more directly than choice. These observations are and should be used in economics. But they are not the focus of this chapter.

2. We are not advocating that economists be directly involved in all policy design. But we do advocate that they be involved in developing the conceptual underpinnings of policy design. And normative analysis that allows for the possibility of mistakes is an important part of that conceptual underpinning.

3. As we emphasize, our approach relies on some action-unobservable assumptions, and these assumptions may implicitly involve value judgments. But since the standard

approach also relies on action-unobservable assumptions, in this sense it is equally problematic.

4. For an expanded treatment of the arguments in this section, see Köszegi and Rabin [2008].

5. For formalizations of the gambler's fallacy and examples of the applicability of such a theory, see Rabin [2002] and Rabin and Vayanos [2005].

6. Identifying beliefs about choice from an infinite set is only slightly more complex. Suppose X is a compact set in a metric space, and utility is continuous with respect to this metric. The only complication relative to a discrete choice set is that there may be choices that are arbitrarily close in preference to the favorite option in X, and a small payment may induce the person to choose one of these near-optima instead. Once again, however, letting $\epsilon \to 0$ in the limit identifies an option in X that the person believes she would be willing to choose.

7. This issue is all the more important in light of some recent work on paternalism, e.g., Camerer, Issacharoff, Loewenstein, O'Donoghue, and Rabin [2003], O'Donoghue, and Rabin [2003], and Sunstein and Thaler [2003], whose major theme is to design policies that aid people avoiding a particular kind of mistake while doing little plausible harm to any previously known type of rational person. While it is often easy to design such policies, it is far less clear that a proposed policy will not do more harm than good to other types of irrational agents.

REFERENCES

Barber, Brad M., and Terry Odean. 2001. Boys Will Be Boys: Gender, Overconfidence, and Common Stock Investment. *Quarterly Journal of Economics* 116(1): 261–292.

Becker, Gordon M., Morris H. DeGroot, and J. Marschak. 1964. Measuring Utility by a Single-Response Sequential Method. *Behavioral Science* 9: 226–32.

Camerer, Colin, Samuel Issacharoff, George Loewenstein, Ted O'Donoghue, and Matthew Rabin. 2003. Regulation for Conservatives: Behavioral Economics and the Case for "Asymmetric Paternalism." *University of Pennsylvania Law Review* 151(3): 1211–1254.

Gul, Faruk, and Wolfgang Pesendorfer. 2001. Temptation and Self-Control. *Econometrica* 69(6): 1403–1435.

Kadane, Joseph B., and Robert L. Winkler. 1988. Separating Probability Elicitation from Utilities. *Journal of the American Statistical Association* 83(402): 357–363.

Karni, Edi. 1999. Elicitation of Subjective Probabilities When Preferences Are State-Dependent. *International Economic Review* 40(2): 479–486.

Köszegi, Botond, and Matthew Rabin. 2008. Choices, Situations, and Happiness. Mimeo, University of California, Berkeley, January.

Laibson, David. 1997. Golden Eggs and Hyperbolic Discounting. *Quarterly Journal of Economics* 112(2): 443–477.

Loewenstein, George, Ted O'Donoghue, and Matthew Rabin. 2003. Projection Bias in Predicting Future Utility. *Quarterly Journal of Economics* 118(4): 81–123.

Odean, Terry. 1999. Do Investors Trade Too Much? *American Economic Review* 89: 1279–1298.

O'Donoghue, Ted, and Matthew Rabin. 1999. Doing It Now or Later. *American Economic Review* 89(1): 103–124.

———. 2003. Studying Optimal Paternalism, Illustrated by a Model of Sin Taxes. Mimeo, UC Berkeley.

Rabin, Matthew. 2002. Inference by Believers in the Law of Small Numbers. *Quarterly Journal of Economics* 117(3): 775–816.

Rabin, Matthew, and Dimitri Vayanos. 2005. The Gambler's and Hot-Hand Fallacies in a Dynamic Inference Model. Working Paper, London School of Economics.

Sunstein, Cass, and Richard Thaler. 2003. Libertarian Paternalism. *American Economic Review* 93(2): 175–179.

CHAPTER 9

THE ECONOMIST AS THERAPIST: METHODOLOGICAL RAMIFICATIONS OF "LIGHT" PATERNALISM

GEORGE LOEWENSTEIN AND EMILY HAISLEY

INTRODUCTION

MUCH economic behavior is, or at least appears to be, rational and self-interested. People balance price and quality when they decide where to shop and what to buy. They decide how much schooling to get and what to study based at least in part on likely returns to different forms of training and in part on their enjoyment of different topics and types of work. They carefully consider investment decisions and hire experts to get good advice. Even if some may view voting itself as irrational, economic interests seem to play at least some role in patterns of voting.

There are areas of life, however, in which people seem to display less than perfect rationality. For example, although the United States is one of the most prosperous nations in the world, with a large fraction of its population closing in on retirement, the net savings rate is close to zero and the average household has $8,400 worth of credit card debt.[1] Fifty percent of U.S. households do not own any equities,[2] but the average man, woman, and child in the U.S. lost $284 gambling in 2004—close to $85 billion in total.[3] Many workers don't "max out" on 401k plans despite company matches (effectively leaving free money "on the table"), and what they do invest often goes undiversified into their own company's stocks or into fixed income investments with low long-term yields. At lower levels of income, many individuals and families sacrifice 10–15% of their paycheck each month to payday loans, acquire goods through rent-to-own establishments that charge effective interests rates approximately in the hundreds of percent, or spend large sums on lottery tickets that return approximately fifty cents on the dollar. Worldwide, obesity rates and associated diseases are high and rising rapidly. Yet people with, or at risk for, life-threatening health conditions often fail to take the most rudimentary steps to protect themselves. One recent estimate is that modifiable behaviors such as tobacco use, overeating, and alcohol abuse account for nearly one-third of all deaths in the United States [Flegal, Graubard, Williamson, and Gail, 2005; Schroeder, 2007]. Moreover, realization of the potential benefit of proven mediations, some targeted at the same medical problems caused by adverse heath behaviors, is stymied by poor adherence rates among patients. For example, by one year after having a heart attack, nearly half of the patients prescribed cholesterol-lowering medications have stopped taking them [Jackevicius, Mamdani, and Tu, 2002].

As economists, how should we respond to the seemingly self-destructive side of human behavior? We can deny it and assume as an axiom of faith that people can be relied upon to do what's best for themselves. We can assume that families paying an average of $1,000 per year financing credit card debt are making a rational trade-off of present and future utility, that liquidity constraints prevent investing in employer-matched 401k plans, that employees have good reasons for investing in their own company's stock instead of a diversified portfolio, that individuals' coefficients of relative risk aversion are high enough to justify investing in bonds instead of equities, that low-income families have good reasons for spending a large fraction of their paycheck on payday loans, usurious interest rates at rent-to-own establishments, and state lotteries, and that people are obese because they have calculated that the pleasure from the extra food, or the pain from the forgone exercise, is sufficient to compensate for the negative consequences of obesity. Indeed, some economists argue exactly that.[4]

Even among economists, however, this may no longer represent a majority view. Stimulated in part by developments in behavioral economics, increasing numbers of economists are questioning whether people really are such reliable pursuers of self-interest, and are coming to recognize that in some predictable situations people are prone to systematic errors.

In some cases, these errors arise from a lack of information, insight, or limited computational ability. For example, people may not recognize that company matches on pension funds effectively represent "free money"; they may not understand why it doesn't make sense to put one's nest egg in one's employer's stocks, and they may not realize that stocks, on average, yield a higher return than bonds. In other cases, people are well aware of the best course of action but due to self-control problems or limited self-insight are unable to implement it [e.g., Loewenstein, 1996]. Obesity and cigarette smoking may best fit into this latter category; few people have any illusions about the health risks of smoking or obesity, and many smokers and obese individuals do not believe that the benefits exceed the costs (which is why they often spend large amounts of time and money on attempts to quit). But in many cases this knowledge is insufficient to motivate behavior change.

"Light" Paternalism

Part of the historic antagonism of economists toward behavioral economics may have been driven by a fear that documenting flaws in human decision making would inevitably lead to calls for paternalism. If so, it seems that such fears were well founded. Beyond documenting such apparent violations of rationality and their consequences for economic behavior, behavioral economists have indeed begun to take the next logical step: they have begun to devise "paternalistic" policies designed to steer economic behavior in more self-interested directions. Paternalistic policies have the goal of benefiting people on an individual basis, premised on the idea that people cannot be relied upon to invariably pursue self-interest. Whereas the conventional justification for government regulation is to limit *externalities*—costs people impose on other people that they don't internalize—to promote the public good, the justification for paternalism is to limit *internalities*—costs that people impose on themselves that they don't internalize [Hernstein, Loewenstein, Prelec, and Vaughan, 1993]. Although some of the behaviors that are targeted by paternalistic policies do generate externalities (e.g., the failure to wear a motorcycle helmet imposes psychic and monetary costs on people other than the rider), paternalistic policies are generally aimed at helping the person whose behavior is altered. Existing examples of paternalistic regulations include banning narcotics, protection of the economically desperate with usury laws, health and safety regulations (for dangerous occupations), warnings on cigarettes, public health advertising, FDA drug approval, and the social security system.

In contrast to these existing forms of "heavy-handed" paternalism, however, behavioral economists have been advocating a new form of what could be called "light" paternalism. Going by labels such as "libertarian paternalism" [Thaler and Sunstein, 2003] and "asymmetric paternalism" [Camerer, Issacharoff, Loewenstein, O'Donoghue, and Rabin, 2003; Loewenstein, Brennan, and Volpp, 2007], the common goal of these approaches is to steer human behavior in more beneficial directions while minimizing coercion, maintaining individual autonomy, and maximizing choice to the greatest extent possible. Light paternalism aims to enhance decision making without restricting it.

In their treatment of "libertarian paternalism," for example, Thaler and Sunstein [2003] note that paternalism is often simply not avoidable. In many situations, they point out, organizations or governments must make decisions that will necessarily affect the choices and welfare outcomes of their constituents. It would seem ridiculous not to consider how such decisions will impact the welfare of those affected. They illustrate the point with the hypothetical case of a company cafeteria manager who must either place healthy items before unhealthy items in a cafeteria line or the reverse, but does not have the option of doing neither. Thaler and Sunstein [2003] argue that in such situations it makes perfect sense for managers to adopt the option that they believe is better for employees—namely, placing the healthy food ahead of the unhealthy food. Another example that has received considerable attention is default options for 401(k) retirement plans. If it is beneficial to invest in a 401k plan, but people tend to stick with the status quo, then it may make sense to change the usual default from not contributing (with the possibility of signing up) to contributing (with the possibility of opting out). The organization must make a choice about whether the default option is enrolled or unenrolled and, if enrolled, at what contribution level. Even if the organization were to have no default option and force employees to select whether they want to be in or out, this still qualifies as a decision of the organization that would lead to a different rate of enrollment and thus affects the welfare of its employees [see Choi, Laibson, Madrian, and Metrick [2005], and Halpern, Ubel, and Ash [2007], for a discussion in the context of healthcare].

The central insight of Camerer et al.'s [2003] notion of "asymmetric paternalism" is that it is often possible to produce benefits for people who make suboptimal decisions while imposing minimal or no restrictions on those who make rational decisions that optimize their own welfare. In the most pure cases of asymmetric paternalism, people behaving suboptimally are benefited without imposing any costs on those behaving optimally. To continue with the example of defaults on 401k plans, if people, contrary to the dictates of conventional economics, are influenced by the default option, then changing the default could potentially benefit them; if people are not influenced by the default, then changing it will have no effect on behavior and little if any cost.[5] Such policies not only provide benefits to agents who make mistakes without hurting those who are making a deliberate decision, but should also appeal to economists both who do and who do not believe in rationality. Economists who believe that people are less than perfectly rational will perceive such policies as beneficial, while economists who believe in rationality should see them as, at worst, little more than a low-cost nuisance. Policies of this type use relatively subtle psychological factors to influence behavior, making it possible to accomplish policy goals without imposing more draconian mandatory measures such as raising the contribution rate of social security. Exactly such an approach was adopted in the Pension Protection Act of 2006, which encourages companies to automatically enroll employees into 401(k) plans, and which passed with bipartisan support in an otherwise highly contentious political year. Other examples of policy interventions that fit the criteria for pure asymmetric paternalism include decision framing and expanding choice to offer commitment devices that aid self-control problems (as discussed below).

Critiques of Light Paternalism

Despite the desire to enlist the support of economists who oppose more heavy-handed forms of paternalism, light paternalism is not without its critics. For example, Glaeser [2006] argues that the bureaucrats who guide paternalistic policies cannot be counted on to be any more rational than those affected by the policies and can be counted on to be less interested in the welfare of those affected than in their own welfare. There is certainly some validity to the point, yet there are predictable situations in which the more detached perspectives of policy makers or experts can be more rational than those of individual decision makers. For example, the individual may be faced with tempting choices that are hard to resist but at odds with his or her long-term interests. Policy makers can predict that people will yield to these temptations and may be able to steer such individuals toward making better choices. Similarly, policy makers may have the information processing resources to figure out the best course of action when it comes to complex decisions, such as when it makes sense to receive different types of health care procedures, in situations in which individuals often make mistakes due to the difficulty of interpreting information.

In a different vein, Sugden [2005] and Klick and Mitchell [2006] argue that there is an inherent value to autonomy—to letting people make mistakes (and, one would hope, learn from them). This may be true in many cases but does not apply when there is no opportunity to learn from experience, as would be the case if one discovered that one's retirement savings were insufficient only upon nearing retirement age. Moreover, this argument seems to reject the very premise of light paternalism—that it is possible to implement paternalistic policies that *do not* restrict individual autonomy or, at worst, do so very minimally. Additionally, paternalistic policies do not preclude learning. Steering individuals toward a welfare-enhancing choice in one situation will be met with positive reinforcement and facilitate learning, which can inform the individual's decisions in other situations.

Finally, in chapter 1, Gul and Pesendorfer do not provide any kind of principled argument against light paternalism, but one that is based purely on convention. They argue that whether such interventions help or hurt economic agents is irrelevant because economists simply should not be in the business of directing social policy. "The standard approach" to economics, Gul and Pesendorfer argue, "assumes a separation between the economist's role as social scientist and the role that some economists may play as advisors or advocates." They dub the economist who crosses that dividing line an "economist/therapist."

Although Gul and Pesendorfer seem to view "therapist" as a pejorative label, we see no reason to not embrace it. Therapy is, in fact, not a bad metaphor for the new types of policies that behavioral economists have been proposing. Much like a therapist who attempts to steer clients toward more beneficial thoughts and behaviors without forcing them to do anything, all of these variants of light paternalism retain the ultimate autonomy of the individual while at the same time attempting to guide individuals toward courses of action that are seen as advantageous. Just as a psychotherapist endeavors to correct for cognitive and emotional disturbances that detract from the mental health of the patient, the economist/therapist endeavors to counteract cognitive and emotional barriers to the pursuit of genuine self-interest.

Methodological Issues Underlying Light Paternalism

Although light paternalism is a "growth industry" in economics, it is not yet sufficiently "mature" as an enterprise to have developed standard operating procedures or for its practitioners to have fully thought out the range of methodological issues that it raises. The purpose of this chapter is to begin to address this void in the literature by exploring some of the issues that light paternalism raises for economic methods.

The first issue is how a particular pattern of behavior should be judged as a mistake and, relatedly, how the success of paternalistic policies designed to rectify such mistakes should be evaluated. That is, an informed application of paternalism, whether light or not, requires some form of welfare criterion. Clearly, the traditional welfare criterion used by economists, which involves satisfying people's preferences to the maximum extent possible, cannot be used to evaluate policies that are premised on the view that people do not always choose what is best for themselves. We discuss the question of what type of welfare criterion should be used to evaluate paternalistic interventions.

Second, paternalism, and especially light paternalism, introduces new motives for attempting to understand the psychological processes underlying economic behavior. An enhanced understanding of process can help to explain why people make mistakes in the first place and, more importantly, can provide insights into what types of policies are likely to be effective in correcting the mistakes. We describe how an understanding of psychological process can inform, and already has informed, light paternalistic policies.

Third, in part because light paternalism is such uncharted territory, there is an acute need for testing different possible policies before implementing them on a large scale. There are good reasons why such tests should be carried out in the field rather than in the lab. Hence, the new paternalism points to the need for an expansion of field experiments—a trend that has already begun [Dellavigna, forthcoming].

In addition to methodological issues, there are pragmatic issues concerning who will implement light paternalistic policies, especially when they involve positive expenditures. We discuss how economic interests can be rechanneled to support endeavors consistent with light paternalism. In some cases, it may be in the interests of private sector industries to offer products or create incentives that help individuals to do what is in their own best interests. In other cases, the government can help align the interests of individuals and private industry. We conclude this chapter with a discussion of how recent trends in economic research on light paternalism relate to positive and normative economics.

In the course of discussing these methodological issues underlying light paternalism, we review a wide range of such interventions that have already been tested, as well as some that are still in the development phase. Therefore, a secondary purpose of this review is to give readers unfamiliar with the topic an overview of the wide range of light paternalistic interventions that are already being implemented and tested.

What Welfare Criterion?

In their paper introducing the notion of libertarian paternalism, Thaler and Sunstein [2003: 175] state that "a policy counts as 'paternalistic' if it is selected with the goal of influencing the choices of affected parties in a way that will make those parties better off," and then continue, "We intend 'better off' to be measured as objectively as possible, and we clearly do not always equate revealed preference with welfare." But what does it mean to measure "better off" "objectively"? As Thaler and Sunstein hint, preference-based measures of welfare are not up to the job because they equate utility with preference and hence automatically assume that anything a person voluntarily chooses to do must be welfare enhancing. Clearly, it does not make sense to assess whether someone is committing an error using a measure that is premised on the assumption that people do not commit errors.

In their discussion of asymmetrical paternalism, Camerer et al. [2003] propose, as the ideal, purely asymmetric paternalistic policies that help people who behave suboptimally but have little or no negative impact on who behave optimally. Some examples that fit this criterion include establishing defaults and framing alternatives so as to steer individuals toward advantageous alternatives, and possibly offering commit options to people with self-control problems.[6] However, Camerer et al. [2003] acknowledge that purely asymmetric policies are not always possible.[7] To extend the applicability of the approach, they propose a looser criterion which simply requires that the net benefit to irrational consumers must exceed the aggregate costs both to rational consumers and any other affected entities such as businesses or taxpayers. This criterion shifts the debate regarding paternalism from philosophical issues about autonomy and freedom to pragmatic issues of benefits and costs (with loss of autonomy potentially treated as a cost). Evaluating costs and benefits, however, once again requires some concept of welfare, and one that does not encode anything an individual does, or would do, as welfare improving by assumption. Several different types of welfare have been proposed that have this property.

Experience Utility

One possible approach, advocated first by Daniel Kahneman, and subsequently embraced by a number of economists, is to base evaluations of welfare on empirically reported happiness, or what Kahneman labels "experience utility" (as distinguished from "decision utility," which corresponds to the modern notion of preference inferred from choice). Layard [2005], for example, argues that maximizing happiness rather than income should be the goal of government policy, and others have argued that happiness data should be used to identify appropriate societal trade-offs between, for example, inflation and unemployment [Di Tella, MacCulloch, and Oswald, 2003] or between money and airport noise [van Praag and Baarsma, 2005]. Others argue for making happiness a goal of policy, on the basis of evidence that happiness leads to such positive consequences as higher incomes, better work performance, citizenship behaviors, stronger more stable relationships, and better health [Diener and Seligman, 2004]. Happiness has a major advantage over revealed preference as a welfare criterion: it is independent of the choices that people make, and hence can be used to evaluate which choices are welfare enhancing and which detract from welfare. However, as discussed in detail by Loewenstein and Ubel [forthcoming], using self-reported happiness as a policy criterion has several problems.

One problem is that people adapt to both unfortunate and fortunate circumstances, such that after sufficient time they return to their original happiness "set point" (see Frederick and Loewenstein [1999] for review). For example, dialysis patients do not experience significantly different levels of happiness than do healthy controls, even when measured "on line" by multiple reports elicited randomly at different points in the day [Riis, Loewenstein, Baron, et al., 2005]. If we were to use experienced utility as a metric for evaluating welfare, we could not conclude that chronically poor health was an undesirable outcome, a result that few would endorse. Moreover, a recent study found that although colostomy patients reported similar levels of happiness to people who did not have colostomies, they also expressed a willingness to give up 15% of their remaining life span if it could be lived with normal bowel function (i.e., no colostomy) [Smith, Sherriff, Damschroder, Loewenstein, and Ubel, 2007]. Despite being about as happy as healthy people, these patients indicated that they placed a high value on having their former health restored. Measures of welfare based on experience utility would fail to pick up such preferences.

Additionally, there are serious problems with all existing measures of happiness. For example, people tend to naturally "norm" happiness scales to their general circumstances or those of the people around them [Kahneman and Miller, 1986; Ubel, Loewenstein, Schwarz, and Smith, 2005]. Happiness scales are also sensitive to a wide range of nonnormative factors, such as current mood, the weather, and earlier questions in the survey [Kahneman and Krueger, 2006]. Finally, existing measures of happiness may miss brief periods of intense grief or regret that might have a substantial negative effect on well-being. Even the best measure of experience utility, using experience sampling techniques, can only measure happiness several times a day. In sum, while happiness measures may provide useful inputs into public policy, it would be a major mistake to base such policies solely on measures of happiness.

Limiting Welfare to "Valid" Choices

An alternative approach, advocated by Bernheim and Rangel (chapter 7), is to adhere to a choice-based measure of welfare (i.e., "decision utility" in Kahneman's parlance) but to limit the range of choices that "count" as indicative of welfare. Intuitively, their idea is that a person's choices usually promote their well-being, but in some limited situations, such as when a person is overwhelmed by drives or emotions, they may not. Their proposal, therefore, is to adopt a welfare criterion that, in effect, surgically removes "bad" choices from the set of choices that count.

The crux of the problem is then to specify which choices count and which do not. Bernheim and Rangel consider several alternative means of selecting which choices should count, such as "preponderance" (only selecting choices that are made with some frequency) and "self-officiating" (allowing the individual to decide which subset of choices should be taken as valid indicators of welfare), but find objections to all. Ultimately, they conclude that determining which choices are commensurate with welfare and which are not will require "noncidoice data," such as evidence from brain scans to determine when decision making is overwhelmed by visceral states or distorted by "circumstances where it is known that attention wanders, memory fails, forecasting is naive, and/or learning is inexplicably slow." As they express it, "In these instances, we say that the [generalized choice criterion] is suspect."

Although such an approach might be useful in theory, we suspect that it will be many years, if ever, before we are able to interpret patterns of brain activation to make inferences about what types of choices should count as welfare enhancing. How, for example, could patterns of brain activation help to differentiate the many legitimate, intense, pleasures that short-circuit rational thinking (and, indeed, are sometimes all the more pleasurable for doing so) from intense impulses that lead us to behave contrary to self-interest. Likewise, it seems questionable that social scientists will come up with a way to distinguish between the excitement of buying something one really wants and the excitement of squandering part of one's nest egg on a worthless trinket. In practice, we suspect, adjudicating between self-interested and non-self-interested choices will need to be done at least partially on the basis of an evaluation of which behaviors are most likely to confer long-run happiness—that is, on the basis of experience utility. Despite their explicit rejection of experience utility as a welfare criterion, therefore, we suspect that adoption of Bernheim and Rangel's criterion would inevitably lead to an implicit reliance on judgments of experience utility, albeit in a more subjective and less systematic fashion.

Informed Decision Utility

Another possible approach discussed, but not advocated, by Loewenstein and Ubel [forthcoming] involves honoring people's choices as a utility-maximizing welfare criterion, but only if attempts are made to ensure that the decision maker is truly informed. Like the approach proposed by Bernheim and Rangel in chapter 7, this is a choice-based approach, but one that seeks to improve the quality of choice by providing decision makers with information rather than by selecting out a subset of choices that are deemed representative of welfare based on nonchoice data. Informed decision utility would include, but goes well beyond, such measures as food and drug labels. Beyond information labels, such an approach might involve providing warnings about potential decision biases, such as how framing an outcome as a loss or a gain can lead to inconsistent choice.

Further, in situations in which information, however detailed and accurate, fails to provide a real anticipation of consequences, elaborate interventions could be devised to truly inform decision making. For example, one existing program intended to discourage childbearing by those who are not ready for it provides teenagers who are deemed at risk for pregnancy with dolls that require constant attention. The rationale is that, absent such a vivid experience, girls may have an overly romantic view of parenting, even if they are provided with more pallid information about the demands of parenting. Similarly, while smokers may appreciate the health risks of smoking at an abstract level, and may even overestimate such risks, they may not truly understand what it is like to die of lung cancer. In such a situation, again, more innovative interventions might be necessary to truly inform decision making.

The informed decision utility approach, however, suffers from two significant problems. The first is very similar to the fundamental weakness of the approach proposed by Bernheim and Rangel; in practice it is unlikely to avoid the need for recourse to judgments of experience utility. Given the wide range of different informational interventions that are possible, it will be necessary to decide which ones are worthwhile and which are not. The very act of providing information may frame a decision in a particular way that influence decisions in a particular direction, so it will also be necessary to decide how information intended to inform decision utility should be presented. For example, differences in small risks can be made to seem dramatic if they are presented in terms of ratios or percentages (e.g., "regular exercise can reduce your risk of disease X by 100%") as opposed to absolute terms (e.g., "regular exercise can reduce your risk of disease X by .0001— from .0002 to .0001"). Deciding which decisions to inform and how to inform them, therefore, will require some independent welfare criterion, the lack of which is the very problem that informed decision utility was intended to solve. As was true for the choice-subset notion proposed by Bernheim and Rangel, therefore, we suspect that in practice such decisions are going to be informed, at least in part, by recourse to judgments about which types of information will make decision makers happy or well off in some other sense—that is, by experience utility.

The second problem is that informational interventions are effective against only one of the two broad categories of mistakes that people make—those that result from incorrect information—and not against the other: self-control problems. As noted in the introduction to this chapter, there are many situations in which people lose control of their own behavior and knowingly behave in ways that they know are not in their own long-term self-interest. While information might help people to avoid such situations, once one is in the situation, the most accurate information that it is possible to impart is unlikely to have much if any impact on behavior.

Capabilities

Yet another approach, advocated by Amartya Sen [1985, 1992] and elaborated on by Martha Nussbaum [2000] is the capabilities approach. This approach is specifically intended to deal with, among other problems, that of adaptation. It rejects the revealed-preference framework for measuring welfare because people adjust their preferences as they adapt to poor social and physical conditions, characterized by poverty or injustice that, most people would agree, objectively reduce the quality of life. In other words, preference and desire can be diminished by "habit, fear, low expectations, and unjust background conditions that deform people's choices and even their wishes for their own lives" [Nussbaum, 2000: 114]. Sen [1985] gives the example that a person living in impoverished conditions may learn to have "realistic desires" and derive pleasure from "small mercies" and, as a result, may have more desires met than a person in dramatically better living conditions with overambitious desires. Note that this problem with a revealed-preference framework is similar to the problem of adaptation that we discuss in relation to using experienced utility as a welfare criterion. Just as adaptation causes problems for hedonic measures of welfare because people adapt hedonically to situations that virtually everyone would agree are adverse, it can cause problems for preference-based measures if people adapt their preferences to their circumstances and, as a result, become satisfied in situations that would be widely deemed to be unsatisfactory.

The solution proposed by Sen and Nussbaum is to construct a normative theory of welfare that is based on human capabilities—that is, what people are capable of achieving based on the opportunities and living conditions afforded then. Nussbaum delineates several "central human functional capabilities," such as health, freedom from assault, political voice, property rights, equal employment, and access to education, which resemble basic human rights, as well as others that involve self-actualization, such as emotion expression, affiliation with others, and recreation.

The capabilities approach avoids the problem of hedonic adaptation, which is one of the central weaknesses of the experience utility approach. It also avoids the problem of the standard revealed preference approach of treating anything that someone does as welfare enhancing. However, the capabilities approach suffers from crippling problems of its own. Specifically, the approach is impractical to implement because policy makers are unlikely to reach a consensus about which capabilities should be valued and, even if a set of valued capabilities can be agreed upon, the relative values of those capabilities. However, there are similarities between this welfare criterion and the one we propose below. At some point, policy makers should have some discretion to impose "values," such as the improvement of health or the reduction of poverty, on others, even if these changes are not deemed necessary by a preference-based or experienced utility welfare criterion—particularly if it can be done without limiting individual autonomy.

An Imperfect but Pragmatic Approach

What welfare criterion, then, should be used? We suspect that in most instances the problem will not be as severe as it seems. Although the threshold for light paternalism can be and should be lower than that for more heavy-handed forms of paternalism, we would still advocate that even light paternalistic policies should only be put into play when welfare judgments tend to be relatively straightforward. This is the case when one of the following conditions is met:

1. *Dominance:* In some cases, such as the failure of employees to take advantage of company matches on retirement accounts, a simple dominance criterion will suffice. In the case of company matches, as long as employees have monotonic

preferences—that is, prefer more income over less income—they will be better off if they maximize their own contribution, at least up to the level of the maximum company match. The underutilization of 401(k) matching programs most convincingly illustrates that many people do not save optimally, since failing to take advantage of such a match effectively "leaves money on the table." This is the case even after taking into account tax penalties for early withdrawal. The mistake is particularly egregious, and by no means rare, when an employee past retirement age does not make the maximal allowable contribution, since in this case the contribution could be made, matched, and then both the contributed funds and the matched funds withdrawn the next day without penalty [Choi, Laibson, and Madrian, 2005]. Thus, from the perspective of the employee, a default contribution equal to the level of the maximum company match makes perfect sense.

A somewhat weaker form of dominance is, "stochastic dominance," which involves minimizing risk at any level of return, or maximizing return at any level of risk. The case of including one's own company's stock in a retirement portfolio would seem to come close to violating stochastic dominance.

2. *Clearly negative outcomes:* Given certain circumstances, people make decisions that lead them down a detrimental path. The resulting outcomes are clearly undesirable, unintended, and not in the decision maker's self-interests. In these cases, a precise welfare criterion is not required because it is clear that people would be better off if they could avoid these negative pitfalls. For example, using a regression discontinuity model, Skiba and Tobacman [2006] found that people who use payday loans have a higher chance of filing for Chapter 13 bankruptcy relative to people who were not approved for the loan. Bankruptcy is a clearly negative outcome leading to filing costs, reorganization of debt, and a 10-year stigma on one's credit report. The shocking statistic that there are more payday loan establishments in the United States than there are McDonalds suggests, at minimum, that government policies which encourage or offer alternative forms of credit could be welfare enhancing for many people.[8]

3. *Self-officiating:* Despite Bernheim and Rangel's dismissal of this criterion in chapter 7, which effectively lets people choose their own goals and then helps them to achieve them through restrictions, incentives, or information to aid self-control, we think this criterion is generally a good one, assuming that the choice of goals is not done in the heat of the moment. If people who are overweight consistently believe that they would be better off were they not overweight, and consistently report that some proposed light paternalistic policy would make them better off, this would seem to be another relatively straightforward situation in which light paternalism can be justified. Thus, for example, if employees at a company themselves decided that they would be better off if, to avoid exposure to temptation, no soda machines were on the premises, a self-officiating criterion would dictate that soda machines should be removed. This is, admittedly, a form of heavy-handed paternalism. A lighter version would

keep the soda machines on premises but engineer a system that renders them operable only by employees who have elected ahead of time to give themselves access.

Bernheim and Rangel are very explicit in advocating a welfare criterion based on choice rather than on preference. Our own opinion is that the welfare criterion for evaluating paternalistic policies should be based on preference. Much as a psychotherapist would likely take at face value a client's professed desire to become happier, more sociable, or less anxious, even if she engaged in patterns of thinking and behavior that led to the opposite result, we would argue that the economist-as-therapist should treat verbal statements of preference as useful information, even if choice is not in line with professed preference. If people express a desire to lose weight but make choices that cause them to gain weight; if they express a desire to be financially solvent but make choices that lead to burdensome debt; if they want to stop smoking but continue to smoke; if they want to take prescription medications but fail to do so, these are all situations in which paternalistic interventions could be helpful. Indeed, the very hallmark of a situation in which paternalism may be justified is a divergence between stated preference and choice. Only in cases where such divergence exists should light paternalistic policies be devised, and they should endeavor to bring choice more in line with stated preference.

As further developments in the measurement of welfare occur, it may ultimately be possible to come up with less conservative measures of welfare that allow for a useful balancing of costs and benefits. Perhaps more fine-grained, domain-specific measures of experienced utility will help get around current problems with the measurement of happiness, allowing for the identification of a broader range of beneficial light paternalistic interventions. Until that happens, however, we would advocate that even light paternalistic policies be enacted only in the clear-cut situations just enumerated.

THE IMPORTANCE OF PROCESS

Light paternalism provides new motivation for looking inside the "black box" of human behavior. A better understanding of the processes underlying economic behavior can help to identify when light paternalistic interventions would be helpful, and, perhaps more importantly, can help to inform the policies themselves. As we show below, many light paternalistic interventions exploit nonstandard behavioral regularities (e.g., loss aversion, hyperbolic time discounting, and the status quo bias), which ordinarily undermine the optimality of decision making, to instead enhance it.

To illustrate the point, consider the Save More Tomorrow (SMarT) program designed and implemented by Thaler and Benartzi [2004]. The program was designed to deal with the problem that many employees fail to take advantage of the tax breaks and company matches on 401(k) plans, and, as a result, fail to save adequately for retirement. The failure to save adequately for retirement stems in part from hyperbolic time discounting (which overweighs the pleasures of current consumption over the pleasures of deferred consumption), loss aversion (because putting money into 401(k) plans is seen as a cut in take-home pay), and the status quo bias (which, when the default contribution rate was zero, encouraged noncontribution).

Employees at companies that participate in the SMarT plan are asked if they would increase their 401(k) contribution rates beginning at the time of their next pay raise. Since the contribution rate does not increase until after a raise, employees do not perceive the increased savings as a cut in take-home pay. Once employees sign up for the plan, they remain enrolled, and the process repeats each year until they reach the maximum contribution rate, unless they opt out. The SMarT plan is designed to make biases that typically discourage saving, such as hyperbolic time preferences, loss aversion, and the status quo bias work instead to promote saving.

Hyperbolic time preference, a concept first identified by Strotz [1955], refers to the tendency for people to be more impatient in the present (when trading off present against future gratifications) than they are with respect to the future (when trading off future against even more future gratifications). As Strotz [1955:177] expressed it, hyperbolic time discounting implies that individuals who

> naively resolve now what they "will do" in the future, commonly do not schedule the beginning of austerity until a later date. How familiar the sentence that begins, "I resolve, starting next[. . .]"! It seems very human for a person who decides that he ought to increase his savings to plan to start next month, after first satisfying some current desires; or for one to decide to quit smoking or drinking after the week-end, or to say that "the next one is the last one."

The SMarT program plays directly on these inclinations, presenting people with the option of doing what comes naturally—spending in the present but saving in the future—a plan that is especially attractive to people with hyperbolic time preferences.

The program also takes account of loss aversion, which describes the tendency for people to put greater weight on the psychological cost of a loss than on the psychological benefit of an equivalent gain. Due to loss aversion, people are more likely to tolerate a forgone gain than a loss of equal value. The program removes saving from future wage increments (perceived as a forgone gain) rather than having people simply contribute out of income (perceived as a loss).

If that were the whole story, of course, the SMarT plan would not work, because when tomorrow became today people would once again prefer spending over saving. However, at this point another factor comes into play that weighs against such an outcome: The program exploits the status quo bias to maximize continuing adherence by putting into place a decision rule (save a certain fraction out of future wage increases) that remains in effect unless it is explicitly rescinded.

This combination of ingredients seems to work. Initial evaluations of the program found that enrollment was very high (78%), that very few who joined dropped out, and that there were dramatic increases in contribution rates (from 3.5% to 11.6% over 28 months).

Harnessing Decision Biases to Improve Decision Making

Redirecting patterns of behavior that usually hurt people to help them instead is a common pattern among light paternalistic interventions. In this subsection, we discuss a variety of behavioral regularities that can be exploited by the economist/therapist.

The Importance of Immediate Feedback and Reinforcement

In the discussion of hyperbolic time discounting in connection with the SMarT plan, the emphasis was on not imposing immediate out-of-pocket costs on program participants. An even more important implication of hyperbolic time discounting is the need to design interventions that provide participants with very immediate costs and benefits—that is, reinforcement—as well as feedback about their behavior.

Thus, for example, hyperbolic time discounting probably plays a role in drug addiction (because the benefits of taking a drug are immediate and the consequences delayed), and one of the most effective treatments of addiction exploits hyperbolic time discounting to provide addicts with short-term financial incentives to quit [Higgins, Wong, Badger, Ogden, and Dantona, 2000]. Addicts are given coupons for consumer goods each day when they come in for treatment if their urine sample is negative for drug use. Most of the addicts treated in this program have experienced devastating losses as a result of their addiction, and would seem to have every incentive for quitting. But these small payments often succeed where much larger benefits fail, probably because they are delivered with a frequency that resembles that of drug-taking itself. A general principle is that many suboptimal patterns of behavior are caused by the overweighting of immediate costs and benefits, and hence any attempt to deliver incentives to overcome such patterns needs to provide incentives that can be small but must be frequent.

A line of research in which this insight is already well understood has involved using financial incentives to combat behaviors resulting from self-control problems. Financial incentives have been used to get people to stop smoking [Volpp, Gurmankin, Asch et al., 2006], lose weight [Jeffrey, Thompson, and Wing, 1978; Jeffrey, Gerber, Rosenthal, and Lindquist, 1983], stop taking addictive drugs such as heroin, cocaine, and cigarettes [e.g., Higgins et al., 2000; Heil, Tidey, Holmes, and Higgins, 2003], and get better grades [Angrist, Lang, and Oreopoulos, 2006]. Such interventions can be seen as an even more extreme version of "light" paternalism in that, not only is participation voluntary, but also the introduction of financial incentives (assuming they are rewards and not punishments) actually puts individuals into financial positions that are better than their positions before the intervention. Although people may know that in the long run it is in their best interests to diet, take their medications, or stop using illicit drugs, they often have difficulty implementing such decisions. Financial incentives seem to help mainly by offering short-term payoffs that bring the short-term incentives in line with long-term self interests.[9]

This insight can and should be, but to the best of our knowledge has yet been, applied to savings behavior.[10] Thus, many interventions to increase saving involve attempts to make the prospect of a destitute (or prosperous) retirement more salient to individuals, for example, by presenting vivid images of people suffering poverty in retirement. Such interventions are unlikely to have much of an impact because the prospect of retirement is so remote when people need to begin saving, and because any one day or even month of saving constitutes an inconsequential "drop in the bucket." Savings interventions that provide people with more immediate and frequent reinforcement are more likely to succeed. Short-term success in implementing saving plans could be reinforced by providing people with daily or weekly feedback of the form: "If you continue to save at this rate, this is where you will be at retirement." And achieving short-term saving goals—even at a daily or weekly level—could be reinforced through small rewards, including lottery prizes. Much as addicts respond to small, immediate gift vouchers, even after failing to respond to the seemingly much larger life benefits of being drug free, it is very likely that small short-term rewards for saving could have an impact that the objectively much larger prospect of a prosperous retirement does not.

Overweighting of Small Probabilities

It is well established that people tend to overweight small probabilities, which contributes to, among other things, the attractiveness of playing the lottery. Although playing the lottery is often viewed as self-destructive, the overweighting of small probabilities can be exploited to individuals' benefits by using it to magnify the value of rewards. Thus, in an ongoing collaboration with Kevin Volpp, Stephen

Kimmel, and Jalpa Doshi at the University of Pennsylvania, the first author has been providing people with a lottery-based incentive to take warfarin—a medication that dramatically lowers the likelihood of a second stroke at minimal cost and with few side effects if taken regularly. Patients get an electronic drug dispenser that electronically signals a central office if the correct drawer has been opened on a particular day, indicating that the patient, in all probability, took the pill. Every evening, a number is drawn and, if the number matches the patient's personal lottery number and the drawer was opened during the day, the patient receives a substantial cash prize. The incentive mechanisms plays not only on the overweighting of small probabilities, but also on regret aversion—the distaste for being in a situation in which one would have experienced a better outcome had one taken a different action. It does so by informing participants who fail to take their drug during the day and who win the lottery that they would have won had they taken the drug. The research on drug adherence is funded by an insurance company that is interested in the possibility that the program could be cost-effective if the cost of promoting adherence is lower than the cost of caring for the people who would have stokes as a result of failing to adhere to their drug regimen. Playing on the overweighting of small probabilities and regret aversion increases the "bang for the buck" and hence the likelihood that the program will be cost-effective. Initial results are promising; two pilot-tests of the intervention, each involving 10 patients followed for one month, resulted in an increase in adherence rates from a baseline of 66% to adherence rates of 96% in one study and 97% in the other.

Loss Aversion

A second program, currently being pilot tested with obese U.S. veterans who want to lose weight, and developed by Volpp, Loewenstein, and Carnegie Mellon University graduate student Leslie John, is an incentive scheme for promoting weight loss that involves "deposit contracts." In an innovative study, Mann [1972] found that participants who deposited money and other valuables with a therapist and signed contracts in which return of their valuables was contingent on progress toward pre-specified weight loss lost tremendous amounts of weight: an average of 32 pounds. A subsequent study that also involved deposit contracts produced similarly stunning results, with 47% losing more than 20 pounds and 70% losing more than 15 pounds. In contrast, interventions in which people have simply been paid for weight loss have produced more modest results.

In our in-progress intervention, people who are already motivated to lose weight (a precondition for this being treated as an instance of light paternalism) are invited to deposit an amount up to $90 per month ($3 per day), which the experimenters match one for one. The individual then receives a payment of two times the daily amount deposited for every day that his weight falls below a line that entails losing one pound per week. Deposit contracts play on loss aversion, but instead of playing on the underweighting of forgone gains (as does the SMarT program), it plays on the relatively greater weighting of out-of-pocket costs, which renders especially distasteful the prospect of losing one's own deposited money, as well as the experimenter's match. Deposit contracts also play on optimism, which encourages obese people who want to lose weight to put their own money at risk in the first place. The hope is that, when combined with the subsequent motivational force of loss aversion, the optimism about future weight loss will become self-fulfilling.

Framing Effects

Diverse lines of research show that changing superficial features in the presentation of a decision can produce predictable shifts in preference. Such "framing effects" can be exploited to help people make beneficial decisions and, at the very least, should be taken into consideration when presenting people with important information they need to make decisions about government programs, investment decisions, medical decisions, and so forth. Making use of framing effects is consistent with asymmetric paternalism in that it does not limit choice in any way, but can be used to help people make beneficial decisions. Similarly, it is consistent with the guiding principle of libertarian paternalism that information must be presented in some way to the public, so why not present it in a fashion that is advantageous to its recipient? Recent research by Schwartz, Bertrand, Mullainathan, and Shafir [2006] takes advantage of framing effects and loss aversion to increase take-up into employer-sponsored health care flexible spending accounts, which are economically beneficial for the vast majority of employees. Contribution rates were higher when the decision was framed as a loss ("Stop losing money now") compared to when the decision was framed as a gain ("Start saving money now").

Goal Gradients

In another program at an even more preliminary stage of development, the two authors have been developing innovations to increase the efficacy of Individual Development Accounts (IDAs). IDAs are matched savings accounts that allow low-income families to accumulate assets to purchase a home, pay for education, or start a small business. One of these innovations involves changing the schedule of deposit goals from a constant goal each month to a schedule based on the goal gradient hypothesis, first proposed by Hull [1932], which states that effort and motivation increase as one gets closer to completing a goal. This principle has been shown to apply to consumer behavior in reward programs, including the finding that even the illusion of progress toward a goal or, in this case, a reward can increase purchases [Kivetz, Urminsky, and Zheng, 2006].[11] Consistent with the goal gradient hypothesis, the schedule of savings deposits starts very small, increases slowly, and is highest right before the savings goal is met. This feature also makes the plan attractive to people with inconsistent time preferences who weigh immediate consumption much more heavily than future consumption. Initial payments will reduce current consumption only marginally, while the larger payments at the end of the plan reduce consumption more significantly but are heavily discounted.

Summary

The foregoing examples illustrate how, consistent with chapters in this volume that argue against a strict revealed preference approach, an understanding of human psychology can help us both to understand the causes of self-destructive behavior and to devise policies intended to counteract it. New developments will inevitably lead to creative new policies. For example, new research on the neural underpinnings of intertemporal choice [e.g., McClure, Laibson, Loewenstein, and Cohen, 2004] are drawing attention to the important role played by affect in many self-control problems. By drawing on insights about affect—namely, the tendency for "hot" emotions to "cool off" over time—this research may help inform and further the reach of cooling off regulations which already exist in a wide range of domains (e.g., when it comes to door-to-door sales). A challenge for future research will be to kindle the motivational force of hot emotions for beneficial rather than self-destructive ends.

The Need for Expanded Field Research

Conventional economists sometimes accuse behavioral economics of being rife with different effects (e.g., as discussed above, loss aversion, hyperbolic time discounting, and regret aversion), with competing effects sometimes coming into play simultaneously, making it difficult to predict the net impact of a particular exogenous change. There is some validity to this charge, although this state of affairs may reflect the real complexity of human psychology rather than any limitation of behavioral economics. People have different identities and behave differently depending on which identity is activated in a particular situation [LeBoeuf and Shafir, 2005]. They come to decisions "armed" with an array of different "choice heuristics," and which they employ depends on what type of situation they view themselves as facing [Frederick and Loewenstein, 2006]. At a more physiological level, behavior is the product of multiple neural systems that often act in concert but in some cases come into conflict [e.g., Sanfey, Loewenstein, McClure and Cohen, 2006]. The consequence is that small changes in circumstances or institutions can sometimes have large unforeseeable effects on behavior.

The multiplicity of psychological effects decreases the predictability of individual responses to policy interventions, and, as economists understand particularly well, interactions between individuals create further opportunities for unpredictable effects. To avoid unintended consequences, therefore, there is a pressing need for careful testing of specific interventions before they are implemented on a broad scale. Careful small-scale pilot testing is essential to ensure that the benefits of a large-scale implementation will outweigh the societal costs. Although we do not endorse what seems to be an emerging hostility toward laboratory studies [e.g., Levitt and List, 2008], there is probably no substitute for field studies when it comes to testing light paternalistic interventions.

An example of a paternalistic intervention with unexpected and unintended consequences was the "Move to Opportunity" experiment that was conducted in several major U.S. cities in the 1990s [Katz, Kling, and Liebman, 2001]. Although not an example of light paternalism, the study is useful for illustrating the utility of field experiments as a tool for evaluating any kind of paternalistic intervention. Families receiving subsidized housing were randomly assigned to one of three conditions: a group given a restricted housing voucher that could only be used in low-poverty neighborhoods (less than 10% below the poverty line), a group given an unrestricted housing voucher, and a no-voucher control group. The purpose of the study was to provide the first unconfounded test of the impact of neighborhood characteristics on economic and noneconomic outcomes. Although not framed by its developers as a test of paternalism, providing restricted vouchers can be interpreted as a form of paternalism, since they limit the choices of those who receive them, presumably with their best interest in mind.

The results of the Move to Opportunity experiment were surprising [Kling, Liebman, and Katz, 2007]. Although moving to a more economically advantaged neighborhood did have some beneficial effects, especially for girls, it also had some surprising negative effects that were concentrated mainly among boys. Girls had beneficial outcomes in the areas of mental health, educational outcomes (staying in school, reading and math achievement), risky behaviors (alcohol use, cigarette use, and pregnancy), and physical health. However, for boys there were substantial negative effects on physical health and risky behaviors. Results for adults were also disappointing. Contrary to expectations, there was no evidence of economic improvement in earnings, employment, or welfare usage for adults. Follow-up interviews indicate that these effects may be due to disrupted social networks and transportation difficulties. However, there were significant beneficial effects for adult obesity and mental health.

The Move to Opportunity study underlines the importance of testing paternalistic interventions on a small scale, but in the field. Although moving poor families into affluent neighborhoods may have clear benefits, such as increasing the safety of children, there may be a host of unintended consequences that could not have been anticipated at the outset. Moreover, the disappointing results from the Move to Opportunity study underscore the importance of collecting information about process, which was the theme of the preceding section. Beyond the disappointing results of the program itself, an unfortunate aspect of the research component of the program was the failure to collect sufficient qualitative data to shed light on why the program produced some of the perverse results that it did. Such process data could be used as an input into developing an improved follow-up program.

Whatever its limitations when it came to monitoring process variables, the Move to Opportunity program did provide extremely good outcome measures, which enabled a very clear delineation of its effects. This is an essential practice that should be applied more diligently in other field evaluations of light paternalism, and that applies most significantly to what is unquestionably the most important application of light paternalistic policies to date: interventions to increase saving.

As already touched upon, a number of researchers have tested interventions designed to encourage people to save more of their income. Note that these interventions are paternalistic in the sense that they assume that people do not naturally save as much as they want to or should. They are "light" in the sense that all are voluntary; none force people to save money. Although some do impose restrictions on withdrawals from savings, these are purely voluntary. These studies have employed a wide range of methods.

Several "natural experiments" (or "quasi experiments" as the psychologists who developed the techniques refer to them; e.g., Campbell [1969]), have examined the effects of increasing default contributions on increasing participation and contribution rates to 401(k) plans (see Choi, Laibson, and Madrian [2004] for review). These studies track changes in the savings and investment behavior of employees at companies that abruptly change some aspect of their policy. Presumably, such a change in policy does not coincide with an equally sudden and simultaneous change in the preferences of employees. Such studies show that simply by changing the default from unenrolled to enrolled dramatically increases enrollment, even though in either case the employee retains total decision-making autonomy, making this a near-perfect example of asymmetric paternalism [Choi et al., 2004; Madrian and Shea, 2001]. Employees are also highly influenced by the default level of contribution and the default for the asset allocation among available investment funds, underscoring the need to set optimal default contribution rates and diversification strategies.

Other research examining interventions to promote saving has involved field experiments in which a variable of interest was manipulated exogenously. For example, Duflo and Saez [2002] examined the impact of an educational intervention to increase enrollment [Duflo and Saez, 2003]. A random sample of employees in a subset of departments were offered a $20 payment for attending an informational fair, and their 401(k) contributions were tracked as well as those of their coworkers. The most interesting finding from the study was that social information plays an important role in participation in 401(k) plans. Enrollment was significantly higher in departments where some individuals received the monetary inducement to attend the fair than in departments where no one received the inducement. However, increased enrollment within these treated departments was almost as high for individuals who did not receive any monetary inducement as it was for individuals who did, demonstrating the influence of social information.

Another field experiment focusing on saving examined the interest in, and response to, the introduction of a voluntary commitment savings product that restricted access to deposits [Ashraf, Karlan, and Yin, 2005]. Existing customers of a bank in the Philippines were randomly assigned to one of three conditions: a commitment group who were given the option of opening the restricted account, a marketing group who received a special visit to encourage savings, and a control group who were not contacted. Twenty-eight percent of the commitment group enrolled in the restricted account. After 12 months, individuals in the commitment group were significantly more likely to have increased their savings by 20% than were participants in the marketing group or the control group. Average savings balances of the commitment group increased by 81% relative to the control group. Further, this study sheds light on which individuals are most likely to enroll in restricted savings accounts. Results of a preexperiment survey show that impatience over immediate trade-offs, but patience over future trade-offs (consistent with hyperbolic discounting), predicts program enrollment, particularly for women.

A major, although seemingly unavoidable, limitation of all of these studies is the paucity of outcome measures that were collected. All of the studies of saving behavior examined the impact of, for example, changing retirement savings defaults on the affected account (the account for which the default rule is changed) but did not look at the impact on the overall financial position of the individuals and families involved. The problem with such a limited focus is that the change in retirement saving may have had other undesirable effects that were not measured by existing studies. If the increase in retirement saving comes out of frivolous consumption, that might be a good thing, but what if it leads to an increase in credit card debt, or a cutback of spending on nutrition or children's education? Without knowing the answer to these questions, it is difficult to come to any confident conclusion about the benefits of the seemingly "successful" programs to increase retirement saving. Indeed, even if it were shown that increasing retirement saving did not come at the expense of increased debt or decreased investments in human capital, it still would be difficult to evaluate the effects of such programs in a comprehensive fashion. For example, if the increase in retirement saving came out of vacation trips, is this necessarily a good thing? Might it be better for a family to take nice vacations while the children are young and then to live on a shoestring during retirement?

Another limitation of most of the field experiments that have been conducted is their failure to manipulate program parameters in a fashion that, if an intervention were successful, would provide insight into what specific features of the intervention matter. For example, the Save More Tomorrow plan, which combines several features, has been proven successful in increasing saving. However, the relative importance of each specific feature is unclear. Thus, perhaps a program that committed people to save in the future but did not deduct that saving from future pay increases would work just as well as the current SMarT plan. Without studies that randomly assign participants to different configurations of plan features, we will never know the answer to questions of this type.

Beyond field research examining the impact of light paternalistic interventions, there is a need for basic research on topics that will inform the design and evaluation of effective policy. First, and consistent with the discussion above, the question of the optimal welfare criterion is in some sense an empirical question. Research could potentially address questions such as which criteria most closely mirror people's lay theories and values (e.g., whether people are more comfortable with choice-based or happiness-based policy decisions) and could also examine the types of trade-offs between autonomy and guidance that people endorse.[12] Additionally, to understand the trade-offs between different welfare criteria, it is important to have basic research on reliable and valid welfare measures. Progress has been made on the development of methodology to measure experience utility, such as with the use of ordinal scales to minimize the problem of scale recalibration and the use of experience sampling techniques [see Kahneman and Krueger, 2006; Riis et al., 2005]. Future research could focus on measures that correspond to different welfare criteria. For example, the self-officiating welfare criterion entails an attempt to ascertain what an individual desires most of the time, but preferences often fluctuate. Just as experience sampling has been used to capture fluctuations in happiness over time, it could also be used to measure fluctuations in preferences over time.

Second, consistent with the need for expanded research on process discussed above, there is a need for basic research on topics that will inform the design of policy. For example, we still have an extremely imperfect understanding of the psychological factors leading to undersaving, overeating, and a variety of other problems. To what extent is undersaving due to the overweighting of immediate gratifications, to procrastination (the intention to start saving tomorrow and the belief that one will do so), the "drop-in-the-bucket" effect (the view that one small indulgence or act of self-denial will have a negligible impact on one's overall level of saving), to overoptimism about future revenue sources, or a host of other possible contributing factors. A better understanding of why people fail to save could aid in the design of light paternalistic interventions. Similarly, many light paternalistic interventions involve giving people feedback and/or rewards for behaving in a self-interested fashion. However, we still have little understanding of what types of rewards are most motivating (e.g., lotteries vs. cash payments vs. in-kind rewards) or about what types of rewards pose the greatest threat of crowding out people's intrinsic motivation to do what's best for themselves.

Third, there is a need for new technologies to aid in the implementation and assessment of paternalistic interventions. For example, devices that measure weight, blood sugar levels, and blood pressure and that, like the electronic pill dispenser we have been using to improve warfarin adherence, permit two-way communications with a central administrator, could introduce a range of new possibilities for light paternalistic interventions.

IMPLEMENTING LIGHT PATERNALISM: RECHANNELING ECONOMIC INTERESTS

Currently, there are a wide range of economic interests aligned, in effect, against consumers—entities that profit when, for example, consumers consume large amounts of food or alcohol, smoke cigarettes, play the lottery, incur credit card debt, or overdraw their bank accounts (incurring overdraft charges that provide a substantial flow of revenues to banks). These efforts are not necessarily driven by malicious motives; a company that failed to play on consumer weaknesses but faced competitors that did would be likely to lose business (see Loewenstein and O'Donoghue [2006] and Issacharoff and Delaney [2006] for a discussion of this issue).[13]

Admittedly, there are economic forces arrayed on the other side, for example, the diet industry, sellers of nicotine patches, and financial companies that benefit when people amass financial assets. But the forces that play on consumers' weaknesses tend to be much stronger than those that bolster consumer defenses, and the motives of those arrayed on the other side are often ambivalent.[14] For example, nicotine patches are sold to people who are addicted to cigarettes, so their makers have, at one level, an interest in promoting addiction. Likewise, although the sellers of commercial diets would probably attract more customers if they were effective in promoting weight loss, they make the most money by selling hope rather than actual results. Hospitals similarly have the goal of curing sickness, but they have little motivation in promoting preventive medicine, which would just hurt their bottom line. An important goal for economists interested in light paternalistic solutions to such problems, therefore, is not only to devise clever solutions to suboptimalities in consumer behavior but to figure out creative ways to implement and fund such solutions.

In some situations, incentives for light paternalistic policies could be put into place via legislation or other forms of government regulation. For example, companies could be given tax breaks that are dependent on employee contribution rates to 401(k) plans, in which case they could potentially be motivated to change defaults or, perhaps, introduce the SMarT plan. Through tax incentives or granting agencies, governments can promote business models that make it easier for individuals to act in their own best interests, such as nutritious and affordable fast food. The so-called "fat tax" is an example of a much more heavy-handed intervention that could work against the ever-declining prices of high-calorie foods, a situation that many economists hold responsible for growing levels of obesity.

In other situations, however, it is going to require the creativity of economists to play matchmaker and to identify areas of mutual interest that might not have spontaneously emerged without their intervention. Take obesity, for example. Although, as described, there are a number of economic entities (including, possibly, the medical industry) that stand to gain from obesity or the behaviors that cause it, there are also some economic interests that lose when people gain weight. Prominent among those who stand to lose are insurance companies. Although, as an industry, insurance companies may be indifferent to whether people are thin or fat, individual life insurance companies would benefit if their customers lost weight. If creative, low-cost interventions could be designed, therefore, it is quite possible that insurance companies would be motivated to underwrite the costs. Insurance companies would also be in a position to lobby for legislation that would allow them to adjust their rates based on the weight of a prospective customer, which would pass the economic benefits of weight loss on to consumers or their employers.

As another example, take drug adherence. Here, health insurers could potentially be motivated to provide funding for interventions that had the potential to reduce health costs. In fact, as already alluded to, the first author, along with researchers at the University of Pennsylvania, has secured funding from an insurance company to pilot test an intervention intended to increase adherence to warfarin— an antistroke medication. Pharmaceutical companies also have a direct stake in drug adherence although their interests are somewhat more conflicted than those of insurance companies.

Saving is an example where there is a confluence of interests between customers and the bank. Further, people's difficulty in saving and desire to save more create a circumstance in which banks can even extract rents by aiding customers in saving more. A recent study conducted in the Philippines examined the impact of hiring deposit collectors, bank employees who come to customers' house to pick up savings deposits, a practice that is prevalent in some developing countries [Ashraf, Karlin, and Yin, 2006]. The use of deposit collectors increased savings by 25% relative to control groups, and people were willing to pay for this service. The study suggests that people are willing to pay because the service reduces the transaction costs of having to go to the bank, facilitates adherence to financial planning, and restricts the spending of spouses. Banks in the United States are just starting to take advantage of people's difficulty in saving to develop marketable products, such as American Express's "Savings Accelerator Plan" for their One Card that contributes 1% of eligible purchases into a savings account.

As a final example, consider lotteries. Despite the fact that state lotteries return only 50 cents on the dollar—the lowest payout rate of any form of legal gambling [Clotfelter and Cook, 1989]—in fiscal year 2003 Americans spent almost $45 billion on lotteries, or $155 for every man, woman, and child in the United States. Lotteries are played disproportionately by low-income individuals, with many studies finding that poor people put a larger fraction of their income into lotteries and others finding that they actually spend a larger absolute amount per capita. The purchase of lottery tickets by the poor could be considered a type of "poverty trap"—a cycle of behavior that prevents poor people from improving their situations.

The most obvious solution to this problem might seem to be to regulate the lottery, but that is very unlikely to happen since the lottery generates a sizable amount of revenue for states, and because any restriction of availability is likely to lead to the reemergence of illegal, unregulated alternatives. A "rechanneling of economic interests" would entail that the financial services industry market investment alternatives that have lottery-like properties—i.e., that have a small cost and a small probability of yielding a large payout—but that, unlike lotteries and other forms of gambling, yield a positive expected return. Trying to "pull" people away from gambling and toward investing could potentially be much more effective than trying to "push" people away from gambling. The potential money amounts to be reaped are staggering, and allocating this money to capital formation instead of operating lotteries would be socially productive.

We believe that the key to selling these low-cost, high-risk investments is to make it possible to invest small amounts at a time and make the investments convenient to purchase on a daily basis. We have conducted experiments on state lottery ticket purchases in a low-income population and found that rates of ticket purchases are high when people make purchase decisions one at a time, that is, myopically. This finding can be explained in part by what is termed the "peanuts effect" [Prelec and Loewenstein, 1991; Weber and Chapman, 2005]. For each decision, the dollar they spend on a ticket is underweighted—that is, merely considered a "peanut"—and so they go for the gamble. However, rates of purchases are significantly lower when the decision to purchase several tickets is aggregated into a single decision. Then people are less likely to write off the amount necessary to purchase several tickets as insignificant.

This insight into decision making under uncertainty can be used to help low-income individuals to invest and to save. Though people may not be willing to take a substantial sum of money to invest (or may not have the self-control to save the minimum balances necessary to open an investment account), they may be willing to devote small amounts of money, spread out over time, to investments options. The startup costs are quite high for the convenient sale of low-cost investments. However, there is a lot of potential to market other types of investments in addition to those designed to dissuade gambling, such as investments in equity index funds and savings in money market accounts.

The convenient sale of low-cost investments in a system that minimizes transaction costs by providing only a few investment options has great potential to increase the money that the average individual devotes to investing and saving, especially for low-income individuals and for those who typically play the lottery. At a minimum, investment companies should market investments as an alternative to gambling. An ad could feature two people, one who spends a dollar a day on the lottery, and show the money being put on a pile and then shrinking or burning, and one who invests it, and show the money accumulating gradually into a huge pile.

CONCLUSION: A METHODOLOGY OF NORMATIVE ECONOMICS

Milton Friedman, in his famous 1953 paper "The Methodology of Positive Economics," distinguished between two approaches to economic methods, which he termed positive and normative economics.[15] Friedman defined positive economics as a "body of systematized knowledge concerning what is," which, he continued, could "provide a system of generalizations that can be used to make predictions about the consequences of any change in circumstances." Normative economics, in contrast, encompassed a "body of systematized knowledge discussing criteria of what ought to be," and a "system of rules for the attainment of a given end." [Friedman, 1953: 3].

Although Friedman devoted most of his essay to a discussion of the methodology of positive economics, he did not dismiss the value of normative economics. Rather, he lamented that normative economics would be unavoidably contentious, because, he believed, issues of values were much more difficult to resolve than issues of fact.[16] Friedman himself, of course, never shied from the normative [Krugman, 2007]. In fact, as typified by his famous *Free to Choose*, much of his professional life was devoted to arguing about what ought to be and what system of rules would be most successful in achieving his vision of the good society. Believing as he did in rational choice and the benefits of free markets, his conclusions were generally fairly predictable: eliminate regulations and eliminate any barriers to unrestricted competition.

In the last several decades, however, a new view of human behavior has taken root among many economists, one that recognizes through methods of positive economics limitations in people's pursuit of self-interest. Research on the psychology of decision making, the role of affect in decision making, and neuroeconomics have led to the recognition that human behavior can in some cases be suboptimal or even self-destructive, and have contributed to our understanding of when, why, and how deviations from self-interest occur. The new research has, in turn, spawned a whole new area of normative economics focused on the two elements of normative economics identified by Friedman: the measurement of welfare and the design of economic and social systems that maximize welfare.

Although embracing an interventionism that conservative thinkers such as Milton Friedman generally disdain, the new light paternalism can be viewed as in fact quite sympathetic to their arguments and philosophy. Eschewing traditional forms of heavy-handed command and control, light paternalism endorses diversity in policy experimentation, the use of market incentives rather than mandates, and the use of improved informational and feedback mechanisms to verify effects, push objectives, and guard against unintended consequences. Although light paternalism is still in its infancy, it has already produced insights into regulation and incentive design that are likely to have far-reaching consequences. Economists, we believe, should be and, as we have documented, to a very great extent already are in the business of "discussing criteria of what ought to be" and attempting to devise economic institutions that maximize the likelihood that what ought to be in fact occurs. If this brands us economist/therapists, we embrace the label with pride.

NOTES

We thank Dan Akst, Eric Agner, Andrew Caplin, Peter Huang, Sam Issacharoff, Ed Glaeser, Ted O'Donoghue, Andy Schotter, Nachum Sicherman, Cass Sunstein, and Kevin Volpp for helpful comments and suggestions.

1. See www.spendonlife.com/content/CreditCardDebtEliminationAndFactsAbout DebtInAmerica-1-223-3.ashx.

2. According to the Investment Company Institute, this includes equity and mutual fund holdings in employee-sponsored retirement plans (www.ici.org/statements/res/ rpt_05_equity_owners.pdf).

3. American Gaming Association (www.americangaming.org/Industry/factsheets/ statistics_detail.cfv?id=7).

4. Murphy [2006].

5. There is a third class of people who could potentially be made worse off by a default. For example, a high savings default would not be optimal for people carrying high credit card debt, and these people may fail to "rationally" opt out of default. This point is further discussed in a later section that highlights the need for pilot testing and good outcome measures to ensure against net negative consequences of paternalistic policies.

6. However, one potential problem with precommitment options is that people who are in "cold states"—e.g., not hungry or not craving drugs—may be unable to fully appreciate the force of their own future motivation and hence may be excessively prone (i.e., more prone than would be optimal) to commit their own future behavior [see, e.g., Badger et al., 2007; Nordren, van der Plight, and Harreveld, in press).

7. Legislation that regulates information disclosure, e.g., the Federal Truth in Lending Act, is close to purely asymmetric and would probably satisfy this criterion. Other forms of information disclosure might be more questionable. For example, food labels can make one miserable if one fails to diet [Loewenstein and O'Donoghue, 2006]. Cooling off periods that require a mandatory waiting period for certain purchases or activities, such as marriage, are even less strictly asymmetric. Cooling off periods are designed to prevent people from making mistakes when they are in a state of arousal that they will later regret, but they do impose real costs on those who must delay their purchase. In such situations, asymmetric paternalism can be justified only if the benefits (in this case, the utility that otherwise would have been lost from making purchasing errors) exceeds the costs for people who engage in the behavior regardless of visceral state (in this case, the cost of having to delay the purchase by those who do, in fact, want to make it).

8. There are approximately 30,000 payday loan outlets in the United States, which is about double the number of McDonald's restaurants.

9. A review of 47 studies on the effect of financial incentives to encourage preventative health care reveals that overall these interventions are successful, at least in the short run [Kane, Johnson, Tawn, and Butler, 2004]. The incentives were effective 74% of the time for simple preventive measures, such as vaccinations, and 72% of the time for complex preventative measures that required sustained behavioral change, such as weight loss. A variety of different types of incentives (cash, coupons, free medical care, lotteries, gifts, and punishment) were effective.

10. Individual development accounts offer financial incentives for saving through monthly matching and have been an extremely promising tool for helping low-income families build assets. However, like employee matching of 401(k) contributions, matching is not immediate and frequent enough to be an optimal reinforcer.

11. The motivational effect of the illusion of progress toward a goal was demonstrated by greater purchase acceleration when people were given a "buy 12 coffees, get one free" card with two preexisting bonus stamps than when they were given a "buy 10 coffees, get one free" card.

12. For an example of using empirical research to elicit values about policy trade-offs, see Ubel and Loewenstein [1996] and Ubel, Loewenstein, Scanlon, and Kamlet [1996].

13. Although not necessarily malevolent, in some cases these forces can take on sinister forms. For example, the "Center for Consumer Freedom (Promoting Personal Responsibility and Protecting Consumer Choice)" (www.consumerfreedom.com/index.cfm) describes itself (see the "About Us" link) as a "nonprofit coalition of restaurants, food companies, and consumers working together to promote personal responsibility and

protect consumer choices" and as being in opposition to "the growing cabal of 'food cops,' health care enforcers, militant activists, meddling bureaucrats, and violent radicals who think they know 'what's best for you' [that] are pushing against our basic freedoms."

14. This is true even when it comes to the biggest success story to date for light paternalism: savings behavior. The first author had the experience of pitching an idea for increasing employee retirement saving to a company that offered an employer match, only to be discreetly informed that it wasn't in the company's interest to encourage its employees to save more since an increase in company matches would only detract from the bottom line.

15. In doing so, he drew on the earlier work of John Neville Keynes [1891].

16. In contrast to his respectful views of normative economics, Friedman was less favorable toward economists who ignore data altogether. Writing in 1953, Friedman failed to anticipate the remarkable methodological advances that were to occur in the next half-century, some of them enabled by the development of the computer. "One effect of the difficulty of testing substantive economic hypotheses has been to foster a retreat into purely formal or tautological analyses. . . . economic theory must be more than a structure of tautologies if it is able to predict and not merely describe the consequences of action" [Friedman, 1953, 11–12].

Moreover, Friedman believed that many apparent disputes over values actually revolve around issues of fact and hence could be resolved empirically—that is, through the methods of positive economics. As an example, he cited disputes over the desirability of minimum wage legislation that seemingly revolved around values but, which he posited, hinged on, and hence could be resolved by knowledge of, the impact of an increase in the minimum wage on employment. While not denying the significance and utility of normative economics (which he hardly could have done without risking the label of hypocrite), Friedman believed it would be possible to diminish the scope of normative economics by expanding that of positive economics. Casual empiricism, as well as empirical research, however, suggests that issues of value are rarely resolved by recourse to data [see, e.g., Mitroff, 1974]. Empirical testing usually has a sufficient subjective element such that clever investigators can, by framing the question in the right way, or by using the right methods, come up with the answer they seek (see Glaeser, chapter 13). Thus, for example, Plott and Zeiler [2005] show that, with a magical mixture of experimental manipulations, they are able to reduce the magnitude of the endowment effect. Indeed, even on the issue that Friedman used to illustrate the capacity of positive economics to supplant normative economics—the impact of an increase in the minimum wage on employment—there has been a remarkable tendency for empirical research conducted by proponents of raising the minimum wage to conclude that doing so has minimal or even positive impact on employment, with the opposite pattern observed in the research of opponents. Fuchs, Krueger, and Poterba [1998] conducted a survey of labor and public economists at leading research universities that elicited, among other things, respondents' beliefs about the impact of an increase in the minimum wage on youth employment, their degree of support for an increase in the minimum wage, and various questions about values and political orientation. Despite many decades of research on the topic, they found a remarkable lack of convergence among researchers regarding the impact of a minimum wage hike on employment. Moreover, there was also little evidence that settling the positive issue would, in fact, help to resolve the normative one. Support for an increase in the minimum wage was strongly correlated with a researcher's social and political values but barely related to economists' beliefs about the impact of an increase in the minimum wage on employment.

REFERENCES

Angrist, Joshua, Daniel Lang, and Philip Oreopoulos. 2006. Incentives and Services for College Achievement: Evidence from a Randomized Trial. Online. Available: www.stanford.edu/group/SITE/Web%20Session%207/Oreopoulos_Abstract.pdf#search=%22.

Ashraf, Nava, Dean Karlan, and Wesley Yin. 2005. Tying Odysseus to the Mast: Evidence from a Commitment Savings Product in the Philippines. *Quarterly Journal of Economics* 121: 635–672.

———. 2006. Deposit Collectors. *Advances in Economic Analysis and Policy* 6(2): 1–22.

Badger, Gary J., Warren K. Bickel, Louis A. Giordano, Eric A. Jacobs, and George Loewenstein, 2007. Altered States: The Impact of Immediate Craving on the Valuation of Current and Future Options. *Journal of Health Economics* 26: 865–876.

Camerer, Colin, Samuel Issacharoff, George Loewenstein, Ted O'Donoghue, and Matthew Rabin. 2003. Regulation for Conservatives: Behavioral Economics and the Case for "Asymmetric Paternalism." *University of Pennsylvania Law Review* 151(3): 1211–1254.

Campbell, Donald. 1969. Reforms as Experiments. *American Psychologist* 24: 409–429.

Choi, James J., David Laibson, and Brigitte C. Madrian. 2004. Plan Design and 401(k) Savings Outcomes. *National Tax Journal* 57: 275–298.

———. 2005. $100 Bills on the Sidewalk: Suboptimal Savings in 401(k) Plans. National Bureau of Economic Research NBER Working Paper 11554.

Choi, James J., David Laibson, Brigitte C. Madrian, and Andrew Metrick. 2005. Optimal Defaults and Active Decisions. National Bureau of Economic Research NBER Working Paper: 11074.

Clotfelter, Charles T., and Philip J. Cook. 1989. *Selling Hope: State Lotteries in America.* Cambridge, MA: Harvard University Press.

DellaVigna, Stefano. Forthcoming. Psychology and Economics: Evidence from the Field. *Journal of Economic Literature.*

Diener, E., and M. Seligman 2004. Beyond Money: Toward an Economy of Well-Being. *Psychological Science in the Public Interest* 5: 1–31.

Di Tella, Raphael, Robert J. MacCulloch, and Andrew J. Oswald. 2003. The Macroeconomics of Happiness. Review of Economics and Statistics 85: 809–827.

Duflo, Esther, and Emmanuel Saez. 2002. Participation and Investment Decisions in a Retirement Plan: The Influence of Colleagues' Choices. *Journal of Public Economics* 85: 121–48.

————. 2003. The Role of Information and Social Interactions in Retirement Plan Decisions: Evidence from a Randomized Experiment. *Quarterly Journal of Economics* 118: 815–842.

Flegal, Katherine M., Barry I. Graubard, David F. Williamson, and Mitchell H. Gail. 2007. Cause-specific Excess Deaths Associated with Underweight, Overweight, and Obesity. *JAMA: Joural of the American Medical Association* 298: 2028–2037.

Frederick, Shane, and George Loewenstein. 1999. Hedonic Adaptation. In *Well-Being: The Foundations of Hedonic Psychology*, ed. Daniel Kahneman, Ed Diener, and Norbert Schwarz, 302–329. New York: Russell Sage Foundation.

————. 2006. Preference Authority in the Evaluation of Sequences. Center for Behavioral Decision Research Working Paper, Carnegie Mellon University.

Friedman, Milton. 1953. The Methodology of Positive Economics. In *Essays in Positive Economics.* Chicago: University of Chicago Press.

Fuchs, Victor R., Alan B. Krueger, and James M. Poterba. 1998. Economists' Views about Parameters, Values, and Policies: Survey Results in Labor and Public Economics. *Journal of Economic Literature* 36: 1387–1425.

Glaeser, Edward L. 2006. Paternalism and Psychology. *University of Chicago Law Review* 73: 133–156.

Halpern, Scott D., Peter A. Ubel, and David A. Asch. 2007. Harnessing the Power of Default Options to Improve Health Care. *New England Journal of Medicine* 357: 1340–1344.

Heil, Sarah H., Jennifer W. Tidey, Heather W. Holmes, and Stephen T. Higgins. 2003. A Contingent Payment Model of Smoking Cessation: Effects of Abstinence and Withdrawal. *Nicotine and Tobacco Research* 5: 205–213.

Herrnstein, Richard, George Loewenstein, Drazen Prelec, and William Vaughan. 1993. Utility Maximization and Melioration: Internalitites in Individual Choice. *Journal of Behavioral Decision Making* 6: 149–185.

Higgins, Stephen T., Conrad J. Wong, Gary J. Badger, Doris E. Ogden, and Robert L. Dantona. 2000. Contingent Reinforcement Increases Cocaine Abstinence During Outpatient Treatment and One Year of Follow-up. *Journal of Consulting and Clinical Psychology* 68: 64–72.

Hull, Clark L. 1932. The Goal-Gradient Hypothesis and Maze Learning. *Psychological Review* 39: 24–43.

Issacharoff, Samuel, and Erin F. Delaney. 2006. Credit Card Accountability. *University of Chicago Law Review* 73: 157–182.

Jackevicius, Cynthia A., Muhammad Mamdani, and Jack V. Tu. 2002. Adherence with Statin Therapy in Elderly Patients with and without Acute Coronary Syndromes. *JAMA: Journal of the American Medical Association* 288:462–467.

Jeffrey, Robert W., Wendy M. Gerber, Barbara S. Rosenthal, and Ruth A. Lindquist. 1983. Monetary Contracts in Weight Control: Effectiveness of Group and Individual Contracts of Varying Size. *Journal of Consulting and Clinical Psychology* 51: 242–248.

Jeffrey, Robert W., Paul D. Thompson, and Rena R. Wing. 1978. Effects on Weight Reduction of Strong Monetary Contracts for Calorie Restriction or Weight Loss. *Behaviour Research and Therapy* 16: 363–369.

Kahneman, Daniel, and Alan B. Krueger. 2006. Developments in the Measurement of Subjective Well-Being. *Journal of Economic Perspectives* 20: 3–24.

Kahneman, Daniel, and Dale Miller. 1986. Norm Theory: Comparing Reality to Its Alternatives. *Psychological Review* 93: 136–153.

Kane, Robert L., Paul E. Johnson, Robert J. Town, and Mary Butler. 2004. A Structured Review of the Effect of Economic Incentives on Consumers' Preventive Behavior. *American Journal of Preventive Medicine* 27: 327–352.

Katz, Lawrence F., Jeffrey R. Kling, and Jeffrey B. Liebman. 2001. Moving to Opportunity in Boston: Early Results of a Randomized Mobility Experiment. *Quarterly Journal of Economics* 116: 607–654.

Keynes, John N. 1891. *The Scope and Method of Political Economy.* London: Macmillan and Co.

Kivetz, Ran, Oleg Urminsky, and Yuhuang Zheng. 2006. The Goal-Gradient Hypothesis Resurrected: Purchase Acceleration, Illusionary Goal Progress, and Customer Retention. *Journal of Marketing Research* 43: 39–58.

Klick, Joanathan, and Gregory Mitchell. 2006. Government Regulation of Irrationality: Moral and Cognitive Hazards. *Minnesota Law Review* 90: 1620–1663.

Kling, Jeffery R., Jeffery B. Liebman, and Lawrence F. Katz. 2007. Experimental Analysis of Neighborhood Effects. *Econometrica* 75: 83–119.

Krugman, Paul. 2007. Who Was Milton Friedman? *New York Review of Books* 54: 27–30.

Layard, R. 2005. *Happiness. Lessons from a New Science.* London: Allen Lane.

LeBoeuf, Robyn A., and Eldar B. Shafir. 2005. Decision Making. In *The Cambridge Handbook of Thinking and Reasoning,* ed. Keith J. Holyoak and Robert G. Morrison, 243–265. New York: Cambridge University Press.

Levitt, Steven D., and John A. List. 2008. What Do Laboratory Experiments Measuring Social Preferences Reveal about the Real World? *Journal of Economic Perspectives.*

Loewenstein, George. 1996. Out of Control: Visceral Influences on Behavior. *Organizational Behavior and Human Decision Processes* 65: 272–292.

Loewenstein, George, Troyen Brennan, and Kevin G. Volpp. 2007. Asymmetric Paternalism to Improve Health Behaviors. *JAMA: Journal of the American Medical Association* 298: 2415–2417.

Loewenstein, George, and Ted O'Donoghue. 2006. We Can Do This the Easy Way or the Hard Way: Negative Emotions, Self-Regulation, and the Law. *University of Chicago Law Review* 73: 183–206.

Loewenstein, George, and Peter A. Ubel. Forthcoming. Hedonic Adaptation and the Role of Decision and Experience Utility in Public Policy. *Journal of Public Economics,* Special Issue on Happiness and Public Economics.

Madrian, Brigitte C., and Dennis F. Shea. 2001. The Power of Suggestion: Inertia in 401(k) Participation and Savings Behavior. *Quarterly Journal of Economics* 116: 1149–1525.

Mann, Ronald A. 1972. The Behavior-Therapeutic Use of Contingency Contracting to Control an Adult Behavior Problem: Weight Control. *Journal of Applied Behavioral Analysis* 5: 99–102.

McClure, Samuel M., David I. Laibson, George Loewenstein, and Jonathan D. Cohen. 2004. Separate Neural Systems Value Immediate and Delayed Monetary Rewards. *Science* 306: 503–507.

Mitroff, Ian I. 1974. *The Subjective Side of Science: A Philosophical Inquiry into the Psychology of the Apollo Moon Scientists.* New York: Elsevier.

Murphy, Kevin. 2006. Keynote Address. 2006 Healthchallenge Think Tank, McGill University.

Nordgren, Loran F., Joop van der Pligt, and Frenk van Harreveld. In press. The Instability of Health Cognitions: Visceral States Influence Self-Efficacy and Related Health Beliefs. *Health Psychology.*

Nussbaum, Martha. 2000. *Women and Human Development: The Capabilities Approach.* Cambridge: Cambridge University Press.

Plott, Charles R., and Kathryn Zeiler. 2005. The Willingness to Pay–Willingness to Accept Gap, the "Endowment Effect," Subject Misconceptions, and Experimental Procedures for Eliciting Valuations. *American Economic Review* 95: 530–45.

Prelec, Drazen, and George Loewenstein. 1991. Decision Making over Time and under Uncertainty: A Common Approach. *Management Science* 37: 770–786.

Riis Jason, George Loewenstein, Jonathan Baron, Christopher Jepson, Angela Fagerlin, and Peter A. Ubel. 2005. Ignorance of Hedonic Adaptation to Hemo-dialysis: A Study Using Ecological Momentary Assessment. *Journal Experimental Psychology: General* 134: 3–9.

Sanfey, Alan, George Loewenstein, Sam M. McClure, and Jonathan D. Cohen. 2006. Neuroeconomics: Cross-Currents in Research on Decision Making. *Trends in Cognitive Science* 10: 108–116.

Schroeder, Steven A. 2007. Shattuck Lecture. We Can Do Better–Improving the Health of the American People. *The New England Journal of Medicine* 357 (12): 1221–1228.

Schwartz, Janet, Marianne Bertrand, Sendhil Mullainathan, and Eldar Shafir. 2006. Boosting Program Take-up: An Experiment with Flexible Spending Accounts. Paper presented at the Behavioral Decision Research in Management Conference, Santa Monica, June 15–17.

Sen, Amartya. 1999. *Development as Freedom.* Oxford: Oxford University Press.

———. 1985. *Commodities and Capabilities.* Amsterdam: North-Holland.

Skiba, Paige, and Jeremy Tobacman. 2006. Measuring the Effect of Access to Credit: Evidence from Payday Loans. Paper presented at the Society for Judgment and Decision Making Conference, Houston, November 17–20.

Smith, Dylan M., Ryan L. Sherriff, Laura J. Damschroder, George Loewenstein, and Peter A. Ubel. 2007. Misremembering Colostomies? Former Patients Give Lower Utility Ratings Than Do Current Patients. *Health Psychology* 25: 688–695.

Strotz, Robert H. 1955. Myopia and Inconsistency in Dynamic Utility Maximization. *Review of Economic Studies* 23: 165–180.

Sugden, Robert. 2005. Capability, Happiness and Opportunity. Paper presented at Capabilities and Happiness: An International Conference, Department of Economics, University of Milano-Bicocca, June 16–18.

Thaler, Richard H., and Shlomo Benartzi. 2004. Save More Tomorrow: Using Behavioral Economics to Increase Employee Savings. *Journal of Political Economy* 112: 164–187.

Thaler, Richard H., and Cass R. Sunstein. 2003. Libertarian Paternalism. *American Economic Review* 93: 175–179.

Ubel, Peter, and George Loewenstein. 1996. Distributing Scarce Livers: The Moral Reasoning of the General Public. *Social Science and Medicine* 42: 1049–1055.

Ubel, Peter, George Loewenstein, Dennis Scanlon, and Mark Kamlet. 1996. Individual Utilities Are Inconsistent with Rationing Choices: A Partial Explanation of Why Oregon's Cost-Effectiveness List Failed. *Medical Decision Making* 16:108–116.

Ubel, Peter A., George Loewenstein, Norbert Schwarz, and Dylan Smith. 2005. Misimagining the Unimaginable: The Disability Paradox and Healthcare Decision Making. *Health Psychology* 24: 57–62.

Van Praag, Bernard M. S., and Barbara E. Baarsma. 2005. Using Happiness Surveys to Value Intangibles: The Case of Airport Noise. *Economic Journal* 115: 224–246.

Volpp, Kevin G., Andrea Gurmankin., David A. Asch, Jesse A. Berlin, John J. Murphy, Angela Gomez, Harold Sox, Zhu Jungsan, and Caryn Lerman. 2006. A Randomized Control Trial of Financial Incentives for Smoking Cessation. *Cancer Epidemiology Biomarkers and Prevention* 15: 12–18.

Weber, Bethany J., and Gretchen B. Chapman. 2005. Playing for Peanuts: Why Is Risk Seeking More Common for Low-Stakes Gambles? *Organizational Behavior and Human Decision Processes* 97: 31–46.

PART IV

NEW DIRECTIONS
FOR POSITIVE
ECONOMICS

CHAPTER 10

LOOK-UPS AS THE WINDOWS OF THE STRATEGIC SOUL

VINCENT P. CRAWFORD

BECAUSE human decisions are the result of cognitive processes, theories of human behavior rest at least implicitly on assumptions about cognition. Neuroeconomics reflects the belief that using evidence on neural correlates of cognition will lead us to better theories of decisions.

Gul and Pesendorfer (chapter 1; henceforth GP) argue that, on the contrary, because economic theory was intended to explain only decisions, it should be tested only by observing decisions. They view neuroeconomics as a radical departure from economics in part because neural data concern involuntary, unconscious processes. Such processes are not decisions, so "our" theories cannot be about them.[1] Moreover, they argue, trying to extend our theories to explain neural data would require sacrificing important strengths of rational-choice analysis.

This chapter attempts to narrow the gap between these views by discussing some recent experiments that elicit subjects' initial responses to games with the goal of identifying the structure of their strategic thinking—subjects' attempts to predict others' decisions by taking their incentives into account.[2] Strategic thinking can, of course, be studied in experiments that elicit decisions alone, via designs in which different models of cognition imply different decisions, as in Stahl and Wilson [1994, 1995; henceforth "SW"], Nagel [1995], and Ho, Camerer, and Weigelt [1998; henceforth HCW]. But the experiments I discuss study strategic thinking more directly, by monitoring and analyzing subjects' searches for hidden but freely accessible payoff information, as in Camerer, Johnson, Rymon, and Sen [1993] and Johnson, Camerer, Sen, and Rymon [2002; henceforth collectively CJ], Costa-Gomes, Crawford, and Broseta [2001; henceforth CGCB], and Costa-Gomes and Crawford [2006, 2007; henceforth CGC]. My discussion draws extensively on CGC [2007], which reports and analyzes the information search data from CGC [2006].

CJ's, CGCB's, and CGC's analyses of search rest on explicit models of cognition and therefore raise some of the same issues that GP raise about neuroeconomics. But unlike neural correlates of cognition, search is a voluntary, conscious process. Rational-choice analysis can therefore be used to describe it, eliminating one source of resistance to studying cognition. Further, the clarity of the insights into behavior these analyses yield is a "proof of concept" that shows how much can be gained by expanding the domain of analysis beyond decisions. Although the analysis of search data sidesteps some important issues raised by studying neural data, I hope that considering it will bring us closer to agreement on how, and whether, to do neuroeconomics.

CJ's, CGCB's, and CGC's analyses suggest a concrete answer to GP's challenge: Why study cognition if our goal is only to understand and predict decisions? In CGC's decision data, for instance, most subjects deviate systematically from equilibrium, and their deviations are not well explained by noisy generalizations of equilibrium such as McKelvey and Palfrey's [1995] quantal response equilibrium ("QRE"). Following SW and CGCB, CGC described their behavior via a structural nonequilibrium model in which each subject's decisions are determined, in all games, by one of a small set of decision rules, or types (as they are called in this literature). The possible types were restricted to general principles of decision making, so that the theory's predictions would be potentially as portable to new games as equilibrium predictions. CGC showed that to the extent that subjects' deviations from equilibrium decisions can be distinguished from randomness, which is considerable, they are best explained by types that are rational and self-interested and that understand the game, but that base their beliefs on simplified models of others' decisions. In other words, subjects' deviations from equilibrium had mainly to do with how they model others' decisions, not with nonstandard preferences or irrationality.[3] Further, CGC's analysis of subjects' searches for hidden payoff information shows that extending the domain of the theory to include cognition and information search as well as conventional decisions allows more powerful tests and precise identification of subjects' types, sometimes directly revealing the algorithms subjects use to process payoff information into decisions and/or distinguishing intended decisions from errors.[4]

One could still choose to use subjects' decisions alone to model their behavior via revealed preference, as in GP's proposal. This requires a generalization of their proposal, because as stated, it refers only to individual decision problems.

In games, given the lack of a rational-choice model of nonequilibrium beliefs, revealed preference would need to be augmented by assumptions about players' beliefs, presumably by assuming that beliefs are in equilibrium.[5] However, as CGC's and previous experiments make clear, such an approach is unlikely to predict reliably beyond sample: in initial responses to new games, subjects' simplified models of others' decisions would yield different patterns of deviation from equilibrium. Only by coincidence would those patterns be well described by equilibrium (or QRE) with subjects' preferences as inferred from previous games. No empirically serious model of initial responses to games can ignore cognition, and relegating data other than conventional decisions to an inspirational role arbitrarily limits the use of a powerful tool for understanding and predicting decisions and may yield a biased view of behavior.

This critique highlights an important issue in judging GP's proposal. GP take the main problem of economics to be uncovering preferences, with rationality in the decision-theoretic sense (and in games, equilibrium) assumed. By contrast, CGC's and previous experiments on initial responses to games test (and mostly affirm) rationality, induce preferences (and leave little room for doubts about risk or social preferences), and focus instead on discovering the general principles that govern strategic thinking. Although many applications involve games whose players have enough clear precedents to justify equilibrium via learning, applications involving novel strategic situations, and where strategic thinking is the main source of uncertainty, are not uncommon. The costs and benefits of GP's proposal should be evaluated in the latter applications as well as in the cases involving individual decisions they use to develop and illustrate their proposal.

The rest of the chapter is organized as follows. I begin by reviewing CJ's and CGCB's designs and results, with the goal of introducing the key design and modeling issues in studying cognition via information search in the contexts in which they first emerged. I then review CGC's [2006] use of decision data to identify subjects' types and the evidence that the main source of their deviations from equilibrium is cognitive, not preference based. Next I introduce CGCB's and CGC's [2006, 2007] model of cognition and search and use CGC's search data to illustrate its use in interpreting search data. Following this, I address questions raised by CGC's [2006] analysis of decisions that seem likely to continue to resist analysis via decisions alone, but that search analysis might answer. Last, I outline a deeper explanation of the assumptions that underlie CGCB's and CGC's model of cognition and search, which views search strategies as rational decisions under plausible assumptions about the benefits and costs of search and constraints on working memory.[6] Throughout the chapter, I assume that subjects are rational, risk-neutral decision makers, but I allow "social" preferences that reflect altruism, spite, fairness, or reciprocity when they seem important, as indicated below.

EARLY EXPERIMENTS THAT STUDIED COGNITION IN GAMES BY MONITORING INFORMATION SEARCH

In this section I review CJ's and CGCB's experimental designs and results. Their and CGC's experiments randomly and anonymously paired subjects to play series of different but related two-person games, with different partners each play and no feedback between plays. The goal was to suppress learning and repeated-game effects in order to elicit subjects' responses, game by game, to each game as if played in isolation, and so to reveal strategic thinking as clearly as possible.[7]

The structure of the games was publicly announced except for hidden, varying payoff parameters, to which subjects were given free access, game by game, one at a time, before making their decisions.[8] With low search costs, free access made the entire structure effectively public knowledge, allowing the results to be used to test theories of behavior in complete-information versions of the games.[9] Varying the payoff parameters makes it impossible for subjects to remember the current game's parameters from previous plays and so gives them incentives to search for the information their decision rules require. It also allows stronger separation of the decisions implied by equilibrium and leading alternative decision rules than in designs such as Nagel's or HCW's, in which subjects play the same game over and over again.

Camerer, Johnson, Rymon, and Sen's Alternating-Offers Bargaining Experiments

CJ [1993, 2002] pioneered the use of search for hidden payoff parameters to study cognition in games, eliciting subjects' initial responses to series of three-period alternating-offers bargaining games.[10] Previous experiments yielded large, systematic deviations from the subgame-perfect equilibrium offer and acceptance decisions when players have pecuniary preferences, such as those observed in ultimatum experiments. The deviations were attributed to cognitive limitations preventing subjects from doing the required backward induction, or believing that their partners would; to subjects having social preferences that modify their pecuniary payoffs; or both. Most researchers now agree that both factors are important, but in the early 1990s this was less clear.

CJ addressed the cognitive aspect of this question more directly by creating a design to study cognition via search and by deriving cognitive implications of alternative models of behavior and using them to analyze the search data. Within a publicly announced structure, they presented each bargaining game to subjects in extensive form as in figure 10.1, as a sequence of three pies and the associated

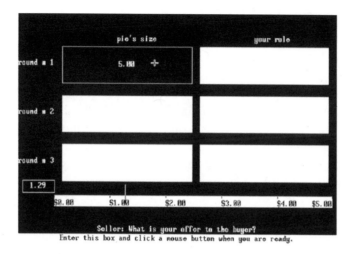

Figure 10.1. Display for Johnson, Camerer, Sen, and Rymon's [2002] alternating-offers bargaining experiments. From Johnson, Camerer, Sen, and Rymon [2002, figure 1].

offer and acceptance decisions. Discounting was simulated by shrinking the pies over time, from roughly $5.00 in round 1 to roughly $2.50 in round 2 and $1.25 in round 3, but the pies were varied slightly from game to game, to preserve subjects' incentives to search.

The pies were normally hidden in "boxes" as for rounds 2 and 3 in figure 10.1, but subjects were allowed to look them up as often as desired, one at a time. In figure 10.1 the subject has opened the box to look up the $5.00 round-1 pie.[11] Subjects' knowledge of the structure of the games and their free access to the pies allowed them to evaluate their own and their partners' pecuniary payoffs for any combination of offer and acceptance decisions.

If free access to the pies induces public knowledge of pecuniary payoffs, and if it is also public knowledge that subjects maximize their own expected pecuniary payoffs, then the results can be used to test theories of behavior in complete-information versions of the game, which has a unique subgame-perfect equilibrium whose offer and acceptance decisions are easily computed by backward induction. Even if players have privately observed social preferences, the incomplete-information version of the game has a generically unique sequential equilibrium whose strategies are easily computed by backward induction. In each case, the subgame-perfect or sequential equilibrium initial offer depends on both the second- and third-round pies, so the search requirements of equilibrium are mostly independent of preferences.[12] From now on I use "subgame-perfect equilibrium" to include pecuniary payoff maximization.

In CJ's baseline treatment, in which subjects were rewarded according to their payoffs playing the games against each other, subjects' decisions were far from the subgame-perfect equilibrium, replicating the results of previous studies and suggesting that requiring subjects to look up the pies did not significantly affect their decisions.

CJ took the analysis a step further by using a model of cognition and search to analyze the search data. They first noted that 10% of their baseline subjects never looked at the third-round pie and 19% never looked at the second-round pie. Thus, even if those subjects' decisions conform to equilibrium (given some specification of preferences, with or without a social component), they cannot possibly be making equilibrium decisions for the reasons the theory assumes. In a nonmagical world, their compliance with equilibrium cannot be expected to persist beyond sample.

This observation motivates a basic general restriction on how cognition drives search, which—anticipating CGCB's term for it—I call "occurrence": If a subject's decision rule depends on a piece of hidden payoff information, then that piece must appear in her/his look-up sequence. Occurrence, as a cognitive restriction, goes against GP's proposal, but it is still uncontroversial enough to be widely accepted by theorists. In this case at least, the epistemic foundations of equilibrium have implications for the interpretation of decisions it is hard to justify ignoring.

If occurrence were the whole story, there would be little to gain from studying cognition via search. Because CJ's subjects who never looked at the second- or third-round pies tended to make decisions far from subgame-perfect equilibrium, there is little risk of misinterpreting them; even so, occurrence helps by ruling out explanations in which subjects' decisions are in sequential equilibrium for extreme distributions of social preferences. Inferences based on occurrence are sometimes useful in CGCB's and, as we will see, CGC's analyses as well, but the full power of monitoring search depends on analyzing the order, and perhaps the duration, of subjects' look-ups.

CJ's analysis of order and duration is based on the argument that in their design the backward induction that is the easiest way to compute sequential or subgame-perfect equilibrium decisions has a characteristic search pattern, in which subjects first look up the third-round pie, then the second-round pie (possibly rechecking the third), and so on, with most transitions from adjacent later to earlier round pies. Their argument rests on the empirical generalization that most subjects use the interface as a computational aid, making the comparisons or other operations on which their decisions are based via adjacent look-ups and relying on repeated look-ups rather than memory. This observation motivates another basic restriction, which—again anticipating CGCB's term—I call "adjacency": the hidden parameters associated with the simplest of the operations on which a subject's decision rule depends will appear as adjacent look-ups in his look-up sequence.[13]

Adjacency, unlike occurrence, requires assumptions that not all theorists find compelling. It is theoretically possible for a subject to scan the pies in any order, memorize them, and then "go into his brain" to figure out what to do, in which case the order and duration of his look-ups will reveal nothing about cognition. (Here, brain imaging has a potential advantage over monitoring search because involuntary correlates of such a subject's thinking may still be observable.)

Fortunately, subjects' searches in designs such as CJ's, CGCB's, and CGC's exhibit strong regularities that make adjacency a reasonable working hypothesis. When challenged, CJ defended their adjacency-based characterization of backward-induction search by running a "robot" treatment with the same games as their baseline, in which subjects were told that they were playing against a computer that simulated a rational, self-interested player. This was followed after four periods by a "robot/trained subjects" treatment in which the same subjects received training in backward induction (but not search) and continued to play against robots as before. The latter subjects' search patterns were close to the backward-induction pattern [CJ 2002, figure 6]. Although the shift in search patterns was small prior to training, these results provide support for CJ's characterization, adjacency, and, of course, occurrence. As illustrated below, further (and sometimes stronger) support for adjacency is provided by CGCB's trained subjects, CGC's robot/trained subjects with high compliance with their assigned type's guesses, and CGC's baseline subjects with high compliance with their apparent rule's guesses (see tables 10.2 and 10.3 below for more details).

CJ's robot subjects' offer and acceptance decisions were shifted away from the baseline patterns toward subgame-perfect equilibrium, but were still far from it. Their robot/trained subjects' decisions were approximately in subgame-perfect equilibrium [CJ 2002, table II]. These shifts can be attributed to the robot treatment's "turning off" social preferences, assuming subjects don't think of experimenters or their funding agencies as "people" ; the robot treatment's eliminating strategic uncertainty; and/or cognition. CJ suggest that the deviations from equilibrium in the baseline are due to a combination of social preferences and cognition, with both important.

Returning to cognition and search, CJ's baseline subjects' searches were nearly the opposite of the searches of robot/trained subjects and CJ's characterization of backward induction search: baseline subjects spent 60–75% of the time looking up the first-round pie and only 20–30% looking up the second-round pie and 5–10% looking up the third-round pie, with most transitions forward, from earlier to later rounds. Importantly, subjects who looked up the second- and third-round pies more often, or had more backward transitions, also had a weak tendency to make, or accept, offers closer to the subgame-perfect equilibrium [CJ 2002, figures 4 and 5]. Thus, CJ's baseline subjects' deviations from backward induction search were correlated with their deviations from subgame-perfect equilibrium decisions, in the direction that an epistemic, procedural view of subjects' decision making would suggest. Although the correlation is weak, this result is an exciting first indication that subjects' search patterns might reveal something about their strategic thinking.

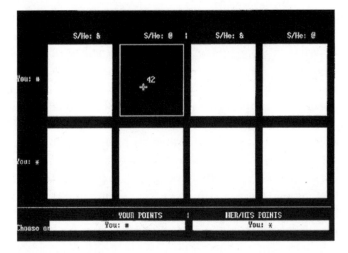

Figure 10.2. Display for a 2 × 2 Game in Costa-Gomes, Crawford, and Broseta's [2001] matrix-game experiments. From Costa-Gomes, Crawford, and Broseta [2001, figure 1].

Costa-Gomes, Crawford, and Broseta's Matrix-Game Experiments

CGCB adapted CJ's methods, building on SW's [1994, 1995] designs, to study cognition via search in a series of eighteen 2 × 2, 2 × 3, or 2 × 4 matrix games with unique pure-strategy equilibria, some of which can be identified by iterated dominance and some without pure-strategy dominance. The games were designed to turn off social preferences, and CGCB's results show little evidence of them. I therefore assume that CGCB's subjects maximized their own expected pecuniary payoffs.

Within a publicly announced structure, CGCB presented each game to subjects via MouseLab, as a matrix with players' payoffs spatially separated to ease cognition and clarify inferences from search. The payoffs were hidden, but subjects were allowed to look them up as often as desired. In the 2 × 2 game in figure 10.2, the subject, framed as the row player, has opened the box with his own payoff, 42, when he chooses decision # and his partner chooses @.[14] If free access induces public knowledge of the payoffs and it is public knowledge that subjects maximize their expectations, then the structure is public knowledge and the results can be used to test theories of behavior in complete-information versions of the games.

Although there are close connections between epistemic analyses of equilibrium decisions in extensive- and normal-form games, their cognitive foundations are very different. The different presentation of payoff information in CGCB's matrix games allows them to explore aspects of strategic thinking that do not come into play in CJ's bargaining games. Moreover, although CGCB's games have small strategy spaces, their sequence of 18 games creates a large space of possible decision histories, which allows their design to separate the implications of leading normal-form theories of decisions more strongly than in previous designs in which subjects play series of different matrix games with small strategy spaces, as in SW [1994, 1995], or in which they repeatedly play the same normal-form game with large strategy spaces, as in Nagel and HCW.

Finally, and most important here, the 8–16 hidden payoffs in CGCB's design create a large space of possible information searches, which allows the design to separate leading theories' implications for search as well as decisions. In CJ's design, a subject's searches can vary in only one important dimension: backward or forward in the pies. Measuring a subject's searches in this dimension can convey a limited amount of information about his strategic thinking—though this information can be quite revealing. In CGCB's games, by contrast, a subject's searches can vary in three important dimensions: up-down (or not) in his own payoffs, left-right (or not) in his partner's payoffs, and the frequency of transitions from his own to his partner's payoffs. With the subject framed as the row player in figure 10.2, it is clear that, assuming adjacency, the first of these dimensions is naturally associated with decision-theoretic rationality, the second with using others' incentives to predict their decisions, and the third with interpersonal payoff comparisons. It would be difficult to imagine an empirically successful theory of initial responses to this kind of game in which those three traits were not independently variable and important. Only a design with a search space as rich as CGCB's can separate the implications of alternative theories for both search and decisions strongly enough to identify their relationships.

In addition to a baseline treatment that paired subjects to play the 18 games with other subjects, CGCB conducted a trained subjects treatment, identical to the baseline except that each subject was trained and rewarded for identifying equilibrium decisions. This treatment confirms that subjects trained and motivated to find equilibrium guesses could do so, and provides data on equilibrium search behavior that are helpful in evaluating CGCB's model of cognition and search.

CGCB's games have unique equilibria that are easily identified by direct checking, best-response dynamics (which always converges in their games), or (in most of their games) iterated pure-strategy dominance. Yet, as in previous studies of initial responses to matrix games, CGCB found systematic patterns of deviation from equilibrium, with high equilibrium compliance in games solvable by one or two rounds of iterated dominance but much lower compliance in games solvable by three rounds or the circular logic of equilibrium without dominance [CGCB, table II]. These patterns are not well explained by noisy generalizations of equilibrium such as QRE. CGCB explained them via a structural nonequilibrium model of initial responses in the spirit of SW's, Nagel's, and HCW's models, in which each subject's decisions are determined, in all games, by one of a small set of types, which determines his decisions, with error, in each game. The possible types were restricted to general principles of decision making, so that the theory's predictions would be potentially as portable to new games as equilibrium predictions.

The leading types in CGCB's analysis include L1 (for level 1, as named by SW), called naive in CGCB and L1 here from now on, which best responds to a uniform random L0 "anchoring type" ; L2, which best responds to L1; Equilibrium, which makes its equilibrium decision; D1 (dominance 1), which does one round of deletion of dominated decisions and then best responds to a uniform prior over the other's remaining decisions; D2, which does two rounds of iterated deletion and then best responds to a uniform prior over the other's remaining decisions; and Sophisticated, which best responds to the probabilities of other's decisions, as estimated from subjects' observed frequencies, included to test whether subjects have prior understanding of others' decisions that transcends simple rules.[15] Because CGCB gave first priority to separating strategic from nonstrategic types, L1's decisions were perfectly confounded with those of a maximax type CGCB called Optimistic. CGCB's econometric analysis of decisions alone estimated high frequencies of L1, L2, and D1. Because those types mimic equilibrium in simple games but deviate systematically in more complex games, this estimated type distribution allows the model to explain the aggregate relationship between complexity and equilibrium compliance.

Turning to CGCB's analysis of search, the main difficulty was imposing enough structure on the enormous spaces of possible decision and search histories to describe subjects' behavior in a comprehensible way. Although CJ identified a correlation (and a "right" direction for it) between subjects' decision and search deviations from subgame-perfect equilibrium in their alternating-offers bargaining games, their analysis does not show how to define or identify such a relationship in the higher-dimensional spaces of possible decisions and searches created by CGCB's design.

CGCB addressed this issue by using the types as models of cognition and search as well as decisions. They took an explicitly procedural view of decision making, in which a subject's type and the associated cognitive process determine his search, and his type and search then determine his decision, game by game.[16] They characterized the link between cognition and search via the occurrence and adjacency restrictions described above, which generalize the ideas behind CJ's characterization of backward-induction search to a much wider class of games, patterns of hidden payoff information, and types. With these restrictions on cognition and search, the types provide a kind of basis for the spaces of possible decision and search histories, imposing enough structure to make it meaningful to ask whether subjects' decisions and searches are related in a coherent way.

Incorporating search into the econometric analysis yields a somewhat different view of subjects' deviations from equilibrium than previous analyses of decisions. It shifts CGCB's estimated type distribution toward L1 at the expense of Optimistic and D1, leaving L1 and L2 as the only empirically important types. Part of this shift occurs because L1's searches, unlike L1's decisions, are clearly separated from Optimistic's, and L1's search implications explain more of the variation in subjects' searches and decisions than Optimistic's, which are too unrestrictive to be useful. Another part of the shift occurs because L1's search implications explain more of the variation in subjects' searches and decisions than D1's, which are much more restrictive than Optimistic's but too weakly correlated with subjects' observed decisions. D1 loses frequency to L2, as well, even though their decisions are only weakly separated in CGCB's design, because L2's search implications explain more of the variation in subjects' searches and decisions. Thus, analyzing search not only yields more precise estimates of subjects' types, but also can correct distortions in type estimates based on decisions alone that stem from a design's failure to fully separate types.

These shifts illustrate an important principle. Because the number of experimental treatments and subjects that can be run is limited, data are scarce relative to the plausible theories of behavior, and trade-offs in discriminating among theories are inevitable. Gathering search (or other nondecision data) as well as decision data can make such trade-offs less stringent. Although gathering and analyzing nondecision data have their own costs, the optimal amount to gather is not always zero.

Overall, CGCB's analysis of decisions and search gives a strikingly simple view of behavior, with L1 and L2 making up 90% of the population. This type distribution and the clear relationships between subjects' cognition as revealed by search and their decisions support my claim that their deviations from equilibrium in these games are due mainly to how they think about others.

Costa-Gomes and Crawford's Two-Person Guessing Game Experiments

CGC [2006, 2007] adapted CGCB's methods to elicit subjects' initial responses to a series of 16 dominance-solvable two-person guessing games, cousins of Nagel's and HCW's n-person guessing games. In this section, I review CGC's design and their results for decisions, which provide even stronger evidence that the deviations from equilibrium in initial responses to games are due mainly to strategic thinking. In the following section, I review CGC's analysis of cognition and search.

CGC's Design

In CGC's games, newly designed for the purpose of studying cognition via decisions and search, two players make simultaneous guesses. Each player has his own lower and upper limit, both strictly positive, as in some of HCW's games, to ensure finite dominance solvability. Unlike in previous designs, however, players are not required to guess between their limits: to enhance the separation of types via search, guesses outside the limits are automatically adjusted up to the lower limit or down to the upper limit as necessary. Thus, the only thing about a guess that affects the outcome is the adjusted guess it leads to. Each player also has his own target, and (unlike in Nagel's and HCW's "winner-take-all" games) his payoff is higher, the closer his adjusted guess is to his target times his partner's adjusted guess.

In the most important departure from previous guessing designs, the targets and limits vary independently across players and games, with the targets either both less than one, both greater than one, or (unlike in previous designs) mixed.[17] The resulting games are asymmetric and dominance solvable in 3 to 52 rounds, with essentially unique equilibria determined (but not always directly) by players' lower limits when the product of the targets is less than one or their upper limits when the product is greater than one. In game 13 in figures 10.4–10.7, for instance, player i has limits 300 and 500 and target 0.7, and player j has limits 100 and 900 and target 1.5 [CGC, table 3]. The product of targets is 1.05 > 1, player i's equilibrium guess is at his upper limit 500, and player j's equilibrium guess is at his best response to 500 of 750, below his upper limit.

From the point of view of studying decisions, CGC's design combines the main strengths of SW's and CGCB's designs, with subjects playing sequences of different but related games, and the main strengths of Nagel's and HCW's designs, games with very large strategy spaces. This combination greatly enhances the separation of equilibrium and other leading types' decisions.

CGC's games explore different aspects of strategic thinking than CJ's, CGCB's, or Nagel's and HCW's games. Of particular note is the subtle way in which the location of the equilibrium is determined by the product of players' targets, which adds greatly to the power of the design to distinguish equilibrium from boundedly rational strategic thinking. The only important difference between some of CGC's games is whether the product of targets is slightly greater or slightly less than one. Equilibrium responds very strongly to this difference, but low-level Lk, or Dk, types, whose guesses vary continuously with the targets, respond much less. Also noteworthy is the strong separation of Lk's and $Dk-1$'s decisions, which are perfectly confounded in most of Nagel's and HCW's treatments and only weakly separated in their other treatments and in CGCB's design.

In addition to a baseline treatment that paired subjects to play the 16 games with other subjects, CGC conducted six different robot/trained subjects treatments, identical to the baseline except that each subject was trained and rewarded as a type: L_1, L_2, L_3, D_1, D_2, or Equilibrium. These treatments assess the types' cognitive demands, confirming, for instance, that subjects trained and motivated to make equilibrium guesses could do so; and provide data on the search behavior of subjects of known types that are helpful in evaluating the model of cognition and search.

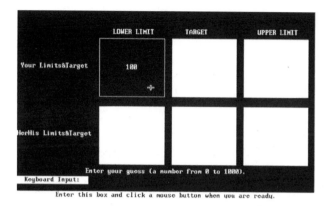

Figure 10.3. Display for Costa-Gomes and Crawford's [2006, 2007] two-person guessing games. From Costa-Gomes and Crawford [2006, figure 6].

In all treatments, within a publicly announced structure, CGC presented each game to subjects as an array of targets and limits, with those payoff parameters hidden but subjects allowed to look them up as often as desired, one at a time, using MouseLab's click option as in CGCB. In figure 10.3, the subject has opened the box to look up his own ("Your") lower limit, 100.

CGC's Analysis of Decisions

The strong separation of types' implications for guesses [CGC 2006, figure 5] and the clarity of CGC's baseline subjects' responses allow many of their types to be confidently identified from guesses alone. Of 88 subjects, 43 have clear "fingerprints" in that they made guesses that complied exactly (within 0.5) with one type's guesses in 7–16 of the games (20 L1, 12 L2, 3 L3, and 8 Equilibrium).[18] Figure 10.4 [CGC 2006, figure 2] shows the fingerprints of the 12 whose apparent types were L2. Of their 192 ($= 12 \times 16$) guesses, 138 (72%) were exact, which means they tracked the complex pattern of the games' L2 guesses with a remarkable degree of accuracy. I stress that these baseline subjects, unlike the robot/trained subjects, were taught nothing about strategic thinking: The models of others' guesses implicit in their apparent types were self-generated.

Given how strongly CGC's design separates types' guesses, and that guesses could take 200–800 different rounded values, these 43 subjects' compliance is far higher than could occur by chance. Further, because the types specify precise, well-separated guess sequences in a very large space of possibilities, their compliance rules out alternative interpretations of their guesses.[19] In particular, because the types build in risk-neutral, self-interested rationality and perfect models of the game, the deviations from equilibrium of the 35 whose apparent types are L1, L2, or L3 can be attributed to nonequilibrium beliefs, not irrationality, risk aversion, altruism, spite, or confusion.

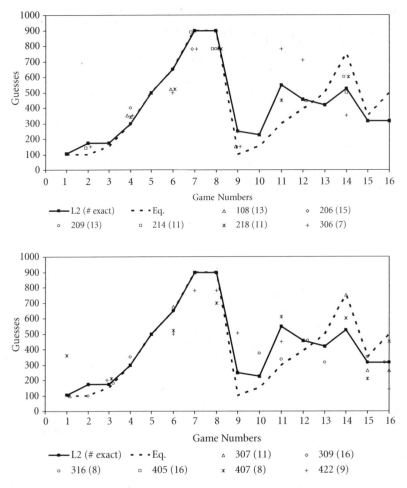

Figure 10.4. "Fingerprints" of 12 apparent level-2 (L2) baseline subjects. Only deviations from L2's guesses are shown 138 (72%) of these subjects' 192 guesses were exact L2 guesses. From Costa-Gomes and Crawford [2006, figure 2].

CGC's other 45 subjects' types are less apparent from their guesses, but L1, L2, and hybrids of L3 and/or Equilibrium are still the only types that show up in econometric estimates.[20] The fact that most subjects follow low-level L*k* types, which mimic equilibrium in games that are dominance solvable in small numbers of rounds but deviate systematically in some more complex games also explains the inverse relationship between strategic complexity and equilibrium compliance observed in CGCB and previous experiments [CGCB, table II].

CGC's results for decisions provide very strong evidence that subjects' deviations from equilibrium in initial responses to games are due mainly to nonequilibrium strategic thinking, not preferences or irrationality. As noted in the introduction to this chapter, one could still use subjects' guesses alone to model their behavior via revealed preference, but such a model would misattribute the cause of the deviations and so would predict well beyond sample only by coincidence.

Costa-Gomes and Crawford's Analysis of Cognition and Search

CGC's [2006, section II.E; 2007] model of cognition and search refines CGCB's model, adapting their occurrence and adjacency restrictions to give a tractable characterization of each type's search requirements. With regard to search, CGC's design combines the strengths of CJ's presentation of games as functions of a small number of hidden parameters within an intuitive common structure, which allows subjects to focus on predicting others' responses without getting lost in the details of the structure; and CGCB's high-dimensional search spaces, which make search more informative and allow greater separation via search. CGC's design strongly and independently separates the implications of leading types for search and decisions, which makes it easier to identify relationships between them and multiplies the power of the design. Finally, it makes each type's search implications independent of the game, which simplifies the analysis.[21]

This section begins with a discussion of the issues that arise in specifying a model of cognition and search. It then presents CGC's leading types' search requirements and illustrates how they are derived. Finally, it presents sample search data for some of CGC's robot/trained and baseline subjects. As these data will be used to show, CGC's design and characterization of types' search implications make it possible to read the algorithms that a large minority of subjects used to choose their guesses directly from their search sequences. Other subjects' cognition is not apparent from their searches, but CGC's [2006] measures of their compliance with leading types' search implications have considerable discriminatory power in the econometric analysis, often allowing those subjects' types to be reliably estimated from searches alone, without regard to guesses.

Specification Issues

Studying cognition via search requires a model of how cognition determines subjects' look-up sequences. Previous articles have taken quite different positions on this issue. CJ's analysis gave roughly equal weight to look-up durations and total numbers of look-ups ("acquisitions") of each pie and to the numbers of transitions between look-ups of adjacent pies. Rubinstein's [2007] analysis considered only durations. Gabaix et al. [2006] focused on total numbers of look-ups rather than durations, but also considered some aspects of the order of look-ups. CGCB's and CGC's analyses focused instead on which look-ups subjects make, in the sense of occurrence, and on the order of look-ups in the sense of adjacency, relegating durations to a secondary role.

On another dimension, CJ's and Rubinstein's analyses and most of Gabaix et al.'s aggregated search data across subjects and over time, while CGCB and CGC took the position that cognition and search are so heterogeneous that it is essential to study them at the individual level.

CGCB's and CGC's focus on occurrence and adjacency follows naturally from a procedural view of decision making and the empirical tendency, now confirmed by a large body of MouseLab data, of most subjects to perform the operations on hidden parameters on which their decisions are based via adjacent look-ups, relying on repeated look-ups rather than memory. In this view—perhaps too extreme—duration is unimportant because the information content of a look-up is independent of its length as long as it suffices for cognition; look-ups too short for comprehension (< 0.18 sec) were filtered out in the analyses discussed here. Although duration might still be correlated with time spent thinking about a particular parameter, which might be important in a more refined model of cognition, search, and decisions, a procedural view does not suggest such a correlation, and CGCB's and CGC's subjects sometimes left boxes open for long periods while staring out the window and so on, which would weaken any such correlations.[23] Total numbers of look-ups are important but are captured indirectly through CGC's notion of search compliance.

CGC's Model of Cognition and Search

In CGC's model of cognition and search, each leading type implies a generically unique, pure adjusted guess in each game, which maximizes its expected payoff given the beliefs regarding others' guesses implicit in the type. (The leading types all specify best responses to some beliefs.) Each type is thereby naturally associated with algorithms that process hidden payoff information into decisions, which CGC used as models of cognition. Given the need to go beyond occurrence and the lack of an accepted theory of cognition and search, the goal was to add enough restrictions to extract the signal from subjects' search sequences but not so many that they distort its meaning. CGC derived types' minimal search implications under conservative assumptions, based on occurrence and adjacency, about how cognition determines search [CGC 2006, section I.B].

The leading role in these derivations is played by a type's ideal guesses, those that would be optimal given the type's beliefs, ignoring its limits. Given the quasi-concavity of CGC's payoff functions, a subject can enter his ideal guess and know that his adjusted guess will be optimal without checking his own limits. Thus, a type's ideal guess not only determines its adjusted guess and the resulting outcome but also determines the type's minimal search implications.

Table 10.1. Types' Ideal Guesses and Minimal Search Sequences [Costa-Gomes and Crawford, 2006].

Type	Ideal guesses	Minimal search sequence
L1	$p^i[a^j + b^j]/2$	$\{[a^j, b^j], p^i\} \equiv \{[4, 6], 2\}$
L2	$p^i R(a^j, b^j; p^i[a^i + b^i]/2)$	$\{([a^i, b^i], p^j), a^j, b^j, p^i\} \equiv \{([1, 3], 5),$ 4, 6, 2\}
L3	$p^i R(a^j, b^j; p^j R(a^i, b^i; p^i[a^j + b^j]/2))$	$\{([a^j, b^j], p^i), a^i, b^i, p^j\} \equiv \{([4, 6], 2),$ 1, 3, 5\}
D1	$p^i(\max\{a^j, p^i a^i\} + \min\{p^i b^i, b^j\})/2$	$\{(a^j, [p^i, a^i]), (b^j, [p^i, b^i]), p^i\} \equiv \{(4, [5, 1]), (6, [5, 3]), 2\}$
D2	$p^i[\max\{\max\{a^j, p^i a^i\}, p^j \max\{a^i, p^i a^j\}\} + \min\{p^j \min\{p^j b^i, b^i\}, \min\{p^j b^i, b^j\}\}]/2$	$\{(a^i, [p^i, a^j]), (b^i, [p^i, b^j]), (a^j, [p^i, a^i]), (b^j, [p^i, b^i]), p^j, p^i\} \equiv \{(1, [2, 4]), (3, [2, 6]), (4, [5, 1]), (6, [5, 3]), 5, 2\}$
Equilibrium	$p^i a^j$ if $p^i p^j < 1$ or $p^i b^j$ if $p^i p^j > 1$	$\{[p^i, p^j], a^j\} \equiv \{[2, 5], 4\}$ if $p^i p^j < 1$ or $\{[p^i, p^j], b^j\} \equiv \{[2, 5], 6\}$ if $p^i p^j > 1$
Sophisticated	(No closed-form expression, but CGC took Sophisticated's search implications to be the same as D2's]	$\{(a^i, [p^i, a^j]), (b^i, [p^i, b^j]), (a^j, [p^j, a^i]), (b^j, [p^j, b^i]), p^j, p^i\} \equiv \{(1, [2,4]), (3, [2,6]), (4, [5,1]), (6, [5,3]), 5, 2\}$

Note: $R(a, b; x) \equiv \min\{b, \max\{a, x\}\} \equiv \max\{a, \min\{b, x\}\}$ denotes x's adjusted guess with limits a and b.

The left-hand side of table 10.1 [CGC 2006, table 4] lists the formulas for the leading types' ideal guesses in CGC's games, which are easily derived as in CGC [2006, section I.B], using CGC's notation for the limits and targets, a^i for the player's own lower limit, b^i for the player's own upper limit, and p^i for the player's own lower target, with analogous notation using superscript j for the player's partner's limits and target. The right-hand side of table 10.1 lists the leading types' minimal search implications expressed as sequences of parameter look-ups, first in CGC's notation and then in terms of the associated box numbers (1 for a^i, 2 for p^i, 3 for b^i, 4 for a^j, 5 for p^j, 6 for b^j) in which MouseLab records subjects' look-up sequences in our design. Table 10.1 shows look-ups in the order that seems most natural, but that order is not required in the analysis.[24]

The search implications are derived as follows. Evaluating a formula for a type's ideal guess requires a series of arithmetic operations, some of which—the innermost operations, whose parameters are in square brackets in the right-hand side of table 10.1, such as $[a^j, b^j]$ for L1—are basic in that they logically precede other operations. Like CGCB, CGC assumed that subjects perform basic operations via adjacent look-ups, remembering their results, and otherwise relying on repeated look-ups rather than memory. Basic operations are then represented by adjacent look-ups that can appear in either order but cannot be separated by other look-ups. The look-ups of other operations can appear in any order and are (conservatively) allowed to be separated. In table 10.1 such operations are represented by look-ups within braces or parentheses.[25]

An L1 player i, for instance, best responds to the belief that player j's guess is uniformly distributed between his limits. This yields a guess for j that is never adjusted, and that averages $[a^j + b^j]/2$. CGC [2006, section I.B] shows via a certainty equivalence property of CGC's games (observation 2) that L1's ideal guess is $p^i[a^j + b^j]/2$, which will be automatically adjusted, if necessary, to $R(a^i, b^i; p^i[a^j + b^j]/2) \equiv min\{b^i, max\{a^i, p^i[a^j + b^j]/2\}\}$. The only basic operation is $[a^j + b^j]$. An L1 player i therefore has minimal look-up sequence: $\{[a^j, b^j]\}$ (to compute j's average guess), p^i (to identify i's ideal guess)$= \{[4, 6], 2\}$, of which $[4, 6]$ cannot be separated.

An L2 player i best responds to the belief that player j is L1, taking the adjustment of j's guess into account. An L1 player j's adjusted guess is $R(a^j, b^j; p^j[a^i + b^i]/2)$, so an L2 player i's ideal guess is $p^i R(a^j, b^j; p^j[a^i + b^i]/2)$, which will be automatically adjusted to $R(a^i, b^i; p^i R(a^j, b^j; p^j[a^i + b^i]/2))$. An L2 player i therefore has look-up sequence $\{([a^i, b^i], p^j)$ (to predict j's L1 ideal guess), a^j, b^j (to predict j's L1 adjusted guess), p^i (to identify i's ideal guess)$\} = \{([1, 3], 5), 4, 6, 2\}$.[26] This illustrates the fact that CGC's design separates the search implications of different types as strongly as it separates their implications for guesses [CGC 2006, figure 5].

In CGC's [2006] econometric analysis of search, not discussed here, search compliance for a given subject, type, and game is measured by the density of the type's complete minimal search sequence in the subject's look-up sequence for the game, allowing for the heterogeneity of search behavior.[27] CGC's measure is a significant advance on CGCB's measure, which is based on the percentages of a type's occurrence and adjacency requirements satisfied by the entire sequence.

Sample Search Data

Table 10.2 gives a sample of the information search data for CGC's robot/trained subjects, and table 10.3 gives an analogous sample for baseline subjects of various assigned or apparent types (see table 10.1 for the search implication for each type). Table 10.4 shows how the numbers in tables 10.2 and 10.3 are used to represent different MouseLab boxes. In each case, the subjects were chosen for high exact compliance with their types' guesses, not for compliance with any theory of search; subjects' frequencies of exact guesses are in parentheses after their types. Only the orders of look-ups are shown, and only from the first two or three games, but those games are representative.

Recalling that the theory allows any order of look-ups grouped within brackets, braces, or parentheses, the searches of high-guess-compliance robot/trained or baseline subjects conform closely to CGC's theory, with a subject's assigned or apparent type's minimal sequence unusually dense in his observed sequence.[28] The only exception is the Equilibrium subjects, who search far longer and in

Table 10.2. Selected Robot/Trained Subjects' Information Searches.

Subject	Type/Alt[a]	Game 1[b]	Game 2[b]
904	L1 (16)	1234564623	1234564321
1716	L1 (16)	14646213464623	46246213
1807	L1 (16)	462513	46213225
1607	L2 (16)	1354621313	1354613546213
1811	L2 (16)	1344465213*46	13465312564231356252
2008	L2 (16)	1113131313135423	131313566622333
1001	L3 (16)	46213521364*24623152	4621356425622231462562*62
1412	L3 (16)	1462315646231	462462546231546231
805	D1 (16)	1543564232132642	51453561536423
1601	D1 (16)	25451436231	5146536213
804	D1 (3)/L2 (16)	1543465213	5151353654623
1110	D2 (14)	1354642646*313	135134642163451463211136 414262135362*146546
1202	D2 (15)	246466135464641321342462 4226461246255*1224654646	123645132462426262241356 462*135242424661356462
704	DEq (16)	123456363256565365626365 6526514522626526	123456525123652625635256 262365456
1205	Eq (16)	1234564246525625256352*465	123456244565565263212554 14666265425144526*31
1408	Eq (15)	12312345644563213211	1234564561236435241
2002	Eq (16)	142536125365253616361454 61345121345263	1436253614251425236256563

[a] Shows the assigned type of each subject and, in the case of subject 804, an alternative assignment as well. The subjects' frequencies of making their assigned types' (and, where relevant, alternative types') exact guesses are in parentheses after the type.
[b] An asterisk in a subject's look-up sequence means that the subject entered a guess without immediately confirming it.

more complex patterns than CGC's theory suggests, perhaps because its minimal Equilibrium search requirements allow more luck than these subjects enjoyed.[29] Baseline L1, L2, and perhaps L3 and Equilibrium subjects' searches are very close to those of their robot/trained counterparts, suggesting that (unlike in CJ) training had little effect on their search behavior.[30] Perhaps Equilibrium search in normal-form games is less unnatural than backward-induction search in CJ's extensive-form games. For the simpler types L1, L2, and perhaps L3, the algorithms that subjects use to identify their types' guesses can be directly read from their searches.

CGC's [2006, section II.E, table 7] econometric analysis shows that such inferences are usually consistent with estimates based on guesses alone, and that search compliance as measured here is also useful in identifying the types of subjects whose types are not apparent from their searches. For some subjects, econometric estimates based on guesses and search together resolve tensions between guesses-only and search-only estimates in favor of a type other than the guesses-only estimate.

Table 10.3. Selected Baseline Subjects' Information Searches.

Subject	Type/Alt[a]	Game 1[b]	Game 2[b]	Game 3[b]
101	L1 (15)	146246213	46213	462*46
118	L1 (15)	24613462624132*135	2462622131	246242466413*426
413	L1 (14)	1234565456123463*	12356462213*	264231
108	L2 (13)	135642	1356423	1356453
206	L2 (15)	533146213	53146231	5351642231
309	L2 (16)	1352	1352631526*2*3	135263
405	L2 (16)	144652313312546232 12512	1324562531564565 4546312315656262	3124565231*123654 55233**513
210	L3 (9) Eq (9) D2(8)	123456123456213456 254213654	1234564655622316 54456*2	1234556456123
302	L3 (7) Eq (7)	221135465645213213 45456*541	2135465662135454 6321*26654123	265413232145563214 563214523*654123
318	L1 (7) D1 (5)	13245646525213242* 1462	132465132*462	1346521323*4
417	Eq (8) L3 (7) L2 (5)	252531464656446531 6412524621213	25523662*3652435 63	5213636415265263* 652
404	Eq (9) L2 (6)	462135464655645515 21354*135462426256 356234131354645	46246135252426131 5463562	462135215634*52
202	Eq (8) D2 (7) L3 (7)	1234562546136213421 *525	1234564456132554 6251356523	1234561235623
310	Eq (11)	123126544121565421 254362*21545 4*	1235462163262314 56*62	123655463213
315	Eq (11)	213465624163564121 325466	1346521246536561 213	132465544163*3625

[a] Shows the assigned type of each subject and, in some cases, an alternative assignment as well. The subjects' frequencies of making their assigned types' (and, where relevant, alternative types') exact guesses are in parentheses after the type.
[b] An asterisk in a subject's look-up sequence means that the subject entered a guess without immediately confirming it.

Table 10.4. MouseLab Box Numbers.

Person	a	p	b
You (i)	1	2	3
S/he (j)	4	5	6

Those estimates confirm the presence of significant numbers of subjects of types L1, L2, equilibrium, or hybrids of L3 and/or equilibrium in the population, and the absence of significant numbers of subjects of other types. Once again, subjects' deviations from equilibrium can be attributed mostly to nonequilibrium strategic thinking, not preferences or irrationality.

For some subjects, search is an important check on type inferences based on guesses. Baseline subject 309, whose 16 exact L2 guesses seem overwhelming evidence that his type is L2, violated L2 occurrence by missing one of its required look-ups in each of games 1–5 (table 10.3 shows his look-ups for games 1–3). Just as for CJ's subjects who never looked at the second- or third-round pie, in games 1–5 this subject could not have been making L2 guesses for the reason the theory assumes, and his compliance could not be expected to persist beyond sample. Fortunately, 309 had a Eureka! moment after game 5, and from then on complied almost perfectly with L2's search requirements as well as its guess requirements.[31]

FURTHER QUESTIONS SEARCH ANALYSIS MIGHT ANSWER

To illustrate some of the further possibilities for search analysis, this section discusses two questions raised by CGC's [2006] analysis of decisions that resist analysis via decisions alone. These questions are addressed in CGC [2007].

What Are CGC's Baseline Apparent Equilibrium Subjects Really Doing?

Figure 10.5 [CGC 2006, figure 4] graphs the guesses of CGC's eight baseline subjects with seven or more exact equilibrium guesses. The 16 games are ordered by strategic structure as in CGC [2006, table 3] (not in the randomized order in which subjects played them), with the eight games with mixed targets (one greater and one less than one) in the right half of the figure. Of these subjects' 128 guesses in the 16 games, 69 (54%) were exact equilibrium guesses. In CGC's [2006] likelihood-based econometrics, given their a priori specification of possible types and the large strategy spaces of CGC's games, this is overwhelming evidence that their types are equilibrium. But as figure 10.5 makes clear, their equilibrium compliance was far higher for games without mixed targets (55 out of 64 possible exact equilibrium guesses, or 86%) than for games with mixed targets (14 out of 64, or 22%). Thus, it is (even nonparametrically) clear that these subjects, despite equilibrium compliance that is off the scale by normal standards, are actually following a rule that only mimics equilibrium, and only in games without mixed targets.

The puzzle is deepened by noting that all the ways game theorists teach people to identify equilibria (best-response dynamics, equilibrium checking, and iterated dominance) work equally well with and without mixed targets. Further, CGC's equilibrium robot/trained subjects who were taught these three ways to identify their equilibrium guesses have roughly the same equilibrium compliance with and without mixed targets [figure 10.6; CGC 2007]. Thus, whatever the baseline apparent

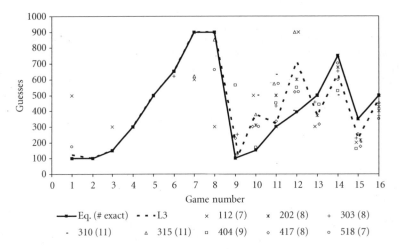

Figure 10.5. "Fingerprints" of eight apparent Equilibrium baseline subjects. Only deviations from Equilibrium guesses are shown; 69 (54%) of these subjects' 128 guesses were exact Equilibrium guesses. From Costa-Gomes and Crawford [2006, figure 4].

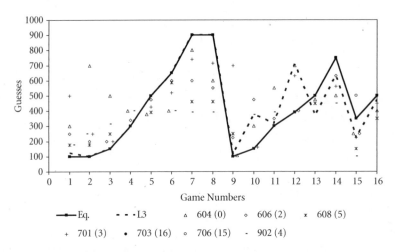

Figure 10.6. "Fingerprints" of 10 Equilibrium robot/trained subjects. Only deviations from Equilibrium guesses are shown; three subjects (603, 704, 705) had 16 exact guesses, and 92 (58%) of these subjects' 160 guesses were exact Equilibrium guesses.

equilibrium subjects were doing, it is not one of the first things a game theorist would think of. (Subjects' debriefing questionnaires did not reveal what it was.) Nonetheless, the rule or rules they follow have a decidedly nonrandom structure: all 44 of those subjects' deviations from equilibrium (the solid line in figure 10.5) when it is separated from L3 (dotted line), with or without mixed targets, are in the direction of (and sometimes beyond) their L3 guesses, though this could reflect the fact that in CGC's games, L3 guesses are always less extreme than equilibrium guesses.

CGC's [2007] analysis tries to resolve the puzzle by using the search data to answer the following questions:

1. How do the baseline apparent Equilibrium subjects find their equilibrium guesses in the games without mixed targets: best-response dynamics, equilibrium checking, iterated dominance, or something else that doesn't "work" with mixed targets? Refining CGC's [2006] characterization of Equilibrium search to separate the three methods and redoing the estimation with the refined compliance measures, separately for games with and without mixed targets, should be revealing. The absence of baseline D_k subjects suggests that iterated dominance, even finitely truncated, is unlikely. Best-response dynamics, perhaps truncated after one or two rounds, seems more likely.

2. How do the baseline apparent Equilibrium subjects' search patterns differ in games with and without mixed targets? How do the differences compare to the differences for baseline L1, L2, or L3 subjects? CGC's 20 apparent baseline L1 subjects' compliance with L1 guesses is almost the same with and without mixed targets [CGC, 2006, figure 1], which is unsurprising because whether or not the targets are mixed is irrelevant to subjects who do not try to model others' responses to incentives. But the 12 apparent L2 [figure 10.4; CGC, 2006, figure 2] and 3 apparent L3 [CGC, 2006, figure 3] subjects' compliance with their types' guesses is much lower with than without mixed targets. This is curious, because for L2 and L3, unlike for Equilibrium, games with mixed targets require no deeper understanding.

3. How do Equilibrium robot/trained subjects with high compliance find their equilibrium guesses even in games with mixed targets? How do their searches in those games differ from baseline apparent Equilibrium subjects' searches? CGC strove to make Equilibrium robot/trained subjects' training as neutral as possible, but something must come first, and they were taught equilibrium checking first, then best-response dynamics, then iterated dominance. To the extent that these subjects used one of those methods, it explains why they have equal compliance with and without mixed targets. But if some of them used something else that deviates from equilibrium mainly in games with mixed targets, it might provide important clues to what the baseline equilibrium subjects did.

Why Are L*k* the Only Types Other Than Equilibrium with Nonnegligible Frequencies?

CGC's [2006] analysis of decisions and search estimated significant numbers of subjects of types L1, L2, equilibrium, or hybrids of L3 and/or equilibrium, and nothing else that does better than a random model of guesses for more than one subject.

Why do these types predominate, out of the enormous number of possibilities? Why, for instance, are there no significant numbers of Dk types, which are closer to what game theorists teach?

CGC's [2007] analysis tries to answer this question by using search and other methods to look more deeply into the following phenomena:

1. Most robot/trained subjects could reliably identify their type's guesses, even for types as difficult as Equilibrium or $D2$. Individual subjects' exact compliance with their type's guesses was usually bimodal within type, on very high and very low. Even so, there are several signs of differences in difficulty across types.

2. None of CGC's 70 robot/trained Lk subjects ever failed their type's understanding test, while 1 of 31 failed the $D1$ test, 1 of 20 failed the $D2$ test, and 7 of 36 failed the Equilibrium test.

3. For those who passed the test, compliance was highest for Lk types, then Equilibrium, then Dk types. This suggests that Dk is harder than Equilibrium, but more analysis is needed to tell if this was an artifact of the more stringent screening of the Equilibrium test.

4. Within the Lk and Dk type hierarchies, compliance was higher for lower k as one would expect, except that $L1$ compliance was lower than $L2$ or $L3$ compliance. This may be because $L1$ best responds to a random $L0$ robot, which some subjects think they can outguess, but $L2$ and $L3$ best respond to a deterministic $L1$ or $L2$ robot, which doesn't invite gambling.

5. Remarkably, 7 of our 19 robot/trained $D1$ subjects who passed the $D1$ understanding test, in which $L2$ answers are wrong, then "morphed" into $L2$s when making their guesses, significantly reducing their earnings (figure 10.7 and subject 804 in table 10.2; recall that $L2$ and $D1$ are cousins, both making 2-rationalizable guesses). This kind of morphing is the only kind that occurred, which seems compelling evidence that Dk types are unnatural. But a comparison of Lk's and $Dk-1$'s search and storage requirements may have something to add.

A RATIONAL-CHOICE MODEL OF OPTIMAL SEARCH FOR HIDDEN PAYOFF INFORMATION

This section outlines a simple rational-choice analysis in support of the occurrence and adjacency assumptions that underlie CGCB's and CGC's models of cognition and search. The analysis is general in that it takes as given the formula that

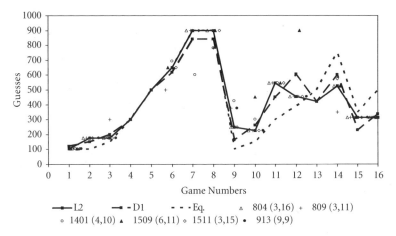

Figure 10.7. "Fingerprints" of six robot/trained subjects who "morphed" from dominance-1 (D1) to level-2 (L2). Only deviations from D1's guesses are shown; 28 (29%) of these subjects' 96 guesses were exact D1 guesses, and 72 (75%) were exact L2 guesses.

relates a type's decision to the hidden parameters. It views search for hidden payoff information as just another kind of rational decision, deriving subjects' demand for it from the benefits of making better decisions under plausible assumptions about the benefits and costs of search and storing numbers in working memory.

The model rests on two assumptions about cognition and search:

1. The costs of look-ups are small. There is a great deal of evidence that subjects in experiments with hidden but freely accessible payoff parameters perceive the cost of looking them up as negligible, scarcely larger than the cost of reading them in a printed table. Having to look things up has small effects on their decisions (as shown in CGCB's and CGC's [2006] open boxes control treatments); subjects usually make many more look-ups than efficient search requires, and they usually make some motivated purely by curiosity.

2. There is a flow cost of keeping numbers in working memory, which starts small for the first number but even then is larger than the cost of a look-up, and which increases with the number of stored numbers. Total memory cost is the time integral of the flow cost and is therefore proportional, other things equal, to total storage time, and increasing in the number of stored numbers. (If working memory were free, nothing would prevent the scanning and memorization referred to in my discussions of CJ and CGCB, but this is plainly unrealistic.)

Occurrence follows immediately from assumption 1. A rational player looks up all costlessly available information that might affect his beliefs. When, as in these designs, information comes in discrete quanta with nonnegligible effects on beliefs and the optimal decision, this conclusion extends to information available at low cost.[32]

Given occurrence, adjacency [in CGC's sense that the basic (innermost) operations in square brackets in the right-hand side of Table 10.1 are represented by adjacent look-ups] follows from assumption 2. Under this assumption, a player minimizes the total memory plus look-up cost by processing the basic operations needed to evaluate the expression for his ideal guess before other operations with whose results they are to be combined, storing the results (meanwhile "forgetting" the parameters they combine), and then combining them. Basic operations take precedence over other operations because "distributing" them increases memory cost.[33] For example, in evaluating the expression $p^i[a^j + b^j]/2$ for L1's ideal guess, processing $[a^j + b^j]$ first, storing the result, and then combining it with p^i yield the following sequence of numbers of numbers in working memory: 1, 2, 1, 2, 1. The distributed alternative of processing $p^i \, a^j$, storing the result, and then processing $p^i \, b^j$ and combining it with $p^i \, a^j$ yields the sequence 1, 2, 1, 2, 3, 2, 1, which dominates the first sequence. The first method also saves the cost of looking up p^i a second time, but this is much less important.

Although occurrence and adjacency are only necessary conditions for optimal search, I stop with them because they have considerable empirical support, they make the main patterns of subjects' search behavior in CJ's extensive-form and CGCB's and CGC's normal-form games intelligible, and they seem more transparent than other conditions for optimality and thus more likely to be descriptive of subjects' search behavior.

I close by noting that although this model supports CJ's, CGCB's, and CGC's use of occurrence and adjacency, it says nothing directly about how to measure search compliance in an econometric analysis. CGC's use of the density of a type's minimal search sequence in the part of the observed sequence where the subject tends to make his relevant look-ups (his search "style," in CGC's terminology) is a judgment call, which seems to be well supported by inspecting the data.

Conclusion

CJ's, CGCB's, and CGC's analyses of cognition in games via monitoring subjects' searches for hidden but freely accessible payoff information bridge part of the gap between neuroeconomics and conventional economics because they rest on explicit models of cognition, but search, unlike neural correlates of cognition, can be viewed as a rational choice. This chapter has used those analyses to make two points about the potential uses of neural data in economics.

First, standard assumptions of rational choice and equilibrium have yielded successful explanations of many phenomena, which as GP note can usefully be tested via revealed preference analysis of decision data. But there are other, equally important phenomena that appear to stem from failures of the implicit assumptions about cognition that underlie standard analyses, for which tests that don't take cognition explicitly into account are likely to be biased and misleading.

Second, with unbounded capacity for experimentation, it might be possible to discover all we need to know about behavior by observing decisions alone. But this is an arbitrary constraint, and CJ's, CGCB's, and CGC's analyses show that expanding the domain of analysis beyond decisions can yield a clearer view of behavior than is practically achievable by observing only decisions.

NOTES

This chapter is based on joint work with Miguel Costa-Gomes, University of Aberdeen, and Bruno Broseta, Red de Institutos Tecnológicos de la Comunidad Valenciana, particularly on Costa-Gomes and Crawford [2006, 2007]. I thank Miguel Costa-Gomes for our many discussions over the years, and Andrew Caplin for his very helpful comments on a previous draft. The experiments and analysis on which this chapter is based were funded in part by the U.S. National Science Foundation under grant SES-0100072 and the U.K. Economic and Social Research Council under grant R/000/22/3796.

1. GP do allow an "inspirational" role for data other than decisions, but they exclude such data from theory testing.

2. Why study strategic thinking when with enough experience in a stationary environment, even amoebas—or human reinforcement learners, who need not even know that they are playing a game—usually converge to equilibrium? Many applications of game theory involve situations with no clear precedents. (Should you sell U.S. airline stocks when the market reopens after 9/11, or buy them on the anticipation that others will overreact?) Comparative statics and design questions inherently involve new games with new equilibria, which players cannot reach by copying behavior from analogous games. In such situations, subjects' initial responses are often plainly "strategic" but nonetheless deviate from equilibrium. Even in settings in which players can be expected to converge to equilibrium, the structure of strategic thinking can influence the rate of convergence and equilibrium selection.

3. This conclusion is consistent with SW's, Nagel's, HCW's, and CGCB's results, but their evidence is less clear.

4. CGCB's and CJ's analyses make this point in different ways. Camerer (chapter 2), Caplin (chapter 15), and Schotter (chapter 3) argue cogently, in complementary ways, for the use of nonchoice data and outline frameworks to guide their use in analyses. Köszegi and Rabin (chapter 8) discuss using decision data to distinguish intended decisions from errors.

5. Or, if the rules and possible preferences allow multiple equilibria, the equilibrium identified by some agreed-upon selection principle. Although GP's chapter focuses entirely

on individual decisions, private communications suggest that they accept the need for extending their proposal to games by assuming equilibrium.

6. The proposed explanation differs greatly from classical search theory in purpose, but only slightly in methods.

7. "Eureka!" learning remains possible, but it can be tested for and seems to be rare. Initial responses yield insights into cognition that also help us think about how to model learning from experience, but that is another story.

8. Access was via a MouseLab interface that automatically records a sequence of parameter opening and closing times, which makes it possible to test models of the order and/or duration of parameter look-ups. Subjects were not allowed to write, and the frequencies with which they looked up the parameters made clear that they did not memorize them. Subjects were taught the mechanics of looking up parameters and entering decisions, but not information-search strategies. MouseLab is an automated way to track search as in eye-movement studies of individual decisions (Payne, Bettman, and Johnson [1993]; www.cebiz.org/mouselab.htm). Wang, Spezio, and Camerer [2006] illustrate the use of a modern, more powerful eye-tracking method.

9. A partial exception is that CJ's experiments evoked nonpecuniary social preferences like those in ultimatum experiments, and these and subjects' risk aversion are uncontrolled and privately known. Privately known social preferences are easily accommodated in the analysis of CJ's results, and risk aversion was probably insignificant.

10. CJ's [1993, 2002] designs differed in some ways, for example framing in losses versus in gains, that are not important for my purposes and are not discussed here. At roughly the same time in the early 1990s, Camerer and Johnson [2004] did a MouseLab study of forward induction in extensive-form games. Algaze (Croson) [1990] reported a very brief study of search for hidden payoff information in matrix games. Neither of the latter papers is discussed here.

11. CJ used a "rollover" option in MouseLab, in which subjects could open the box that concealed a pie by moving the cursor into it, revealing the pie for as long as the cursor was in the box. Subjects could also use the interface to look up their roles in each round, but these were known, and those look-ups were not reported or analyzed.

12. Only "mostly" because with only pecuniary preferences, the first-round pie, as long as it is large enough, does not affect the equilibrium initial offer. With social preferences, the first-round pie may be relevant because it may influence the responder's acceptance decision.

13. This informal definition, like the one for occurrence, is intentionally vague regarding how often look-ups or operations appear to accommodate variations in CJ's, CGCB's, and CGC's use of occurrence and adjacency. The notions are made more precise in CGCB's analysis and, as explained below, CGC's. Note that both are general restrictions on how cognition drives search, which can be applied across a variety of games and decision rules.

14. Instead of the rollover option CJ used, CGCB used a "click" option, in which subjects could open a box by moving the cursor into it and left-clicking the mouse. Before he could continue, a subject had to close the box by right-clicking, which could be done from anywhere in the display.

15. Lk's and $Dk - 1$'s decisions both survive k rounds of iterated elimination of dominated decisions and so in two-person games are k-rationalizable [Bernheim 1984].

Although Dk − 1 types are closer to how theorists analyze games, Lk types seem more natural and predominate in applications.

16. Because a type's search implications depend not only on what decisions it specifies, but also on why, something like a types-based model seems necessary here. In CJ [1993], types are implicit in the discussion and limited to two, which might be called "subgame-perfect equilibrium" and "other." CJ [2002] adapted CGCB's analysis by defining extensive-form "types" modeled after CGCB's and SW's normal-form types, using them to construct a more structured data analysis than CJ's [1993].

17. In previous designs, the targets and limits were the same for both players and varied only across treatments.

18. Eleven of these subjects were from an "open boxes" treatment, not discussed here, identical to the baseline but with the parameters continually visible. The results of this treatment (and analogous treatments in CJ and CGCB) confirm that making subjects look up the parameters does not significantly affect their decisions, so the data can be pooled with baseline decision data, as here. CGC's open boxes subjects have numbers that begin with a 5.

19. By contrast, in SW's or CGCB's matrix-game designs, even a perfect fit does not distinguish a subject's best-fitting type from nearby omitted types; and in Nagel's and HCW's guessing-game designs, with large strategy spaces but with each subject playing only one game repeatedly, the ambiguity is worse.

20. Nagel's results are often viewed as evidence that subjects perform finitely iterated dominance, as in Dk − 1. But Lk's and Dk − 1's decisions are perfectly confounded in Nagel's main treatments and weakly separated in Nagel's and HCW's other treatments and in CGCB's design. CGC's clear separation of Lk from Dk − 1 allows them to conclude that Dk types don't exist in significant numbers, at least in this setting, and thus that subjects respect low levels of iterated dominance as a by-product of following Lk types, not because they explicitly perform it. Sophisticated, which is clearly separated from equilibrium, also doesn't exist in significant numbers. CGC's [2006, section II.D] specification test rules out significant numbers of other types omitted from the specification.

21. By contrast, the lack of a simple common structure in CGCB's design makes rules' search implications vary from game to game in ways so complex you need a "codebook" to identify them.

22. CGCB and CGC made no claim that durations are irrelevant, just that durations don't deserve priority. CGCB [table IV] present some results on durations under the heading of "gaze times."

23. Wang, Spezio, and Camerer's [2006] eye-tracking methods have an advantage in avoiding this ambiguity.

24. In CGC's design, unlike in CGCB's, Equilibrium's minimal search implications are simpler than any boundedly rational type's implications. This makes it harder to explain deviations from equilibrium by cognitive complexity. But we will see that high-compliance Equilibrium robot/trained subjects search more than high-compliance robot/trained subjects of other types, so CGC's Equilibrium search implications may not reflect its complexity.

25. L1's search implications illustrate an important advantage of the automatic adjustment feature of CGC's design. L1's ideal guess depends on its own target but only its partner's limits, while L2's and D1's depend on both players' targets and limits and

Equilibrium's depends on both players' targets and a combination of its own and its partner's lower or upper limits. In other designs, such as CGCB's, L1's decisions almost inevitably depend only on its own payoff parameters, and more sophisticated types' decisions depend on both own and other's parameters. Thus, the automatic adjustment feature allows CGC to separate solipsism from the strategic naivete of L1. CGC's data give no evidence of solipsism, but a great deal of evidence of naivete. CGC's data also show that most subjects understood and relied upon automatic adjustment, which was carefully explained to them.

26. With automatic adjustment, an L2 player i does not need to know his own limits to play the game or think about the effects of his own guess being adjusted, only to predict j's L1 guess. By contrast, an L1 player i doesn't need to know his own limits, only j's. Because the possible values of the limits are not public knowledge, an L2 player i cannot infer that adjustment of player j's ideal guess can occur only at his upper (lower) limit when $p^j > 1$ ($p^j < 1$). An L2 subject who incorrectly infers this may omit $a^j = 4$ ($b^j = 6$) when $p^j > 1$ ($p^j < 1$).

27. As is evident from Tables 10.2 and 10.3, subjects' look-up sequences vary widely in what CGC called "style": Most robot/trained and baseline subjects with high exact compliance consistently look first at their type's minimal search sequence and then continue looking, apparently randomly, or stop and enter their guess (for example L2 robot/trained subject 910, L3 subject 1008, and D1 subject 1501 in Table 10.2; and L2 baseline subjects 108 and 206 in Table 10.3). But some such subjects look randomly first and turn to the relevant sequence at the end (L1 robot/trained subject 904). CGC's [2006, Section II.E] econometric analysis uses a binary nuisance parameter to distinguish these "early" and "late" styles and filter them out to obtain a better measure of search compliance.

28. CGC's specification analysis turned up only one clear violation of their proposed characterization of types' search implications, which is instructive. Baseline subject 415 (not shown in table 10.3), whose apparent type was L1 with nine exact guesses, had zero L1 search compliance in 9 of the 16 games because he had no adjacent $[a^j, b^j]$ pairs. His look-up sequences, however, were rich in (a^j, p^i, b^j) and (b^j, p^i, a^j) triples, in those orders, but not in such triples with other superscripts. This strongly suggests that 415 was an L1 who happened to be more comfortable with three numbers in working memory than CGC's characterization of search assumes, or than their other L1 subjects were. But because this violated CGC's assumptions on search, this subject was "officially" estimated to be D1.

29. One of the methods CGC allow for identifying equilibrium guesses is equilibrium checking, which has the least search requirements among all methods. Equilibrium checking can identify the equilibrium guess very quickly if the player has the luck to check the equilibrium first [CGC 2006, appendix H; CGC 2007]. Allowing this is unavoidable without risking incorrectly concluding that a subject has violated Equilibrium's search implications.

30. CGC's baseline subjects with high compliance for some type are like robot/untrained subjects, which do not usually exist because one cannot tell robot subjects how they will be paid without training them in how the robot works. These "naturally occurring" baseline robot subjects provide an unusual opportunity to separate the effects of training and strategic uncertainty, by comparing their behavior with robot/trained subjects' behavior.

31. Subject 309 omitted look-ups 4 and 6 (his partner's lower and upper limits) in game 1 and look-up 4 in games 2–5. This suggests that he did not yet understand the need

to check his partner's lower limit to be sure of his L2 guess even when his own target, or the product of targets, was greater than 1. However, he omitted look-up 4 even in game 4 where both targets were less than 1, showing that his error was probably more complex. That these omissions did not lead to non-L2 guesses in games 1–5 is an accident of our design with no greater significance.

32. Note that because MouseLab allows a subject to enter a tentative guess without confirming it (the asterisks in the data in tables 10.2 and 10.3), thereby saving storage cost, the variations in search style described in note 24 are consistent with optimality when look-up costs are negligible even if storage costs are not.

33. This effect is related to the reason that backward induction is the most efficient way to solve a finite-horizon dynamic programming problem such as those that subjects faced in CJ's design: other ways are feasible, but wasteful of storage and computational capacity (though the latter is assumed to be freely available here).

REFERENCES

Algaze (Croson), Rachel. 1990. A Test of Presentation Effects on Strategy Choice. B.A. honors thesis, University of Pennsylvania.

Bernheim, B. Douglas. 1984. Rationalizable Strategic Behavior. *Econometrica* 52: 1007–1028.

Camerer, Colin, and Eric Johnson. 2004. Thinking about Attention in Games: Backward and Forward Induction. In *The Psychology of Economic Decisions*, Vol. 2: *Reasons and Choices*, ed. Isabel Brocas and Juan Carrillo. Oxford: Oxford University Press.

Camerer, Colin, Eric Johnson, Talia Rymon, and Sankar Sen. 1993. Cognition and Framing in Sequential Bargaining for Gains and Losses. In *Frontiers of Game Theory*, ed. Kenneth Binmore, Alan Kirman, and Piero Tani, 27–47. Cambridge, MA: MIT Press.

Costa-Gomes, Miguel, and Vincent Crawford. 2006. Cognition and Behavior in Two-Person Guessing Games: An Experimental Study. *American Economic Review* 96: 1737–1768.

———. 2007. Studying Cognition via Information Search in Two-Person Guessing Game Experiments. Mimeo. University of California, San Diego.

Costa-Gomes, Miguel, Vincent Crawford, and Bruno Broseta. 2001. Cognition and Behavior in Normal-Form Games: An Experimental Study. *Econometrica* 69: 1193–1235.

Gabaix, Xavier, David Laibson, Guillermo Moloche, and Stephen Weinberg. 2006. Costly Information Acquisition: Experimental Analysis of a Boundedly Rational Model. *American Economic Review* 96: 1043–1068.

Ho, Teck Hua, Colin Camerer, and Keith Weigelt. 1998. Iterated Dominance and Iterated Best Response in Experimental "p-Beauty Contests." *American Economic Review* 88: 947–969.

Johnson, Eric, Colin Camerer, Sankar Sen, and Talia Rymon. 2002. Detecting Failures of Backward Induction: Monitoring Information Search in Sequential Bargaining. *Journal of Economic Theory* 104: 16–47.

McKelvey, Richard, and Thomas Palfrey. 1995. Quantal Response Equilibria for Normal-Form Games. *Games and Economic Behavior* 10: 6–38.

Nagel, Rosemarie. 1995. Unraveling in Guessing Games: An Experimental Study. *American Economic Review* 85: 1313–1326.

Payne, John, James Bettman, and Eric Johnson. 1993. *The Adaptive Decision Maker.* Cambridge: Cambridge University Press.

Rubinstein, Ariel. 2007. Instinctive and Cognitive Reasoning: A Study of Response Times. *Economic Journal* 117: 1243–1259.

Stahl, Dale, and Paul Wilson. 1994. Experimental Evidence on Players' Models of Other Players. *Journal of Economic Behavior and Organization* 25: 309–327.

———. 1995. On Players' Models of Other Players: Theory and Experimental Evidence. *Games and Economic Behavior* 10: 218–254.

Wang, Joseph, Michael Spezio, and Colin Camerer. 2006. Pinocchio's Pupil: Using Eyetracking and Pupil Dilation to Understand Truth-Telling and Deception in Games. Mimeo. California Institute of Technology.

CHAPTER 11

REVEALED PREFERENCE AND BOUNDED RATIONALITY

DOUGLAS GALE

REVEALED PREFERENCE

WHEN Paul Samuelson introduced the idea of revealed preference, I have little doubt that he was only trying to ground economic theory in observable behavior, as required by the positivism of the 1930s, and do away with unnecessary concepts.

> The discrediting of *utility* as a psychological concept robbed it of its only possible virtue as an *explanation* of human behaviour in other than a circular sense, revealing its emptiness as even a construction. As a result the most modern theory confines itself to an analysis of indifference elements, budgetary equilibrium being defined by equivalence of price ratios to respective indifference slopes.
>
> Consistently applied, however, the modern criticism turns back on itself and cuts deeply. For just as we do not claim to know by introspection the behaviour of utility, many will argue we cannot know the behaviour of ratios of marginal utilities or of indifference directions. [Samuelson, 1938: 61]

Samuelson hypothesized that what we observe is an individual choosing a consumption bundle $x \in \mathbf{R}^{\ell}_+$ from a budget set defined by the constraint $p \cdot x \leq w$, where w is the individual's wealth and p is the vector of prices at which commodities are traded. Suppose that we observe a finite sequence of price vectors $\{p_i\}_{i=1}^{n}$ and the corresponding sequence of choices $\{x_i\}_{i=1}^{n}$. We do not observe preferences or any other motivating factors, only the prices and the chosen quantities. What can we say about motives for this behavior? Samuelson implicitly assumed a stable preference ordering, that is, assumed that the individual's preferences were not changing over time. As a result, one could say that if a bundle x were chosen when x' was available, the individual had revealed that he preferred x to x'. Formally, if $p \cdot x \geq p \cdot x'$, then x is *directly revealed preferred* to x'. The revealed preference relation is just the transitive closure of the direct revealed preference relation: given a sequence $\{x_i\}_{i=1}^{n}$ of commodity bundles, if x_i is directly revealed preferred to x_{i+1} for $i = 1, \ldots, n-1$, then we can say that x_1 is *revealed preferred* to x_n. To ensure that this revealed preference relation is consistent, we must assume there are no cycles. The Generalized Axiom of Revealed Preference (GARP) states that if x is revealed preferred to x', then x' cannot be strictly revealed preferred to x. Formally, if x is revealed preferred to x', then $p' \cdot x \geq p' \cdot x'$, where p' is the price vector at which x' is chosen.

It can be shown that if a demand relation satisfies GARP, then it must be generated by utility maximization in the sense that there exists a well-behaved utility function that represents the revealed preference relation and that the chosen bundles maximize this function subject to the prevailing budget constraints [Afriat, 1967]. This seems pretty innocuous as a basis for demand theory. What has made revealed preference theory controversial is its use as a paradigm of economic explanations in other areas of economics. Let us leave on one side the argument heard at the conference that neuroscience can make economic researchers' lives easier by providing tools that do more efficiently what older methods have done inefficiently in the past. Instead, I want to address the question of whether preferences can legitimately be inferred from observations of choice behavior. The arguments offered to support this view often sound rather silly. For example, it is pointed out that American tourists in London are involved in more traffic accidents than the locals because they tend to look the wrong way when crossing the road. Does this mean, it was asked rhetorically, that Americans are revealing a preference for being run over by London taxis? Although it would be easy and reasonable to dismiss such arguments as juvenile snarkiness, they raise interesting questions about how to model behavior when individuals are not perfectly rational.

The classical revealed preference framework makes several implicit assumptions that are limiting. First, there is no uncertainty in this framework. Second, it is a framework dealing with what Simon [1982] called "substantive rationality", as distinct from what he termed "procedural rationality". Third, there are no costs of making decisions. Obviously, if an action has uncertain consequences, one cannot conclude that the individual revealed a preference for the realized outcome, as distinct from the action that led to that outcome. Similarly, limited computational ability may cause an individual to adopt simple heuristics that approximate her "true" optimal behavior. This approximately optimal behavior may be inconsistent with a well-defined preference ordering, although the underlying preferences are not. Finally, even a perfectly rational individual may find it easier to adopt simple habits rather than attempt in every circumstance to optimize relative to her true preferences. In other words, perfect rationality is not optimal.

No one seriously doubts that people make mistakes, that they sometimes make choices without thinking about all the possible consequences, or that they sometimes regret their actions. One could go further and agree with psychologists that emotions play a role in decision making and that individuals do not always behave like a rational economic person. However, before accepting that this amounts to a damning critique of economic methods, we need to ask how well behavioral approaches will perform in explaining a broad range of social phenomena. It is one thing to point out anecdotal failures of economic modeling. It is another to prove that economics is systematically incapable of providing a coherent and accurate account of economic behavior, and still another that "behavioral economics," whatever that may be, offers a better empirical account of the same data. While being happy to admit that there are more things on heaven and earth than are dreamt of in neoclassical economics, I see no reason to think that they cannot mostly be approximated by neoclassical methods, suitably extended. One example is the use of maximizing methods to model procedural rationality. In the next section I give a sketch of such a model and then briefly describe some empirical applications.

BOUNDED RATIONALITY

When subjects enter an experimental laboratory, they bring with them behavioral rules (heuristics or rules of thumb) that have proved helpful in the past. These heuristics may be genetically wired, or they may be the result of education, imitation, and trial and error. Whatever the source, they are behavioral rules that the experimentalist takes as given. When a subject's behavior looks "as if" it is Bayes rational, I believe it is because the experimental design is sufficiently simple and transparent and the subject's heuristics are sufficiently well adapted that they approximate the optimal behavior. The question, then, is whether the model of Bayes rational behavior is useful in interpreting and organizing the data. I believe that it is. Moreover, there are few alternatives when it comes to confronting the data with some theory.

There are many approaches to modeling boundedly rational behavior. In work with Syngjoo Choi, Ray Fisman, and Shachar Kariv, we have taken the approach that heuristics or rules of thumb are tools that individuals use to simplify the complex problems they face in everyday life. Simon [1982] defines an individual to be procedurally rational if he uses procedures or rules to achieve a given objective. This excessively broad characterization is not very useful for our purposes, so we adopt a narrower definition according to which a procedurally rational individual uses simple rules, that we call heuristics, in order to maximize his objective function.[1] Before getting to the applications, I give a sketch of our general approach to modeling bounded rationality, including the distinction between substantive and procedural rationality.

An Abstract Model

To illustrate the general approach, I use the example of an individual who has to solve a static decision problem. The individual is assumed to have a preference ordering that can be represented by a von Neumann Morgenstern (VNM) utility function $U : X \to \mathbf{R}$, where $X \subset \mathbf{R}^\ell$ is the set of possible choice with generic element $x \in X$. The set of feasible choices depends on a vector of parameters $p \in P \subset \mathbf{R}^m$ and is denoted by $B(p) \subset X$ for every vector p. So the individual's decision problem, given the parameter p, is to choose an element $x \in X$ that maximizes $U(x)$ subject to the constraint $x \in B(p)$.

This problem may be too complex for the individual to solve. That is, she may not be able to identify the true maximizer for each vector p. Instead, individuals tend to exhibit programmed behaviors that can be represented by stochastic choice rules. Suppose there is a set of random choice functions $\left\{ \tilde{f}_k : k = 1, \dots . K \right\}$, where $\tilde{f}_k : \mathcal{B} \to X$ and $\mathcal{B}$ contains the possible choice sets, that is, $B(p) \in \mathcal{B}$ for every p. The choice functions must satisfy a feasibility condition, namely, $\tilde{f}_k(B) \in B$ for every $B \in \mathcal{B}$.

Where our theory departs from others is in the assumption that the choice of the heuristic $\tilde{f}_k$ is motivated by the attempt to maximize the expected value of the underlying VNM utility function U. More precisely, we assume that each heuristic $\tilde{f}_k$ has an associated value function, $v_k : P \to \mathbf{R}$, defined by putting

$$v_k(p) = E\left[U \circ \tilde{f}_k(B(p)) \right]$$

for every p in P. In other words, $v_k(p)$ is the expected utility that would result from choosing the heuristic $\tilde{f}_k$ when the choice set is $B(p)$. Even if the individual is restricted to the finite set of simple rules or heuristics, we should not assume that he will be able to unerringly pick the best rule in every case. Instead, we assume that he is more likely to pick a rule if it has a higher payoff, but he is not certain to do so. In general, we want the the probability that heuristic k is chosen, conditional on the parameter vector p, to be increasing in relative payoffs, say,

$$\Pr\left[\kappa = k \middle| p \right] = G_k\left(v_1(p), \dots, v_K(p) \right). \tag{11.1}$$

For example, we could use the familiar logistic law

$$\Pr\left[\kappa = k \mid p\right] = \frac{\exp\left\{\beta v_k\left(p\right)\right\}}{\sum_{k'=1}^{K} \exp\left\{\beta v_{k'}\left(p\right)\right\}},$$

(11.2)

which says that the probability of choosing heuristic k is proportional to the exponentiated payoff from heuristic k. The parameter $\beta > 0$ measures the accuracy of the individual's effort to maximize expected utility. If β is close to zero, the probability distribution given by equation 11.2 is almost independent of the payoffs. He is almost equally likely to choose any heuristic. On the other hand, as β increases, more and more of the probability mass is concentrated on the optimal heuristic until, in the limit as $\beta \to \infty$, he becomes a pure maximizer.

The problem with this approach and the reason, one presumes, that writers such as Simon reject it, is that it appears to assume hyperrationality on the part of the individual decision maker. Apart from the errors in the choice of heuristic, modeled for example by the logistic function, the decision maker is treated as a rational maximizing agent. In fact, he is solving a *more* complex version of the original decision problem. Instead of choosing the preferred element from the choice set $B\left(p\right)$, he has to figure out the consequences of choosing a particular heuristic, then calculate the expected utility of that heuristic, then select the best of the heuristics, and finally, implement it. This sounds like a much more demanding form of rationality, one that takes us even further away from a realistic account of bounded rationality.

There are two ways to address this issue. The first requires us to make a conceptual distinction between assuming that someone chooses an "optimal" heuristic and assuming that he "solves" the decision problem of choosing the optimal rule. For example, these rules may be hardwired in his brain, and his knowledge of the payoffs from each heuristic may be instinctual or acquired by trial and error. As a metaphor, suppose we think of the individual's behavior as the result of an evolutionary process (i.e., an "as if" evolutionary process) in which the individual randomly selects different heuristics in different situations and gradually adapts his behavior in response to the resulting payoffs. For example, suppose an individual has an initial value function v_k^0 for each heuristic k. These functions could be constant functions, and they could be the same for each heuristic. At date 0, a random parameter $\tilde{p}^0$ is observed, and the individual chooses a heuristic k according to the probability law 11.2 using his current value functions $\{v_k^0\}$. After observing the random outcome $\tilde{f}_k\left(B\left(p^0\right)\right)$, the value functions $\{v_k^0\}$ are updated using some adaptive algorithm (*not* necessarily Bayesian updating). Call the new functions $\{v_k^1\}$. At date 1, a random parameter $\tilde{p}^1$ is observed, the individual chooses a heuristic k using the new value functions $\{v_k^1\}$, which are then updated, based on the payoff received, to provide a new set of functions $\{v_k^2\}$. Repeating this procedure at each date, we generate a sequence of functions $\{v_k^t\}$. Under certain regularity conditions, the stochastic process $\{v_k^t\}$ converges to the true value function, v_k, with probability one.

The second way to answer the charge of hyperrationality is to point out that the most useful theory for empirical work is not necessarily the most sophisticated or intellectually interesting. The advantage of our framework is that it can be implemented in practice and helps us in accounting for and interpreting the data. This is not really surprising, since it follows the successful neoclassical recipe of explaining everything in terms of constrained maximization by adding constraints to the problem. In other words, the proof of this "as if" pudding is in the eating, which in our case means that it should be judged by how well it helps us deal with data.

Decision Making under Uncertainty

Choi, Fisman, Gale, and Kariv [2006] (henceforth CFGK), have applied these general principles to an experimental problem of decision making under uncertainty. In their experiment, subjects are presented with a standard portfolio choice problem. There are two states of nature, $s = 1, 2$, that occur with known probabilities π and $1 - \pi$, respectively. There are Arrow securities corresponding to each state. A security promises one dollar if state s occurs, and nothing otherwise. A subject chooses a nonnegative portfolio $x = (x_1, x_2)$ satisfying the budget constraint

$$p_1 x_1 + p_2 x_2 = 1, \tag{11.3}$$

where x_s is the demand for security s and p_s is the price of security s. By homogeneity, there is no loss of generality in assuming that the subject's income is normalized to equal unity. A graphical experimental interface displays a sequence of 50 randomly generated budget sets from which the subject makes her choice by "pointing and clicking." The experimental output for each subject is a series $\{(p^i, x^i)\}_{i=1}^{50}$, where p^i is the parameter vector and x^i is the portfolio choice at the ith decision.

One of the most striking features of the data produced by CFGK is the heterogeneity of the subjects' behavior, which indicates the inadvisability of trying to estimate average preferences from pooled data. Although the behavior differs a lot from subject to subject, there are certain stylized behaviors that appear over and over again. Sometimes subjects choose the riskless portfolio at the intersection of the budget line and the 45 degree line where $x_1 = x_2$, behavior that could be rationalized as exhibiting infinite risk aversion. Sometimes they choose portfolios on the boundary of the nonnegative orthant where $x_1 = 0$ or $x_2 = 0$, behavior that could be rationalized by the assumption of risk neutrality. Sometimes they are responsive to relative prices and try to exploit the trade-off between risk and return by shifting along the budget constraint in one direction or the other. This is the kind of behavior that one would expect from rational agents with positive but finite risk aversion.

While some subjects exhibited one of these stylized behaviors most of the time, others were harder to characterize. Although it proved impossible to classify all the different types of behavior, all the subjects exhibited some elements of the three heuristics mentioned above.

With this motivation, CFGK estimated a *type-mixture model* (TMM) to provide a unified account of both procedural rationality and substantive rationality. Following the general approach outlined above, subjects were assumed to be expected utility maximizers who chose from a set of three heuristics, the "diagonal" heuristic, the "boundary" heuristic, and the "smooth responsiveness" heuristic. The TMM simultaneously accounts for subjects' underlying preferences, in particular, their risk aversion and the choice of decision rules.

Although the model is very sparsely parameterized, it does a good job of accounting for the data. From a methodological point of view, the most important point is that, although the behavior of some subjects cannot be reconciled with expected utility maximization, we can explain the behavior by assuming underlying expected utility (EU) preferences, together with the assumption that subjects try to approximate optimal behavior by choosing "optimally" from a limited set of heuristics. Clearly, a simple-minded application of revealed preference might lead to the conclusion that agents could not be expected utility maximizers. But a theory of procedural rationality provides us with both an underlying account of substantive rationality that is consistent with EU theory and an empirical model that can account for the data.

Estimating Cognitive Hierarchies in Social Learning Experiments

In the preceding application, a clear theoretical analysis allows one to understand the elements of a complex experiment and to make maximum use of the resulting data. Sometimes an experiment is designed to test a single "fact" and theoretical analysis may be less important in such cases where the data may be expected to "speak for itself." But the most interesting economic questions are not of this kind. Often we are interested in the subjects' interaction, for example, playing a game, and we may want to know something about their motivations or expectations or strategies, things that are not directly observable. The role of theoretical analysis in helping us understand what is going on in a complex game is well illustrated by Choi, Gale and Kariv [2005] (henceforth CGK), which adapted a protocol from Anderson and Holt [1997] to "test" the theory of social learning in networks proposed by Gale and Kariv [2003].

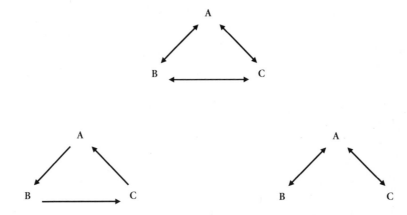

Figure 11.1. Different types of network: complete (top), circle (left), and star (right)

Social learning refers to the process of information acquisition that occurs when one person observes a choice made by another person. Examples would be observing the make of car the neighbors drive, seeing the number of people going into a popular restaurant, or hearing that a neighboring farmer has planted a new type of wheat. All of these observations provide economically relevant information and may influence the decisions of the observer. In practice, each individual observes the choices made by a only limited set of other individuals, which we call her "neighborhood." Information diffuses through the social network as each individual observes her neighbors, updates her beliefs, revises her behavior, and is observed in turn by other individuals.

In this protocol, two states of nature are represented by two urns, a red urn and a white urn. The red urn contains two red balls and one white ball. The white urn contains two white balls and one red ball. At the beginning of the game, one of the urns is chosen by "nature." Each urn has an equal probability of being chosen. The subjects in the experiment do not know the identity of the chosen or "true" state, but they know the contents of the urns and the probability with which each is chosen.

After the true state has been determined, subjects receive private information in the form of a random draw from the true urn. More precisely, with some probability $0 < q \leq 1$, a subject is informed, and with probability $1 - q$, he is uninformed. An informed subject receives a private signal, which is either red or white. The probability of red is 1/3 if the true state is white and 2/3 if the true state is red. An uninformed subject does not receive any signal.

There are three individuals in each game, located at positions A, B, and C on a simple graph. There were three types of graphs used in the study, a complete network, a star network, and a circle network. The graphs are illustrated in figure 11.1, where an arrow pointing from individual i to individual j indicates that i can observe j's actions.

Once the individuals have been informed, there are six stages (decision turns) of the game, in each of which the subjects are asked to guess the true state of nature. Note that the state is the same throughout the six periods. The subjects do not receive private signals after the beginning of the game, but they do observe the actions of (some of) the other subjects.

At the first decision turn, the subjects make a decision (red or white) based on private information (if they are informed) or their priors (if they are uninformed). After the decision has been made, a subject observes the choices of his neighbors. In the complete network, she observes the choices of the two other subjects in the network. In the star network, the subject in the center observes the choices of the two peripheral subjects, whereas the peripheral subjects only observe the choice of the subject in the center. In the circle, each subject observes the choice of the subject who is her neighbor in the clockwise direction.

After observing the neighbor's choice, the subject is asked again to guess the true state. If she wishes, she can use the information she has obtained from her neighbor's choice to update her beliefs. Once everyone has chosen the urn she thinks is most likely, the subjects again observe their neighbor's choices. This procedure is repeated until the subjects have made six decisions about the true state of nature.

In the experimental design of CGK, subjects are rewarded if they guess the state correctly. More precisely, at the end of each game, one decision turn is chosen at random and the subject receives a positive payment (two dollars) if he guessed the true state in that turn and nothing otherwise. Assuming a subject prefers a higher probability of being rewarded, he should choose the state with the higher likelihood, conditional on his information.

The large-scale features of the data from this experiment are fairly consistent with the Bayesian learning theory developed in Gale and Kariv [2003], but there are signs of heterogeneity that are inconsistent with the symmetric behavior required by Bayesian updating. In fact, it appears that different subjects exhibit different levels of cognitive ability. Some make choices almost randomly, others make use of their private information and do not learn from neighbors, and others are much closer to the behavior associated with rational Bayesians.

Choi [2005] uses a cognitive hierarchy framework to model heterogeneous behavior in the data from the study by CGK. He identifies a small number of heuristics and treats them as behavioral "types" in a TMM. In any game, a subject's type is given and determines how much information the subject can process. Choi's model assumes that subjects have rational expectations and, faced with a distribution of types as opponents, they respond optimally given the information they process. Choi estimates the probability distribution of types for each treatment (network × information) using maximum likelihood methods.

It turns out that assuming that some subjects are boundedly rational still leaves an important role for rational behavior. The model of cognitive hierarchy fits the data better and allows the rational agents, what Choi calls "sophisticated Bayesians," a large role in the estimated model. The probability that an individual subject is a sophisticated Bayesian is quite high, and furthermore, because it is not necessary to explain departures from Bayesian updating by noise, the sophisticated Bayesians fit the data better. Again, recognizing departures from substantive rationality reveals the true rational types more clearly and provides stronger evidence that this is the "right" model.

Conclusion

The approach advocated here uses well-specified theoretical models as the basis for experimental designs, but recognizes that subjects are boundedly rational and inevitably make mistakes. On the one hand, it is silly to reject a model just because it cannot predict experimental behavior with complete accuracy. On the other hand, a model should provide more than a vague comparative static prediction. Ideally, one wants an experiment to be rich enough to provide a real challenge for the model, and one wants the model to account for the data. Since a theory based on substantive rationality will never fit the data exactly, a well-articulated account of bounded rationality is necessary to bridge the gap between the initial theory and the data. I and my colleagues have suggested estimating a structural model of bounded rationality to do the best possible job of accounting for the data and to allow us to recover the individuals' underlying preferences from observed behavior.

Taking theory seriously has numerous implications for the design of experiments. One implication is that we need to present subjects with a richer menu of decision problems or games. This will produce a richer data set, which in turn will allow us to identify heuristics used by individual subjects, to distinguish systematic biases from simple mistakes, and to make a more stringent test of the theoretical model.

Instead of making fun of the naivete of revealed preference, we should be using more sophisticated models to study behavioral phenomena in terms of maximizing behavior.

NOTE

1. It should be noted that Simon (1986) explicitly disavowed this approach to modeling bounded rationality. Maximizing an objective function subject to additional constraints was still, in his view, a case of substantive rationality rather than procedural rationality.

REFERENCES

Afriat, Sydney N. 1967. The Construction of a Utility Function from Expenditure Data. *Econometrica* 6: 67–77.

Anderson, Lisa R., and Charles A. Holt. 1997 Information Cascades in the Laboratory. *American Economic Review* 87: 847–862.

Choi, Syngjoo. 2005. A Cognitive Hierarchy Model of Learning in Networks. Mimeo, New York University.

Choi, Syngjoo, Douglas Gale, and Shachar Kariv. 2005. Learning in Networks: An Experimental Study. Mimeo, New York University.

Choi, Syngjoo, Raymond Fisman, Douglas Gale, and Shachar Kariv. 2006. Substantive and Procedural Rationality in Decisions under Uncertainty. Mimeo, New York University.

Gale, Douglas, and Shachar Kariv. 2003 Bayesian Learning in Social Networks. *Games and Economic Behavior* 45(2): 329–346.

Samuelson, Paul. A. 1938. A Note on the Pure Theory of Consumers' Behaviour. *Economica* 5: 353–354.

Simon, Herbert. A. 1982. *Models of Bounded Rationality*, Vol. 2. Cambridge, MA: MIT Press.

CHAPTER 12

··

THE SEVEN PROPERTIES OF GOOD MODELS

··

XAVIER GABAIX AND DAVID LAIBSON

SCIENTISTS spend most of their time formulating and analyzing models. A model is a description—or representation—of the world. Most models are based on assumptions that are known to be only approximately true (and exactly false). For example, consider the most commonly used models of the earth: flat, spherical, and ellipsoid. These models do not account for the bumps and grooves. A perfect replica of the earth would reproduce every contour, but such a representation would be impractical. You don't need to know the height of Beacon Hill to take a subway across Boston. Tourists use a flat subway map—the model that is just complex enough for the problem at hand.

This chapter describes the seven key properties of useful economic models: parsimony, tractability, conceptual insightfulness, generalizability, falsifiability, empirical consistency, and predictive precision.[1] Successful economic models have most of these properties, although almost no economic models have them all. Some of these seven properties are already well accepted among economists: parsimony, tractability, conceptual insightfulness, and generalizability. The other properties— falsifiability, empirical consistency, and predictive precision—are not universally accepted.

We believe that these seven properties are fundamental. Some economists instead argue that classical optimization assumptions—such as rationality and dynamic consistency—are necessary ingredients of a good economic model.

We believe that these optimization assumptions do discipline economic analysis and often produce many of the seven properties listed above. For instance, parsimony, tractability, conceptual insightfulness, and generalizability all tend to follow from classical optimization assumptions. However, such classical assumptions are not the only path to a good model. We believe that classical optimization assumptions are better treated as hypotheses that should be tested and not fundamental or necessary properties of economic models. Anticipating one set of objections, we also discuss how to conduct normative analysis even if economists cannot rely on optimization principles such as revealed preferences.

We conclude this chapter by discussing the appropriate empirical scope of economic models. We argue that restrictions on the scope of economic research contradict the history of science, as well as the conceptual orientation of economics itself.

SEVEN KEY PROPERTIES OF ECONOMIC MODELS

Economic models are conceptual frameworks that aid in the understanding, description, and/or prediction of human behavior. Formal empirical analysis, casual observation, and introspection all play a role in demonstrating the correspondences between economic models and the world.

In this section, we define the seven key properties of good models. We note that these properties are not always mutually consistent. Consequently, these properties sometimes need to be traded off against each other.

1. Parsimony
2. Tractability
3. Conceptual insightfulness
4. Generalizability
5. Falsifiability
6. Empirical consistency
7. Predictive precision

Parsimonious models are simple models in the sense that they rely on relatively few special assumptions and they leave the researcher with relatively few degrees of freedom.[2] Parsimonious models are desirable because they prevent the researcher from consciously or subconsciously manipulating the model so that it overfits the available facts. Overfitting occurs when a model works very well in a given situation but fails to make accurate out-of-sample predictions. For example, if a model incorporates a large set of qualitative psychological biases, then the model is non-parsimonious, since selective combination of those biases will enable the researcher

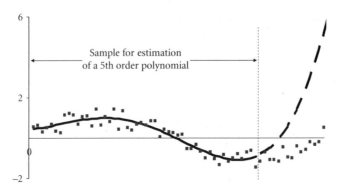

Figure 12.1. An example of overfitting.

to tweak the model so that it "explains" almost any pattern of observations. Likewise, if a model has many free parameters—for instance, a complex budget constraint or complex household preferences—then the model is relatively nonparsimonious. When models are flexible and complex, the researcher can combine the myriad elements to match almost any given set of facts. Such flexibility makes it easy to explain in-sample data, producing the false impression that the model will have real (out-of-sample) explanatory power (see figure 12.1).

Tractable models are easy to analyze. Models with maximal tractability can be solved with purely analytic methods—that is, paper and pencil calculations. At the other extreme, minimally tractable models cannot be solved even with a computer, since the necessary computations/simulations would take too long. For instance, optimization is typically not computationally feasible when there are dozens of continuous state variables—in such cases, numerical solution times are measured on the scale of years or centuries.

Conceptually insightful models reveal fundamental properties of economic behavior or economic systems. For example, the model of concave utility identifies the key property of risk aversion. The concept of concave utility is useful even though it makes only qualitative predictions. An optimizing framework such as a Nash equilibrium is also conceptually insightful even though it relies on an assumption that is empirically false—perfect rationality. The concept of Nash equilibrium clarifies some abstract ideas about equilibrium that are important to understand even if the Nash framework is an incomplete explanation of real-world behavior. Finally, many models are conceptually useful because they provide normative insights.

Generalizable models can be applied to a relatively wide range of situations. For example, a generalizable model of risk aversion could be used to analyze risk aversion in settings with small or large stakes, as well as risk aversion with respect to losses or gains. A generalizable model of learning could be used to study learning dynamics in settings with a discrete action set, or a continuous action set, or an action set with a mixture of discrete and continuous actions. A generalizable model of intertemporal choice could be used to study decisions with consequences that occur in minutes or decades.

Falsifiability and prediction are the same concept. A model is falsifiable if and only if the model makes nontrivial predictions that can in principle be empirically falsified. If a model makes no falsifiable predictions, then the model cannot be empirically evaluated.

Empirically consistent models are broadly consistent with the available data. In other words, empirically consistent models have not yet generated predictions that have been falsified by the data. Empirically consistent models can be ranked by the strength of their predictions. At one extreme, a model can be consistent with the data if the model makes only weak predictions that are verified empirically. At the other extreme, models can achieve empirical consistency by making many strong (i.e., precise) predictions that are verified empirically.

Models have *predictive precision* when they make precise—or "strong"— predictions. Strong predictions are desirable because they facilitate model evaluation and model testing. When an incorrect model makes strong predictions, it is easy to empirically falsify the model, even when the researcher has access only to a small amount of data. A model with predictive precision also has greater potential to be practically useful if it survives empirical testing. Models with predictive precision are useful tools for decision makers who are trying to forecast future events or the consequences of new policies.

A model with predictive precision may even be useful when it is empirically inaccurate. For instance, policy makers would value a structural model that predicts the timing of recessions, even if the model usually generated small predictive errors. An alternative model that correctly predicted that a recession would occur at some unspecified time over a 10-year horizon would not be as useful. In general, models that make approximately accurate strong predictions are much more useful than models that make exactly accurate weak predictions. Figure 12.2 provides a visual illustration of this point.

Predictive precision is infrequently emphasized in economics research. Academic economists have instead elevated such properties as parsimony, tractability, conceptual insightfulness, and generalizability. We believe that this tendency arises because people tend to celebrate the things they do best. Economists have had a comparative advantage in developing elegant mathematical models. Economists— including behavioral economists—have been far less successful in developing general models that make precise quantitative predictions that are approximately empirically accurate. In this sense, economic research differs from research in the natural sciences, particularly physics. We hope that economists will close this gap. Models that make weak predictions (or no predictions) are limited in their ability to advance economic understanding of the world.

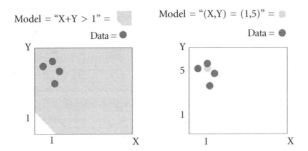

Figure 12.2. An example of high and low predictive precision. (a) Model is falsifiable and empirically consistent and does not have predictive precision. (b) Model is falsifiable and empirically inconsistent and has predictive precision.

Is Optimization a Necessary Ingredient for an Economic Model?

We have summarized seven key characteristics of a good model. Some economists have argued that modeling criteria such as those that we have discussed are incomplete. These economists formally define an economic model as a mathematical representation that has many of the features above and certain axiomatic optimization properties. For instance, rational beliefs and dynamic consistency have been proposed as axioms that define what it means to do economics. We do not agree with such a formulation.

We believe that economics is ultimately like any other science. Scientific models are mathematical approximations of the world. In every other scientific field, these approximations are judged by something akin to the seven criteria listed above and not by a model's adoption of particular axiomatic assumptions.

In the history of science, every axiomatic litmus test has been discarded. In retrospect, it is easy to see that axioms such as the flat earth, the earth at the center of the universe, or the Euclidean structure of space should not have been viewed as inviolate. It is likely that every axiom that we currently use in economics will suffer the same fate that these earlier axioms suffered. Indeed, it is now believed that no branch of science will ever identify an inviolate set of axioms [Kuhn, 1962]. This does not mean that we should abandon axioms, only that we should not use axiomatic litmus tests to define a field of scientific inquiry.

Relaxing economists' commitment to optimization axioms poses several problems. Optimization has provided discipline—that is, parsimony. But optimization is neither necessary nor sufficient for parsimony. For example, physics models are not constrained by optimization and are nevertheless highly parsimonious. Moreover, there are many optimization models that are not parsimonious since they make many special assumptions—about budget constraints and preferences—to explain a single behavioral regularity.

Without optimization axioms, economists will not be able to rely on traditional normative tools such as revealed preference. Instead, economists must develop models in which true preferences interact with other factors—such as biases, errors, and dynamic inconsistency—to produce economic behavior. Economists will need to simultaneously model true preferences—hereafter called normative preferences— and the confounding factors that prevent individuals from maximizing these normative preferences. Such integrative models are not new. Since the work of Luce [1959], economists have been developing formal mathematical models that incorporate both normative preferences and decision-making errors.[3]

To impute normative preferences, economists should adopt a two-step strategy that generalizes the classical revealed preference framework. First, specify a model that includes both normative preferences and a positive theory of behavior (incorporating such factors as decision-making errors and/or dynamic inconsistency that force a wedge between revealed preferences and normative preferences). Second, use choice data to estimate the model, thereby imputing the latent normative preferences.[4]

What Is the Appropriate Scope of Economic Research?

All natural sciences have developed by incorporating the study of smaller and smaller units of analysis. Biologists began with organisms, and then studied cells, cellular organs, and molecules (most importantly DNA). Physicists and their intellectual precursors began with visible objects and subsequently studied atoms and sub-atomic particles. Similar intellectual progressions have also occurred in the social sciences. For instance, psychologists have recently embraced both neuroscience and molecular genetics. Some anthropologists are also using these new methods.

We believe that economic research will also incorporate smaller units of analysis. Economics is usually described as the study of the allocation of scarce resources. Economists identify the individual decision maker as the key actor in this resource allocation process. Neuroscience[5] and cognitive genetics[6] will enable economists to develop a more complete understanding of the decision-making process. Ultimately, such research will advance economists' goal of predicting human behavior. Neuroscience and genetics data are not necessary ingredients for economic research, but such biological data will speed up the economic research process by providing convergent types of evidence that complement traditional behavioral studies. These new data sources will enable economists to more quickly formulate, develop, and test models of decision making and interindividual variation.

CONCLUSION

This chapter describes the seven key properties of successful economic models: parsimony, tractability, conceptual insightfulness, generalizability, falsifiability, empirical consistency, and predictive precision. However, even highly successful models do not have all seven properties. Many of the properties are in conflict with one another. For example, generalizing a model sometimes makes a model unfalsifiable—the most general form of the theory of revealed preference cannot be rejected by behavioral data.

We encourage economists to give more weight to the property of predictive precision. Models that make quantitatively precise predictions are the norm in other sciences. Models with predictive precision are easy to empirically test, and when such models are approximately empirically accurate, they are likely to be useful.

NOTES

We thank Andrew Caplin for helpful advice. Ian Dew-Becker and Brian Wells provided valuable research assistance. We acknowledge financial support from the National Science Foundation (HSD 0527518) and the National Institute of Aging (P01 AG005842).

1. Many other authors have attempted to characterize the purposes of models. Our formulation has been directly and indirectly influenced by preceding analyses by Popper [1934, 1963], Merton [1973], Friedman [1953], Kuhn [1962], and Stigler [1965]. For a related contemporary analysis, see Jasso [2004]. Stigler [1965] is the most important precedent for the analysis in this chapter. Stigler identifies three characteristics of economic theories that are accepted by "leading economists": generality, manageability, and congruence with reality.

2. These ideas are reflected in Occam's Razor, a principle attributed to the logician William of Ockham: "All things being equal, the simplest solution tends to be the best one."

3. See Bernheim and Rangel (chapter 7) for an extended discussion of these issues.

4. See Beshears et al. [2007] for a more detailed discussion of these issues.

5. See Camerer et al. [2007] for a recent review.

6. See Ding et al. [2006] and Benjamin et al. [2007].

REFERENCES

Benjamin, Daniel, J., Christopher F. Chabris, Edward Glaeser, Vilmundur Gudnason, Tamara B. Harris, David Laibson, Lenore Launer, and Shaun Purcell. 2007. Genoeconomics. In Biosocial Surveys, ed. Maxine Weinstein. Washington, D.C: National Academy of Sciences.

Beshears, John, James J. Choi, David Laibson, and Brigitte C. Madrian. 2007. How Are Preferences Revealed? Mimeo, Harvard University.

Camerer, Colin, Jonathan Cohen, Ernst Fehr, Paul Glimcher, David Laibson, George Loewenstein, and Read Montague. 2007. Neuroeconomics. In *The Handbook of Experimental Economics*, ed. John Kagel and Alvin Roth. Oxford: Oxford University Press.

Ding, Weili, Steven Lehrer, J. Niels Rosenquist, and Janet Audrain-McGovern. 2006. The Impact of Poor Health on Education: New Evidence Using Genetic Markers. NBER *Working Paper* 12304. Cambridge, MA: National Bureau of Economic Research.

Friedman, M. 1953. *Essays in Positive Economics*. Chicago: University of Chicago Press.

Jasso, Guillermina. 2004. The Tripartite Structure of Social Science Analysis. *Sociological Theory* 22(3): 401–431.

Kuhn, Thomas S. 1962. *The Structure of Scientific Revolutions*. Chicago: University of Chicago Press.

Luce, R. Duncan. 1959. *Individual Choice Behavior*. New York: Wiley.

Merton, Robert K. 1973. *The Sociology of Science*. Chicago: University of Chicago Press.

Popper, Karl R. 1934. *The Logic of Scientific Discovery*. English translation. New York: Basic Books, 1959.

———. 1963. *Conjectures and Refutations: The Growth of Scientific Knowledge*. New York: Basic Books.

Stigler, George J. 1965. *Essays in the History of Economics*. Chicago: University of Chicago Press.

CHAPTER 13

RESEARCHER INCENTIVES AND EMPIRICAL METHODS

EDWARD L. GLAESER

A central theme of economics is respect for the power of incentives. Economists explain behavior by pointing toward the financial gains that follow from that behavior, and we predict that a behavior will increase when the returns to that behavior rise. Our discipline has long emphasized the remarkable things—from great inventions to petty crimes—that human beings can do when they face the right incentives.

But while economists assiduously apply incentive theory to the outside world, we use research methods that rely on the assumption that social scientists are saintly automatons. No economist would ever write down a model using the assumptions about individual selflessness that lie behind our statistical methods. A small but strong literature that dates back to Sterling [1959] and Tullock [1959], and that is most strongly associated with Edward Leamer, counters this tendency and examines the impact of researcher initiative on statistical results. But while many of the key points of this literature (especially those associated with data mining and specification searches, as in Leamer [1974] and Lovell [1983]) are both understood and accepted, the only obvious impact of this literature is a healthy skepticism about marginally significant results. Certainly, there is no sense in which standard techniques have been adjusted to respond to researcher incentives.

Indeed, the modest number of econometric papers in this area is probably best understood as the result of the very modest interest of empirical researchers in using techniques that correct for data mining and other forms of researcher initiative. After all, the impact of such techniques is invariably to reduce the significance levels of results. The same incentives that induce researchers to data mine will induce them to avoid techniques that appropriately correct for that data mining.

The importance of these issues increases during periods of rapid change in empirical techniques. New technologies increase the ability of researchers to produce less than reliable results. Computerization made it possible to run thousands of regressions, which made it much more likely that the results that were being presented represented a tiny, selected sample of the regressions that had been run. An increased attention to instrumental variables likewise increased the scope for researchers to produce spuriously significant results by creating the possibility of selecting particularly effective instruments. Today, rapid methodological advances in laboratory experiments, brain imaging, genetics, and geographic imaging all offer both the advantages of new information and the danger of new ways for researchers to present selected results.

One traditional approach to data mining has been experience-based rules of thumb. Everyone knows to be skeptical about a new growth regression purporting to present a new variable that predicts growth [see Sala-I-Martin, 1997]. This area is particularly dangerous since the ratio of potential independent variables to observations is quite high. In other contexts, many economists just favor a much higher standard for statistical significance, such as a t-statistic of 3 or 4, rather than a t-statistic of 2. But these experience-based rules are hard to apply to the new methodologies that are coming on line.

I believe that there are three natural approaches to these new research technologies. First, we should always be particularly cynical about the first set of results in these areas. Second, as a profession, we should emphasize the need to make underlying data as accessible as possible. Replication will give us the experience that we need to evaluate the pitfalls of these new techniques. Third, we need to develop a more robust econometric theory that actually respects researcher incentives. Such theory should be able to furnish predictions about which types of methodological advances are most likely to create the biggest problems.

In this chapter, I make 10 points about researcher incentives and statistical work. The first and central point is that we should accept researcher initiative as being the norm and not the exception. It is wildly unrealistic to treat activity such as data mining as being rare malfeasance; it is much more reasonable to assume that researchers will optimize and try to find high correlations. This requires not just a blanket downward adjustment of statistical significance estimates but more targeted statistical techniques that appropriately adjust across data sets and methodologies for the ability of researchers to affect results. Point estimates as well as t-statistics need to be appropriately corrected.

The second point is that the optimal amount of data mining is not zero, and that even if we could produce classical statisticians, we probably would not want to. Just as the incentives facing businessmen produce social value added, the data mining of researchers produces knowledge. The key is to adjust our statistical techniques to realistically react to researcher initiative, not to try and ban this initiative altogether.

The third point is that research occurs in a market where competition and replication matter greatly. Replication has the ability to significantly reduce some of the more extreme forms of researcher initiative (e.g., misrepresenting coefficients in tables), but much less ability to adjust for other activity, such as data mining. Moreover, the ability to have competition and replication correct for researcher initiative differs from setting to setting. For example, data mining on a particular micro data set will be checked by researchers reproducing regressions on independent micro data sets. There is much less ability for replication to correct data mining in macro data sets, especially those that include from the start all of the available data points.

Fourth, changes in technology generally decrease the costs of running tests and increase the availability of potential explanatory variables. As a result, the ability of researchers to influence results must be increasing over time, and economists should respond for regular increases in skepticism. At the same time, however, improvements in technology also reduce the cost of competitors checking findings, so the impact of technology on overall bias is unclear.

Fifth, increasing methodological complexity will generally give the researcher more degrees of freedom and therefore increase the scope for researcher activity. Methodological complexity also increases the costs to competitors who would like to reproduce results. This suggests that the skepticism that is often applied to new, more complex technologies may be appropriate.

My sixth point is the data collection and cleaning offer particularly easy opportunities for improving statistical significance. One approach to this problem is to separate the tasks of data collection and analysis more completely. However, this has the detrimental effect of reducing the incentives for data collection that may outweigh the benefits of specialization. At the least, we should be more skeptical of results produced by analysts who have created and cleaned their own data.

A seventh point is that experimental methods both restrict and enlarge the opportunities for researcher action and consequent researcher initiative bias. Experiments have the great virtue of forcing experimenters to specify hypotheses before running tests. However, they also give researchers tremendous influence over experimental design, and this influence increases the ability of researchers to affect results.

An eighth point is that the recent emphasis on causal inferences seems to have led to the adoption of instrumental variable estimators that can particularly augment researcher flexibility and increase researcher initiative bias. Since the universe of potential instruments is enormous, the opportunity to select instruments creates great possibilities for data mining. This problem is compounded when there are weak instruments, since the distributions of weak instrument t-statistics can have very fat tails. The ability to influence significance by choosing the estimator with the best fit increases as the weight in the extremes of the distribution of estimators increases.

A ninth point is that researcher initiative complements other statistical errors in creating significance. This means that spurious significance rises spectacularly when there are even modest overestimates in statistical significance that are combined with researcher initiative. This complements and also creates particularly strong incentives to fail to use more stringent statistical techniques.

My tenth and final point is that model-driven empirical work has an ambiguous impact on researcher initiative bias. One of the greatest values of specialization in theory and empirics is that empiricists end up being constrained to test theories proposed by others. This is obviously most valuable when theorists produce sharp predictions about empirical relationships. On the other hand, if empirical researchers become wedded to a particular theory, they will have an incentive to push their results to support that theory.

A SIMPLE FRAMEWORK

Consider a researcher who is trying to produce famous results that appear to change the way that we see the world. The researcher's objective function is $\theta \cdot S(f(E) + R) - E$, where θ is the exogenous importance of the question; $S(\cdot)$ reflects the extent that the public attributes importance to the result; R is the real significance of the research, which is a random variable not known by the public, characterized by distribution $g(R)$; E is the nonnegative effort of the researcher in enhancing its significance; and $f(\cdot)$ is a monotonically increasing function mapping effort into more impressive results.

The function $S(\cdot)$ is meant to reflect Bayesian inference on behalf of the pubic about the real value of R. For example, if $f(E) = 1$, for all E, then $S(f(E)R) = f(E)R = R$, and there would be no incentive to put in any effort. More generally, the researcher's first-order condition is $\theta \cdot S'(f(E) + R))f'(E) = 1$, which determines an optimal choice of effort E^*. This problem is solved if $S(f(E) + R) = f(E) + R - f(E^*)$. In this case, the researcher sets $\theta f'(E^*) = 1$. Here there is no misinformation; the public corrects perfectly for the researcher effort. The social loss is just the wasted researcher effort. This model predicts that there will be more researcher effort on more important problems and that the public will correctly be more skeptical about new results in important areas. I believe that this situation roughly characterizes situations with established researchers and established methodologies.

I now assume instead that the researcher has access to a new research technology, that is less perfectly understood by the public. In this case, $f(E) = \alpha\phi(E)$, where $\phi(E)$ is a known function and α is productivity parameter. If α is known, then in equilibrium $S(\alpha\phi(E) + R)) = \alpha\phi(E) + R - \alpha\phi(E^*)$ and E^* is defined by $\theta\alpha\phi'(E^*) = 1$. Again, there is no misinformation, but the amount of researcher effort and associated cynicism is increasing with the value of α. New research technologies that increase the ability of worker effort to produce significant results will lead to more effort, more results that overrepresent significance, and, in equilibrium, more discounting of worker results.

The more complicated and interesting case occurs when the parameter α is unknown to the general public and known to the researcher. I assume that there is a distribution $h(\alpha)$, that is known. If R is unknown to the researcher when the choice of E is made, then the equilibrium is characterized by the optimal effort equation

$$\theta\alpha\phi'(E^*) \int S'(\alpha\phi(E^*) + R)g(r)d(r) = 1,$$

and the Bayesian inference equation

$$S(x) = \frac{\int (x - \alpha\phi(E^*(\alpha)))g(x - \alpha\phi(E^*(\alpha)))h(\alpha)d(\alpha)}{\int g(x - \alpha\phi(E^*(\alpha)))h(\alpha)d(\alpha)}.$$

In this case, the uncertainty about the new research technology loses information because the public does not know how much the new technology changes the ability of researchers to affect significance.

This small framework has made four points. First, the degree of skepticism about results should be a function of the returns for providing significant results. Second, new technologies that increase the ability of researchers to influence results should increase skepticism. Third, new technologies, until they are fully understood, will lead to confusion because it is hard to figure out whether high levels of significance reflect reality or an increased ability of researcher effort to skew findings. I now move to a series of points about the impact of researcher effort. The first point follows directly from the model.

> *Point 1*: Researchers will always respond to incentives and will be more
> skeptical than standard statistical techniques suggest.

Empirical researchers are not automata. They make decisions about what puzzles to study, what variables to investigate, what specifications to estimate, what data to use, and how to collect that data. Every decision permits flexibility and can potentially increase extent to which results are exciting and seem significant. The decisions that are made greatly affect the way that we should interpret results and create what I will refer to as "researcher initiative bias."

The best-studied example of researcher initiative bias is data mining [Leamer, 1978; Lovell, 1983]. In this case, consider a researcher presenting a univariate regression explaining an outcome, which might be workers' wages or national income growth. That researcher has a data set with k additional variables other than the dependent variable. The researcher is selecting an independent variable to maximize the correlation coefficient (r) or r^2 or the t-statistic of the independent variable (which equals $r/\sqrt{1-r^2}$), all of which are identical objective functions. I will assume that each of these explanatory variables is independently and identically distributed. Finally, I will assume that the researcher is constrained to present a univariate relationship that will then be judged on its ability to explain the data.

If the true correlation between every one of the k independent variables and the dependent variable is zero, and if all of the independent variables are independent, then the probability that the researcher will be able to produce a variable that is significant at the 95% level is $1-95^k$. If the researcher has 10 potential independent variables, then the probability that she can come up with a false positive is 40%. If the researcher has 100 independent variables, then the probability with which he can come up with a false positive is more than 99%. Even 99% confidence levels yields a 64% probability of a false positive if the researcher has 100 variables over which she can search.

Lovell [1983] provides a rule of thumb: "[W]hen a search has been conducted for the best k out of c candidate explanatory variables, a regression coefficient that appears to be significant at the level $\bar{\alpha}$ should be regarded as significant at only the level $\alpha = 1 - (1-\bar{\alpha})^{\frac{c}{k}}$" [3]. This provides us with a convenient way of adjusting significance levels for data mining. Alternatively, the formula can be inverted to determine the appropriate t-statistic needed to guarantee a significance level recognizing that the researcher chooses the best c out of k instruments.

Using this approach, to get a significance level of $\bar{\alpha}$, one needs to insist on a t-statistic that delivers a conventional statistical significance level of $\alpha = 1-(1-\bar{\alpha})^{\frac{c}{k}}$. For example, in the case where the researcher is choosing the best out of 10 candidate explanatory variables, and we want results to be statistically significant at the 95% level, we should save our interest for coefficients that are significant at the 99.5% level, which would require a t-statistic of 2.6. If the researcher had 100 potential explanatory variables to draw from, and we wanted a 95% confidence level, then we would insist on a t-statistic of around 3.3.

This approach assumes no other forms of flexibility and assumes that the independent variables are uncorrelated. High degrees of correlation among the potential explanatory variables will make the bias less severe. Other forms of flexibility, such as the ability to choose functional form or selectively clean data, will increase the bias, and as I discuss further below, often these types of flexibility will be complements in the production of bias. More generally, there will be a great deal of heterogeneity across settings in the ability to engage in both data mining and other forms of researcher initiative—in the language of the framework, the parameters α and θ. Ideally, if these parameters are known, this would lead to a straightforward adjustment of significance levels. The problem is, in fact, far more difficult, since the reader knows quite little about the actual ability of the researcher to influence significance.

Denton [1985] follows Sterling [1959] and makes it clear that exactly the same statistical problems occur with data mining and publication bias. For example, if 10 different statisticians work independently testing only one variable in the classic way, and if the only work that is published is that which is statistically significant at the 95% level, then this is equivalent to having a single researcher choose the best of 10 potential variables. This publication bias is best seen as the result of journal editors using their initiative to obtain their own objectives. Journal editors also face incentives to present exciting significant work, and this causes them to publish only papers that have significant results, which will create exactly the same bias that occurs when the selection occurs at the researcher level.

The fact that both journal editors and authors have an incentive to collaborate in producing exciting results that seem statistically significant may perhaps explain why the econometric field of addressing research initiative bias has grown so slowly. There is no quick fix for this problem, and addressing it requires the vast majority of researchers to admit that they routinely violate the admittedly unrealistic norms suggested by classical statistics. Econometrics, like every other field, responds to demand, and the demand for techniques to correct statistical significance downward has historically been limited.

One example of the relative modesty of this field is that while these papers have convinced at least some readers to hold out for t-statistics greater than 2, there has been little attempt to develop the appropriate ways of correcting point estimates as well as significance levels. Yet the researcher initiative bias compromises both significance tests and point estimates. At the extreme, a regression coefficient should be seen as the biggest coefficient among a distribution of coefficients rather than an average coefficient among that distribution. If the researcher is just trying to produce significant results, this will bias coefficients away from zero. If the researcher has an ideological bias that pushes toward one type of result, this will create bias in a single direction.

For example, assume again that the true relationship between each of k candidate variables and the outcome variable is zero, and that the standard deviation of the coefficient estimates is σ; then, the expected value of the maximum coefficient in this group is approximately $\sigma \left[\sqrt{2 \ln k} - \frac{\ln(\ln(k)) + \ln(4\pi) - 1.544}{2\sqrt{2 \ln k}} \right]$. The term in brackets equals 1.72 when k is equal to 10. As such, the expected value of a best regressor drawn from a sample of 10 uncorrelated regressors is 1.72 standard deviations. If the regressors had an average coefficient of "b," then the expected largest regressor would be 1.72 standard deviations higher than b. This gives us a hint of how one might correct for data mining in our coefficient estimates as well as our significance tests. A more thorough approach would require complete specification of the reader's assumptions about what the researcher can do, and then use Bayesian inference.

This hint is only that, and to address this issue squarely we need to develop better methods for dealing with researcher initiative bias. These methods are needed partially to be realistic: all of the most well-meaning attempts to get empiricists to act exactly like classical statisticians are doomed to failure because of the amount of discretion that is unavoidable. But these methods are also necessary, because as I argue in the next section, it is not obvious that we would want empiricists to follow the classic rules of statistical inference even if we could get them to do so.

Point 2: The optimal amount of data mining is not zero.

Classical statistics suggests that every hypothesis that is ever tested should be written up and published. After all, only in that case will we be sure that we are seeing an unbiased sample of the true set of estimates. However, economic models have an uncountable number of potential parameters, nonlinearities, temporal relationships, and probability distributions. It would be utterly impossible to test everything. Selective testing, and selective presentation of testing, is a natural response to a vast number of possible tests. Moreover, in cases where economic questions have reached iconic status (the impact of education on wages, e.g.), the utopian classical scenario may actually come close to being true. After all, when the question becomes sufficiently important, there is an interest in both positive and negative results. Of course, even in this case, estimates that lack sufficient precision to inform the debate often die without publication, but my suspicion is that most sensible tests of fully established questions are generally published. In these cases, as well, it is presumably true that the real correlation between the variables of interest is not zero, which also acts to reduce the degree of publication bias.

The situation is far different when we are in the more primitive situation of trying to come up with new explanations for an outcome of interest. Consider the problem facing a social planner who has a set of researchers whose activities can be completely controlled. Assume further that the planner's only ambition is to inform the world about the true causes of variation in the outcome. I assume further that there is a single (incredibly large) data set with a fixed number of variables, and we are interested in the ability of these variables to explain a single dependent variable. Would this dictator instruct his researchers to act like classical statisticians, or would he favor an approach that looks like data mining?

To fill in the model, assume that the planner's total allocation of researcher time equals "T" and that it takes "z" units of time for each researcher to run a test and understand its meaning and "q" units of time for the researcher to write up each set of results in a coherent manner and present it to the public. I am essentially assuming that each new test requires its own paper. I abstract from the costs of editor and referee time and the hard costs of publication. If the planner instructs the researcher to act like a classical statistician, she will write $T/(q + z)$ papers informing the public of $T/(q + z)$ correlations.

If each independent variable has an expected r-squared of ρ^2, and if all of the x variables are completely independent, then the expected amount of total explanatory power created by the $T/(q + z)$ variables introduced to the public is $T\rho^2/(q + z)$. I am assuming that the number of tests involved is sufficiently small that this number is comfortably greater than one. In this case, the amount of knowledge that the public thinks that it has is the same as the amount of knowledge that it actually does have because the reported r^2 are unbiased estimates of the true r^2.

Consider, alternatively, the situation in which the planner instructs the researcher to run "m" tests and report the "n" most significant of those tests where $mq + nz$ equals T. I assume that the decision about how many tests to run is determined before learning the results of any of these tests, so the value of n is also predetermined and equals $(T - mq)/z$. There will be a cutoff point, denoted $(\bar{\rho})^2$, that is determined by the n most significant variables. The basic intuition behind the social benefit of data mining is that there is very little benefit in reporting a variable that literally has an r^2 of zero to a social planner trying to reveal information about the causes of the outcome. If a regression found that wearing blue shirts had no correlation with cancer, then would it really make sense to publish that result?

Assume, somewhat implausibly, a binary distribution that each one of the variables either had an r^2 of zero or $\bar{\rho}^2$ each with equal probability, and that a regression also yielded binary results so that variables appeared to have power or not and there was a probability of error in each variable of "e." We can then compare the strategy of reporting all of the variables or reporting only those variables that seem to be significant. If we report all of the results, the expected number of variables that the public will think matter equals $T/2(q + z)$. There will be some confusion over which variables are significant and which ones are not.

Conversely, if the researcher reports only the variables that appear significant, the public will have learned of $T/2(q + z)$ variables that are significant. The public will not have learned about all the negatives, some of which are false. But if there are actions that can be taken in response to observed correlations, then certainly the second strategy is better. In either case, the public must adjust its beliefs about the positive results downward to account for the possibility of a false positive, and in this case, the adjustment factor does not change between the two strategies. It is just that with data mining more information gets to the public.

Obviously, the advantages of data mining in this little example increase with the size of z. When writing up results is costless relative to running the experiments, then there is little advantage to be gained from selectively presenting results. However, when z is larger, then the gains from data mining are higher. This may explain why data mining appears to be more prevalent in economics than in many of the laboratory sciences. Our presentational requirements are much harder, and our experiments—at least those with observational data—are much cheaper. As a result, no social planner would insist that every insignificant result be presented to the public.

Of course, this is just one admittedly extreme example of how data mining can be good. In other cases, it can be an unqualified bad. For example, if the social planner is directing his researchers to all do independent tests on the same variable, then suppressing data is generally socially bad (unless the suppressed data are a random sample of the revealed data). Moreover, if the ability of people to correct the errors in observed estimates declined when data were selectively published, that would also represent a problem. If, for example, individuals did not know the ex ante probability of getting significant or insignificant results, then providing the insignificant results would have social value.

One technique that seems to offer the advantages of data mining with limited costs is the computer science technique of machine learning. This method clearly specifies the form that the data mining takes. If the algorithm is known, statistical significance can be adjusted appropriately.

Point 3: Competition and replication can help, but its impact will differ significantly from setting to setting.

The role that competition among scientists will have on researcher initiative bias was discussed by Tullock [1959], who argued that competition would counteract the version of publication bias that occurs when 20 researchers each use different data sets to run the same experiment but when only the one significant result gets published. Tullock argued that in this case the other 19 researchers would come forward and discuss their insignificant results. The conclusion Tullock drew from this is that publication bias is more likely to occur in a situation where there is a single datum and 20 possible explanatory variables. In that case, there is no obvious refutation that could be published over the false positive. The best that can be done is to publish articles emphasizing the number of potential explanatory variables in the data set [as in Sala-I-Martin, 1997] or the fragility of the results to alternative specifications [as in Levine and Renelt, 1992].

Tullock is surely right that there are cases where competition among peers is likely to either deter researcher initiative bias or at the least limit its impact ex post, and there are other cases where this competition is unlikely to have any impact. The debiasing power of competition lies in the fact that once an article is published showing a fact, then it becomes interesting to publish an article refuting that fact, even in cases where the negative result would not have been interesting on its own. This competition will be stronger in large fields than in small ones, and more effort will be put into debunking famous facts than ones that are less important. This seems at least reasonably efficient.

However, the ability of replication and competition to reduce researcher initiative bias will differ greatly across the types of initiative and across the nature of the data. For example, the cheapest form of researcher initiative bias is just faking the numbers in a regression table. This method provides an easy way of achieving any statistical significance that the researcher might want to achieve. However, as long as the data are public, there is little chance that an important paper written with completely faked tables will survive any scrutiny. I believe that there is almost no wholesale fabrication of results for this reason.

A second way of producing misleadingly significant results is to choose an extreme specification that yields significant yet highly fragile coefficients. This method of misleading is considerably safer than wholesale fabrication because if caught, the researcher is not actually guilty of lying. Moreover, in the subsequent debate that will surely surround claims and counterclaims, it will be difficult for outsiders to sort out who is right. Even a knife-edge specification can usually be given some sort of coherent defense.

Classic data mining is even harder to refute. After all, the correlation is actually there in the data. As the Denton-Lovell dialogue makes clear, a misleadingly significant result can come from one data mining econometrician or 20 classical statisticians, so there is certainly no reasonable public censure that accompanies claims of such behavior (although one could imagine such censure if norms about specifying hypotheses shifted enough). If the first data set is the only one that exists, the only response is to mention that there were many variables and this is the one that was most significant, and to hope that readers downgrade their assessments of the research accordingly.

Competition can check data mining primarily when new and independent data sets exist. For example, once a fact is established on U.S. wages, then a test of that fact using British wages serves as an unbiased test of the first hypothesis, and once the first fact is established as interesting, the second fact will generally be considered interesting enough to be published. The existence of multiple sets therefore helps us to counter publication bias, and this suggests one reason why micro results that can be reproduced in other data sets seem more reliable than macro data sets. The evolution, for example, of industrial organization from broad cross-industry regressions to within-industry studies surely increases the possibility that replication across industries can serve as a check on researcher initiative bias. Of course, the new data set must be both independent and similar enough to the existing data set for results to be seen as relevant tests of the first finding.

This reasoning also helps us to consider what sort of macroeconomic facts are more or less likely to have researcher initiative bias corrected by replication. For example, cross-country income regressions are particularly prone to this bias because there is little change in this distribution year to year and no chance of duplicating these regressions with some other sample. Cross-country growth regressions are somewhat less vulnerable because new data come out at regular intervals.

A fact established on income growth between 1960 and 1990 can then be tested using income growth between 1990 and 2000. The new growth rates are not truly independent of early growth, but they are more likely to be independent than income levels, which are spectacularly correlated across decades. Within-country time series is deeply problematic, as well, because of the high levels of year-to-year correlation of many variables. Replication has some ability to correct researcher initiative bias if time series from other countries can be used or if the variable changes at high enough frequencies so that new information is produced rapidly over time.

In general, there can be little doubt that competition among researchers can act as a check on researcher initiative bias, and steps taken to ease replication are surely beneficial. For example, making data widely available seems like a particularly useful step in promoting replication. As I discuss further below, keeping replication costs low is also a case for simple methodologies.

As beneficial as competition among researchers generally may be, it should be emphasized that the competing researchers are also maximizing their own objectives, which may or may not be the perfect presentation of truth. Once a famous result has been established, there are strong incentives for debunking that result, and researchers will respond to those incentives and take their own initiative. As a result, it surely makes sense to have some skepticism toward the skeptics.

Two obvious examples of how refutation can be biased are again data mining and specification search. One technique of refuting a statistically significant finding is to search and find the right combination of variables that make the variable of interest appear statistically insignificant. These regressions will be informative, but since the researcher specifically sought to find the variables that would drive the result, standard significance does not apply. The new variables will generally appear to be more significant than they actually are, and the original variable may, as a result, appear less significant than it is in reality.

Specification changes also offer a large number of degrees of freedom to potential debunkers and, as such, should also be treated skeptically. It is particularly hard for an outsider to infer the meaning of a result that appears significant in some specifications and insignificant in others. Again, there is need for both more econometric research in this area and more use of the econometric techniques that are available.

Point 4: Improvements in technology will increase both researcher initiative bias and the ability of competition to check that bias.

Lovell's [1983] original work was motivated by the observation that improvements in computing technology and expanded data sets make data mining far easier. He is surely correct. In the framework, those changes can be understood as reflecting an increase in the parameter. Technological change has reduced the costs of searching across different potential explanatory variables and specifications. Since the time of that article, the costs of computing have only continued to fall, and the ability to search across a wide range of specifications and variables has increased. One reasonable response to this is to be increasingly skeptical of results produced over time. According to this view, empirical results of the 1950s are more likely to reflect classical conditions than are results produced over the last five years.

A countervailing force is that the ease of running regressions has also reduced the costs of competition, replication, and sensitivity analysis. In the 1950s, it would have been prohibitively costly to have students reproduce famous empirical results. Today, such student replication is routine and seems like an ideal way to check for certain types of researcher initiative. The rise of empirics outside the United States also offers greater possibility for replicating facts using independent non-U.S. data sets.

> Point 5: Increasing methodological complexity will generally increase researcher initiative bias.

While technological progress will have mixed effects on the amount of researcher initiative bias, methodological progress—unless it is aimed directly at the problem of researcher initiative bias—is likely to just increase the potential for researcher initiative. There are two effects that come from new and improved methodologies. First, they clearly increase the degrees of freedom available to the researcher. Unless the methodology has truly become de rigeur, the researcher now has the freedom to use either the old or the new techniques. If the researcher can choose to present only one of these types of results, then the researcher's action space has increased and so has the expected amount of researcher initiative bias.

A second reason for increased bias is introduced by the existence of particularly complex empirical methodologies. Methodological complexity increases the costs of competitors refuting or confirming results. The simpler the technique, the cheaper it will be for someone to try to duplicate the results either with the same or with some other data set. At the extreme, an unvarnished figure allows the reader to reproduce an ocular data test in real time. However, as methods become more complex, it becomes harder to reproduce results or even figure out the amount of discretion available to the researcher.

The appropriate response to the freedom and replication costs created by new methods is far from trivial. In some cases, insisting the older, simpler techniques be used as well can help, but the partisans of newer methods can sometimes justly claim that when new methods produce different results, this represents progress. The real solution must lie in the econometrics profession taking researcher initiative seriously and designing corrections that are based on the degrees of freedom enjoyed by an enterprising researcher.

> Point 6: The creating and cleaning of data increase the expected amount of researcher initiative bias.

A particularly potent opportunity for researcher initiative lies in the collection and cleaning of data. Leamer's [1983] essay on taking the "con out of econometrics" particularly dwells on the dangers of producing data. Any time the researcher is closely involved in the design of the data gathering process or, even worse, its implementation, there is abundant scope for taking actions to increase expected r^2 and thereby bias results. A researcher gathering cross-national data on a subset of countries could easily decide to avoid certain countries that are unlikely to vindicate her ideas on cost-related grounds. This biasing activity can even be subconscious, so a clear conscience is not even enough to ensure that some biasing did not take place.

Introducing bias through the selective cleaning of data may be even easier. In many cases, there are abundant excuses to eliminate or alter particular data points on seemingly legitimate grounds.[1] After all, most data are flawed one way or another. Selectively cleaning data points, even when truth is replacing falsehood, introduces clear biases into estimated results. Even choosing to clean all of the data points, if this decision is made after results are observed, introduces a bias since presumably the decision to clean is more likely when the results do not match the researcher's objectives.

The one reason why skewed data cleaning may end up being less problematic than skewed data production is greater ease of replication. Since the cost of data cleaning is so much lower, once the basic data set is available, it becomes easier for researchers to apply their own cleaning mechanism or use the raw data. Indeed, there are many instances of debates about selective cleaning of data and far fewer debates about selective production of data.

Specialization offers one fix for the skewed data production problem. When data analysis is separated from data production, researchers lose the ability to manipulate. There is still a legitimate fear that data producers will skew results so that data will be more exciting to future researchers, but this seems somewhat less likely. However, enhancing the division of labor also substantially reduces the incentives for data creation. After all, the reason that so many researchers put in time and energy to produce data is in the hope that it will create new information. Certainly, if we are faced with the choice between no information and biased information, the latter option is preferred.

Point 7: Experimental methods restrict hypothesis shopping but increase researcher discretion in experimental design and data collection.

One of the most exciting trends in empirical methods over the last 40 years has been the introduction of true experiments into economics. Many of the first economic experiments were like psychological experiments conduced in the "lab" using students as subjects. More modern experiments take place in the field; sometimes these experiments are small in scale (sending out randomized vitas to potential employers), and sometimes they are extremely large (giving out housing vouchers to a random sample of the population as in the Moving to Opportunity program). The introduction of experimental methods both reduces and increases the scope for researcher initiative bias.

The positive impact of experimental methods on researcher initiative bias comes through limiting the scope for data mining. Experiments are always designed with a clear hypothesis, which is then embedded in the experimental manipulation. The clear statement of a hypothesis before any data gathering occurs makes data mining much more difficult. When experiments are sufficiently expensive that each experiment is written up, then data mining essentially disappears. The primary source of selection bias will then occur at the journal stage, when insignificant results may have difficulty finding a home in print.

The reverse side of experimental economics is that experimenters have enormous degrees of freedom in experimental design. A whole host of experiments have shown how easy it is to manipulate student behavior in a lab setting. Field experiments also give great scope for experimenter initiative. Moreover, once the data are collected, the experimenter can readily clean the data with a variety of irrefutable justifications. This discretion is also present in field experiments, although the large number of people involved in some of them means that the ability of any one researcher to skew results may be limited.

As such, the basic trade-off with experimental methods is that greater discretion in data gathering in experimental design and data collection is traded off against reduced discretion in shopping hypotheses. There are a number of nuances to this basic view. First, after testing the basic hypothesis, many researchers launch into a search for interactions. Since there may be a large number of variables that can potentially interact with the experimental treatment, estimates of interaction effects are much more likely to suffer from research initiative bias.[2] This is a clear area where better econometric methods are needed for appraising the statistical significance of estimated interactions.

A second nuance is the impact of experimental cost on researcher initiative bias. Lower costs mean that it becomes easier for the experimenter to run several experiments and report only one. Lower costs also make it easier for other experimenters to reproduce important results in their own lab. My guess is that the positive effect of reduced costs that works through replication is more important than the negative effect that comes from greater experimenter discretion.

Point 8: The search for causal inference may have increased the scope for researcher initiative bias.

Perhaps the greatest change in empirical methods over the past 20 years has been the increased emphasis on causal inference. While researchers in the 1970s and 1980s were often comfortable documenting correlations among clearly endogenous variables, today such work is much rarer and often confined to less prestigious research outlets. There is no question that increased attention to causal inference represents progress, but in many cases, the empirical approach to endogeneity has greatly expanded the degrees of freedom available to the researcher and consequently the scope for researcher initiative bias, especially in the use of instruments, and especially in those collected and cleaned by analysts themselves.

One impact of the rise of causal inference has been a renewed focus on older hypotheses, such as the connection between schooling and education. The tendency to address established questions limits hypothesis shopping. A second impact has been the rise of true experiments, such as Moving to Opportunity. Although there are worries about the freedom allowed in experimental design, as I discussed above, this trend also forces researchers to specify hypotheses ex ante.

The most worrisome aspect of causal inference is the prevalence of instrumental variables drawn from observational data selected, or even collected by the researcher. In that case, the scope for researcher effort is quite large, although some of this freedom is restricted when the researcher focuses on a clean public policy change that is directly targeted at a particular outcome. The problem will be most severe when the variables are general characteristics that may have only a weak correlation with the endogenous regressor.

At the very least, the choice of instruments creates the standard problem of the ability to find the instrument (or set of instruments) that produces results. In this case, instrumental variables have essentially reintroduced the data mining problem into the debate on an established hypothesis where freedom of choice in dependent and independent variables had been purged from research. By allowing the researcher to choose any number out of a wide range of possible instruments, instrumental variables estimation creates great scope for selecting a set of instruments that produce the desired results. It would be shocking (to economists, at least) if that freedom does not occasionally produce striking results.

This basic problem with instrumental variables is compounded by other statistical problems, especially the weak instruments problem [Staiger and Stock, 1997]. One of the consequences of weak instruments is that the distribution of t-statistics becomes nonnormal and, in some cases, develops especially fat tails. The problem of researcher initiative bias concerns selecting those coefficients at the upper end of a distribution. Extra weight in the right-hand side of a distribution makes it much easier to select a particularly large value. As a result, the problem of weak instrument bias, makes it particularly easy for researchers to find estimators that have particularly large t-statistics, which further biases results.

Another way of thinking about this problem is that the impact of instrument bias is increased by covariance between the instrument and the independent variable, divided by covariance between instrument and the dependent variable. The univariate instrumental variable estimator is $\text{Cov}(Y, Z)/\text{Cov}(X, Z)$, where Y is the dependent variable, X is the endogenous regressor, and Z is the instrument. If there is some reason for spurious correlation between Z and Y, this will be divided by the covariance between X and Z. Another way of writing this formula is $\frac{\text{Cov}(y,z)}{\text{Var}(z)} / \frac{\text{Cov}(x,z)}{\text{Var}(z)}$, which means that the regression coefficient when Y is regressed on Z is divided by the regression coefficient when X is regressed on Z. When the denominator is small, any biases in the numerator get blown up. As such, either selection of the instrument Z to have a high correlation with Y, or selective cleaning of that instrument can have a much larger impact when the correlation between Z and X is modest, even if the instruments pass conventional weak instrument tests.

How should researchers adjust to the presence of researcher initiative bias in instrumental variables? On one level, the existence of researcher initiative just presents a caution against this technique, especially when the instruments are not clearly experimental treatments. Certainly, it is especially worrisome when instrumental variable estimators diverge substantially from ordinary least squares estimators, but it is in those cases that we find instrumental variable estimates most interesting. Again, we need new statistical tools, especially those that combine the robust literature on weak instruments with more realistic assumptions about researcher behavior. A more complete Bayesian approach that recognizes researcher initiative may offer some hope.

Point 9: Researcher initiative bias is compounded in the presence of other statistical errors.

The complementarity between researcher initiative bias and weak instruments highlights a more general issue: in many cases, there is a complementarity between researcher initiative and other statistical errors in producing falsely significant results. Let us return to Lovell's basic data mining example and assume now that the researcher is erroneously underestimating standard errors (e.g., by failing to cluster for correlation at the local level). In the absence of researcher initiative, this failure to correct standard errors makes it x percent more likely that a variable will be statistically significant at the 95% level. The probability of a false positive is therefore $.05 + x$.

If the researcher has access to k independent variables, the probability that a false positive will be found on at least one of them is then $1 - (.95 - x)^k$. If $x = .01$ and $k = 10$, then the probability of a false positive increases with this 1% error from .4 to .46. The 1% increase in false positives is magnified six times through data mining. As long as the error occurs in each of variables tested or each of the specifications tried, then the ability to try many variables or many specifications will compound the impact of the bias.

There are two obvious consequences of this complementarity. First, this complementarity makes it all the more important to eliminate other sources of false statistical significance. Second, the existence of researcher initiative may make researchers less willing to take steps that would tighten up their standard errors and make significance less likely. Since these errors can have a really spectacular impact on the ability to generate positive results, they will continue to be attractive.

Moreover, we should expect the perpetuation of such errors, particularly in settings where data mining is easy and replication difficult.

> *Point* 10: The impact on researcher initiative bias of increasing the connection between theory and empirics is ambiguous.

One of the central divides in modern empirical work is the appropriate degree of connection between economic theory and empirical work. A closer connection between theory and empirics can have both positive and negative effects on the amount of researcher initiative bias. On the negative side, theoretically motivated researchers may be more committed to finding a particular type of result. Atheoretical, empirical researchers presumably care less about the sign of their effects, and this may decrease the incentives for researcher initiative. This effect suggests an increased connection between theory on bias.

On the other hand, models, especially when they are written by researchers other than the empiricists themselves, specify particular hypotheses and even particular functional forms. This leads to a reduction in researcher discretion and a consequent reduction in researcher initiative bias. The division of labor is also important, because models produced after results are generated offer no such hope for reducing bias.

Together, these two points suggest that theory-driven researchers are pushed toward finding a particular result in line with the theory, and that empiricists without theory are prone to running too many specifications. Both forms of researcher initiative need to be considered, and there certainly is no clear implication that we need either more or less theory in empirics.

CONCLUSION

The tradition in statistical work of assuming that researchers all follow the rules of classical statistics is at odds with usual assumptions about individual maximization and reality. Researchers choose variables and methods to maximize significance, and it is foolish either to act as if this is a great sin or to hope that this will somewhat magically disappear. It would be far more sensible to design our empirical methods the way that we design our models: embracing human initiative in response to incentives. In most cases, this initiative is good for research, and even such things as data mining have substantial upsides. After all, none of us would like to read through paper after paper of insignificant results.

However, the problems that come from researcher initiative are also quite significant and grow more so during periods of rapid technological change, such as today. The first response to this problem is just skepticism. We should recognize that many early results using a new technique may not stand up well. The second response is to particularly subsidize data creation and transmission. Replication offers the best route toward experience in these new techniques, and this experience will help us understand how to correct for a biased presentation of results.

The third approach is to develop a body of econometric techniques that enables us to adjust for the researcher incentives. There is the beginning of an empirical approach along these lines in the work of Edward Leamer, who is clearly the pioneer in this field. We need a series of both tests and techniques that respond to researcher initiative bias. Only in that way will the many benefits of researcher creativity be tied to less biased estimation.

NOTES

This chapter was written for the NYU Conference on Economic Methods. I am grateful to the Taubman Center for State and Local Government for financial support. My thoughts on this topic are the result of conversations over years with many people, but I am particularly indebted to Robert Barro and Lawrence Katz. Andrew Caplin, Guido Imbens, Lawrence Katz, and especially Edward Leamer provided helpful advice.

1. Robert Barro has been a particularly forceful advocate of restricting researcher discretion in data cleaning.
2. Many researchers are very well aware of this issue, but my own thinking on it has been particularly shaped by Lawrence Katz.

REFERENCES

Denton, F. T. 1985. Data Mining as an Industry. *Review of Economics and Statistics* 67(1): 124–127.

Leamer, E. 1974. False Models and Post-data Model Construction. *Journal of the American Statistical Association* 69(345): 122–131.

———.1978. Speacification scarones: Ad Hoc Interference is Nonexperimental data, John Wiley and Sons. Inc.

———.1983. Let's Take the Con Out of Econometrics. *American Economic Review* 73(1): 31–43.

Levine, R., and D. Renelt 1992. A Sensitivity Analysis of Cross-Country Growth Regressions. *American Economic Review* 82(4): 942–963.

Lovell, M. 1983. Data Mining. *Review of Economics and Statistics* 65(1): 1–12.

Sala-I-Martin, X. 1997. I Just Ran Two Million Regressions. *American Economic Review* 87(2): 178–183.

Staiger, D., and J. Stock. 1997. Instrumental Variables with Weak Instruments. *Econometrica* 65(3): 557–586.

Sterling, T. 1959. Publication Decisions and Their Possible Effects on Inference Drawn from Tests of Significance—Or Vice Versa. *Journal of the American Statistical Association* 54(285): 30–34.

Tullock, G. 1959. Publication Decisions and Tests of Significance—a Comment. *Journal of the American Statistical Association* 54(287): 593.

CHAPTER 14

CHOICE AND PROCESS: THEORY AHEAD OF MEASUREMENT

JESS BENHABIB

AND

ALBERTO BISIN

A New Method

THE traditional method of decision theory, founded on revealed preferences, restricts its focus to predicting and explaining *choice* and is agnostic about the *process* underlying choice itself. Recent research in economics (typically under the heading of "neuroeconomics" or of "behavioral economics") aims instead at developing joint implications on choice as well as on processes.

In this chapter, we argue that models of decisions designed to produce joint implications for both choice and process constitute a new and exciting area of research for decision theory.

We also argue, however, that the literature would gain from the adoption of structural empirical methods to guide the analysis and test the models. The conceptual hiatus between axiomatic decision theory in economics and models of decision processes in neuroscience in fact suggests the necessity of a structural approach to better lay out and clarify the often implicit identifying assumptions adopted in either discipline.

We finally attempt to illustrate, by means of examples in the context of intertemporal decision theory, how a structural analysis of choice and process can add explanatory and predictive power to decision theory.

Why a New Method?

The traditional method adopted in economics has its foundations in *revealed preferences*. It is the product of the ordinal revolution in I. Fisher [1892] and V. Pareto [1906].[1] This method has been most recently discussed by Gul and Pesendorfer (chapter 1) in a lucid and provocative manner as an alternative to behavioral economics and neuroeconomics.

In the pure example of this method, a decision maker is presented with choices among acts. An act describes the consequence that the decision maker will obtain for every realization of a state of nature. A theory of choice is a complete list of what the decision maker will choose for any possible option that she is facing. Since listing the choices obscures their systematic nature, the list is summarized in a set of axioms. The typical decision theory is then a representation theorem, that is, the statement that the decision maker chooses according to the axioms if and only if she chooses *as if* she were maximizing a certain value function.

In this view, the representation of the preferences has purely the nature of a conceptual construct and has no independent informational value in addition to what is already contained in the axioms. For the method of revealed preferences, the only admissible evidence to test a decision theory over a set of options is the agent's real choice from subsets of that set.

It is certainly good methodological practice not to test a theory based on data the theory itself was not designed to fit. As we do not reject representative agent macroeconomic models based on the observation of agents' heterogeneity, we should not reject the standard axiomatic decision theory if we fail to identify a max U process in the brain.

Nonetheless, we argue here that a clear-cut methodology making use of explicit models of process as well as psychological or neurophysiological data can provide the decision theorist with useful tools to explain choice. More specifically, we claim that, even if we agree that our objective as economists is to explain choice per se, not process, nonetheless the study of choice processes has in principle additional explanatory power for decision theory.

If, however, we find ourselves to date hard pressed to name existing models and data on decision processes that have fundamentally contributed to our understanding of choice, this is, in our opinion, because most empirical work in neuroeconomics is not tightly guided by models making joint predictions on choice and process. We therefore observe that, in practice, progress in producing explanatory power to understand choice is likely to require *structural analysis*, more theory ahead of measurement.[2]

Before proceeding with the arguments, we wish to clarify two terms we repeatedly use in this chapter, "*explain*" and "*structural analysis.*" By "*explain*" we mean, with Gul and Pesendorfer (chapter 1), "identify choice parameters [...] and relate these parameters to future behavior and equilibrium variables." In other words, an explanation is such when it has predictive power, outside of sample. By "structural analysis," we mean the specification of a formal model that maps a set of parameters, assumed stable, to a set of observable (measurable) variables, and the estimation of the parameters by statistical inference methods. The structure of the model explicitly represents the a priori assumptions underlying the analysis. In the context of the study of choice and process, a structural model has implications for both choice and process variables.

When Is Theory and Measurement of Process Useful?

The aim of this section is to examine the conditions under which economic analysis may be improved by theorizing about and observing psychological states and decision processes.

To set a frame of reference for the ensuing arguments, consider the typical decision problem in the spirit of revealed preference. A decision maker chooses from subsets A_1, A_2 of an abstract choice set **A**. His behavior is formally represented by a choice function $C(\cdot)$ whose domain is the set of subsets of **A** and whose range is **A**. Standard decision theory would study the implications, in terms of choice, of a series of axioms on choice itself taken to define rationality. The fundamental axiom of rational choice is *consistency* (a.k.a. independence of irrelevant alternatives):

if $A_1 \subseteq A_2 \subseteq$ **A** and $C(A_2) \in A_1$, then $C(A_1) = C(A_2)$

The choice function $C(\cdot)$ satisfies consistency if and only if it can be represented by a preference ordering $\geq$ such that $C(A)$ contains the maximal element of $\geq$ in A.

Notice that the explanatory power of standard decision theory results from an axiom such as "consistency" underlying (having predictive power regarding) choice in many different environments, for example, from intertemporal choice to choice under uncertainty.

Psychological States and Preferences

Let S denote a set of *psychological states,* a list of emotions, for instance.[3] Suppose that in fact the decision maker's choices are affected by emotions, and her behavior consists in fact of a list of choice functions $C_s(\cdot)$, for any state s in S. Then a decision theorist, observing choices while varying $A \in$ **A** but oblivious of the fact that states are also varying, might conclude that the observed choice function does not satisfy the consistency requirement necessary for representation, even though consistency might instead be satisfied for each $C_s(\cdot)$. In this context, psychological states might count as primitives of the decision problem and observation of the states might represent a necessary constitutive component of a coherent revealed preferences exercise: preferences are *revealed* at the varying of the choice set A (typically through variations in prices and income) as well as at the varying of the psychological state s.

But suppose instead that, even though the decision maker's choice depends on psychological states s that are not observed in the revealed preference exercise, a representation of $C(\cdot)$ is obtained. In a certain sense, this is the showcase of the "as if" argument: no matter that choice might be related to the decision maker's psychological states, she chooses as if she were maximizing a well-defined preference ordering. We claim that even in this case a structural analysis of psychological states states $s \in S$ is useful to improve the explanatory power of decision theory.

To illustrate this argument, it is useful to introduce a simple formal example. Consider the typical decision problem induced by the choice of a consumption allocation $x \in \mathfrak{R}_+^n$ in a budget set $px \leq I$, where $p \in \mathfrak{R}_+^n$ is the price vector and $I \in \mathfrak{R}_+$ is income. The decision theorist observes a sequence of choices associated to different prices p and income I. Assuming linearity (for simplicity; our argument does not depend on this assumption) and allowing for observation errors ϵ, the decision theorist observes

$$x = \beta \begin{bmatrix} p \\ I \end{bmatrix} + \epsilon, \tag{14.1}$$

where β is a vector of unknown parameters and ϵ a random variable. The aim of the decision theorist is to explain choice (for clarity, let us say explain/predict choice), that is, x. This requires a regression analysis to estimate β.

Psychological states are summarized by a variable $s \in S$, which depends on the data of the decision problem, $\begin{bmatrix} p \\ I \end{bmatrix}$. For instance, the consumer can feel excited if his income is large (increases) or if a series of goods are sold at a bargain (a low price). In summary, states satisfy

$$s = \gamma \begin{bmatrix} p \\ I \end{bmatrix} \tag{14.2}$$

(adding noise does not change the argument).

Suppose that the psychoneural process that is summarized by the variable s interacts directly (and interestingly) with choice. Suppose, for instance, that

$$\beta = \alpha s; \text{ that is, } x = \alpha \gamma \begin{bmatrix} p \\ I \end{bmatrix} + \epsilon. \tag{14.3}$$

Notice that in this formulation the decision maker's choice function has a preference representation even if the decision theorist is oblivious to states s. This manifests in the fact that the decision theorist can certainly estimate $\beta = \alpha\gamma$ without independently estimating the specific values of α and γ per se.

But, could the decision theorist improve her explanation/prediction of x by making use of her observation of s? The answer is certainly affirmative, in a statistical sense, since an independent estimate of γ can be, in general, efficiently used to improve the estimate of $\beta = \alpha\gamma$ and therefore to deepen our understanding of the relationship between the determinants of choice, $\begin{bmatrix} p \\ I \end{bmatrix}$, and choice x itself. While measurement of psychological states is not an easy task, proxies such as heart rate and galvanic skin response have been successfully employed in neuroscience (see, e.g., Damasio [1999]).

The metaphor we adopted, decision theory as a regression, is certainly a stretch, but it demonstrates effectively, in our opinion, that data on process are certainly useful as a complement to data on choice as soon as we require decision theory to provide explanation/prediction for behavior out of sample. Outside of the metaphor, structural models of the interaction between choices and psychological states could have, in principle, implications for diverse areas of decision theory, from intertemporal choice to choice under risk and uncertainty, and therefore contribute to a unifying explanation of several experimental puzzles.

The regression metaphor allows us also to stress that it is the structural model of the interaction of choice and process that really potentially adds to our abstract understanding of choice itself. Consider a formulation of the decision problem in which s is a random variable correlated with choice x, that is, with ϵ. Then, observing s would certainly reduce the noise in the prediction of x, like the introduction of any new explanatory variable in a regression will do. But it would not contribute to our analysis of choice more than the observation that "hot weather increases the demand for ice cream." We are not after adding s to as many regressions as possible; rather, we are after the structural explanation of choices. It is structural models of the determination of psychological states and emotions, as well as of their interaction with choice, which can in principle deepen our understanding of choice.

Procedural Rationality

While decision theory stands traditionally on choice axioms, an interesting literature has produced axiomatic analysis of choice processes, inspired by the work of Herbert Simon in the 1950s (collected in Simon [1982]; see Rubinstein [1998] for a fascinating introduction to this literature).

As an illustration (we follow Rubinstein [1998] here), consider again the standard decision problem. Rather than directly postulating properties of choice (through axioms) and then deriving an "as if" representation, a theory of procedural rationality describes a choice process (a *procedure*) and then derives its implied restrictions on choice. A typical procedure is, for example, *satisficing*:

> Let O denote an ordering on $\mathbf{A}$, let T be a subset of $\mathbf{A}$, and let $A \in \mathbf{A}$ denote a choice set; then $C(A)$ contains the first element of A, according to the order O, which belongs to T (and the last element of A if A and T are disjoint).

The primitives of the procedure include T and O. The properties of the choice function $C(\cdot)$ obviously depend on a crucial manner on T and O. For instance, allowing T and O to depend on the choice set A implies that $C(\cdot)$ might not satisfy the *consistency* axiom, and that a standard representation in terms of preference maximization might not exist. The same obtains if T and O depend on psychological states $s \in S$. Behavior such as framing (the dependence of choice in experiments on the way choice problems are posed) might be rationalized by a satisficing procedure, by letting the order O depend on unobservable psychological states induced by the way choice problems are posed.[4]

A decision theory formulated in terms of a procedure such as satisficing has most explanatory power inasmuch as it includes a model of the determination of the set T and of the ordering O, for all $A \subseteq \mathbf{A}$ and psychological states $s \in S$. *Identifying choice parameters* in this context might require, then, data on process, such as those collected through the eye-tracking procedures for saccade tasks commonly adopted in vision and attention studies in neuroscience (see, e.g., Deubel and Schneider [1996]) or the mouse tracking procedure (e.g., Camerer, Johnson, Rymon, and Sen [1993]).

To better illustrate the kind of structural models we claim are useful in this context, consider the following abstract class of procedural environments:

> Let $A \in \mathbf{A}$ denote a choice set; two distinct procedures P_1 and P_2 map A into respective elements of A; a third procedure selects which of P_1 and P_2 controls choice, that is, if $C(A) = P_1(A)$ or $C(A) = P_2(A)$.

A procedure of this sort can abstractly capture a large class of cognitive decision processes that involve competing procedures and a selection mechanism. Often, the competing procedures are modeled to represent the classic automatic-controlled (or visceral-cognitive) dichotomy and the selection mechanism is represented by some form of attention control.

Procedures of this sort could represent well *choice mistakes*, "systematic phenomena which disappear once decision makers learn of their existence" [Rubinstein, 1998: 22]. A typical example is tourists looking left when crossing the street in the United Kingdom, but many other examples flood the experimental psychology literature. *Choice mistakes* provide, in fact, a useful clarifying example of the new method we delineate in this chapter. Gul and Pesendorfer (chapter 1) suggest that, according to the standard method of revealed preferences, mistakes of this sort can be rationalized simply by means of "subjective constraints on [their] feasible strategies." This is because such mistakes would be "relevant only if they could be identified through economic data." We claim instead that a structural model of the choice process leading to such mistakes would constitute a better methodological practice. It would avoid adding an ad hoc "subjective constraint" every time needed, and it could provide explanatory power to understand choice in several different interesting contexts in which attention control might be relevant (see also the discussion in the next section regarding intertemporal choice).

A model of the procedures P_1 and P_2 as well as of the selection mechanism, the primitives of the procedure, is necessary to provide unifying explanations for choice mistakes. But what are the components such a model? What is *automatic*, what is *cognitive*, and what is *attention*?

While we do not know of an axiomatic analysis of this class of procedures, models of this kind of behavior have been developed, and their structural empirical implications have been studied in neuroscience. The *language* of modeling in neuroscience is different than in economics: it involves simulating the dynamic activation properties of a neuronal network rather than deriving the logical implications of axiomatic relations. Nonetheless, these models provide natural constructs for the structural analysis of choices and of choice processes.

As an illustration, consider Cohen, Dunbar, and McClelland's [1990] cognitive control model of automatic and controlled processes in the Stroop task, after the experiments by Stroop in the 1930s.[5] The Stroop task consists in naming the ink color of either a conflicting word or a nonconflicting word (e.g., respectively, saying "red" to the word "green" written in red ink, and saying "red" to the word "red" written in red ink). Cohen et al.'s [1990] model is based on *parallel distributed processing* (PDP).[6] PDP models consist of a collection of different processing units distributed over a network whose architecture represents processing modules and pathways. Each processing unit is characterized by a pattern of activation that dynamically propagates over the network, from the exogenous inputs to the output. For instance, letting the index i run over all the processing units that input into element j, the activation of j at time t, $a_j(t)$, is written as follows:

$$a_j(t) = \tau \sum_i a_i(t)w_{ij} + (1 - \tau) \sum_i a_i(t-1)w_{ij},$$

where w_{ij} represent the weight (or strength) of the connection between unit i and j.

Cohen et al. [1990] model word-reading and color-naming as competitive processing pathways in the network, which are simultaneously activated by the word image. Furthermore, a different pathway is activated by the explicit goal of the cognitive task, say, color-naming, which cognitively controls the output of the task by differentially activating the appropriate processing pathway and inhibiting the other one.

This model is crucially supplemented by a specific learning model that determines endogenously the weights of the connections w_{ij} in the network. An *automatic* pathway is defined as one that has been repeatedly active in the past, so that the learning process has generated high connecting weights, and the output is quickly generated from the input. In Cohen et al. [1990], word-reading, which is a very common task in the subjects' practice outside the lab, is modeled as an automatic process that produces a rapid response. The controlled processing aspect of the task can, however, override the stronger word-reading process by inhibiting the automatic reading association.[7]

The model implies a pattern of reaction times to conflicting and nonconflicting words that is consistent with the pattern observed in experiments with Stroop: (i) reaction times for reading tasks are unaffected by the ink color, (ii) reaction times for conflicting words are longer than for nonconflicting words, and (iii) reaction times are longer, for either conflicting and nonconflicting words, than the reaction times of simple reading tasks.[8]

While these models has been developed to understand behavior in cognitive rather than decision-theoretic tasks, we suggest that this class of models could very usefully be adapted to study choice processes. We believe that formal models of automatic and controlled processes can provide a unifying explanation of choice mistakes as well as of several other puzzling choice phenomena documented in the experimental lab, in several decision-theoretic environments ranging from intertemporal choice (see the following section) to choice under uncertainty [see Loewenstein and O'Donoghue, 2005].

Intertemporal Choice: The Method in Practice

In the preceding section, we argue that models and data on psychological states and choice processes are, in principle, useful to decision theory. In this section, we survey as an illustration the literature concerning intertemporal choice. We identify in the lack of structural analysis a bottleneck of neuroeconomics in this context.

The standard economic approach to the study of intertemporal decisions involves agents maximizing their present *exponentially* discounted utility. Exponential discounting postulates that the present discounted value of a reward u received with a t-period delay is $\delta^t u$ for some $\delta < 1$.[9] Recently, however, behavioral economists have criticized this approach on the basis of a vast amount of behavioral regularities (called "anomalies") documented in experimental psychology that indicate that agents may have a preference for present consumption, a "present bias," that cannot be rationalized with exponential discounting.[10] The most important of such regularities is called "reversal of preferences." It occurs when a subject prefers $x now rather than $x + \Delta$ in a day, but he prefers $x + \Delta$ in a year plus a day rather than $x in a year.

Various alternative decision theories have been developed that rationalize such data, and reversal of preferences in particular. For instance, Laibson [1996] and O'Donoghue and Rabin [1999] favor a quasi-hyperbolic specification of discounting, which posits that the present discounted value of a reward u received with a t-period delay is $\beta \delta^t u$ for some $\beta, \delta < 1$. Others (e.g., Ainsle [1992]) favor a hyperbolic specification, implying a discounted value of the form $(1/1 + \delta t)u$. Finally, Gul and Pesendorfer [2001] develop an axiomatic theory of temptation and self-control that rationalizes present bias by extending the domain of choice to sets of actions.

All these are standard decision-theoretic models in that they induce restrictions/implications only on choice, and not on processes, and they are formulated as a preference representation.[11] They can therefore be tested in the experimental lab with choice data.[12] As we argued in the preceding sections, however, this is not enough to conclude that data on process are not useful: data on process can, in principle, help explain choice. We next survey selectively some attempts at doing just that in practice in the context of intertemporal choice.

For instance, Wilson and Daly [2004] document higher discounting for men after having observed photographs of women that they reported as attractive. This finding can be appealingly interpreted as a manifestation of dependence of discounting on psychological states; the photographs are "inducing a 'mating opportunity,'" in the words of the authors [S177]. No model of such dependence is, however, developed that can be tested with choice or with process data. Consequently, the authors are silent on the possible relationship between psychological states and the discounting anomalies that we seek an explanation for.[13]

Much more important and central to our understanding of the interaction between choice and process are two recent studies at the forefront of neuroeconomics, McClure, Laibson, Loewenstein, and Cohen [2004] and Glimcher, Kable, and Louie [2006].

Both McClure et al. [2004] and Glimcher et al. [2006] produce and study brain imaging data to explicitly distinguish between some of the different preference representations in the context of intertemporal choice tasks. In particular, McClure et al. [2004] claim evidence for the quasi-hyperbolic representation of discounting. They postulate that such representation results from the influence of two distinct neural processes, one that is differentially activated in the presence of immediate rewards, and one that is commonly activated when the decision maker engages in intertemporal choices. They then measure brain activation of several subjects in an intertemporal choice task by functional magnetic imaging (fMRI) techniques and identify econometrically areas of differential activation when the choice task involves an immediate reward. McClure et al. [2004] then categorize such areas of the brain as β-*areas*, interpreting them as representing present bias, and more generally interpret the existence of such areas as evidence in favor of the existence of two neural processes involved in intertemporal choice.

McClure et al. [2004] provide no structural analysis of choice and process underlying the different neural processes. No choice data are reported. No formal model of the neural processes that are postulated to underlie choice is proposed, and hence, no formal implications are derived regarding the pattern of activation of different areas of the brain. Furthermore, no clear a priori theoretical presumption links quasi-hyperbolic discounting with two distinct neural processes.[14] As a consequence, the empirical results of McClure et al. [2004] are prone to different interpretations and can hardly identify the properties of the underlying choice process that they observe in their fMRI study, including the existence of two neural processes involved in intertemporal choice. In this sense, Glimcher et al. [2006] argue that the activation patterns found in McClure et al. [2004] are, in fact, consistent with the hypothesis that brain activation simply correlates with an hyperbolic representation of the decision maker's discounting preferences, the implicit choice process in this case simply being represented by discounted utility maximization (without recourse to two neural processes).

Glimcher et al. [2006] instead estimate discounting preferences with choice data, finding that a hyperbolic representation is not statistically rejected. They then proceed to measure brain activation by fMRI and find a clear correlation pattern of activation measurements, in areas of the brain typically associated with option valuation, with the discounting representation estimated with choice data. This is interpreted as evidence for an explicit preference maximization procedure underlying intertemporal choice. Lacking a structural model of choice and process, however, the data can once again hardly identify the (single or multiple) neural processes involved in intertemporal choice.

In summary, the neuroeconomics literature has made great progress in studying brain imaging data of decision makers engaged in intertemporal choice tasks. Structural models to guide the empirical analysis are still lacking, however, that can provide the decision theorist with the explanatory power to distinguish between different choice representations of discounting and hence, ultimately, to explain intertemporal choice anomalies.

In the quest to explain intertemporal choice anomalies, a few models of choice and process have been developed and studied. Unfortunately, until now these models have been studied empirically only with choice data from the experimental lab and not yet with data on process itself. We illustrate this point by explicitly discussing two such models, Rubinstein [2003] and Benhabib and Bisin [2004].

Rubinstein [2003] considers a simple procedural model of the binary choice over rewards x at different delays t. The procedure studied is a *similarity* procedure:[15] facing the binary choice over (x, t) and (x', t'), the decision maker first looks for dominance, for example, choosing (x, t) if $x \geq x'$ and $t \geq t'$ (with at least one strict inequality—note that the ordering $\geq$ is a preference ordering, not the "greater or equal" ordering); lacking dominance, the decision maker looks for *similarity*, for example, choosing (x, t) if x *is similar to* x' and $t > t'$; if the two previous procedures are inconclusive, choice is made using yet another procedure.

Several choice experiments are designed that can distinguish hyperbolic discounting from the similarity procedure (once complemented with a specific notion of the relation *is similar to*) and choice data are provided that support the similarity procedure.

Note also that, in accordance with the methodological claim we are exposing, that is, that models of process have the potential of providing unifying explanation of various phenomena in experimental choice behavior, a related similarity procedure has been studied by Rubinstein [1998] in the context of choice over risky lotteries. While rich implications of the similarity procedure can certainly be derived on process data (e.g., on reaction times), we know of no research along these lines.[16]

Benhabib and Bisin [2004] provide instead an intertemporal choice model in which choice is the result of the interaction of automatic and controlled processing.[17] When specialized to the binary choice over rewards at different delays, the typical choice experiment that gives rise to the *anomalies* in experiments, Benhabib and Bisin's [2004] model induces a present discounting representation of a reward u at delay t of the form $\delta^t u - b$, where b represents the psychological cost induced by the need to exercise self-control, interpreted as a psychological restraint from the impulse of choosing the immediate reward. The cost of delay b is a fixed cost, that is, is independent both of the size of the reward and of the amount of the delay.[18] Benhabib, Bisin, and Schotter [2005] estimated discount preferences with experimental choice data and found statistical evidence that in fact favors this representation over both quasi-hyperbolic and hyperbolic discounting.

A different test of Benhabib and Bisin's [2004] model can be performed, once again, with experimental choice data, by considering a simple environment in which an agent has to decide how much to consume today out of available income z. When their analysis is specialized to this simple environment, they obtain the following representation:

$$\max \left\{ \max_{x \leq z} u(x) - b, u \left(\arg \max_{x \leq z} v(x) \right) \right\}, \tag{14.4}$$

where $u(x)$ and $v(x)$ are smooth, concave real functions representing, respectively, the cognitive and automatic components of preferences. The cognitive component of preferences controls choice if and only if its valuation minus the self-control cost b

is larger than the automatic valuation $u\left(\arg\max_{x\le z} v(x)\right)$. Under some regularity assumption,[19] this representation has the identifying behavioral implication: the choice $x(z)$ is not increasing in z, but rather has a decreasing jump. The jump represents the behavioral regularity that small temptations are not controlled, while large ones are.

In work in progress, Benhabib, Bisin, and Kariv are exploring this implication in the experimental lab. About a half of the 20 subjects for which data have been collected display the behavior predicted by the model.

While Benhabib and Bisin's [2004] model of intertemporal choice and process has been tested with choice data, as we reported above, the model also has potentially several clear-cut implications about process that can be derived by formulating a parallel distributing processing model along the lines of the Stroop model in Cohen, Dunbar, and McClelland [1990] and that can be tested, for example, by recording reaction times data during an intertemporal choice task. This has not yet been done.

The theory of intertemporal choice is a fascinating laboratory: it has (i) choice *anomalies* to explain; (ii) sophisticated models, from axiomatic to algorithmic, to put to data; and (iii) a wealth of data, from the experimental choice data to brain imaging data, to test its models. All the ingredients for the application of the new method we have discussed are ready to be mixed.

While intertemporal decision theory appears representative of other areas of neuroeconomics in terms of the methods used, structural models of choice and process are being developed at the frontier, for instance, in the study of reward prediction errors in learning [Caplin and Dean, 2007] and in the study of random utility [Maccheroni, Marinacci and Rustichini, 2006].

CONCLUSIONS

In this chapter we have argued that, in our opinion, no logical reasons exist to exclude models and data on choice processes from decision theory. On the contrary, the structural analysis of models and data on process represents, in our opinion, the fascinating frontier of decision theory.

While standard decision theory has been very successful in rationalizing a rich set of behavioral data from lab experiments by a combination of weakening of the axioms and enlarging of the choice set,[20] it seems to us that this success has come at the expense of explanatory power, that is, of a unified theory of decision making. A new method exploiting the study of choice processes as well as choices, in our opinion, contains the promise of unifying the explanations of many behavioral puzzles observed in the experiments.

With respect specifically to the theory of intertemporal choice, we have noted that the structural analysis of choice and process that we claim could advance our understanding of choice seems to be yet missing: the most advanced brain imaging techniques are adopted without the guide of theoretical analysis, resembling what economists call "fishing for factors," while the few models that in fact focus on the interaction of choice and process are tested only with choice data, wasting much of their explanatory/predictive power.

We conclude this chapter by claiming an added rhetorical advantage for a methodology for decision theory that goes beyond "as if" representations by directly formulating models of choice processes that can be tested with data on process. The representation of preferences in the standard theory of revealed preferences is often, by its very nature, an informal description of a process. The elegance of the representation, its accordance with introspective beliefs about the decision processes which *inspire* it[21]—in summary, its *intuitive appeal*—is typically crucial for a decision theory to be accepted. The necessarily informal (but important) role that such concepts as *intuitive appeal* or *inspiration* end up performing in the method of revealed preferences is in our view a substantial limitation of the method itself. Wouldn't it be much better to lay all the cards down for inspection?

NOTES

Many of the ideas exposed in this chapter evolved in the course of discussions with Aldo Rustichini, who appeared as co-author in previous versions of the paper. Thanks to Andrew Caplin, Chris Flinn, Ariel Rubinstein, and Yuval Salant for useful discussions.

1. Intellectual interest in the study of decision processes can, however, be traced to the classic period, from W. S. Jevons's "Brief Account," [1866] or chapters II and III of his *Theory* [1871], to J. Bentham's *Principle's of Morals and Legislation* [1780], or to A. Smith's *Theory of Moral Sentiments* [1759].

2. The classic formulation of the methodology of structural empirical analysis is in Koopmans [1947] and Marschak [1952]. A recent discussion is contained in Keane [2006].

3. See Kahneman and Krueger [2006] for a survey of the theoretical constructs and the measurement issues behind the notion of psychological states.

4. Relatedly, see Rubinstein and Salant [2006] for the axiomatic treatment of choices from lists.

5. The distinction between automatic and controlled processing is common in neuroscience and is articulated, e.g., in Schneider and Shiffrin [1977] and in Norman and Shallice [1980].

6. See Rumelhart and McClelland [1986] for an extensive presentation and discussion of PDP models in neuroscience.

7. See Miller and Cohen [2001] for a general introduction to attention control models and their structural empirical analysis.

8. Furthermore, patients with frontal impairment have difficulties with the Stroop task; see Cohen and Servan-Schreiber [1992] and Vendrell et al. [1995].

9. See Koopmans [1960] and Fishburn and Rubinstein [1982] for the classic axiomatic treatment of intertemporal choice.

10. See, e.g., Ainsle [1992] and Frederick, Loewensteinm, and O'Donoghue [2002] for comprehensive surveys.

11. See Ok and Masatlioglu [2006] for general axiomatic representations of these discounting preferences.

12. This is done, e.g., by Benhabib, Bisin, and Schotter [2005].

13. See Smith and Dickhaut [2004] for empirical evidence on the effect of emotions on bidding in auctions.

14. Intuitively, however, the power of the test relies on their finding that β-*areas* are mostly located in the limbic system, which is an area of the brain typically associated with impulsive choice rather than cognitive processing.

15. See Tversky [1977] for the early introduction of similarity relations in decision making.

16. But see Rubinstein [2007], which relates cognition and reaction times in several strategic environments.

17. While Benhabib and Bisin [2004] model the choice process directly, without providing its axiomatic foundation, see Nehring [2006].

18. Note that the quasi-hyperbolic representation can be written as $\delta^t u - (1 - \beta)\delta^t u$. It therefore implies instead a variable cost associated to nonimmediate rewards, that is, a cost proportional to the value of the reward u.

19. In particular, assuming

$$x^* = \arg\max_{x \leq z} \ u(x) < \arg\max_{x \leq z} \ v(x)$$

allows the interpretation, essentially without loss of generality, of "temptations" as "preferences for a larger x"; so z measures then, parametrically, the "size" of the temptation.

20. Notable examples include Kreps and Porteus [1978] on early resolution of uncertainty, Gilboa and Schmeidler [1989] on uncertainty aversion, Gul and Pesendorfer [2001] on present bias, among many others.

21. In this sense, Gul and Pesendorfer (chapter 1) accept a reference to process in decision theory as *inspiration*.

REFERENCES

Ainsle, G. 1992. *Picoeconomics*. Cambridge: Cambridge University Press.

Benhabib, J., and A. Bisin. 2004. Modelling Internal Commitment Mechanisms and Self-Control: A Neuroeconomics Approach to Consumption-Saving Decision. *Games and Economic Behavior* 52(2): 460–492.

Benhabib, J., A. Bisin, and A. Schotter. 2005. Hyperbolic Discounting: An Experimental Analysis. Mimeo, New York University..

Bentham, J. 1780. *An Introduction to the Principles of Morals and Legislation*. London.

Camerer, C., E. Johnson, T. Rymon, and S. Sen. 1993. Cognition and Framing in Sequential Bargaining for Gain and Losses. In *Frontiers of Game Theory*, ed. K. Binmore, A. Kirman, and P. Tani, 27–48. Boston: MIT Press.

Caplin, A., and M. Dean 2007. Dopamine and Reward Prediction Error: An Axiomatic Approach to Neuroeconomics. *American Economic Review* 97(2): 148–152.

Cohen J. D., and D. Servan-Schreiber. 1992. Context, cortex and dopamine: A connectionist approach to behavior and biology in schizophrenia. Psychological Review 99: 4577.

Cohen, J. D., K. Dunbar, and J. L. McClelland. 1990. On the Control of Automatic Processes: A Parallel Distributed Processing Model of the Stroop Effect. *Philosophical Transactions of the Royal Society (London) B* 351: 1515–1527.

Damasio, A. R. 1999. *The Feeling of What Happens*. Orlando, FL: Harcourt Brace.

Deubel, H., and W. X. Schneider. 1996. Saccade Target Selection and Object Recognition: Evidence for a Common Attentional Mechanism. *Vision Research* 36: 1827–1837.

Fishburn, P., and A. Rubinstein. 1982. Time Preference. *International Economic Review* 23: 677–694.

Fischer, I. 1892. Mathematical Investigations in the Theory of Value and Prices. *Transactions of the Connecticut Academy of Sciences and Arts* 9(1): 1–124.

Frederick, S., G. Loewenstein, and T. O'Donoghue. 2002. Time Discounting and Time Preference: A Critical Review. *Journal of Economic Literature* 40: 351–401.

Gilboa, I., and D. Schmeidler. 1989. Maxmin Expected Utility with a Non-unique Prior. *Journal of Mathematical Economics* 18: 141–153.

Glimcher, P. W., J. Kable, and K. Louie. 2006. Neuroeconomic Studies of Impulsivity: Now or Just as Soon as Possible? Mimeo, New York University.

Gul, F., and W. Pesendorfer. 2001. Temptation and Self-Control. *Econometrica* 69(6): 1403–1436.

Jevons, W. S. 1866. Brief Account of a General Mathematical Theory of Political Economy. *Journal of the Royal Statistical Society* 29: 282–287.

———. 1871. *The Theory of Political Economy*. London: Macmillan.

Kahneman, D., and A. B. Krueger. 2006. Developments in the Measurement of Subjective Well-being. *Journal of Economic Perspectives* 20(1): 3–24.

Keane, M. P. 2006. Structural vs. Atheoretic Approaches to Econometrics. Mimeo, Yale University.

Kreps, D., and E. L. Porteus. 1978. Temporal Resolution of Uncertainty and Dynamic Choice Theory. *Econometrica* 46(1): 185–200.

Koopmans, T. C. 1947. Measurement Without Theory. *Review of Economics and Statistics* 29: 161–172.

———. 1960. Stationary Ordinal Utility and Impatience. *Econometrica* 28: 287–309.

Laibson, D. 1996. Golden Eggs and Hyperbolic Discounting. *Quarterly Journal of Economics* 112: 443–477.

Loewenstein, G., and E. D. O'Donoghue. 2005. Animal Spirits: Affective and Deliberative Processes in Economic Behavior. Mimeo, Cornell University.

Maccheroni, F., M. Marinacci, and A. Rustichini, 2006. Preference-Based Decision Processes Mimeo, University of Minnesota.

Marschak, J. 1952. Economic Measurement for Policy and Predictions. In *Studies in Econometric Methods*, ed. W. C. Hood and T. C. Koopmans, 1–26. New York: Wiley.

McClure, S. M., D. Laibson, G. Loewenstein, and J. D. Cohen. 2004. Separate Neural Systems Value Immediate and Delayed Monetary Rewards. *Science* 306: 503–507.

Miller, E. K., and J. Cohen. 2001. An Integrative Theory of Prefrontal Cortex Function. *Annual Review of Neuroscience* 24: 167–202.

Nehring, K. 2006. Self-Control Through Second Order Preferences. Mimeo, Universty of California Davis.

Norman, D. A., and T. Shallice. 1980. Attention to Action: Willed and Automatic Control of Behaviour. Centre for Human Information Processing Technical Report 99. University of California, San Diego 99.

O'Donoghue, E.D., and M. Rabin. 1999. Doing It Now or Doing It Later. *American Economic Review* 89: 103–124.

Ok, E., and Y. Masatlioglu. 2006. A General Theory of Time Preferences. Mimeo, New York University.

Pareto, V. 1906. *Manuale di Economia Politica, con una Introduzione alla Scienza Sociale.* Milano.

Rubinstein, A. 1998. *Modeling Bounded Rationality.* Cambridge, MA: MIT Press.

———. 2003. "Economics and Psychology"? The Case of Hyperbolic Discounting. *International Economic Review* 44(4): 1207–1216.

———. 2007. Instinctive and Cognitive Reasoning: A Study of Response Times. *Economic Journal* 117: 1243–1259.

Rubinstein, A., and Y. Salant. 2006. A Model of Choice from Lists. *Theoretical Economics* 1(1): 3–17.

Rumelhart, D. E., and J. L. McClelland, eds. 1986. *Parallel Distributed Processing: Exploration in the Microstructure of Cognition.* Cambridge, MA: MIT Press.

Schneider, W., and R. M. Shiffrin. 1977. Controlled and Automatic Human Information Processing: 1. Detection, Search, and Attention. *Psychological Review* 84: 1–66.

Simon, H. 1982. *Models of Bounded Rationality.* Cambridge, MA: MIT Press.

Smith, A. 1759. *The Theory of Moral Sentiments.* Edinburgh: A. Kincaid and J. Bell.

Smith, K., and J. Dickhaut. 2004. Economics and Emotions: Institutions Matter. *Games and Economic Behavior* 52(2): 316–335.

Tversky, A. 1977. Features of Similarity. *Psychological Review* 84: 327-352.

Vendrell P, Carme J, Pujol J, Jurado MA, Molet J, Grafman J (1995) The role of prefrontal regions in the Stroop task. Neuropsychologia33: 41352.

Wilson, M., and M. Daly. 2004. Do Pretty Women Inspire Men to Discount the Future? *Biology Letters (Proc. Roy, Soc. Lond. B)*271: S177–S179.

CHAPTER 15

ECONOMIC THEORY AND PSYCHOLOGICAL DATA: BRIDGING THE DIVIDE

ANDREW CAPLIN

CLASSICAL decision theory is a picture of harmony. Models are designed to predict economically consequential choices, and empirical tests concern their ability to explain these choices. The models themselves are typically solved using optimization techniques with solid axiomatic foundations. These foundations allow for a complete understanding of the qualitative and quantitative relationship of the models to relevant choice data. The consensus within economics concerning this decision-theoretic methodology has had powerful positive externalities, ensuring strong communication across professional subdisciplines. Economics stands out in this respect from other social sciences, in which the approach to model building is more fragmented and in which communication problems are correspondingly more profound.

Despite its harmony, many researchers view classical decision theory as limited in its ability to incorporate psychological factors. As detailed in this chapter, this has led to ever growing interest in nonstandard economic models that sit outside the choice-theoretic tradition. At the same time, diverse new forms of "psychological" data are being developed, concerning features of informational search, eye movements, neurological responses, and answers to novel survey questions. The possibilities for new insights to be gleaned by appropriately combining nonstandard theories with novel psychological data excite many prominent researchers (e.g., Benhabib and Bisin, chapter 14; Camerer, chapter 2; Crawford, chapter 10; Schotter, chapter 3).

While the recent expansion in the scope of economic theory and measurement opens up intriguing new vistas, it also raises profound challenges. In particular, it has disturbed the harmonic situation that previously prevailed. In striking contrast with the classical theory, there are expanding gaps between the new economic models and the psychological data that are used to inspire and to test them. Should these gaps continue to expand, it will pose a significant threat to the hard-won unity of our discipline. The challenge before us concerns how best to open up new avenues of exploration while retaining the essential coherence of economic thought.

In direct response to this challenge, Faruk Gul and Wolgang Pesendorfer (chapter 1; henceforth GP) have proposed a highly disciplined method by which to expand the domain of economics. They propose fixing empirical attention firmly on standard choice data, using choice-theoretic (generally axiomatic) methods to characterize how psychological factors may affect such choices.

While sympathetic to the GP proposal with respect to theoretical methodology, I have an entirely different view concerning the data. Below I explain my belief concerning the great value of incorporating enriched psychological data into economic models. In light of this, I propose an alternative methodology that encourages essentially limitless expansion in the psychological data that economists model, while setting high ideals concerning model-building techniques. The central pillar in the proposed methodology is the use of axiomatic methods along the lines envisaged by Samuelson [1938]. Rather than identifying theories of choice with unobservable "folk" concepts such as utility and its maximization, Samuelson sought axioms by which to characterize the observable implications of these theories. The methodology I propose herein operates in precisely this same manner on far richer data sets. It calls for axiomatic characterizations of potentially intricate psychological data sets, typically including various forms of standard choice data.

The identifying feature of the proposed methodology is that it is "minimalist." As in standard axiomatic choice theory, one characterizes the precise implications of a given theory for a data set of interest and identifies as equivalent all models that produce the same predictions. Such tight characterizations reveal the essential features of the underlying model. Psychological and neurological constructs modeled in this manner will end up being characterized precisely in terms of observable counterparts, as has been the case for utility and choice. In this sense, minimalism represents no more than a broadening of Samuelson's original proposal to richer settings. It places the axiomatic method at the center of theoretical enquiry and imposes no restriction on the formal content of theories.

My deepest hope is that the minimalist methodology will prove of value in interdisciplinary research, which is of rapidly growing importance. Typically, folk concepts are imbued with meaning through repeated use within disciplinary confines. As GP make crystal clear in their discussion of "risk aversion," interdisciplinary differences of interpretation cause communication problems that may be impossible to understand, let alone to overcome. The defining virtue of the minimalist methodology in this regard is that it removes the ambiguities associated with such folk definitions. Any intuitive constructs that minimalist theories introduce must be characterized directly in terms of observables. In this respect, the current proposal is designed not only to retain the unity of economics, but also to permit conceptual unification across current disciplinary boundaries, including the new neuroscientific boundaries between social and natural science.

The importance that I attach to a methodology that allows for social scientific unification may be best understood using language borrowed from the theory of random graphs. Individual pieces of research can be conceptualized as nodes in an evolving social scientific "research graph." The stronger are the links between the nodes in this graph, the longer are the research paths over which each individual researcher can traverse. If social scientists can adopt common linguistic conventions, the end result will be a great strengthening of the connections between the various disparate nodes in this graph. With agreement around a connective methodology such as minimalism, future social scientists may be able to link up and form the kinds of "massive components" needed to overcome challenges that will increasingly disrespect field boundaries. Absent some such agreement, social science as a whole, and economics in particular, will become increasingly fragmented.

In terms of practical implementation, it is clear that a certain maturity of understanding is necessary before it is appropriate to develop axiomatic models. There may be need both for preliminary investigation of new data sources and for exploration of theories that import concepts such as anxiety and fear directly from folk psychology [e.g., Caplin, 2003]. The minimalist methodology is appropriate only when it comes time to unify theory and data. As gaps are found in early models and as new sources of insight open up, theory and measurement will ideally coevolve. As potentially insightful sources of new data emerge, complementary models will be developed that make predictions concerning these data in addition to standard choices. Conversely, new theoretical approaches will be matched with complementary innovations in measurement.

One possible area of tension concerns the implicit downgrading of constrained maximization. While theories involving optimization may be of particular interest due to their simplicity and their connection to the long stream of prior economic analysis, they are not essential to the methodology. Development of axiomatic models that do not rely on optimization is likely to introduce communication problems with those branches of the discipline in which the principle of constrained optimization has been placed on a higher plane than axiomatic reasoning. My hope is that facing such problems head on will result in the methodology being sharpened rather than discarded.

A crucial issue in applying the methodology is how best to take advantage of the implied freedom to construct the data concerning which we develop our theories. Below I illustrate two cases in which this question has been adequately answered. The first example involves a minimalist approach to understanding the impact of subjective informational constraints on decision making, and is detailed in Caplin and Dean [2008b]. The second example involves a minimalist approach to neuroscientific data that have been hypothesized to register the degree of surprise as the environment changes for the better or for the worse. Theoretical foundations for this research are detailed in Caplin and Dean [2008a], with the empirical implementation being detailed in Caplin, Dean, Glimcher, and Rutledge [2008].

PARADISE LOST

In this section I provide doctrinal background on the revealed preference approach to choice theory proposed by Samuelson [1938]. I then outline how and why model builders learned to bypass the constraints that this approach entails. Then follows a review of some of the new psychological data that are increasingly available, and the largely extratheoretical approaches to discriminate among the new models based on these data. The review highlights the strains that are currently being placed on professional unity.

Preferences and Utility

Water is essential to life yet is worth far less than such an obvious nonnecessity as a diamond. Efforts to explain this "diamond–water" paradox led to various strained efforts to purge theories of "exchange value" of any and all references to "use value," or utility. For example, the labor theory of value explained prices as resulting from the direct and indirect inputs of labor required to produce the object of exchange. Water is cheap relative to diamonds because it is so much easier to produce.

It was the marginalist revolution that indicated how to reinsert utility considerations into price theory. According to the marginalist interpretation, the reason that water is so inexpensive is that beyond the units that are readily available, incremental units do little to improve well-being. Were water in short supply, it would have far higher marginal utility and would surely sell for a very high price. Following this logic to its seemingly natural end point, many economists of the late nineteenth century took the low price of water as evidence for the principle of diminishing marginal utility, whereby marginal utility declines with quantity consumed. The apparent need for utility to diminish at the margin justified lengthy investigations into how one might best quantify utility, with various measurement devices being proposed.

Speculations on how best to measure utility were cut short by the advent of the ordinalist approach to choice. According to this approach, choice-relevant likes and dislikes are summarized by a complete and coherent (transitive) preference relationship among prizes. The observation that one can summarize a choice procedure that respects this relationship as equivalent to assigning utility numbers to prizes, and maximizing this function, is the first step in realizing the futility of the search for "true" utility. The clincher is the equally transparent observation that one could use any other utility function that preserved the order as an alternative to describe precisely the same pattern of choice.

In terms of understanding prices, the ordinalist approach showed that the low price of water must be explained based not on diminishing marginal utility, but rather on a diminishing marginal rate of substitution among distinct commodities. This is a property that is reflected in the shape of the indifference curves, which in turn derives entirely from the underlying preference ordering. The ordinalist revolution effectively ended the search for "true" internal utility.

Choices and Utility

In ordinalist logic, the starting point for demand theory is a coherent personal ranking of the potential objects of choice. Samuelson asked a simple question: what exactly are the limits that this theory imposes on demand functions themselves? This question and the subtle answer that it produced gave rise to an implicit critique of the standard ordinalist approach to choice theory. If observations are ultimately limited to choices alone, what is the point in theorizing about inner comparisons? If two distinct theories are identical in terms of the choices that result, are they not to all (economic) intents and purposes equivalent? The revealed preference approach to choice theory follows the logic of this critique to its natural end point and fully identifies theories with their behavioral implications.[1]

In technical terms, the move from ordinalism to revealed preference is relatively minor. Ordinalism takes as its starting point a preference ordering over elements of the choice set, X, taken for simplicity to be finite. Revealed preference takes as its starting point a choice correspondence that details all elements that might end up being chosen from an arbitrary set $A \subset X$. The minimal assumption in this approach is that the choice correspondence satisfies the Weak Axiom of Revealed Preference (WARP): given $A, B \in 2^X$, and $x, y \in A \cap B$,

$$x \in C(A), y \in C(B) \implies x \in C(B).$$

WARP implies that we can use the choice correspondence to define an implied binary relation,

$$x \succsim y \iff x \in C(\{x, y\}),$$

that is itself complete and transitive and therefore permits standard utility representations. The converse is also true: if we derive the choice correspondence from an underlying preference ordering on X, then WARP will be satisfied.

While the technical switch implied by the revealed preference approach seems minor, it is methodologically crucial. Models in this tradition characterize conditions under which observable choices can be calculated using a simple algorithm, such as maximization of a utility function. It is in this sense that economic theories of decision making are "as if" theories. Standard theory does not claim that an agent maximizes a utility function, or possesses a complete, transitive preference ordering. The claim is only that one can model decision makers as if they are utility maximizers if and only if their choices satisfy WARP.

As explored below, revealed preference models have now been developed for choice among many different types of objects, with various different assumptions on the nature of the choices, and correspondingly different methods for computing choices. A proponent of the approach axiomatizes specific properties of choice that are to be captured. All remaining objects in the theory are then derived from the corresponding axioms. I take the following general structure to characterize the class of revealed preference theorems:

> Choices among objects of type * have appealing properties ** if and only if determined by calculations/operations of the form ***.

In this general structure, calculating *** may represent an entirely unrealistic picture of the decision process. Yet the principle of revealed preference places the empirical bar for amending the theory higher. If ** is empirically violated, the task is to identify changes that accommodate this failing. If violations of ** are empirically unimportant, then choice data per se cannot force rejection of the theory. Note also that the underlying "theory" that is being captured in the axioms can be described either as ** or as ***. In the original formulation, the starting point was the theory that individuals maximize utility (***), and the point of the theorem was to characterize choices that are consistent with this class of theory. In many current formulations, it is the property of the choices (**) that is treated as the starting point, and the conclusion concerns the algorithm that this pattern of choice identifies. A final point to note is that the class of such theories is very much tied up with technology, since technological expansion opens up entirely new forms of calculation with which to underpin such theorems.

In addition to the basic characterization theorems, choice theoretic models include statements concerning equivalent representations. These results provide precise limits on what the underlying theories are able to identify from data on the corresponding choices:

> There exist equivalence classes of calculations/operations of the form *** such that choices among objects of type * are identical within any such class, yet differ between classes.

Enter the Unobservable Abstractions

The revealed preference approach to choice pushed economic theory in the direction of observationally based streamlining. All elements that are superfluous to choice are excluded from the theory by definition. This holds in particular for psychological intuitions that do not restrict choice data. However, the asymmetric information and game-theoretic revolutions introduced into economics many model elements that have no obvious basis in observation. With respect to presumed information asymmetries, what observation teaches one whether or not an agent is informed? And while out-of-equilibrium strategies are inherently unobservable, there have been long and sometimes fruitful debates concerning how they are chosen. As game theory has increasingly become the dominant approach to microeconomic interactions, so economic theorists have become accustomed to the gap between what can be theorized about and what can be observed.

It was in this theoretical environment that research in economics and psychology began in earnest. The early developments, while formally motivated by the empirical failures of standard theory (e.g., the Allais paradox), were informed by psychological intuitions concerning missing factors of first-order importance. Kahneman and Tversky [1979] were motivated by various violations of the predictions of the standard model, and their prospect-theoretic utility function incorporates such standard objects as losses, gains, and objective probabilities. However, their broader goal was to develop an approach to choice that reflected the "heuristics," such as anchoring and adjustment, that they hypothesized to be at work in real-world decisions [Kahneman and Tversky, 1974].

A similar combination of formal and informal motives underlies the pioneering work of Strotz [1956] on time inconsistency, which forms a cornerstone of modern economics and psychology. The formal motivation for his work derives from the failure of standard economic models to capture use of commitment devices to reduce future flexibility. The informal motivation concerns the desire to introduce psychologically realistic self-control problems into economics. Models with time inconsistency continue to have such powerful appeal not only because of their predictive power, but also because of their psychological content. In terms of predictions, David Laibson [1997] and Ted O'Donoghue and Matthew Rabin [1999] have done pioneering research on the many behaviors that are easier to explain with models of this form than with standard exponential discounting.

In psychological terms, Loewenstein [1987] and Caplin and Leahy [2001] have shown how time inconsistency can be produced by psychological forces seemingly unrelated to self-control problems, such as anticipatory feelings about future outcomes.

The phenomenon of time inconsistency powerfully illustrates the extent of the departure from revealed preference in economics and psychology. The field has by and large adopted the proposal of Peleg and Yaari [1973] that models with time inconsistency are best solved using game-theoretic concepts, such as perfect equilibrium. Once an individual is regarded as involved in a strategic interaction with future selves, questions are opened up on many levels. What is the appropriate solution concept for the resulting game, and what does this imply about out-of-equilibrium beliefs? Are agents aware of their future preference changes? Finally, while the original Strotz model involves a unified individual who changes preferences over time, alternative conceptualizations are now available in which the individual makes cue-triggered mistakes [Bernheim and Rangel, 2004] or suffers from intrapersonal conflict within a given period (e.g., Benhabib and Bisin [2005], Fudenberg and Levine [2005], and Loewenstein and O'Donogue [2004]). Once one regards individual decisions as the outcome of a dynamic game with more than one player in each period, it is clear that the principle of revealed preference has been left far behind.

Psychological Data and Economic Theory: The Divide

As noted above, models in economics and psychology typically operate both on the behavioral level and on the psychological level. With regard to the purely behavioral aspects of the underlying psychology, it is clear how to bring these models to the data. What is less clear is how to bring the more intuitive content, such as heuristics and self-control problems, to the data. In this regard, it is perhaps fortunate that the growth of the field has coincided with a revolution in data availability. This flood of new data is reflected in various empirical papers in economics and psychology.

In terms of measuring heuristics, Payne, Bettman, and Johnson [1993] developed a program, MouseLab, precisely to provide new evidence on the process of decision making. The MouseLab system is a computer-based way of tracking the order in which information is processed in a choice problem. It presents the subject with a choice among several alternatives, each of which is characterized by a number of attributes. All the attributes are given numerical values. The vector of attributes for each of the options is presented on a screen in a grid form. However, each of the numbers in the grid is obscured. In order to view a number, the subject has to move the mouse cursor over the relevant box. By recording these movements, the experimenter is able to view the order in which information is acquired and the speed with which it is acquired.

One experiment outlined by Payne, Bettman, and Johnson [1993] used Mouse-Lab while varying the choice environment along two dimensions. First, they varied the dispersion of importance of the different attributes from low to high. Second, they varied the degree to which the subject experiences time pressure while arriving at a decision. From the MouseLab system, they recorded various measures of the way that subjects collect information from the grid. They focused on identifying qualitative features of the resulting data, observing, for example, that the high dispersion environment saw more time spent on the most important attribute, and higher variance in time spent on each attribute and alternative. Payne, Bettman, and Luce [1996] ran experiments using MouseLab in which the opportunity cost to time was allowed to vary.

A second new form of data that is increasingly available is response data of various sorts, including survey responses. The ever decreasing cost of Internet surveys suggests that availability of such data is soon to mushroom. One potentially interesting set of psychological questions that have been posed concern planning activities. Ameriks, Caplin, and Leahy [2003] developed a new survey instrument to get insights into planning behaviors and forethought, an area of economics and psychology in which Lusardi [2000] pioneered. They provided results suggesting that those with a high "propensity to plan" generally accumulated greater wealth. Another burgeoning area of research in economics and psychology concerns the analysis of data derived from surveys of happiness [Kahneman et al. 2004].

A third important new source of psychological data derives from neuroscientific evidence [Glimcher and Rustichini, 2004]. McClure, Laibson, Loewenstein, and Cohen [2004] have pioneered in the use of data on brain activation to collect evidence on self-control. Inspired in large part by the findings of Schultz, Appicella, and Ljungberg [1993], the literature on dopaminergic responses has also been used to shed light both on preferences and on beliefs. Other experimental work suggests that the firing of dopamine neurons may record a reward prediction error (the difference between received and expected reward) rather than just the pure expectation of reward [Berns, McClure, Pagnoni, and Montague, 2001 and Bayer and Glimcher 2005].

Unfortunately, these exciting new forms of data are often poorly integrated into the underlying models. Models of heuristic decision making are not rich enough to predict mouse clicks, rendering tests based on these behaviors more indicative than formally useful. The survey questions that are being explored concerning such variables as planning and happiness deal with objects that are undefined in the underlying models. Finally, of all areas, it is the neuroscientific data that is hardest to interpret. Self-control–based models of choice do not include a cortical or limbic blood oxygen level dependent (BOLD) signal function. Models of expectations are similarly silent on the dopaminergic response. The fact that neuroscientific data are being interpreted as relevant to models of choice is particularly disturbing to proponents of revealed preference. Hence, it is no surprise that it was a proposal to expand the use of these data that triggered the current methodological debate [Camerer, Loewenstein, and Prelec, 2005]. How can we prevent economics from being swamped by masses of new data of dubious interest to our progress in understanding choice?

CHOICE THEORY AND PSYCHOLOGY

There is nothing per se irrational about having brain scans, mouse clicks, and survey responses move one toward acceptance of models in which they do not formally appear. A Bayesian can update personal priors based on evidence that is relevant to a "large world" model, yet is not present in the "small world" theory that is being tested. Yet updating beliefs based on such a personal world view has its dangers. Those who hold different priors over the large world may update in an entirely different manner, and no amount of evidence is guaranteed to provide convergence of posteriors. This process of updating based on extratheoretical evidence may have as its end point a highly fractured profession. Absent discipline, our proud and unified social science risks devolving into many little fieldoms, each with its own private language concerning how to interpret evidence.

Surveying the scene with their eyes fixed on observables, GP posed anew the question of Samuelson. If two distinct psychological theories produce the same implications for choice in all situations, are they really different in a way that matters to economists? Believing this question to have a negative answer, GP propose that the standard revealed preference approach to choice theory be restored to its traditional centrality. They propose replacing all theories that invoke direct assumptions on unobservable psychological phenomena with theories that are phrased directly in terms of choice alone. This proposal, and its seemingly devastating implications for economics and psychology, has profoundly caught the attention of the profession.[2]

I illustrate in this section the potential psychological power of the methodology proposed by GP. I first outline the general method by which expansions in the domain of choice are used to increase the psychological range of choice theory. It is precisely the fact that this approach focuses direct attention on the domain of choice that accounts for its advantages in terms of parsimony and elegance over psychologically driven theories of behavior. I then present an example that GP themselves stress as a perfect exemplar of their approach. The underlying subject concerns the impact of mental states such as anxiety and suspense on choice of information. I develop a directly psychological model of these phenomena due to Caplin and Leahy [2001]. I then show how to apply the axiomatic model of Kreps and Porteus [1978] to capture the key behavioral implications of these psychological forces without ever having to define them or to measure them.

The broad point is that one does not need to specify psychological phenomena directly if one's only goal is to study behavior. I illustrate this point again in the context of models of bounded rationality and of the decision process. These examples also make clear why maximization is less essential to choice theory than is the axiomatic approach. Current axiomatic models of boundedly rational decision making are explicitly procedural, and stand or fall on the behavioral implications of these procedures regardless of whether they can be phrased as in some sense optimal.

Domain of Choice and Psychological Range

It was the theory of choice under uncertainty due to von Neumann and Morgenstern [1947] that first indicated the potential psychological power of the choice-theoretic approach. Their expected utility theory model is explicit in conceptualizing objects of economic choice as psychological constructs rather than as physical objects. The implicit hypothesis is that choice under uncertainty is equivalent to choice among objective lotteries. This represents a huge psychological advance over viewing prizes as physical objects. Of course, there is no direct way of knowing if uncertain winnings are in fact perceived as objective lotteries, which is what makes the connection to implied patterns of behavior so crucial.

Savage [1954] took the process of abstraction from the physical prize to a psychological construct one step further, applying axiomatic methods to choice among acts that associate consequences with all states of nature. This removed the need to assume acceptance of commonly understood objective probabilities. The results that Savage demonstrated based on his conceptualization of the domain of choice stand as among the most remarkable achievements in social science. With his axioms, one and the same process of inference from concepts that are purely choice based gives rise not only to the implied structure of preferences but also to the implied structure of subjective beliefs.

The above models illustrate the connection between the domain on which a choice theory operates and the psychology that the theory can encompass. Using as the domain a purely physical prize space disallows psychological phenomena connected with uncertainty. The domain of objective lotteries is clearly richer in this regard, and allows one to capture some of the financial implications of the psychology of risk (e.g., interest in insurance). However, the range of psychological questions that can be shoe-horned into a model with such a simple domain remains limited. For example, the model of Kreps and Porteus [1978] outlined below shows that a richer domain is needed to account for noninstrumental information preferences. The fundamental point is that no theory of choice can be more psychologically sophisticated than is allowed for by the domain on which it is defined. If objects are not differentiated in the domain, there can be no distinction among them at any later stage of the theory.

A domain that is particularly rich in terms of the psychology it allows to be modeled is the set of subsets of a given physical prize space, rather than the prizes themselves. Kreps [1979] used this domain to model preference for flexibility. Yet it is the GP model of temptation and self-control that most profoundly illustrates the rich psychology that this domain liberates [Gul and Pesendorfer, 2001]. As noted above, Strotz [1956] argued that time-inconsistent preferences that overemphasize the present give rise to demand for commitment devices. GP turned this around and asked what interest in commitment devices reveals about preferences over choice sets. The resulting model implies that larger choice sets may not be for the better, yet does not allow for time-changing preferences.

Belief-Based Utility and Psychological Expected Utility

Traditional expected utility theory has the property that information is purely instrumental. Hence, more information can never be either a bad thing, or desirable for its own sake. Yet many psychological arguments suggest that factors such as anxiety, fear of disappointment, love of suspense, and possible regret may affect preferences over information for reasons that go beyond pure instrumentality. To formalize the modeling, consider a medical setting with two possible health states, θ_1 and θ_2, in which outcome θ_2 is having Huntingdon's disease (an incurable degenerative disease with onset at some future date) and outcome θ_1 is not so having. Let $p \in [0, 1]$ denote the probability of not so having, as assessed in the period prior to the actual final resolution of the uncertainty, yet following receipt of a signal $s \in S$ concerning this outcome. Each signal is associated with information that affects the probability that state θ_1 will eventuate: it gives rise to a probability distribution over beliefs.

In the case of Huntingdon's disease, there is a simple genetic test that can be taken to resolve the $p = .5$ chance of having the disease that exists among the offspring of prior victims. Yet many who have been offered the right to uncover their genetic fate have chosen not to take the test. The primary motivating factor in these cases appears to be psychological rather than monetary (commonly the blood has already been sampled, so the only question is whether or not the patient is given the information that the responsible medical authorities already know).

One way to model the forces that give rise to information rejection is to directly model the impact of belief-based prizes on utility. This is the approach adopted in the psychological expected utility (PEU) model of Caplin and Leahy [2001], which explicitly connects such preferences with a particular psychological response to information. In the context of Huntingdon's disease, the model relies on the psychological hypothesis that subjective contentment in the preoutcome period depends on the operative belief state, p. To capture this formally, the PEU model posits existence of a function that calibrates the cost in expected utility terms of the aversive state associated with preoutcome beliefs p. While the name is unimportant, "anxiety" is a reasonable psychological label for the aversive mental state in the preoutcome period.

A simple way to analyze the choice-theoretic implications of the PEU model is to work directly in a prize space comprising all lotteries over preoutcome beliefs and actual outcomes. Pure prizes are belief–outcome pairs of the form (p, θ_j) with $p \in [0, 1]$ and $j \in \{1, 2\}$, and the PEU function is defined on the set of all such pure prizes,

$$Z = \{(p, \theta_j) : 0 \leq p \leq 1; j \in \{1, 2\}\}.$$

According to the model, one lottery over these prizes is preferred to another if and only if it has higher expected utility according to some utility function $u^{ANX} : Z \to R$. In the context of Huntingdon's disease, the natural psychological hypothesis is that the best prize is good news early, while the worst is bad news early. Normalizing as usual, we know that for all belief–prize pairs (p, θ_j) with $p \in [0, 1]$ and $j \in \{1, 2\}$,

$$1 = u^{ANX}(1, \theta_1) \geq u^{ANX}(p, \theta_j) \geq u^{ANX}(0, \theta_2) = 0.$$

There are two reasons that $(1, \theta_1)$ is so good. First, the ultimate outcome is good. Second, receiving the good news early alleviates the anxiety associated with living with fear of impending doom. Similarly, $(0, \theta_2)$ is so bad not only because the ultimate outcome is bad, but also because it forces the agent to live in fear.

To understand the impact of the model on choice of information, note that the probability that belief p will be paired with outcome θ_1 is p. The other possibility, that it will be paired with outcome θ_2, has probability $1 - p$. Hence, one can define the function $K^{ANX}(p)$ as the overall expected utility corresponding to this belief concerning final outcomes,

$$K^{ANX}(p) \equiv pu^{ANX}(p, \theta_1) + (1 - p)u^{ANX}(p, \theta_2).$$

It is this function that determines choice among signals. Given signals $s, s' \in S$, one signal is preferred to another if and only if it produces a lottery over beliefs p that yields higher expected utility according to the function $K^{ANX}(p)$:

$$s \succsim s' \text{ if and only if } E_s(K^{ANX}) \geq E_{s'}(K^{ANX}).$$

Note that information is rejected if this function is concave, and that such a rejection permits of a psychological interpretation. Information is rejected if increased pessimism in the face of a bad signal is regarded by the agent as more aversive at the margin than increased optimism in the face of a good signal is beneficial.

Avoiding Anxiety or Preserving Surprise?

I show now that the PEU model contains redundant elements from a purely choice-theoretic perspective. Consider a PEU model designed to capture positive surprise. Outcome θ_1 is that a birthday party is thrown for a close friend. Outcome θ_2 is that no such party is thrown. The friend's postsignal preoutcome belief that the party will be thrown is p. To model this as a preference over prizes and beliefs, one makes the psychologically natural assumption that the best prize is good news late, while the worst is bad news that is disappointing. Normalizing again, this gives rise to the following restrictions on the underlying expected utility function on belief–prize pairs (p, θ_k) with $p \in [0, 1]$ and $k \in \{1, 2\}$:

$$1 = u^{SUR}(0, \theta_1) \geq u^{SUR}(p, \theta_k) \geq u^{SUR}(1, \theta_2) = 0.$$

As before, informational choice depends on the appropriate weighted average as captured by $K^{SUR}(p)$:

$$K^{SUR}(p) \equiv p u^{SUR}(p, \theta_1) + (1 - p) u^{SUR}(p, \theta_2).$$

Note that the attitude toward information derives from an almost polar opposite psychology in the case of the surprise party compared with the case of Huntingdon's disease. In the former case, pessimism is beneficial, while in the latter it is per se unpleasant. Yet it is easy to construct cases in which revealed preferences among signals are identical. In particular, the following linear case meets all of the intuitive criteria that can be imposed on the psychology of anxiety and of surprise:

$$u^{SUR}(p, \theta_1) = 1 - \alpha^{SURP} p, \text{ with } \alpha^{SURP} \in (0, 1);$$

$$u^{SUR}(p, \theta_2) = (1 - p)\beta^{SURP}, \text{ with } \beta^{SURP} \in (0, 1);$$

$$u^{ANX}(p, \theta_1) = \alpha^{ANX} p + (1 - \alpha^{ANX}), \text{ with } \alpha^{ANX} \in (0, 1);$$

$$u^{ANX}(p, \theta_2) = \beta^{ANX} p, \text{ with } \beta^{ANX} \in (0, 1).$$

With $\beta^{SURP} = 0.15$, $\alpha^{SURP} = 0.35$, $\alpha^{ANX} = 0.1$, and $\beta^{ANX} = 0.5$, the two functions are increasing affine transforms, and hence behaviorally equivalent:

$$K^{SURP}(p) \equiv 0.15 - 0.2p^2 + 0.7p = 0.15 + 0.5K^{ANX}(p).$$

The fact that two entirely different psychologies produce identical choices implies immediately that they are indistinguishable from a standard choice-theoretic perspective. From the perspective of choice theory, psychological motivations are just as hidden as are decision processes. In both cases, the decision theorist can look for the projections of the underlying factors onto the domain of choice and provide models that mimic in this domain any behaviors that may be uncovered through other forms of research. In this interpretation, psychology may be inspiring, but it is not to be modeled.

A Choice-Theoretic Approach

In fitting with the GP proposal, what is needed is a choice-theoretic model that captures the behavioral implications of psychological forces such as anxiety and love of surprise. The model of Kreps and Porteus [1978] (henceforth KP) provides just such foundations and is correctly regarded by GP as an exemplar of their approach to economics and psychology. KP take on exactly the same challenge as does the PEU model: how to allow for beliefs that may directly affect choices. However, they do not make any direct references to psychology. Instead, they take a choice-theoretic approach, looking to summarize properties of choice among signals. In order to do this, KP apply axiomatic methods of choice theory to the domain of temporal lotteries ("lotteries over lotteries over . . .") rather than simple lotteries as in expected utility theory.

The KP model involves axioms such that signals are ranked in a simple and transparent fashion. Specifically, these axioms are equivalent to existence of a function $K : [0, 1] \rightarrow R$ such that given $s, s' \in S$,

$$s \succsim s' \text{ if and only if } E_s(K) \geq E_{s'}(K).$$

One signal is preferred to another if and only if it produces a lottery over beliefs that yields higher expected utility according to this function. This is exactly as in the PEU model, with the only difference being that the function $K(p)$ preserves consistency in the order as between beliefs and outcomes: if prize θ_1 is strictly preferred to prize θ_2 so that $K(1) > K(0)$, then the K function is strictly increasing; it is strictly decreasing if the inequality is reversed, while if $K(1) = K(0)$ all beliefs are equally ranked and all signals are indifferent. Again, as in the PEU model, the function $K(p)$ fully identifies choice among signals. The concave case produces what is known as preference for late resolution of uncertainty, in which a signal that provides no information is preferred to a signal that resolves any of the uncertainty up front. Similarly, the convex case produces preference for early resolution of uncertainty. Linearity is equivalent to neutrality with respect to the temporal resolution of uncertainty.

While at first appearance it may be a source of comfort that the KP model and PEU theory have such strong similarities, the differences between them are profound. The critical distinction is that the domain on which preferences are defined is strictly smaller in the KP model. The KP utility function has in its domain any and all lotteries that may be available to an agent choosing among information gathering strategies. By construction, this domain exhausts all possibilities for private choice.

In contrast, the PEU function is constructed on the domain of lotteries over beliefs and final prizes. This space contains objects to which Bayes's rule does not apply, such as belief–prize pair $(0.5, \theta_1)$ for sure: an ex ante belief that θ_1 and θ_2 are equally likely, yet the realization of outcome θ_1 for sure. Unfortunately, a guarantee that a currently uncertain future will turn out well is not available as an object of choice. It is this extension of the domain of preferences into the realm of fantasy that makes the PEU model fall afoul of the principle of revealed preference.

As noted above, one issue that the enriched domain gives rise to is interpretational ambiguity. An individual who will pay to avoid information is certainly displaying a preference for late resolution of the form modeled by KP. Yet one cannot be similarly confident that the psychological motivation is avoidance of an aversive prior mental state induced by pessimistic beliefs, since precisely the same pattern of behavior can be observed in cases in which pessimistic beliefs are beneficial as opposed to damaging.

The Decision Process and Bounds on Rationality

One motivation for models of bounded rationality is that they are more intuitively appealing than the standard optimizing model. In fact, the first formal model of bounded rationality, the "satisficing" model of Herbert Simon [1955], was introduced as a direct response to the perceived implausibility of the prevailing model of economic man. Simon proposed a theory of choice by which the decision maker has some concept of the characteristics that would make an option satisfactory. The choice set is searched sequentially until an option is found that fulfils those criteria, which is then chosen. A second attempt at designing a model of the decision-making process based on plausibility is Sauermann and Selten's aspiration adaptation model (cited in Selten [1999]). As its name suggests, the model describes a set of rules by which a decision maker adjusts the aspiration level in the process of search until only one choice is left.

While the early bounded rationality theories had an aura of plausibility, it was not clear whether they were different in terms of implied choices from the standard optimizing approach. Later theories were more explicit in differentiating the implied behaviors from those that would be produced in standard choice theory. The "elimination by aspects" model of Tversky [1972] specifies an environment in which a choice object has a number of well-specified attributes, or "aspects." The procedure that Tversky posits is one in which the decision maker orders these aspects and sequentially rules out alternatives that are not satisfactory on the basis of each aspect in turn, until left with a unique choice. It is easy to produce examples whereby application of this decision-making process gives rise to violations of WARP: the theory is behaviorally distinct from standard rationality-based choice theory. Similarly, such heuristic rules as the "search for reasons"

[Rubinstein, 1998] can cause behaviors that violate standard principles of rational decision making.

Heuristics are rational in the sense that they appeal to intuition and avoid deliberation cost, but boundedly rational in the sense that they often lead to biased choices. While there are examples in which various heuristics describe behavior better than does rational decision theory, the question arises as to whether a heuristic would be applied in an environment in which massive losses would result. Many doubt that this would be the case, and as a result have proposed models that allow adaptive selection among heuristics. Payne, Bettman, and Johnson [1993] have used MouseLab to provide evidence suggesting that the choice environment indeed affects the heuristic employed, thereby edging toward a theory of rational choice among these new primitives.

An entirely different approach to bounded rationality involves formalizing specific constraints on the decision maker's abilities, and solving for optimal strategies subject to these constraints. Wilson's [2002] analysis of an agent with bounded memory and Radner and Rothschild's [1975] examination of the allocation of effort solve optimization problems of this variety. Variations on this optimality-based theme include models that are designed to provide simple and plausible solutions for models that are too complex for an agent realistically to solve. Gabaix and Laibson [2000] propose just such a decision rule based on an assumption of myopia, whereby agents choose sequentially among cognitive operations to maximize expected benefit as if they are going to stop and choose in the next period.

Axioms Please

There are by now a bewildering number of different models of the decision-making process, and there is little consensus concerning how best to discriminate among them. In fact, many models of process have the defect that it is unclear what restrictions they place on choice data. The typical way this issue is currently addressed is by designing an experimental environment in which predictions are easy to derive. However, when these models perform poorly, one does not know whether to adjust the assumptions that were made to operationalize the models or the overall modeling approach. In contrast, tests of standard rational choice theory based on WARP operate at a high level of generality. The tests explore whether the data are consistent with a class of decision-making models, rather than just with a specific process in a particular narrow setting.

Given this background, it is not surprising that there is currently an attempt to provide choice-theoretic models of bounds on rationality and the decision-making process.

Tyson [2005] provides an axiomatic treatment of a version of the satisficing procedure. Manzini and Mariotti [2004] consider what they term the "rational shortlist" method of choice. Their axioms characterize a class of decision-making algorithms associated with two orderings rather than one. For any given choice problem, the decision maker uses the first ordering to construct a shortlist comprising all elements that are maximal. The agent then selects from this "shortlist" all elements that are maximal according to the second ordering. A third paper in a similar vein is Ergin's [2003] model of costly contemplation. Ergin considers decisions in which people have to choose choice sets from which they will have to pick an element at a second stage. Thinking harder may provide a finer partition and thus allow a better first-stage decision, but also may require more effort, represented by a cost function c.

While the choice-theoretic modeling of bounded rationality is at an early stage, it is quickly reshaping the theoretical landscape. The parsimony of these early choice-theoretic approaches stands in pleasant contrast to the prior models that were explicitly procedural, yet whose empirical content has proven so hard to divine. Moreover, what is of interest in these models is precisely how they depart from the standard theory of utility maximization. This makes the models particularly important in methodological terms, in showing how axiomatic models that capture psychological forces may allow for behaviors that are qualitatively different from those associated with standard theories based on constrained optimization.

Modeling Psychological Variables

The GP proposal involves an implicit prohibition on modeling psychological variables. Their proposal in this regard is outlined below. The remaining sections show that there are many models available that allow better use to be made of the new psychological data. I first make this argument in the context of models that can be fit using survey responses, and then repeat the argument for models that make direct predictions of various nonstandard data items related to the decision-making process. I then turn to models that are predictive of data on internal states, such as PEU. In all such cases, enriching the theoretical and evidentiary base allows the associated models to perform to a higher standard than those that are restricted to exclude the nonchoice data. Direct modeling of psychological data allows one to fit data on pure choice better than would be possible were these data to be excluded on the basis of a methodological prohibition. Many of the other chapters in this volume provide rich examples along similar lines, in particular, those of Benhabib and Bisin (chapter 11), Camerer (chapter 2), Crawford (chapter 10), and Schotter (chapter 3).

The GP Proposal

GP argue that modeling choice is the central task of economic theory, and those engaged in research in economics and psychology have yet to provide a strong counterargument. Yet even if these are shared priorities, they do not provide an answer to the question of what to do about the new psychological data that are increasingly available. Certainly, one can criticize as ad hoc the common procedure of modeling only choice data, yet commenting on the model fit based on data that are not included in the model. But the GP proposal in this regard is also subject to criticism.

GP allow that one can use any form of data one wants to guide intuitions concerning choice. Thinking of psychological forces such as anxiety and self-control problems may provide inspiration concerning the behaviors to model. Yet psychological forces have no place in the model itself, so psychological data have no role in formally fitting the models. Similarly, it may be that survey answers are suggestive of forces that drive behavior, and that thinking about these forces improves understanding of behavior. One may even use neurological data and data on the process of choice to derive conjectures concerning the likely pattern of choice in various contingencies. However, their proposal is that one should limit the use of these data to precisely such a suggestive role. One can seek choice-theoretic inspiration from psychological data, but psychological variables themselves must ultimately be excluded from the theory.

The GP proposal privileges data on choice above all other forms of data. In fact, the approach is built up as if no additional data were available. If one were indeed to have data only on standard choices, it is hard to see why one would want to construct two distinct explanatory frameworks. When measurement and theory are not tightly matched, differences among competing theories will reside in the unobservables. Those looking for common theoretical ground will remove as many references as possible to these variables. In this sense, the GP proposal represents the logical limit of the theorist's natural desire to remove superfluous elements in a world in which only choice data are available. Yet this leaves their approach ill-suited to a world in which rich new sources of data do in fact exist.

Strategic Survey Responses

Survey responses provide a particularly rich form of data that may demonstrably help in fitting models of choice. After all, models of behavior are constructed in large part to help answer questions about future contingent choices. The fact that exactly the same situation has not been seen previously is what makes it important to have an all-purpose picture of decision making, in particular, for those interested in making policy interventions. The standard method that revealed preference allows for fitting model parameters is extremely limited: moment-matching based on data from past choices. It is easy to find cases in which these data provide little of the information one is seeking. This is particularly so when one is looking to explore the impact of policy changes that are likely to result in something of a break from past patterns of behavior. In many such contexts, the complications involved in designing a realistic experiment make it far too expensive a proposition, at least until and unless some preliminary evidence has been gathered using less costly means, such as conducting surveys.

A simple question that has proven very hard to answer concerns the impact of an estate tax reduction on wealth accumulation. Kotlikoff and Summers [1981] argued that the bequest motive is the primary driver of wealth accumulation, which implies that the estate tax is a crucial determinant of spending in the retirement period. Hurd [1987] has argued that precautionary motives provide an equally attractive explanation for the observed spending pattern among the elderly. Since that time, efforts to distinguish in the data between bequest and precautionary motives have proven so unsuccessful that such prominent researchers as Dynan, Skinner, and Zeldes [2002] have argued that they may be empirically indistinguishable. Hence, standard economic models based on behavior alone provide, at best, weak evidence on which to base any changes in estate tax policy.

In current research, a "strategic survey" methodology is being developed to improve inference in dynamic optimization models of this sort [Ameriks et al., 2007]. This methodology exploits the fact that the decision maker's strategy is potentially far more revealing than is behavior alone.[3] The goal of a strategic survey question is to explore informative aspects of the agent's strategy that may not have been revealed in the prior history. Seeking data on strategies is consistent with the spirit of revealed preference, according to which choice behavior is more revealing than any statement of priorities could ever be. In philosophical terms, the strategic survey methodology is a minimum departure from standard observation of behavior and, as such, represents the natural next step when purely behavioral data are unrevealing.

In Ameriks et al. [2007], we confirm technically the limitations of behavioral data in separating bequest and precautionary motives, and design specific strategic survey questions to shed new light on their relative importance. In technical terms, the critical issue is how to fit a model of behavior and survey responses to data of both different forms. This calls for models of the survey error process: the gap between survey responses and what would in fact occur in the given contingency. As do Kimball, Sahm, and Shapiro [2005] and Ljungqvist [1993], we develop an explicit model of the survey error process in estimating our model. While our ultimate interest lies only in behavior, modeling the survey data is a necessary means to achieving this standard behavioral end. Fitting the model based on past behavior alone would needlessly limit our understanding of future behavior.

The Decision Process

The resources that go into making a decision are scarce. Fully assessing all the possible alternatives in a decision problem takes both time and effort. In some cases, if the alternatives are relatively simple and the stakes for making a good decision are high, this may be a good idea. However, in other cases, where the alternatives are more complicated and the cost of the wrong decision is relatively small, this may be not such a good idea. In these cases, the decision maker may choose to cut some corners, either by choosing to ignore some of the options available, or by not inquiring into some of the aspects of some of the options. If this is the case, a model that hopes to well explain choice must explain how decision makers search for information, how they decide to stop searching, and how they make a decision based on the information that they have. For this reason, models of the decision-making process may provide insight into many aspects of the decision in addition to what is finally chosen.

A simple variable that has often been used to provide additional insight into the decision-making process is time to decide. For example, Gabaix, Laibson, Moloche, and Weinberg [2006] have used decision time and other additional observables to examine the success of their directed cognition model. Within psychology, the work of Dean, Woo, and Maloney [2007] has similarly indicated the impact of decision time on choice. They consider a class of models of aiming at a fixed physical target in which the degree of accuracy depends on the time available to point at this target. Their model produces a time-dependent error around a clear objective, with convergence to an irreducible individual level of error. Their model predicts accuracy far better than one would be able to if one excluded reference to the time constraint and looked merely at the projection of the decision strategy onto the choice space as standardly conceived, which is the geometric region in which the target is constrained to lie. Even more basic in this regard is evidence concerning the time it takes for sensory information such as sights and sounds to effectively register, and the differential speed with which various parts of the brain are now known to operate. A classical illustration of this effect at work lies in the finding that it takes longer to read the word "red" in green letters than in red letters (the Stroop effect discussed by Camerer in chapter 2).

When explicit models of the time taken in making a decision are developed, richer data can in principle be used to better fit the entire set of available data, potentially offering a more robust model of the decision itself. This is the spirit in which Gabaix et al. [2006] use MouseLab to fit nonchoice variables that are predicted by their directed cognition model of information acquisition. The nonchoice variables they model and fit are the number of boxes opened in each column, the number of boxes opened in each row, and the time taken to make a decision. In an analogous manner, Johnson, Camerer, Sen, and Rymon [2002] use MouseLab data in fitting models that characterize the impact of strategic sophistication on the outcomes of various games. Crawford (chapter 10) provides convincing evidence of how richly search data of this form can inform prediction. Camerer (chapter 2) provides a very rich description of psychological data sets that either currently exist or are clearly emergent. He presents rich evidence indicating how much these data may enrich our understanding of decisions. It is quite out of the question for these rich new sources of data and of insight to be ignored.

PEU and Psychological States

While the KP model has advantages over PEU in the purely decision-theoretic context, PEU has complementary strengths. In fact, the direct inclusion of psychological factors in the PEU model opens the door to rich analysis of what determines preferences over signals. To capture this, the model includes a production function relating the evolution of psychological states to the external environment. Making psychologically natural assumptions on this function, Caplin [2003] models the impact of attention grabbing messages on medical choices. Health authorities often use vivid "fear appeals" to stimulate learning and prevention among at-risk agents who might otherwise neglect possible preventive acts, such as cancer screening. PEU theory can capture this by making the level of anxiety depend not only on objective risk, but also on attentional resources that the messages are designed to commandeer.

The empirical research agenda associated with such an application is clear. Since the psychological production function is responsible for driving choice-relevant psychological states, empirical work must focus not only on fitting choices, but also on fitting the production function for choice-relevant psychological states. Just as physical production functions represent the stable underlying structure that survives parameter shifts, so do their psychological counterparts. Only by recovering the underlying production function will we be able to make robust predictions in the face of the many policy changes the model is designed to explore.

Once one takes account of the psychological production function, it is clear that PEU theory may make predictions for data other than standard choices. In this sense, it has a richness that is lacking in the KP model, which seems all to the good. For example, if psychological states can be measured and used in fitting the theory, then it becomes easy in principle to distinguish anxiety-avoidance motives for informational choice from those that are based on the desire to be surprised. While such measurement is very hard with present technologies, the idea that this research should be ruled out on the grounds that it can only be tested based on nonstandard data seems strained.

There are normative as well as positive reasons for developing models in which the domain extends beyond that required for standard private choice. Even though it was shown above that PEU models of anxiety and of surprise may be characterized by identical private decisions, the incentive of an empath to pass on good news is very different (see Caplin and Leahy [2004]). In the former case, the choice will be made to pass on good news early, since optimistic beliefs are always to the good, while in the latter it will be withheld since low expectations are beneficial. In this respect, it seems that it is the domain of the KP model that is too limited, rather than that of PEU being excessive.

REVEALED PREFERENCE AND MINIMALISM

The research outlined above into the joint properties of standard choice data and psychological data will move forward whether or not research methodology adjusts. Yet moving forward with this research absent methodological discipline presents severe dangers to professional unity, as outlined above. The good news is that just such discipline is at hand if we adapt the techniques pioneered in revealed preference theory to cover psychological data. To realize this, all one has to do is to open up the question of what constitutes a choice for the purposes of revealed preference theory. I argue here that modeling verbal evidence as chosen is consistent with a broad interpretation of the principle of revealed preference. I then go further and argue that any and all measurements of human activity can in principle be modeled as chosen, and therefore be incorporated into the mainstream of economic methodology. Following this, I detail the resulting "minimalist" methodology, which retains the insistence on streamlined modeling matched tightly to well-defined data that characterize revealed preference. However, the approach is entirely open in terms of the variables that can be modeled as chosen. Rejection of vast amounts of previously unmeasurable individual data is not only inconceivable in practice but also methodologically incoherent.

Dangers of Model Proliferation

There is an unstoppable momentum behind efforts to build rich new models to predict survey responses, mouse clicks, and neurological responses in addition to standard choices. What is unclear is how much economic content these models will have, and whether they will achieve the high standards of coherence and parsimony that previously characterized economic model building. One problem is that economists have historically tended to focus on behaviors close to our natural concerns, with a clear concept of the motivations driving behavior. The new psychological data that we are trying to model are entirely different. We have little or no experience modeling these data, we have very limited understanding of underlying measurement problems, and we do not have a clear conceptual framework relating the new measurements to standard choices. Given that the new variables are so unfamiliar to us, there is profound risk of ill-discipline in the modeling process and of professional fragmentation. What discipline can be added to keep this expansion from giving rise to a proliferation of different models that are mutually incompatible not only in terms of the details, but also in terms of the overarching approach?

I believe that it is relevant to ask of the new, richer models the precise question that was originally asked in the context of models of choice, and that gave rise to the original revealed preference proposal. Suppose one fits a rich model that predicts standard choices in addition to new psychological data, and one wishes to improve this model. Are the problems fundamental, or do they relate to the underlying conceptualization? If we are to answer questions of this form, we will need to discipline the modeling process to capture the implications for the data of general structural assumptions concerning the data generating process. It is precisely this drive for generality that gave rise to revealed preference theory in the narrower domain of classical choice data. Why not apply precisely the same discipline in the context of the richer psychological data? In order to explore such an approach, we first need to reconsider the limits of the original principle of revealed preference.

Words Are Chosen

Revealed preference modeling may be applied whenever one conceptualizes a choice as having made from among a set of feasible objects. But when is and when is not a choice being made? During the discussion of behaviorism in psychology, the point was made forcefully that verbal statements of all kinds may be conceptualized as chosen behaviors. Ericsson and Simon [1984] proposed recording subjects' "talk aloud" procedures when performing complex decision tasks. They felt that the systematic collection of these types of observations could be used to test models of human reasoning and of decisions. To counter the obvious behavioral counterargument, they argued that there is no reason for behaviorists to rule out such "verbal protocols" as evidence for their theories: "We see verbal behavior as one type of recordable behavior, which should be observed and analyzed like any other behavior." [Ericsson and Simon, 1984: 7]. Willingness to consider verbal statements as evidence does not convey a blind assumption that they are to be taken at face value: "The report 'X' need not be used to infer that X is true" [9].

The argument that answers to the "strategic survey questions" developed in Ameriks et al. [2007] are chosen is particularly in keeping with the spirit of revealed preference theory, rooted as it is in hypothetical rather than actual choices. The essentially hypothetical nature of revealed preference is stressed in particular by Aumann [1998: 935], "The essence of the axiomatic approach is that it . . . relates the given, 'real' situation to a whole lot of other situations, all of them hypothetical. This happens . . . even in Savage's development of probabilities themselves." In a letter to Aumann, Savage himself expressed comfort not only with the need to consider hypotheticals, but also with the need to consider situations that are regarded as impossible: "It is quite usual in this theory to contemplate acts that are not actually available. . . . I can contemplate the possibility that the lady dies medically and yet is restored in good health to her husband" [quoted in Aumann, 1998: 935]. In light of this history, it is particularly hard to understand how the line in revealed preference theory between permissible and impermissible evidence can rule out statements concerning intended future behavior.

Of Human Activity

Any attempt to restrict our attention to "choice data" rests on a shared "folk" under-standing of what is and what is not a choice: "I know when I am choosing." Consciousness is a key ingredient in this folk conception of choice. Unfortunately, consciousness itself is a very poorly understood phenomenon. Experiments in social psychology show that many apparently conscious choices are made automatically, and that ex post explanations for apparently conscious choices may be demonstrably false [Bargh and Chartrand, 1999]. The difficulty in separating human behavior as between automatic and chosen was highlighted by Selten [1999: 4] in the course of a discussion of bounded rationality:

> Much of human behavior is automatized in the sense that it is not connected to any conscious deliberation. In the process of walking one does not decide after each step which leg to move next and by how much. Such automatized routines can be interrupted and modified by decisions but while they are executed they do not require any decision making. . . . One might want to distinguish between bounded rationality and automatized routine. However, it is difficult to do this. Conscious attention is not a good criterion. Even thinking is based on automatized routine. We may decide what to think about but not what to think.

No clear line separates human activities into mechanistic and chosen. The goal of decision theory is, after all, to model "choice" itself mechanically. Hence, there is no reason to limit a priori the outputs of human activity that can be included in axiomatic models. All such activities may be modeled as having been chosen from a feasible set, and the issue of what theory accounts for the observed reali-zation is open. Any separation of human activities as between preprogrammed and chosen is best characterized on a case-by-case basis rather than in the overarching methodology.

A pragmatic issue relating to modeling many nonstandard psychological data is our relative lack of knowledge of, and possibly even interest in, the set of fea-sible alternatives to given observations. For this reason, they may be modeled as tightly complementary with some external feature. One may even wish to keep the language of production theory, while recognizing that this is really just a way in which to remove too many active margins at this stage in our understanding of behavior.

Minimalism

I view the principle of revealed preference as an approach to modeling rather than a set of rigid constraints on measurement and theory. In this interpretation, it imposes no restrictions on the data that can be employed in fitting economic models, but rather guides the modeling of the given data. Specifically, it suggests a very streamlined, or "minimalist," approach to modeling whatever data are ultimately selected.

In loose terms, this approach involves characterization of the exact empirical content of a model for a particular data set. As in standard choice theory, development of a single axiomatization of all measured data is the ideal, since it reduces to an absolute minimum the number of model elements that are needed. Again, as with standard revealed preference, models producing the same data are to be regarded as equivalent: this is the generalized version of the "as if" principle. In fact, the general theorem structure in a minimalist model is unchanged in essentials from that described above for standard revealed preference, with the only difference being the greater range of data that can be measured:

> Measured outputs of type * have appealing joint properties ** if and only if these data are determined by calculations of the form ***.

The need to analyze equivalence classes of representations applies with at least equal force in these models as in standard choice-theoretic models, and the theorem structure is essentially as it was in the case of standard choice theory. If anything, results placing precise limits on what these richer theories are able to identify from the new psychological data may be even more important than in the standard choice theory, since we are at such an early stage of understanding.

> There exist equivalence classes of calculations of the form *** such that measured outputs of type * are identical within any such class, yet differ between classes.

Theories that adhere to the minimalist approach will themselves rest on underlying intuitions, which may in turn be subject to dispute. Such disputes are particularly likely when distinct intuitively based theories are found to be equivalent in terms of the restrictions they impose on a particular data set. Yet by the same token, such equivalence would establish these theories as indistinguishable in the given empirical context, making continued debate inconsequential. To re-energize debate on the relative status of such theories would require a richer empirical environment in which they had distinct implications.

What is needed to effectively differentiate the minimalist methodology from standard revealed preference are direct examples in which the data go beyond standard choices. Some examples are sketched in the next section. In each case, conventional concepts as studied in choice theory serve as the starting point for a theory that encompasses specific additional items of psychological data.

Two Applications

Below I outline a minimalist approach to understanding the impact of subjective information constraints on decision making, as detailed in Caplin and Dean [2008b]. I then outline a minimalist approach to neuroscientific data hypothesized to register the degree of surprise as the environment changes for the better or for the worse. Theoretical foundations for this research are detailed in Caplin and Dean [2008b], with the empirical implementation being detailed in Caplin, Dean, Glimcher, and Rutledge [2008].

Information and the Choice Process

How best to model bounds on rationality and apparently poorly adapted decisions? One possible interpretation of such decisions is that they stem from subjective constraints on information of the form associated with the standard microeconomic model of constrained optimization. An entirely different interpretation is that they stem from application of decision heuristics of the sort identified by Kahneman and Tversky [1974]. Greater consensus is needed on how best to model the internal search process before the theory of bounded rationality can attain the standard of coherence and centrality that characterizes standard search theory, as pioneered by Stigler [1961] and McCall [1970].

Caplin and Dean [2008b] argue that a critical barrier holding back agreement on how best to model the internal search process is evidentiary. To overcome this constraint, they measure and model a new source of information on the search process. In the basic choice process data set, each possible nonempty subset of the commodity set $A \subset X$ is imagined as being presented one and only one time to the decision maker. The model specifies not only the final choice that a decision maker makes, but also how the most preferred object changes in the course of arriving at the final decision. The idealized "choice process" data identify for any choice set and any length of time what the decision maker would choose from that choice set after that length of time. For each discrete time $t \in \mathbb{N}$ (the natural numbers, or strictly positive integers), the decision maker is observed selecting a subset of the elements of A, with the interpretation that if the choice situation was to be terminated at this time, an identified member of this list would be received.

Definition 15.1.

A *choice process environment* (X, C) comprises a finite set X and a correspondence $C : 2^X/\phi \times \mathbb{N} \to 2^X/\phi$, $C(A, t) \subseteq A$, referred to as the "choice process".

A theory of the choice process identifies all successive approximations to the object chosen in a naturalistic setting with no external time constraints. Caplin and Dean characterize the extent to which these enriched data make observable aspects of the internal search that would otherwise be kept private. This characterization matches in many respects the theory of sequential search with perfect recall. The decision maker is endowed with a complete, transitive preference ordering over the objects in the commodity space and explores options sequentially, retaining in hand the best object identified to date. The vision underlying the model is that the set of available alternatives is hard to identify, not their characteristics once identified as available. The process of search is then the process of uncovering precisely what is feasible in a given decision problem.

Definition 15.2.

A *choice process environment* (X, C) permits of an *alternative-based search representation* (u, S) if there exists a utility function $u : X \to \mathbb{R}$ and a correspondence $S : 2^X/\phi \times \mathbb{N} \to 2^X/\phi$, the *search process*, that is expanding [i.e., $S(A, s) \subseteq S(A, t) \subseteq A$ for all $A \in 2^X/\phi$ and $t \geq s$] and such that

$$C(A, t) = \arg \max_{x \in S(A,t)} u(x).$$

This model has the property that only a decision maker who takes the time to search through the entire choice set can be guaranteed to satisfy WARP. Hence, the theory is boundedly rational, in the sense that an "inferior" object may be selected over a "superior" one if search is incomplete. Yet it shares much in common with standard optimal search theory. The model can be specialized to cases in which search terminates when, and only when, a "reservation" utility is achieved. The resulting mode of choice has obvious links not only to the theory of optimal sequential search, but also to Simon's models of satisficing behavior. Moreover, by allowing for a possible impact of search order on choice, the model suggests a largely standard search-theoretic interpretation for such phenomena as reliance on default options and framing effects.

The theory is not intended to have universal applicability. The intricacies of realistic search processes are strongly hinted at in the work of Payne, Bettman, and Johnson [1993]. In their terminology, our search model is "alternative based," with given options being compared with one another across many dimensions before new options are considered. An obvious alternative is "attribute based" search, in which the decision maker compares alternatives on an attribute-by-attribute basis. The goal of the axiomatization is only to characterize environments in which the modeled form of alternative-based search constitutes an adequate description of behavior. Ideally, the nature of observed violations in environments to which the model is poorly adapted will serve as inspiration for future process models.

Theories of the choice process data set introduced above represent only a first step in the process of understanding bounded rationality. One could, in principle, gather richer data on the evolution of preferences via an "indifference process" methodology in which one tracks over time sets of objects that are mutually indifferent. If theoretical considerations make clear that this is a potentially insightful data set, it will motivate the corresponding experimental design task in humans and potentially in other animals. While research into this question is in its very infancy, it illustrates the extent to which social scientific data and theories are endogenous, and can be simultaneously designed to bring out complementarities.

Dopamine and Choice

Dopamine, which is a neurotransmitter, plays a profound role in choice behavior. Experiments from the mid-1950s to the present show that rats and other mammals repeatedly return to locations that have been set up only to stimulate dopaminergic activity [Bernheim and Rangel, 2004]. Rats make this choice over such alternatives as food, water, and opportunities to mate, even in the presence of such disincentives as painful electric shocks. Recent experiments suggest that dopamine's role in choice may be causal: rats given drugs that block dopamine receptors eventually stop feeding. Indeed, an emerging theory of Parkinson's disease in humans is that, by compromising dopaminergic function, it radically alters the incentives to make even previously rewarding choices.

The best-developed theory of how dopamine affects choice is the "dopaminergic reward prediction error" (DRPE) hypothesis. Schultz et al. [1993] demonstrated an increase in dopaminergic activity when a monkey was unexpectedly given a squirt of fruit juice, which aligned with the early theory that dopamine affects choice directly through hedonic impact. Yet they went one step further, motivated in part by the Pavlovian learning model of Rescorla and Wagner [1972]. They found that if the monkey learned to associate a particular sound with the later receipt of the fruit juice, the dopaminergic response occurred when that sound was heard, not when the juice was received. Moreover, when cued rewards failed to arrive, dopamine neurons exhibited a momentary pause in their background firing. These findings suggest that dopamine tracks the path over time of the difference between some form of anticipated and realized reward value. Intriguingly, Schultz, Dayan, and Montague [1997] noted that this "prediction error" signal is precisely what is needed in reinforcement learning algorithms designed by computer scientists to approximate standard dynamic programming value functions [Barto and Sutton, 1982]. This has led many researchers to conclude that this similarity is no coincidence, and that dopamine does indeed measure a reward prediction error that is used to update an evolving value function.

Given the recent findings, it is increasingly clear that dopaminergic activity carries economically important information concerning how beliefs and preferences are formed, how they evolve, and how they play out in the act of choice. Yet communication across field boundaries remains largely out of reach. Many neuroscientific tests of the DRPE hypothesis take the perspective of "classical" or "Pavlovian" conditioning, in which choice plays no role, rendering economic interpretation difficult at best. Another fundamental problem is that the implicit assumption within the neuroscientific community is that the fMRI signal is related to the unobserved "reward" according to an affine transformation. No justification has ever been provided for limiting attention to this simple class of transformations. Neuroeconomic research needs to follow the lead of utility theory and internalize the perils of treating an ordinal reward function as if it was cardinal.

To pursue a minimalist research agenda into dopaminergic function, Caplin and Dean [2008a] use axiomatic methods to characterize the empirical implications of this hypothesis for a data tape with combined information on choice and dopaminergic activity. This enables us to define neurological abstractions directly in terms of their empirical implications, removing the essential language barrier between neuroscientific and economic theory. We outline three economic applications of the resulting dopaminergic framework. First, we outline the potential use of dopamine measurements to provide insight into belief formation, a topic of great interest in experimental economics. The second application relates directly to learning theory, in which Erev and Roth [1998] pioneered application of the reinforcement model of animal learning. Finally, we outline an application to addiction, strongly related to the work of Bernheim and Rangel [2004], and based on the observation that many addictive substances stand out as dopamine "agonists," stimulating high levels of dopaminergic activity upon consumption. While neuroscientists are currently taking the lead in exploring the interaction between dopamine and addiction, we believe that the interaction with economic reasoning is essential if the ultimate goal is to affect choice. An integrative theory such as ours is a necessary prelude to the required form of interdisciplinary research.

We develop the DRPE hypothesis for a case in which probabilities are objective and dopaminergic responses derive from realizations of specific lotteries over final prizes. The ideal data set comprises both any initial act of choice among lotteries, and the dopaminergic response when each possible prize is realized. Definition 15.3 lays out the fundamental building blocks of the theory:

Definition 15.3.

The set of prizes is a metric space Z with generic element $z \in Z$. The set of all simple lotteries over Z is denoted Λ, with generic element $p \in \Lambda$. We define $e_z \in \Lambda$ as the degenerate lottery that assigns probability 1 to prize $z \in Z$ and the set $\Lambda(z)$ as all lotteries with z in their support,

$$\Lambda(z) \equiv \{p \in \Lambda | p_z > 0\}.$$

The function $\delta(z, p)$ defined on $M = \{(z, p) | z \in Z, p \in \Lambda(z)\}$ identifies the dopamine response function (DRF), $\delta : M \to R$.

The DRPE hypothesis hinges on dopaminergic responses being somehow determined by the relationship between "expected" and "experienced" rewards associated with any pair $(z, p) \in M$. The simplest technical translation of the hypothesis involves a function $r : \Lambda \to \mathbb{R}$, which defines the expected reward associated with each lottery and that simultaneously induces the reward function on prizes $z \in Z$ as $r(e_z)$. We define the DRPE hypothesis in three parts: the reward function should contain all information relevant to dopamine release; the dopaminergic response should be strictly higher for a more rewarding than for a less rewarding prize from a given lottery, and from a less rewarding that from a more rewarding lottery to a given prize; and, if expectations are met, the dopaminergic response should not depend on what was expected.

Definition 15.4.

Given a function $r : \Lambda \to \mathbb{R}$, define $r(\Lambda)$ as the range of the function and $r(Z)$ as the set of values taken by the function r across degenerate lotteries,

$$r(Z) = \{r(p) \in \mathbb{R} | p = e_z, z \in Z\}.$$

A DRF $\delta : M \to R$ admits a dopaminergic reward prediction error (DRPE) representation if there exist functions $r : \Lambda \to \mathbb{R}$ and $E : r(Z) \times r(\Lambda) \to \mathbb{R}$ that

1. *Represent the DRF $\delta : M \to R$, in that, given $(z, p) \in M$,*

   $$\delta(z, p) = E(r(e_z), r(p)).$$

2. *Respect dopaminergic dominance, in that E is strictly increasing in its first argument and strictly decreasing in its second argument.*

3. *Satisfies no surprise constancy in that, given $x, y \in r(Z)$,*

$$E(x, x) = E(y, y).$$

Precise characterization theorems are presented in Caplin and Dean [2008a]. Note that the rewards in the above characterizations are defined only in relation to dopaminergic activity, just as in classical revealed preference theory, utility is defined through choice. If the basic DRF permits a DRPE characterization, there exists a definition of reward such that dopamine responds consistently to that definition, while if it does not, no such reward definition can be found. Note also that the above theory will be of little interest to economists unless the reward function is somehow related to choice behavior. The strongest such relation would be if choices among lotteries could be modeled as deriving from maximization of the DRPE reward function. While this case is of obvious interest to economists, it represents an extreme form of the DRPE hypothesis. A more standard scenario involves dopamine as simply one component of a richer overall process of learning and of choice.

The axiomatic methodology may be even more important when modeling novel neuroscientific data than in its standard decision-theoretic setting. It enables one to define theoretical abstractions such as rewards, predictions, and the DRPE hypothesis itself, in a direct and precise empirical language. If the data do not obey the proposed axioms, then the DRPE model is fundamentally wrong, not merely misspecified. Moreover, from a purely neuroscientific viewpoint, the minimalist agenda has value in suggesting experimental protocols directed to the central tenets of the theory, rather than to particular parametrizations. We explore this in Caplin, Dean, Glimcher, and Rutledge [2008].

CONCLUSION

Given the limitations of standard economic models and massive increases in data availability, research methods will surely be revolutionized over the coming decades. The minimalist methodology outlined above is designed to make room for new data while improving communication across subdisciplines of social science. Successful research in line with this methodology has the potential to expand the domain of social science in ways that we are currently unable even to imagine.

NOTES

I thank Mark Dean for his many contributions to the ideas expressed herein, and his collaboration on the associated research projects. I have also learned much from conversations with Paul Glimcher, Miles Kimball, John Leahy, Andy Schotter, and

Ruth Wyatt. I thank the National Science Foundation and the C. V. Starr Center at New York University for research support.

1. The reader will find the term "revealed preference" defined in many different ways in this volume. My own definition is entirely technical: I use it to characterize a class of axiomatic models of observables, as detailed below.

2. It is hard to understand why issues of observability have attracted so little attention in interactive contexts. How could one ever know whether equal and immediate division in a bargaining problem reflected subtle mutually held beliefs concerning out-of-equilibrium behavior, or instead reflected simple application of conventions? It might be argued that the former provide the simplest generalizable account of such outcomes, since conventions are fragile. Hausman [2000] highlights this issue in discussing weak points in the conception of revealed preference. For those who are deeply attached to the latter, it may be seen as highlighting weaknesses in game theory. Yet this debate has not been joined, since the subject of observability has not struck a chord in the strategic context.

3. Barsky, Juster, Kimball, and Shapiro [1997], Kimball and Shapiro [2003], and Kimball, Sahm, and Shapiro [2005] have done much to blaze this methodological trail.

REFERENCES

Ameriks, J., A. Caplin, S. Laufer, and S. Van Niewerburgh. 2007. The Joy of Giving or Assisted Living: Using Strategic Surveys to Separate Bequest and Precautionary Motives. Mimeo, New York University.

Ameriks, J., A. Caplin, and J. Leahy. 2003. Wealth Accumulation and the Propensity to Plan. *Quarterly Journal of Economics* 118: 1007–1048.

Aumann, Robert T. 1998. Common Priors: A Reply to Gul. *Econometrica* 66: 929–938.

Bargh, John, and Tania Chartrand. 1999. The Unbearable Automaticity of Being. *American Psychologist* 54: 462–479.

Barsky, Robert, Thomas Juster, Miles Kimball, and Matthew Shapiro. 1997. Preference Parameters and Behavioral Heterogeneity: An Experimental Approach Using the Health and Retirement Survey. *Quarterly Journal of Economics* 112: 537–579.

Barto, Andrew, and Richard, Sutton. 1982. Simulation of Anticipatory Responses in Classical Conditioning by a Neuron-like Adaptive Element. *Behavioral Brain Research* 4: 221–235.

Bayer, H., and P. Glimcher. 2005. Midbrain Dopamine Neurons Encode a Quantitative Reward Prediction Error Signal. *Neuron* 47: 129–141.

Benhabib, Jess, and Alberto Bisin. 2005. Modeling Internal Commitment Mechanisms and Self-Control: A Neuroeconomics Approach to Consumption–Saving Decisions. *Games and Economic Behavior* 52: 460–492.

Bernheim, B. Douglas, and Antonio Rangel. 2004. Addiction and Cue-Triggered Decision Processes. *American Economic Review* 94: 1558–1590.

Berns, G. S., S. M., McClure, G., Pagnoni, and P. R. Montague. 2001. Predictability Modulates Human Brain Response to Reward. *Journal of Neuroscience* 21: 2793–2798.

Camerer, Colin F., George Loewenstein, and Drazen Prelec. 2005. Neuroeconomics: How Neuroscience Can Inform Economics. *Journal of Economic Literature* 34(1): 9–64.

Caplin, A. 2003. Fear as a Policy Instrument. In *Time and Decision*, ed. R. Baumeister, G. Loewenstein, and D. Read. New York: Russel Sage.

Caplin, A., and M. Dean. 2008a. Dopamine, Reward Prediction Error, and Economics. *Quarterly Journal of Economics* in press.

———. 2008b. Revealed Preference, Search, and Choice. Mimeo., New York University.

Caplin, A., M. Dean, P. Glimcher, and R. Rutledge. 2008. Measuring Anticipated and Realized Rewards: A Neuroeconomic Approach. Mimeo, New York University.

Caplin, A., and J. Leahy. 2001. Psychological Expected Utility Theory and Anticipatory Feelings. *Quarterly Journal of Economics* 116: 55–80.

———. 2004. The Supply of Information by a Concerned Expert. *Economic Journal* 114: 487–505.

Dean, Mark, Shih Wei Woo, and Laurence Maloney. 2007. Trading Off Speed and Accuracy in Rapid, Goal-Directed Movements. *Journal of Vision* 6(1): 53–63.

Dynan, Karen, Jonathan Skinner, and Stephen Zeldes. 2002. The Importance of Bequests and Life-Cycle Saving in Capital Accumulation: A New Answer. *American Economic Review Papers and Proceedings* 92: 274–278.

Erev, Ido, and Alvin E. Roth. 1998. Predicting How People Play Games: Reinforcement Learning in Experimental Games with Unique, Mixed Strategy Equilibria. *American Economic Review* 88(4): 848–881.

Ergin, H. 2003. Costly Contemplation. Mimeo, MIT.

Ericsson, K., and H. Simon. 1984. *Protocol Analysis*. Cambridge, MA: MIT Press.

Fudenberg, D., and D. Levine. 2005. A Dual Self Model of Impulse Control. Mimeo. Harvard University.

Gabaix, Xavier, and David Laibson. 2000. A Boundedly Rational Decision Algorithm. *American Economic Review Papers and Proceedings* 90: 433–438.

Gabaix, X., D. Laibson, G. Moloche, and S. Weinberg. 2006. Costly Information Acquisition: Experimental Analysis of a Boundedly Rational Model. *American Economic Review* 96: 1043–1068.

Glimcher, Paul, and Aldo Rustichini. 2004. Neuroeconomics: The Consilience of Brain and Decision. *Science* 306: 447–452.

Gul, F., and W. Pesendorfer. 2001. Temptation and Self-Control. *Econometrica* 69(6): 1403–1436.

Hausman, D. 2000. Revealed Preference, Belief, and Game Theory. *Economics and Philosophy* 16: 99–115.

Hurd, Michael D. 1987. Savings of the Elderly and Desired Bequests. *American Economic Review* 77(3): 298–312.

Johnson, Eric J., Colin Camerer, Sankar Sen, and Talia Rymon. 2002. Detecting Failures of Backward Induction: Monitoring Information Search in Sequential Bargaining. *Journal of Economic Theory* 104: 16–47.

Kahneman, D., A. Krueger, D. Schkade, N. Schwarz, and A. Stone. 2004. A Survey Method for Characterizing Daily Life Experience: The Day Reconstruction Method (DRM). *Science* 306: 1776–1780.

Kahneman, Daniel, and Amos Tversky. 1974. Judgment under Uncertainty: Heuristics and Biases. *Science* 185: 1124–1131.

———. 1979. Prospect Theory: An Analysis of Decision under Risk. *Econometrica* 47(2): 263–292.

Kimball, Miles S., C. Sahm, and Matthew D. Shapiro. 2005. Using Survey-Based Risk Tolerance. *Working Paper*, University of Michigan.

Kimball, Miles S., and Matthew D. Shapiro. 2003. Labor Supply: Are Income and Substitution Effects Both Large or Both Small? *Working Paper*, University of Michigan.

Kotlikoff, Laurence J., and Lawrence H. Summers. 1981. The Role of Intergenerational Transfers in Aggregate Capital Accumulation. *Journal of Political Economy* 89: 706–732.

Kreps, D. 1979. A Preference for Flexibility. *Econometrica* 47: 565–576.

Kreps, D., and E. Porteus. 1978. Temporal Resolution of Uncertainty and Dynamic Choice Theory. *Econometrica* 46: 185–200.

Laibson, David. 1997. Golden Eggs and Hyperbolic Discounting. *Quarterly Journal of Economics* 112: 443–477.

Ljungqvist, Lars. 1993. A Unified Approach to Measures of Privacy in Randomized Response Models: A Utilitarian Perspective. *Journal of the American Statistical Association* 88(421): 97–103.

Loewenstein, G. 1987. Anticipation and the Valuation of Delayed Consumption. *Economic Journal* 97: 666–684.

Loewenstein, G., and T. O'Donoghue. 2004. Affective and Deliberative Processes in Economic Behavior. Mimeo. Carnegie Mellon University.

Lusardi, Annamaria. 2000. Explaining Why So Many Households Do Not Save. Mimeo, University of Chicago Harris School of Public Policy.

Manzini, P., and M. Mariotti. 2004. Rationalizing Boundedly Rational Choice. IZA Discussion Paper 1239, Bonn Germany.

McCall, J. J. 1970. Economics of Information and Job Search. *Quarterly Journal of Economics* 84(1): 113–126.

McClure, Samuel, David I. Laibson, George Loewenstein, and Jonathan D. Cohen. 2004. Separate Neural Systems Value Immediate and Delayed Monetary Reward. *Science* 306: 603–616.

O'Donoghue, Ted, and Matthew Rabin. 1999. Doing It Now or Later. *American Economic Review* 99: 103–124.

Payne, John W., James R. Bettman, and Eric J. Johnson. 1993. *The Adaptive Decision Maker*. Cambridge: Cambridge University Press.

Payne, J. W., J. R. Bettman, and M. F. Luce. 1996. When Time Is Money: Decision Behavior under Opportunity-Cost Time Pressure. *Organizational Behavior and Human Decision Process* 66(2): 131–152.

Peleg M., and M. E. Yaari. 1973. On the Existence of a Consistent Course of Action When Tastes Are Changing. *Review of Economic Studies* 40: 391–401.

Radner, R., and M. Rothschild. 1975. On the Allocation of Effort. *Journal of Economic Theory* 10(3): 358–376.

Rescorla, R. A., and A. R. Wagner, 1972. A Theory of Pavlovian Conditioning: Variations in the Effectiveness of Reinforcement and Nonreinforcement. In *Classical Conditioning II*, ed. A. H. Black and W. F. Prokasy, 64–99. New York: Appleton-Century-Crofts.

Rubinstein, A. 1998. *Modeling Bounded Rationality*. Zeuthen Lecture Book Series. Cambridge, MA: MIT Press.

Samuelson, P. 1938. A Note on the Pure Theory of Consumer's Behavior. *Economica* 5: 61–71.

Savage, L. J. 1954. *The Foundations of Statistics.* New York: Wiley and Sons.

Schultz, Wolfram, Paul Apicella, and Tomas Ljungberg. 1993. Responses of Monkey Dopamine Neurons to Reward and Conditioned Stimuli During Successive Steps of Learning a Delayed Response Task. *Journal of Neuroscience* 13: 900–913.

Schultz, Wolfram, Peter Dayan, and P. Read Montague. 1997. A Neural Substrate of Prediction and Reward. *Science* 275 : 1593–1599.

Selten, R. 1999. What Is Bounded Rationality? *SFB* Discussion *Paper* B-454. University of Bonn, Germany.

Simon, Herbert. 1955. A Behavioral Model of Rational Choice. *Quarterly Journal of Economics* 69(1): 99–118.

Stigler, George J. 1961. The Economics of Information. *Journal of Political Economy* 69(3): 213–225.

Strotz, Robert. 1956. Myopia and Inconsistency in Dynamic Utility Maximization. *Review of Economic Studies* 23: 165–180.

Tversky, A. 1972. Elimination by Aspects: A Theory of Choice. *Psychological Review* 79(4): 281–299.

Tyson, C. 2005. Contraction Consistency, Cognitive Constraints and the Satisficing Criterion. Working Paper, Oxford University.

Von Neumann, J., and O. Morgenstern. 1947. *Theory of Games and Economic Behavior.* Princeton, NJ: Princeton University Press.

Wilson, Andrea. 2002. Bounded Memory and Biases in Information Processing. Working Paper, Princeton University.

Index